Developmental Science provides an account of the basic principles of the new developmental synthesis. A group of eminent scientists from sociology, psychiatry, psychology, public health, social ecology, and psychobiology believe that a fresh, interdisciplinary orientation is required to achieve progress on critical issues of behavioral theory, method, and application. Toward this end, they formed the Carolina Consortium on Human Development in 1987 as part of an advanced institute for the study of development, the Center for Developmental Science.

This book grew from that long-term collaboration. In addition to the collaborative statement, individual chapters outline implications of the orientation for method and theory in traditional disciplines. The chapters address specific developmental issues, varying across time frames, methodologies, disciplines, cultures, and even species. They provide an inside look at the basic issues that confront modern social and behavioral study, including its strengths and problems.

Cambridge Studies in Social and Emotional Development

General Editor: Martin L. Hoffman, New York University

Advisory Board: Robert N. Emde, Willard W. Hartup, Robert A. Hinde, Lois W. Hoffman, Carroll E. Izard, Nicholas Blurton Jones, Jerome Kagan, Franz J. Mönks, Paul Mussen, Ross D. Parke, and Michael Rutter

Developmental Science

IN MEMORIAM

On the special occasion of this reissuing of *Developmental Science*, we wish to remember the late Robert B. Cairns and his creative role in the book's evolution and in the founding of the Carolina Consortium on Human Development and the Center for Developmental Science.

> *Glen H. Elder, Jr., and E. Jane Costello, co-editors, and the Center for the Developmental Science Faculty, fellows and students*

Developmental Science

Edited by
Robert B. Cairns, Glen H. Elder, Jr., and E. Jane Costello

CAMBRIDGE
UNIVERSITY PRESS

PUBLISHED BY THE PRESS SYNDICATE OF THE UNIVERSITY OF CAMBRIDGE
The Pitt Building, Trumpington Street, Cambridge, United Kingdom

CAMBRIDGE UNIVERSITY PRESS
The Edinburgh Building, Cambridge CB2 2RU, UK
40 West 20th Street, New York, NY 10011–4211, USA
10 Stamford Road, Oakleigh, VIC 3166, Australia
Ruiz de Alarcón 13, 28014 Madrid, Spain
Dock House, The Waterfront, Cape Town 8001, South Africa

http://www.cambridge.org

First published 1996
Reprinted 2001
First paperback printing 2001

Printed in the United States of America

A catalogue record for this book is available from the British Library

Library of Congress Cataloguing-in-Publication Data is available

ISBN 0 521 49585-7 hardback
ISBN 0 521 79459-5 paperback

Contents

Contributors

Adrian Angold
Duke University School of Medicine
Department of Psychiatry
P.O. Box 3454
Durham, NC 27710

Urie Bronfenbrenner
Cornell University
Bronfenbrenner Life Course Center
259 Martha Van Rensselaer Hall
Ithaca, NY 14853-4401

Robert B. Cairns
Center for Developmental Science
University of North Carolina
521 S. Greensboro St. C.B.#8115
Chapel Hill, NC 27599-8115

E. Jane Costello
Duke University Medical Center
Department of Psychiatry
P.O. Box 3454
Durham, NC 27710

Carol O. Eckerman
Duke University
Department of Psychology
Durham, NC 27706

Glen H. Elder, Jr.
University of North Carolina
Carolina Population Center
C.B.#8120, University Square East
Chapel Hill, NC 27599-3270

Jean-Louis Gariépy
University of North Carolina
Department of Psychology
C.B.#3270, Davie Hall
Chapel Hill, NC 27599-3270

Gilbert Gottlieb
University of North Carolina
C.B.#8115
Chapel Hill, NC 27599-8115

David Magnusson
Stockholm University
Department of Psychology
S-106 91
Stockholm, Sweden

Frederick J. Morrison
Loyola University of Chicago
Department of Psychology
Damen Hall 608
Chicago, IL 60626

Peter A. Ornstein
University of North Carolina
Department of Psychology
C.B.#3270, Davie Hall
Chapel Hill, NC 27599-3270

Sarah Putnam
University of North Carolina-
  Greensboro
Department of Human Development
  and Family Studies
Park Building
Greensboro, NC 27412

Arnold J. Sameroff
Center for Human Growth and
  Development
300 North Ingalls Building
University of Michigan
Ann Arbor, MI 48109-0406

Stephen J. Suomi
NIH-NICHD-DIR
9000 Rockville Pike 31/B2B15
Bethesda, MD 20892

Jonathan Tudge
University of North Carolina-
  Greensboro
Department of Human Development
  and Family Studies
Park Building
Greensboro, NC 27412

Jaan Valsiner
University of North Carolina
Department of Psychology
C.B.#3270, Davie Hall
Chapel Hill, NC 27599-3270

Foreword

Urie Bronfenbrenner

Seldom, in reading a scientific manuscript, does one feel impelled to identify it as a potential scientific milestone. In this instance, the milestone may well mark a significant step toward the evolution of a new and more powerful paradigm for the scientific study of human development. To be sure, as the authors of the volume emphasize, any new "paradigm shift" (if such a phenomenon, in fact, will ever exist) still lies far ahead. Nor do the authors claim principal credit for having themselves achieved the progress that has been made. Rather, they call attention to what they have perceived as an emergent convergence and isomorphism, mostly over the past two decades, in the work of scientists in different disciplines, employing seemingly different theoretical perspectives, reporting results specific to delimited substantive domains, and yet, in the authors' view, all producing patterns of findings encompassable within the same general model of developmental structure and process. Moreover, the defining properties of the emergent model contradict, almost point for point, the now prevailing conceptual and operational strategies of choice in each specialized field of inquiry.

To counter any impulse on the part of the reader to dismiss this formulation as too sweeping and abstract to be translatable into concrete testable hypotheses, I hasten to point out that the chapters of this book are replete with research examples pointing to the feasibility of developing rigorous research designs consistent with the defining properties of the emerging paradigm, and to the plausibility of the hypotheses that the paradigm generates.

The nature of the coactive process and its implications for both theory and research design constitute the central thesis and theme of Chapter 2, authored by David Magnusson and Robert B. Cairns. They call the thesis "developmental integration" and present it as the first and most fundamental defining property of the emergent paradigm. "An individual develops and functions psychologically as an integrated organism. Maturational,

ix

experiential, and cultural contributions are fused in ontogeny. Single aspects do not develop and function in isolation, and they should not be divorced from the totality in analysis." In short, the thesis is one of *interdependence both within and across systems* at successive levels of structure and process.

Given the complexity of this formulation, Magnusson and Cairns acknowledge that it poses a problem for operationalization. "The challenge for contemporary theory is to establish a perspective that is systematic enough to integrate the multiple subprocesses of behavior, but precise enough to direct the drive for evidence." But undaunted, they undertake to illustrate the practicality and scientific power of their thesis by citing a research example from the longitudinal study of 1,300 Swedish children conducted over the past twenty years by Magnusson and his colleagues. In their analysis, the investigators demonstrate that "girls who reach menarche very early tend to show multiple signs of behavioral deviancy" (e.g., drinking, cheating in school, and higher levels of sexual activity). Moreover, some of these effects persist into adulthood. "The very early-maturing girls had married earlier, had more children, and had achieved less advanced education relative to the average or late-maturing girls."

But the maturation-deviance linkage is only part of the story. Consistent with holistic perspective, Magnusson and Cairns observe that there are powerful contextual constraints on these effects. In this regard, they note that Caspi and Moffitt (1991) found the same early maturation-deviance phenomenon in the longitudinal study of a sample of New Zealand girls. The effect was obtained, however, only if the girls were enrolled in a coeducational school. Presumably, the opportunities for deviance by differential association were greater in the coeducational setting than they were in all-girl schools. Along the same lines, Robert and Beverley Cairns, in their fourteen-year investigation of seven hundred young persons in the United States discovered that " girls who matured very early tended to hang around with other girls who also matured very early." In the Cairnses' research, "very early sexual maturation was *not* associated with subsequent problem behaviors. In the American samples, age of menarche was not strongly linked to any of the measures of adolescence deviance (e.g., aggression, substance use, low school achievement). Nor were they related to early marriage, teenage parenthood, or lower levels of educational achievement." The bottom line is that there are consequential cross-overs between the biological and social domains within the immediate face-to-face environments of family, school, neighborhood, and society.

In the book's next chapter, Glen Elder dramatically expands the scope of the environment across both space and time, but still in accord with the basic principle of interdependence across disciplinary and subdisciplinary domains. A sociologist who has developed close scholarly ties with both developmental psychologists and historians, Elder has been for more than two decades the principal theoretical and empirical protagonist of what he has called the "life course perspective" in research on human development. In Elder's formulation, the life course is the environmental path (or path segment) that a particular individual or group traverses through life. Paralleling this journey through time, but distinguished from it, is what Elder refers to as a "developmental trajectory." This concept encompasses the continuities and changes in the biopsychological characteristics of particular individuals or groups as they proceed along a given environmental pathway through time.

On first consideration, perhaps the most distinctive feature of Elder's theoretical approach and the one that most saliently extends the interdisciplinary scope of developmental inquiry is his thesis that a person's developmental course is embedded in, and significantly shaped by, conditions and events occurring during the historical periods through which the person lives. In short, history is exploited as an experiment of nature. The corresponding research design compares groups similar in other respects who have been exposed, versus not exposed, to a particular historical event or set of historical conditions. Working from this perspective, Elder and his colleagues have studied developmental changes in individuals and groups resulting from living through the Great Depression; military service and actual combat in World War II, Korea, and Vietnam; the Iowa farm crisis of the 1980s; and the sending of youth to the countryside during China's Cultural Revolution.

Some the results of these investigations are cited in Elder's chapter in this volume, but in the present context, the scientific importance of Elder's work lies not in his empirical findings but in its special contribution to extending the more general theoretical paradigm emerging in the work of the Carolina Consortium. Stated more broadly, Elder's central thesis is the power of social change in shaping the course and outcome of human development. Moreover, Elder claims and demonstrates the validity of this thesis as applying beyond the formative years (the typically delimited focus of developmental psychology) not only to encompass the entire life course but to extend across successive generations of adults.

It is especially instructive to compare Elder's theoretical formulations, and the empirical findings they generate, with those presented in the preceding chapter by Magnusson and Cairns, for the comparison reveals a marked contrast at the level of manifest content counterbalanced by what, upon analysis, emerges as a remarkably analogous underlying theoretical structure. (Indeed, one suspects that the editors had precisely this paradox in mind in juxtaposing the two chapters.) To begin with the contrasts, the two theoretical perspectives are rooted in different disciplines: Magnusson and Cairns draw primarily on social interactional models of psychology and evolutionary biology, Elder, on the work of the Chicago school of sociology, particularly Thomas and Znaniecki's classic four-volume study *The Polish Peasant in Europe and America.* Correspondingly, in their theoretical expositions, both parties speak mainly in the language of their root disciplines. But behind these externals, the posited underlying structures and their dynamic interrelationships are strikingly similar. As the reader will discover, both theoretical models conceive of development as a process of organism-environment interaction over time, in which the organism plays an active role in shaping its own development. Both orientations view the developing person as a dynamic whole rather than in terms of isolated domains of psychological function (e.g. cognition, emotion, motivation, social behavior). Both approaches argue, and illustrate, the necessity of examining development from an interdisciplinary perspective. Within that perspective, both emphasize the recognition of dynamic interdependence within and across systems levels over the course of development. Indeed, one of the best examples of this dynamic is found in Elder's thesis that the lives and developmental trajectories of family members are necessarily intertwined through their shared but also differentiated experience of historical events as a function of their social roles, state in life, and personality characteristics. These interdependencies are captured in concrete form in the following summary of developmental processes and outcomes for families living through the Great Depression.

Families that suffered heavy income losses during the 1930s became more discordant in the marital relationship, owing largely to rising financial disputes and to the more irritable, tense, and volatile state of husbands. The more irritable men became under economic pressure, the more they tended to behave punitively and arbitrarily toward their offspring. Economic stress generally increased the explosive tendency of men, but it did so primarily when they initially ranked high on this characteristic. Yet even when irritable under economic stress, a father was less likely to abuse his children if their mother provided affectional support for them. This maternal role also minimized continuation of a child's problem behavior. Unstable (explosive, volatile) personalities and unstable family (marital, parent-child) relations are mutually reinforcing dynamics across the life course (Elder, Caspi, &

Downey, 1986). These dynamics persist from one generation to the next through a process of individual continuity and intergenerational transmission.

Last but not least, both perspectives acknowledge a paradox in the course of human development over time. On the one hand, both posit and document the occurrence of major psychological changes, both for better and for worse, taking place over the course of development. Thus, the fourth of Magnusson and Cairns's propositions defining their emerging theoretical paradigm affirms: "Novel patterns of individual functioning arise during individual ontogeny." Similarly, Elder points to major changes occurring in the psychological development of both children and adults as the result of such life experiences as growing up in the Great Depression or serving in the military during wartime. On the other hand, the authors of both chapters emphasize the operation of counteractive forces that, overall, produce a high degree of stability and continuity in development of the life course. Thus, Magnusson and Cairns's final proposition reads: "Conservation in development is supported by constraints from without and from within, as well as by the correlated action of external and internal forces. The result is that social and cognitive functioning in development tends to be organized and conservative despite continuous change."

Similarly, one of the five "life-course mechanisms" that undergird Elder's theoretical model serves an analogous function. He calls it the "control" cycle, described as follows:

> This cyclical process has at its center the connection between a person's losing control and that person's efforts to restore control over life outcomes. . . . The process entails the production *and* reduction of discrepancies, disequilibration, and equilibration.
>
> The precipitating event for this process is one that substantially alters the balance between claims and resources. As the balance changes, the actor's control potential is threatened, and adaptive responses are called into play."

The comparison of these two, remarkably rich theoretical chapters reveals yet another and even more striking paradox. In his chapter, Elder observes that "theory in psychology cannot apprehend 'social structure as a constitutive force in development' when it views the social environment from the perspective of the individual." He makes a parallel criticism of contemporary sociological research on cohort and period effects for failing to identify the processes producing the observed changes. He then points to the life course perspective as the theoretical strategy of choice for rectifying shortcomings in both disciplinary domains: "To understand historical forces, then, we need an approach that begins with the transforming environment, not with the individual and a partial selection of social factors. . . . If one's objective is to understand social change in lives and developmental processes, the most effective research strategy would be to begin by studying the particular environmental change and its human implications."

As a developmental psychologist, I can only concur with Elder's characterization of my field, including my own theoretical and research endeavors within it, as one that "views the environment from the vantage point of the developing organism." What I would call into question, at least initially, is Elder's assertion that "theory in psychology cannot apprehend 'social structure as a constitutive force in development' *when* [my italics] it views the social environment from the perspective of the individual." Given a coactive model of development as a process of interaction between the individual and the multilevel environment in which he or she lives, entry from one or another pole of such a reciprocating system should not rule out being captured from the outset in its complementary dynamic field. Given such a bidirectional model, claiming a one-way entry from the environmental side is no more justifiable than insisting that life course development can be investigated and understood only by focusing initially on the individual as a biopsychological organism.

To invoke Elder's argument in reverse, proceeding first solely from the perspective of the environment "underplays" the critical importance of biologically based limits, imperatives, and potentials, both for the species as a whole and differentially for its individual members, that determine how the human organism will respond to particular forms of social change. A growing body of evidence suggests that the social changes taking place today in developed societies, particularly in the United States, are creating environments that are increasingly unfavorable to the realization of human potentials for competence and character. In sum, in the evolving paradigm of developmental science, it would seem important to be equally alert to the contributions of both organism and environment at every stage of the inquiry.

The introduction of a new idea in science can become such a precipitating event, one that "substantially alters the balance between claim and resources" not only in the particular science but also in the particular scientist who introduces a new idea. And in the effort to right the balance, there is the risk of initially overstating one's case. At least that was my own reaction, now almost two decades ago, when in the effort to move my own discipline, developmental psychology, beyond the laboratory into the real world, I described it as "the study of the strange behavior of children in strange situations with strange adults for the briefest possible period of time" (Bronfenbrenner, 1977, p. 513). The irony is that, today, a major thesis of what I am now calling the bioecological model (Bronfenbrenner, 1995; Bronfenbrenner & Ceci, 1994) involves a return to one of the elements I so summarily rejected in the past – namely, a focus on the moment-to-moment interaction between the developing person and the people, objects, and symbols in the immediate setting as the ultimate mechanism through which development occurs – a mechanism, however, that is profoundly influenced by the broader environmental contexts in which such settings are embedded over the life course.

It is not my purpose here to argue the merits and shortcomings of this formulation (both of which exist). Rather, my aim is to suggest that the introduction of important new theoretical ideas, especially in so inexact a field as developmental science, is likely to involve, and may even require, some elements of overstatement and lack of articulation with existing paradigms or other innovative formulations – a process analogous to that of Elder's control cycle. If so, then the lesson of this developmental reality is to encourage and incorporate these ideas, especially in an interdisciplinary context, so that, gradually, they can find their place in the larger corpus of scientific thought and empirical findings.

These same considerations apply, perhaps with even greater force, to the fourth and, in my judgment, most scientifically provocative chapter in the volume, Gilbert Gottlieb's exposition of the implications for developmental science of contemporary theory in developmental psychobiology. The central concept in Gottlieb's formulation is *epigenesis,* which he defines as follows: "Individual development is characterized by an increase of complexity of organization – that is, the emergence of new structural and functional properties and competencies – at all levels of analysis (molecular, subcellular, cellular, organismic) as a consequence of horizontal and vertical coactions among its parts, including organism-environment coactions."

This formulation is accompanied by an exciting array of observational studies and experiments demonstrating the powerful, even dramatic interplay between genetically based dynamic dispositions and variations in the form and extent of their expression as a function of the environment. Initially, that environment is within the organism itself. Witness the following example: "If they are left in place, cells in the upper one-third of an early frog embryo differentiate into nerve cells: If removed from that region, those same cells can become skin cells." Gottlieb then quotes Hans Spemann, the principal discoverer of the phenomenon of embryonic induction, and adds a Puckish comment of his own: " 'We are standing and walking on parts of our body which could have been used for thinking if they had developed in another position in the embryo.' . . . It might have been even more striking – and equally correct – if Spemann had elected to say: 'We are sitting on parts of our body which could have been used for thinking.' "

Moving beyond the prenatal period, Gottlieb describes his own ingenious experiments demonstrating crossover interactions between an organism's internal and external environments. Specifically, he established that "mallard duck embryos had to hear their own vocalizations prior to hatching if they were to show their usual highly specific behavioral response to the mallard maternal assembly call after hatching" – a phenomenon referred to as canalization.

As Gottlieb points out, such findings call into serious question the simplistic additive conceptions of the role of heredity and environment espoused and applied in the field of contemporary behavior genetics. But once again, from a broader scientific perspective, what is most noteworthy about Gottlieb's work is the isomorphism it reveals, and thereby validates, between his theoretical conceptions and those emerging in the preceding chapters of the volume. In this case, the similarity is all the more striking because all of the research cited by Gottlieb was conducted with nonhuman species. Yet he invokes many of the very same constructs and principles employed by Magnusson and Cairns. For example: "So far we have dealt with the concepts of emergence and coaction as they pertain to the development of individuals. The notion of hierarchy, as it applies to individual development, simply means that coactions occur vertically as well as horizontally in all developmental systems. All the parts of the system are capable of influencing all the other parts of the system, however indirectly that influence may manifest itself."

But the recognition of analogical concepts and principles across disciplines does not by itself move developmental science forward unless the formulations in one field can generate new, potentially explanatory hypotheses in the other. In contrast to both Magnusson and Cairns, and to Elder, Gottlieb does not draw any concrete implications from his model for future research on the development of humans. This is regrettable, for it is difficult for researchers not working in the context of his particular substantive domain and theoretical framework to discern just what these implications might be. Is one to assume that, in Gottlieb's view canalization also occurs in the human species – for instance, that there are prenatal experiences that narrow the range of behavioral dispositions in newborn infants after birth? And if the biologically deterministic assumptions of contemporary behavioral genetics are in fact invalid, as he contends, what theoretical and operational models, if any, can be applied to investigate processes and outcomes of gene-environment interaction in humans?

Each of the remaining chapters in this remarkable book is an attempt to provide a coherent answer to the question I just raised. It is not entirely smooth sailing. The careful reader will find more than one occasion when representatives of Carol Eckerman's two modes of developmental research – the "hawks" and the "moles" – live in entirely separate worlds. Some of the larger problems arise when they try to get together. "Tensions arise, for instance, when different domains evolve separate meanings for the same terms or when they compete for hegemony."

In this foreword, I presume to suggest that, in their commendable caution in not going beyond the as yet available research findings in their respective fields, the authors understate the ultimate scientific importance of what they have accomplished. For the dynamic framework they have conceived, both deductively and inductively, is capable of generating testable hypotheses at the level of higher-order systems that posit powerful linkages across traditional disciplinary borders (e.g., biology, psychology, sociology, as well as history, economics, and demography).

Finally, and perhaps most consequentially for the future of developmental science, the emergent model the authors discern not only permits but explicitly requires a reversal of the most pronounced trend in psychological science over the past half century, namely, its return to the "faculty psychology" of a bygone era, but now institutionalized in the form of separate organizations and journals devoted exclusively to research in particular psychological domains such as, e.g., cognition, emotion, motivation, psychopathology, and social behavior.

The members of the Carolina Consortium propose nothing less than the scientifically disciplined integration of these centrifugal trajectories under the unifying banner of development as a process of "coaction" between, on the one hand, individual human beings as active, holistically functioning biopsychological organisms and, on the other hand, the equally dynamic multilevel environmental systems in which they live their lives. This process of coaction is posited as continuing not only over the life course but also across successive generations.

Acknowledgments

This volume grew out of the activities of the Carolina Consortium on Human Development and its parent organization, the Center, an advanced-studies institute for Developmental Science, is supported as a basic behavioral research center by the Division of Neuroscience and Basic Behavioral Science of the National Institute of Mental Health. The postdoctoral and predoctoral training activities of the Carolina Consortium have been funded by the National Institute of Child Health and Human Development. The collaboration this volume represents would not have been possible without the support of these institutes, their scientific administrators, and our peers who judged the endeavor to be worthy.

A large number of colleagues have contributed to the ideas represented in this volume, and many participated in the weekly discussions from which the volume evolved. Our predoctoral and postdoctoral fellows played a key role in the formulation of the ideas and the presentations of the chapters. Our special thanks are extended to Ann McGuire, who was key in the planning phase and who contributed significantly to its organization. Indeed, she could well be included as a coeditor of the volume. Over the years, other Consortium fellows who participated in the discussions and debates included Debra Skinner, Catherine Haden, Philip Rodkin, Tom Farmer, Laura Sadowski, Anne Fletcher, Tamara Halle, Scott Gest, Kelly Bost, Cheryl Ann Sexton, Debra Mekos, Michael Shanahan, Holly J. Neckerman, and Brenda Volling.

The preparation of this book for publication has itself been a collaborative enterprise. We particularly thank Adrienne Himmelberg, Rebecca Premock, Amy Briceño, Tamara Ladd, Sarah Hearne, and Beverley Cairns for their help. The assistance was sandwiched between other research and administrative activities, and it required very early and very late hours.

Our Cambridge University editor, Julia Hough, has been our lifeline through the preparation of this book. We thank her for her encouragement, patience, and strong support.

Individual acknowledgments follow:

Chapter 2: These propositions were framed by the discussions and debates in seminars of the Carolina Consortium on Human Development, and the authors owe much to their colleagues for their contributions. But because debate implies at least some disagreement, they accept responsibility for the specific formulation. The fact that the two coauthors tailored their methods and concepts to fit the needs of longitudinal research is not remarkable. That they independently arrived at similar conclusions on theory and method is. RBC expresses his gratitude to the Spencer Foundation and NIMH for their support in this work.

Chapter 3: Work on this chapter was supported by the National Institute of Mental Health (MH 41327, MH 43270, and MH 51361), a contract with the U.S. Army Research Institute, a grant from the Department of Veterans Affairs Merit Review program, research support from the John D. and Catherine T. MacArthur Foundation Program for Successful Adolescent Development Among Youth in High-Risk Settings, and a Research Scientist Award (MH 00567).

Chapter 4: This chapter is an updated version of a portion of the author's article "Experiential Canalization of Behavioral Development: Theory," which appeared in *Developmental Psychology,* 1991, vol. 27, pp. 4–13, and is reproduced here with the permission of the American Psychological Association.

Chapter 6: Work on this chapter was supported in part by a Research Scientist Award to the first author from the National Institute of Mental Health.

Chapter 7: Preparation of this chapter was supported in part by Grants HD 27176 and MH 43904 from the United States Public Health Service.

Chapter 9: This chapter was written with the support of faculty-scholar awards from the William T. Grant Foundation, as well as support from the Leon Lowenstein Foundation.

Chapter 10: Preliminary versions of this chapter were presented at the Carolina Consortium on Human Development, Chapel Hill, N.C., 21 October 1991, and the Conference on Human Development, Atlanta, Ga., 10 April 1992. We are very grateful to the members of the Carolina Consortium for comments and suggestions, and in particular to Gabrielle Albert, Louis Gariépy, David Goldstein, Ann Hagell, Nancy Hurlbut, Beth Kurtz-Costes, Angela O'Rand, and Brenda Volling.

1 Developmental Science: A Collaborative Statement

The Carolina Consortium on Human Development

Developmental science refers to a fresh synthesis that has been generated to guide research in the social, psychological, and biobehavioral disciplines. It describes a general orientation for linking concepts and findings of hitherto disparate areas of developmental inquiry, and it emphasizes the dynamic interplay of processes across time frames, levels of analysis, and contexts. Time and timing are central to this perspective. The time frames employed are relative to the lifetime of the phenomena to be understood. Units of focus may be as short as milliseconds, seconds, and minutes, or as long as years, decades, and millennia. In this perspective, the phenomena of individual functioning are viewed at multiple levels – from the subsystems of genetics, neurobiology, and hormones to those of families, social networks, communities, and cultures.

We believe that recognizing the complexity of development is the first step toward understanding its coherence and simplicity. In this perspective, patterns of adaptation represent interactions across levels within and without the person. Because the relative weights of these contributors to behavior vary across ontogeny and across domains, longitudinal analyses have particular value in understanding how they are coalesced over development. The pathways of development are relative to time and place; they contribute to – and reflect – temporal changes in culture and society. Developmental investigation focuses attention on the ontogenies of both embryos and ancestors, and on the process by which pathways may be repeated or redirected across successive generations. Toward this end, comparative, cross-cultural, and intergenerational research strategies should be employed in conjunction with standard experimental methods.

The preamble to this chapter summarizes our consensus on the scope and concerns of developmental science. In this volume, we elaborate on the propositions embedded in the preamble and explore their implications for scientific research and social applications.

1

Developmental science has roots in both the biological and social disciplines. The need for a systematic developmental perspective has long been recognized in comparative psychology and behavioral biology. Fresh statements of this kernel assumption have recently evolved in developmental psychobiology, dynamic systems approaches, and models of neurobehavioral development.[1] Simultaneously, the need for a developmental approach to the social and cognitive phenomena was expressed in the work of Baldwin (1897), Cottrell (1942), Piaget (1926), Lewin (1931), and Vygotsky (1962). Over the past two decades, these ideas, too, have been extended and elaborated in social ecology, social development, cognitive development, and life-course analysis.[2]

The modern developmental orientation – including the term "developmental science" itself – has won reasonably broad acceptance over the last decade. Nonetheless, shortcomings remain in attempts to translate it into an effective program of research, training, and application. Part of the problem appears to be the inertia of traditional disciplines and the rigidity of existing research boundaries. To the extent that ideas remain at an abstract level, they do not demand a reorientation of existing academic disciplines and separate domains of knowledge. On this score, advances in scholarship typically precede changes in institutional structure. The study of development is no exception. Discipline and institutional barriers are deeply rooted, and the gap between biological-health training and behavioral-social training has proved difficult to bridge.

A second part of the problem has been the demands of the orientation upon the individuals who aspire to conduct holistic developmental study. To support the concept of interdisciplinary research is one thing; to expect that individuals will embrace and teach the concepts in areas beyond those in which they themselves were trained is another. Not only must oppor-

---

[1] The pioneers in the embryology of behavior and behavioral biology include Kuo (1967), Schneirla (1966), Weiss (1939/1969), and von Bertalanffy (1933/1962). Beyond the chapters in this volume, introductions to recent developments in behavioral biology could include, for instance, developmental psychobiology (e.g., Gottlieb, 1992; Hood, Greenberg, & Tobach, 1995), ethology (e.g., Bateson, 1991; Hinde, 1966), dynamic systems approaches (e.g., Thelen & Smith, 1994; Smith & Thelen, 1993), and developmental neurobiological approaches (e.g., Magnusson, 1996).

[2] Beyond the chapters in this volume, see, for example, statements on social ecology (Bronfenbrenner, 1979; Sameroff & Fiese, 1990), social development (Cairns, 1979; Cairns & Cairns, 1994; Eckerman, 1993a; Magnusson, 1988; 1995), cognitive development (Valsiner, 1987), and life-course analysis (Elder, 1995; Moen, Elder, & Lüscher, 1995).

tunities and facilities for such training be provided, but the candidates and the faculty must be highly motivated to attain skills that go beyond a single discipline.

The perspective is still evolving. The orientation demands a fresh look at research design and analysis. Without a thorough reexamination of methodology and analyses and their relations to theory, investigators may become, unwittingly, attracted to procedures that are ill-suited for studying developmental processes. In this regard, some of the more rigorous experimental designs, measures, and statistics in psychology characteristically control for (or eliminate) variance attributable to age changes or maturational differences. In contrast, the developmental perspective requires research methodologies and analyses that promote the study of ontogenetic integration across levels and over time.

Then there are the issues of the breadth of the time intervals studied and the scope of their measurement. Attention to time intervals brings attention to the possible time-boundedness of observations in a given society. Temporal changes within a culture can invalidate even the most carefully framed generalizations about behavior and social processes, to the extent that these generalizations have been restricted in time and place. But temporal change should not be seen simply as a handicap, as it has sometimes been viewed within psychology. Within the present framework, these temporal shifts are employed to clarify the developmental mechanisms at work and demonstrate their operation in concrete instances of adaptation. One mediating link between ontogenetic and temporal-generational study can be found in the detailed analysis of the processes of intergenerational transmission and intergenerational change.

Magnusson (1988) has called for longitudinal research designs that accurately reflect the integration of processes within individuals and sequential changes over development. Person-oriented as well as variable-oriented analyses should be employed to track individuals over successive ontogenetic stages. To ensure that the hard-won gains in statistical rigor and empirical objectivity are not compromised, precise linkages must be established with traditional methods of statistical analysis. Where differences appear, the reasons for the differences must be carefully explored and their implications monitored (Magnusson & Bergman, 1990).

Issues of human development are central to modern society. Each stage of developmental progress presents special problems for adaptation and health. For example, adolescence is characterized by asymptotic levels of automobile accidents and personal injuries, including those caused by violent crime. It is also the period associated with the onset of drug and alcohol addiction and with a sharp increase in self-destructive behavior. The school failures and drop-out rates of adolescents are directly linked to earlier identified problems in their academic performance and motivation, including specific disabilities in reading.

Adolescence cannot be viewed, however, independently of the stages of development that precede it, nor can it be divorced from later life stages or from the transmission that occurs from one generation to the next. Problem behavior in adolescence is usually continuous with problem behavior in childhood, but it also shapes life chances for the adult years. Such pathways of development constitute a critical part of the story of how behavior patterns are transmitted across generations. Behaviors in childhood may or may not persist into the years of childbearing and child rearing. In order to plot across-time linkages, longitudinal studies of individuals, families, and social groups are required. The longitudinal research design has become recognized as critical for understanding the diverse issues of development, education, and health.

Developmental trajectories occur in changing worlds. There is good reason to expect that people mature and age in different ways according to these changes. Indeed, there are dramatic modifications worldwide in the structure of the family, in the economic support available to children, and in the perceived responsibilities of adults for their aging parents. An adequate account of families requires attention to intergenerational social bonds, including those established between grandparent and grandchild, as well as to parent-child relationships. Virtually every index on trends in American society indicates that changes in family structure will continue unabated into the next century. Behavioral and social investigations have been unable to keep pace with these family trends, despite the dire implications of some of the changes. The costs to society of providing for alternative care, child health, and education will multiply over the next decade. But if the decisions are based on inadequate knowledge, the costs will be even greater.

Although human development is a central issue in this volume, we recognize that an understanding of developmental processes necessarily involves study that is multilevel and integrated. This is in accord with Kuo's (1967) proposal that "The study of behavior is a synthetic science. It includes comparative anatomy, comparative embryology, comparative physiology (in the biophysical and biochemical sense), experimental morphology, and qualitative and quantitative analysis of the dynamic relationship between the organism and the external physical and social environment" (p. 25). Kuo himself studied animals, and several of us who contributed to this volume have focused on nonhumans in our research.

Others of us focus on social, emotional, and cognitive processes in humans. Together, we concur that the "synthetic science" of development should be inclusive rather than exclusive. A distinctive feature of this volume – and the Carolina Consortium discussions that led to its production – is the belief that developmental constructs that have emerged from social and cognitive research in humans can be productively merged with constructs from research on animals and basic processes in infants. We also believe that confrontation can lead to clarification and advances in understanding when the inquiries are open and friendly, when one's colleagues are held in the highest regard, and when the group is bound together by a common, compelling goal. It was in this spirit that the present volume was prepared.

One may question whether the study of young organisms is sufficient reason for the definition of a new science. But the question itself is misleading, in that the essential concerns of development are not limited to children. Development encompasses the entire manifold of the life course, from conception to death, and into the next generation. Children become parents in their own time, and novelties introduced in one generation can become the traditions of the next.

This view of development requires concepts and measures that permit the description of persons-in-context through time and space. We see individuals as integrated and integrating units that are dynamic and change over time. This proposal is in conflict with a reductionistic view that the adaptations of persons could be partitioned into separate variables and elementary units of behavior or biology, and removed from the whole for independent analysis. In the developmental framework that we have adopted throughout this volume, the biologies and actions of persons are mutually constrained over time. The emerging holistic view has multiple consequences for research design, measurement, and analysis.

This latter point is a relevant response to the criticism that the introduction of developmental concepts may be a step backward because of the complexity that is introduced. We disagree. In our view, recognition of the complexity of behavioral development has been, paradoxically, a key to achieving both greater accuracy and parsimony in measurement. By omitting developmental and contextual considerations, traditional psychological models have tried to solve the puzzles of behavior with less than half of the pieces on the board. Allowing more information into the system – including details about ontogeny and context – provides components that are essential to understanding how persons adapt to the concrete realities of life.

What has been new in the last two decades has been the emergence of the results of detailed prospective longitudinal studies of human beings. These findings have forced the reevaluation of traditional conceptions of behavioral functions and of how these functions are organized over time in children, adolescents, and adults. They have also provided new solutions to the problem of how behaviors are organized in context. This concrete information on development has become wedded to psychobiological constructs of ontogeny, and the synthesis that has emerged has in turn created pressure for radical change in traditional measures, designs, and constructs.

The statement on the scope and limits of developmental science provided here is an introduction to the issues addressed in this volume. It was given its preliminary form during discussion and debate among the faculty and fellows of the Carolina Consortium on Human Development. It is a statement that continues to evolve, and the nature of this evolution is reflected in the chapters that follow.

2 Developmental Science: Toward a Unified Framework

David Magnusson and Robert B. Cairns

A fresh synthesis of ideas and findings has recently emerged across the several areas of developmental investigation. As indicated in Chapter 1, this synthesis employs concepts that have issued from longitudinal investigations, life-course studies of contextual change, cognitive development, and developmental psychobiology. Consistent with the collaborative statement, the stuff of development is seen as arising from the dynamic interrelations among systems that exist within and without persons. A nuclear principle of this holistic framework of development is that "the individual is an active, purposeful part of an integrated, complex and dynamic person-environment system. A consequence of this view is that it is not possible to understand how social systems function without knowledge of individual functioning, and it is not possible to understand individual functioning and development without knowledge of the environment" (Magnusson & Stattin, in press). Accordingly, development is not simply a property of individuals – social interactions develop, communities change, and societies evolve. In this chapter, we summarize some principles that provide a bridge between the conceptual framework of developmental science and the concrete methods required for the conduct of developmental research.

In the consensus statement in Chapter 1, we observed that "recognizing the complexity of development is the first step toward understanding its coherence and simplicity." The problem has been that it has been difficult for researchers to move beyond the first step. Accordingly, the holistic perspective described in the collaborative statement presupposes multidisciplinary methods and multilevel measures. These procedures are required to analyze the integrated operation of bidirectional and correlated systems across levels of influence. A developmental orientation implies that observations should be extended over time and generations in order to plot the mechanisms and rates of change and to identify developmental pathways that are formed for persons and contexts.

7

What Develops?

Given the current state of research in behavioral science, it is clearly beyond the scope of any single researcher to investigate simultaneously all of the systems that contribute to behavioral adaptations. Choices have to be made, and the question "What develops?" must be addressed at the beginning of any investigation. Does the problem involve time-related changes in social behavior, perception, neurobiology, communication, disease processes, social networks, or cultures? The dilemma is that these systems simultaneously undergo changes over time, and together they contribute to the social and adaptive functioning of persons and societies. However, in order to achieve precision in empirical analysis and understanding, decisions must be made to bring some features to the foreground and move others into the background. Developmental researchers trained in neurobiology and genetics inevitably adopt different starting points in their investigations than, say, those trained in life-course sociology and anthropology. And this decision on where to begin has inevitable consequences for what kinds of specific generalizations will first emerge.

This volume illustrates the point. Elder (Chap. 3, this volume) demonstrates that generational changes in society provide a window for understanding how environmental changes help produce modifications in family processes and individual development. In contrast, Gottlieb (Chap. 4, this volume) shows that the sensory and perceptual development of the embryonic or neonatal organism provides a productive entry for understanding the bidirectional developmental system. But it is also clear from both Gottlieb's and Elder's chapters that the authors consider the developmental analyses incomplete without explicit accounts of interactions with systems above, or below, the points of entry that they selected. Parallel accounts of convergence, despite different starting points, are found in each chapter of this volume. This is illustrated in comparisons between the social-communication concerns raised separately by Eckerman and Tudge, Putnam, and Valsiner, and the biobehavioral issues raised in companion chapters by Gariépy and Sameroff and Suomi. Morrison and Ornstein raise the issues of developmental pathways in the analysis of cognitive processes, while Costello and Angold speak to a comparable concern in understanding the development of psychopathology.

Differences in starting points should not, therefore, obscure the common ground upon which developmental research proceeds. To this end, we believe that it should be helpful to summarize certain of the assumptions shared by virtually all developmental investigators regardless of their specific area of expertise. The common goal is to understand how the multiple systems that influence individual development – from cultural processes to genetic and physiological events to social interactions – become integrated over time to promote healthy, adaptive functioning or its converse. The orientation is developmental because of a shared concern with the emergence, dynamics, and pathways of change of component systems and of individuals as a whole. Essential developmental questions include how interacting systems influence each other and are brought into alignment over time.

"Coming of Age": Developmental Integration over Time and Space

To illustrate the developmental research strategy, consider the findings from recent longitudinal investigations into the relationship between early pubertal maturation and attitudes and behaviors (Caspi, 1995; Caspi & Moffitt, 1991; Stattin & Magnusson, 1990). In brief, the research indicates a link between developmental changes in rates of maturation, social relationships, and deviant behaviors. Specifically, very early maturation in girls is associated with a variety of deviant behaviors, and this relationship is mediated by the effects of differential affiliation in the girls' social networks.

In a longitudinal investigation of 1,300 Swedish children, Stattin and Magnusson (1990) reported that the girls who reached menarche very early (≤ 11 years of age) tended to show multiple signs of behavioral deviancy. Deviance among these very-early-maturing girls included, at 14 years of age, higher alcohol consumption, more cheating in school, greater amounts of sexual activity, and adoption of antisocial norms relative to the attitudes of late-maturing girls at the same age.

Following a developmental model, these investigators (Magnusson, 1988; Stattin & Magnusson, 1990) reasoned that the effects may have been mediated by social interchanges that were provoked and supported by the early maturation. The girls affiliated more with older peers and adopted developmentally advanced actions and values. The result was that their sexual and social behaviors deviated, for a 15-month period, from age-appropriate standards. Support was obtained in the IDA longitudinal data set for this maturation-affiliation-activity interpretation (Magnusson, 1988; Stattin & Magnusson, 1990). Consistent with the hypothesis, this effect was observed only among early-maturing girls who had affiliated in early adolescence with older males who were out of school and working.

More broadly, it is not merely the rate of onset of sexual maturity that accounts for the prediction of deviance in adolescence. To the contrary, a key mediational variable appears to be the social affiliations that were promoted by the biological changes. It should be emphasized that the specific deviance–pubertal onset relationship was limited to the years of mid adolescence. By age 15, most differences in deviance had diminished. When later-maturing girls reached a similar state of sexual maturity, no differences were observed in female antisocial behavior as a function of rate of maturation. But a follow-up in adulthood showed that some effects associated with early maturation still persisted. The very early-maturing girls had married earlier, had more children, and had achieved less advanced education relative to the average or late-maturing girls.

Essential features of these findings have been replicated in other settings and with other samples. For instance, Caspi and Moffitt (1991) found the same early maturation–deviance phenomenon in the longitudinal study of a sample of New Zealand girls. The effect was obtained, however, only if the girls were enrolled in a coeducational school. Presumably, the opportunities for deviance by differential association were greater in the coeducational setting than they were in all-girl schools.

Such boundary conditions for the maturation-deviance effect point to the role of social context in determining the nature of the phenomenon. Viewed in this light, cross-cultural and cross-generational designs are absolutely required for the systematic developmental study of social interactions. According to Bronfenbrenner (1958), studies of the variations in the effects of child-rearing practices over time and space are critical for understanding the processes of socialization. The same principle doubtless holds for studies of the maturation-deviance effect. In a holistic framework, the variations in outcome across societies could reflect context differences in multiple domains. Toward this end, it would be instructive to identify social contexts where early maturation supports differential peer affiliations but does not lead to increased behavioral deviance.

Such contexts occur in the United States. In a longitudinal study of two samples of American youth, Cairns and Cairns (1994) confirmed that girls who matured very early tended to hang around with other girls who also matured very early.[3] But very early sexual maturation was *not* associated with subsequent problem behaviors. In the American samples, age of men-

---

[3] In this investigation, "very early" referred to girls who reached menarche between 9 and 11.5 years of age. The mean age of menarche was 12.6 years of age in the combined U.S. samples, virtually identical to the mean reported by Magnusson (1988) in his Swedish sample.

arche was not strongly linked to any of the measures of adolescent deviance (e.g., aggression, substance use, low school achievement), nor were they related to early marriage, teenage parenthood, or lower levels of educational achievement. Moreover, the effects of maturation on social affiliation were relatively modest compared to those of other behavioral and demographic factors that had a powerful influence on peer group formation among American girls. The most robust longitudinal predictors of deviance in this investigation were childhood expressions of aggressive behavior and poor school performance. To be sure, affiliation with deviant peers was an important predictor of subsequent problems, but the tendency to affiliate with deviant peers was not associated with very early maturation in girls (Cairns & Cairns, 1994).

The relativity of specific biological-behavioral correlations illustrates the dynamic interrelations among systems within and without persons. In the first half of the 20th century, female adolescent delinquents were arrested primarily for status offenses (sexual promiscuity, incorrigibility). In the second half of the century, there was a sharp diminution in arrests for status offenses – girls now tend to be arrested for the same kinds of violent and property crimes as are boys (Schlossman & Cairns, 1993). Over the same period, correlated generational changes occurred in America in (a) the acceptability of sexual behaviors and (b) the criteria for judgments of feminine attractiveness. These temporal-generational changes in the context of development, in social attributions, and in the dynamics of social influence may account for the modest role that sexual maturation now plays in adolescent deviance among American girls. Consistent with Elder's (Chap. 3, this volume) emphasis on the powerful effects of social change upon social development, there has been a reversal in how adolescent female "deviance" and "delinquency" are defined in American society.

Toward a Unified Framework

Modern studies of human ontogeny are concerned with the establishment of, maintenance of, and change in structures and processes over the life span and across generations. Development, in its most general form, refers to any process of progressive change. When applied to the special issues of activity and adaptation, it must encompass changes in the biological processes of the organism and changes in the organism's social and nonsocial contexts over time (see Baldwin, 1895, 1902; Mills, 1899; Morgan, 1896, for earlier statements on this matter; more recently, the ideas have been extended in Cairns, 1979; Gottlieb, 1991b; King, 1967; Magnusson, 1988, 1995; and Scott, 1977). Accordingly:

1. *An individual develops and functions psychologically as an integrated organism. Maturational, experiential, and cultural contributions are fused in ontogeny. Single aspects do not develop and function in isolation, and they should not be divorced from the totality in analysis.*

In the example of early-maturing girls, the effects of pubertal timing cannot be divorced from the social context in which puberty occurs. It is virtually impossible to identify a social activity in either human beings or animals that does not reflect the simultaneous contribution of forces within and without the organism (Magnusson & Törestad, 1993). To understand social actions, attention must be paid to time and place as well as to physical maturation and neurobiology. A primary concern for science is to create integrated methods for clarifying the development of persons in their particular social context.

This first principle has sometimes been misunderstood to mean that the developmental perspective is simply another holistic approach, not unlike gestalt psychology's protest against behaviorism. To be sure, the details of developmental processes can be comprehended only if the full range of experimental, neurobiological, and analytic strategies are precisely and rigorously employed. However, this principle clearly does *not* require that all investigations must assess all levels simultaneously. Unless the circumstances are unusual, investigators are expected to simultaneously assess two, or possibly three, levels of influence. Investigators are limited by their resources and tools in the concurrent tracking of multiple levels of information. But the limitations of measurement and design should not handicap the study's framework. Developmental study necessarily involves a systems analysis, even though not all system studies are developmental.

The perspective just discussed provides a basis for planning, implementing, and interpreting studies of specific developmental problems. In planning research on a certain problem within this framework three steps are implied. First, the level of the process that is under consideration must be identified. Second, the empirical data to be collected must be appropriate to the level of the process at which the problem has been identified. Third, the results of the study must be interpreted with reference to immediately linked levels of the subsystem under investigation. History is full of examples of how violation of these basic principles led to fruitless debate on central issues. For example, the controversy over the existence of traits and cross-situational consistency in behavior could not result in any meaningful conclusions as long as transsituational consistency in aggregate data at the trait level was used as an argument against the existence of person-situation interactions. Conversely, individual differences in cross-situational profiles, based on situation-specific data, were used as an argument against the existence of personality traits.

This principle addresses the question of how ontogeny is guided. The proposition that the individual develops and functions as a totality and that each aspect of individual functioning gets its meaning from the role it plays in the totality has broad empirical support in modern biological science (Schneirla, 1966; von Bertalanffy, 1933/1962).[4] Thus the optimal functioning of the totality serves as the goal for the development and functioning of the separate parts. No part develops and functions with its own optimal functioning as its sole goal. The cardiac system provides a biological illustration of the operation of self-organizing systems. If either a single component or several components collapse or fail, the remaining components reorganize themselves so that the total cardiac system fulfills it role in the support of the organismic system.

The developmental view has not been dominant in either personality research or social research. Traditionally, research has been designed around single variables and their interrelations. Examples in longitudinal studies would include variables such as "aggression," "intelligence," and "early pubertal maturation." Within the modern developmental framework, the psychological significance of such variables in the developmental processes of the individual cannot be effectively studied if they are divorced from the social and environmental contexts in which they occur.

> 2. *An individual develops and functions in a dynamic, continuous, and reciprocal process of interaction with his or her environment, including relations with other individuals, groups, and the subculture.*

The term "homophily" refers to similarities among members of natural-peer social groups. In childhood and adolescence, persons in the same social group tend to be similar on salient domains of gender, age, physical

---

[4] In the applied natural sciences as well. For instance, empirical research on specific issues in meteorology is planned, implemented, and interpreted within a general theoretical framework integrating information on the stratosphere, the landscape, the wind, and the ocean temperatures and currents.

development, and individual adjustment. Thus leaders in a school or summer camp will rapidly form elite social clusters, whereas, conversely, aggressive youth will develop coercive cliques that, under some conditions, escalate into gangs. Membership in these social clusters is itself a dynamic process. Once an individual is in a social structure, the attitudes and actions of that person become aligned with those of other members of the group.

A major reason for the reshuffling of relationships is environmental change, for example, year-to-year shifts in classroom assignment, changes in residence, or life-course transitions, such as graduation from high school or marriage. In general, actions and social structures have the property of rapid and reversible adjustment to environmental change.

The second proposition follows directly from the first principle and should properly be considered its corollary. It deals with the bidirectionality of social influence and with how individuals are synchronized with each other and with their contexts. The idea is embodied in Bronfenbrenner's (1979) model of social ecology and in Magnusson's (1988) proposal that the person is an active, purposeful agent in continuous, moment-to-moment interaction with the social as well as the nonsocial world.

When we emphasize the reciprocal character of the process in which the individual and the environment are engaged, it is not usually as an interplay of two equal parts. The main organizing principle for an individual in dealing with the outer world is his or her cognition of the social and physical environment and connected motives, goals, values, and emotions. For this individual, this mental mediational system is framed in the process of interacting with the environment. At each stage, it plays a role in organizing the individual's interaction with the environment.

One other question raised by this view of reciprocating persons is the issue of individual integrity and interpersonal synchrony. How does an individual serve two masters at the same time? How is it possible for a person to maintain internal balance, on the one hand, and to adapt to other persons, on the other? In this respect, reciprocity and synchrony imply constraints upon action. Not all forms of synchrony between persons and settings are feasible, and most relationships will be resisted to the extent that major changes are required within the person. Nor is it the case that bidirectionality presupposes mutuality of influence or that the weights of influence will be equivalent at all stages of ontogeny. For example, parents have the ability to structure the environmental contingencies and world to which their offspring must adapt in normal parent-infant relationships. It may be a "two-way street of influence," but the traffic pattern resembles the flow on a highway in one direction and a footpath in the other. Among the more compelling research issues is to determine how the bidirectional processes of social influence change over time, and when and why differential influences are observed in infancy, childhood, adolescence, and maturity. This implies the need to analyze how the individual's mediating cognitive-emotional subsystems develop through maturation and experience and how they function in interactions.

In the accommodations of human development, the actions and counteractions of other persons constitute major extraorganismic sources of behavioral organization. When this proposition is taken seriously, the detailed, longitudinal investigation of social behavior becomes a matter of high priority for the biological sciences as well as for the psychological sciences.

> 3. *Individual functioning depends upon and influences the reciprocal interaction among subsystems within the individual; namely, the organization of interactional perceptual-cognitive, emotional, physiological, morphological, perceptual, and neurobiological factors over time.*

Some features of this proposition are hardly newsworthy. Consider the commonplace observation that weight lifting or exercise programs demonstrate that persons can sculpt their own morphologies if the activity is maintained. Scientific findings are less pedestrian, perhaps because they are less likely to be overtly observed. For instance, it has been firmly established that changes in an individual's social status and living conditions are directly correlated with changes in that person's emotional reactivity, physiology, and neurobiology. More broadly, internal states routinely come into alignment with experiences, and the readiness for further action is affected (Magnusson & Stattin, in press). In several mammalian species, for example, structural and biological changes occur within winners of aggressive bouts, and these changes are the opposite of those that occur in the losers (Cairns, 1979; Cairns, Gariépy, & Hood, 1990; Gariépy, Lewis, & Cairns, in press). The biological state of each organism is brought into line with the individual's current actions and with the anticipated consequences of the next encounter.

This proposition is also a corollary of the first principle. That biological states affect emotions, cognitions, and actions cannot be denied. Nor can effects in the opposite direction be ignored. There is now abundant evidence in animals and humans that actions and experiences align biological states, from the synchrony of menstrual cycles among college women who room together (Hood, 1996, for a recent review) and the cessation of lactation among mothers who chose not to breastfeed (Cairns, 1979). Again, the bidirectionality relation between behavior and biology has not been the dominant view in many areas of neurobiology, medicine, and psychology. Biological reductionism has been the dominant view. There are substantial reasons, however, to expect that the development of psychological processes will prove as much a key to understanding biological processes as vice versa. A methodological implication is that studies in behavioral genetics and neurobiology should begin with detailed accounts of development, especially psychological development. Actions, emotions, and cognitions – the stuff of psychology – have a special status for organismic adaptation and integration. On this score, psychological functioning can be reduced to "biological structure" only in a trivial and misleading sense. It is a mild irony that several areas of biology – sociobiology, ethology, and behavioral zoology – have embraced the primacy of social behavior, whereas the point remains unrecognized by many in psychology.

4. *Novel patterns of individual functioning arise during individual ontogeny.*

Girls develop new techniques of aggressive expression in late childhood, including the ability to ostracize and ridicule peers so that the victim is unaware of the person or persons attacking. This strategy is employed with increasing frequency by girls in late adolescence. In contrast, boys' attacks on their peers are characterized by direct confrontational techniques that leave attackers vulnerable to direct and violent reciprocation (Cairns, Cairns, Neckerman, Ferguson, & Gariépy, 1989).

Tracing backward from a person's adulthood to his or her childhood and infancy reveals few novelties in individual functioning. But it is a different story if one reverses the analysis and works forward, beginning with the embryonic and infancy states and advancing to childhood, adolescence, maturity, and senescence. In the lifetime of each individual, certain actions and thoughts emerge that are entirely novel. These include the development of the ability to locomote, to ingest solid foods, to think, to speak, and to affiliate in groups. In addition, as the research already discussed illustrates, the onset of the ability to procreate is an emergent, novel function that has multiple consequences. Such novelties can either reorganize existing patterns or create entirely new ones.

Standard theoretical constructs and statistical models are poorly equipped to address either type of novelty. Ordinarily this difficulty has been overcome by the use of the same trait to describe seemingly similar activities over the life span. But a problem arises when constructs that adequately describe activities in one stage of development are applied to subsequent stages, despite changes in operational definition. For example, the operations employed to identify "aggressiveness" in 3- to 4-year-old children are qualitatively different from those needed for 9- to 10-year-olds and 17- to 18-year-olds. To use the same construct to refer to qualitatively different activities can obscure the new phenomena and the mechanisms by which they are established. An equally common temptation is to use quantitative transformations – such as standard scores and IQ – that wipe out real differences and create the illusion of a common dimension despite qualitative differences over time. A large effort has been made in traditional psychology to eliminate the effects of time and age.

From this perspective, the concepts of homotypical and heterotypical continuity, which were important distinctions for their time, change meaning. These concepts were bound to and relevant for research in a tradition that discussed individual development mainly in terms of variables and that focused, in empirical research, on relations among variables. The issue thus would be whether, for example, measures of aggression for a sample of boys or girls at age 6 showed a higher correlation 6 years later with measures of aggression than with nonaggressive variables (i.e., homotypic continuity). Alternatively, the measure of early aggression might be most highly correlated with motor disturbance at 12 years (i.e., heterotypic continuity).

An essential element of the view discussed here is that the development of an individual cannot be meaningfully analyzed, explained, or understood in terms of single variables or relations among single variables, expressed as correlations. As we already noted, a fundamental characteristic of the developmental process is that the individual emerges as an integrated, total organism through a dynamic process. Across time, this implies that the total organism undergoes continuous transformation into new patterns of operating factors depending upon which factors operate, their relative roles, and their psychological significance for the totality. Because of this characteristic, traditional ways of studying homotypic and heterotypic continuity by correlation techniques are inappropriate and potentially misleading.

5. *Differences in the rate of development may produce major differences in the organization and configuration of psychological functions. The developmental rate of individual components may be accelerated or delayed relative to other features.*

Individual development reflects a mosaic of ontogenetic trajectories. Sexual development is a case in point. Sexual development is not unitary. Some features of the sexual adaptation of humans – such as gonadal structure and function – resist the effects of variations in experience at puberty. Other aspects of sexual behavior – such as preferred sexual activities and partners – may be strongly influenced in the pubertal years. Different features of sexuality call for different epigenetic landscapes and different formulations of bidirectionality. Acceleration in the age of menarche in humans has been associated with various outcomes, most of which have been viewed as negative for girls and positive for boys (Simmons & Blythe, 1987; Stattin & Magnusson, 1990). Beyond biology, the change in rate of development occasioned by early entry into school (by chance or by geography) has been associated with accelerated cognitive development in children. The advantages are enduring, and they extend beyond scholastic achievement to include advances in basic information processing and intellectual test performance (Morrison, 1991).

These concepts have a common focus upon the rate of development. If modifications in rate occur in the right system at the right time, slight variations can produce manifold differences.[5] The concept of heterochrony – which subsumes the phenomena of both delayed maturation and accelerated development – extends beyond developmental psychology into neurobiology and evolution (de Beer, 1958).

> 6. *Patterns of psychological functioning develop like dynamic systems in that they can be extremely sensitive to the conditions under which they are formed. Thus the emergence of psychological patterns cannot be accounted for solely in terms of the hierarchical organization of more elementary systems, nor can they be reduced to simpler experiential antecedents or more elementary biological units.*

Elements of experience and biology are seen as undergoing organization or reorganization at key points in ontogeny. For instance, many of the behavior problems of Swedish early-maturing girls who affiliate with deviant boys in adolescence are no longer problems in late adolescence. As the configuration of influences change, so do the activity patterns. Yet, as Magnusson (1988) has shown, the effects of some activities in adolescence

---

[5] This statement is linked to the "butterfly effect" in chaos theory (Gleick, 1987) and, earlier, to heterochrony in evolutionary theory (de Beer, 1958; Gould, 1977).

persist into late adolescence, leading to lower academic aspirations and to differences in childbearing, with the early maturers having children sooner.

More generally, this principle holds that during periods of organization and reorganization, preexisting features of the individual and new features of the environment are brought into alignment and synchronized in ways that enhance individual functioning and accommodation. The nature of the organization is thus equally dependent upon the available elements and the internal and external challenges. This conception that things change suddenly and by fits and starts is an element in what has been called "catastrophe theory" (Thom, 1972; Zeeman, 1976). Relatively few phenomena in nature are orderly and well-behaved; on the contrary, the world is full of sudden transformations and divergence. Nonetheless, there is a psychological lawfulness and mathematical order to be found in any analysis of the transformations themselves (Zeeman, 1976).

> 7. *Conservation in development is supported by constraints from without and from within, as well as by the correlated action of external and internal forces. The result is that social and cognitive functioning in development tends to be organized and conservative despite continuous change.*

The aggressive boy who is held back in school in the seventh grade is likely to affiliate the next year with other aggressive boys who have themselves been held back (Cairns & Cairns, 1994). The same holds true for girls. Hence aggressiveness and school failure, and the social problems associated with these patterns, are supported by the adolescents' peer network as well as by their internal dispositions. The social group, once established, becomes the primary reference group for its members' dating and bonding with persons of the opposite sex who show similar behavioral and educational configurations. Correlations among constellations of characteristics combine, in a fail-safe pattern, to support continuity in attitudes and actions.

At first blush, these last two points may appear to negate the earlier propositions of development. We contend, however, that these points are as conservative as they are malleable. The theoretical problem is to explain how conservatism arises in the midst of change, some of which may be described as "chaotic." The first principle implies conservatism and order. When, for example, two persons are synchronized in their actions, the actions of each provide direction for, and constraint on, the other. Should the constraints be violated, the relationship itself is challenged because of the dyssynchrony. In most relationships and in most social groups, there are strong pressures for conformity and strong sanctions against individual changes and novelty.

The challenge for contemporary theory in development is to establish a perspective systematic enough to integrate the multiple subprocesses of activity yet precise enough to direct the drive for evidence. Without such a model, contemporary research has increasingly relied upon advances in statistical modeling to unravel the relevant processes. These procedures (e.g., multivariate analyses and linear structural equations) are attractive because they permit the simultaneous evaluation of multiple variables, they rank variables in weight, and they provide guides for eliminating nonsignificant factors. When the limitations of data or statistics are encountered, simplifying assumptions can be made to reduce the complexity of the model. This analytic strategy has promoted advances in identifying the roles of interactional control, social learning, self-concepts, socioeconomic factors, maturational influences, and psychobiology in behavioral control. Such progress would have been difficult without advanced computer algorithms.

Similarly, the interrelations among subsystems of the organism support mutual consistency and help bring back into alignment those features that do not conform. When the linkages involve *correlated constraints* – a network of associations between social, environmental, and biological forces – there is codetermination of individual functioning (Cairns et al., 1990), which would make for a "unity" in functional organization. It would also limit the range of freedom for individual adaptation. The upshot is that ontogeny is considerably more conservative than has usually been appreciated.

Methods for a Developmental Framework

The adoption of a developmental perspective on the study of psychological phenomena has strong implications for research methods, including the designs employed, constructs embraced, and statistical procedures used. Because these issues of method have been discussed elsewhere in some depth (e.g., Magnusson & Bergman, 1990; Valsiner, 1986; Wohlwill, 1973), we only touch on some of the highlights.

Research Designs

Developmental study presupposes methods that permit the analysis of time-related changes in societies, environments, persons, and biological systems.

These phenomena call for the utilization of the full range of research design: experimental, naturalistic-ethnological, and comparative. In addition, a special burden is placed upon developmental research because the primary features of time and age cannot be manipulated or experimentally reversed.[6] On this score, Jessor and his colleagues have observed: "Understanding the integrity of the life course, tracing its continuity over large segments of time, distinguishing what is ephemeral from what is lasting, grasping the role that the past plays in shaping the future – all these, and more, are issues that yield only to research that is longitudinal and developmental in design" (Jessor, Donovan, & Costa, 1991).

Longitudinal designs lie at the heart of developmental research because they are required to plot the trajectories of change. But they are necessary. For instance, cross-sectional research designs constitute an economical and appropriate research strategy for plotting age-related changes in actions and functions. In addition, the precise analysis of mechanisms of development requires an integration of experimental, comparative, and longitudinal strategies.

Moreover, development is not limited to ontogeny: It encompasses relationships across generations. Each person's activities in her or his own life span are necessarily interwoven through experience and biology with the lives of both their parents and their children. These considerations point to the need for research designs that follow successive ontogenies of parents and offspring in order to compare similarities and differences at particular points in the life span. They are also necessary to analyze successive developmental trajectories. On this score, the expression of genetic similarities in behavior is not limited to the earliest stages of development, as has been commonly assumed in nature-nurture debates. To the contrary, von Baer's laws (1828) imply that the specific differences would be likely to emerge first not in development but at more advanced stages of ontogeny. Features of intergenerational similarity (e.g., pubertal onset, expression of violence, styles of parenting) require comparisons at the same age in the parents and the offspring (e.g., Cairns, McGuire, & Gariépy, 1993).

Given the need to clarify the mechanisms of development, greater attention should be given to designs that combine (a) the longitudinal study of individuals with (b) experimentally induced changes in the environment. In

---

6 This inherent restriction on developmental studies led G. Stanley Hall, one of the modern founders of developmental psychology, to assign its study a second-class status (Hall, 1885).

this regard, J. W. Mills (1899) argued that longitudinal designs should be the first step in developmental research. The second step should be to introduce systematic changes in the course of ontogeny. Despite the difficulties in their implementation, such designs are required for the identification of phases in ontogeny that are highly vulnerable to environmental changes as well as phases that are highly resistant. If such periods are identified, they can locate "windows of vulnerability" when preventive interventions can be productively introduced.

There have been few instances of the combination of intergenerational and experimental longitudinal research. Yet such research is necessary for identifying mechanisms of microevolutionary change. For example, the effects of developmental manipulation can be studied not only in the life spans of individuals but also in the life spans of their progeny. If intergenerational effects are observed, they may be mediated by genetic mechanisms, neurobiological mechanisms, or behavioral transmission across generations.

Pitfalls in Longitudinal Research. Because developmental research requires a large investment in individuals over time, data quality and retention of subjects emerge as primary concerns in the day-to-day conduct of investigations (see Kessen, 1960; Loeber & LeBlanc, 1990; and Magnusson & Bergman, 1990). With each year, the margin of permissible error becomes smaller, and efficiency and accuracy gain in importance. This concern with data quality led us to reexamine the assumption that the researchers who are least trained and least prepared should be the ones to have direct contact with subjects. In some cases, for more highly trained and sophisticated researchers to have contact with subjects the priorities in the distribution of time and talent must be reversed. In our research, we found it useful to include senior researchers in data collection in ways consistent with the need to ensure objectivity in interpretation.

Subject loss and lack of cooperation loom as special problems in longitudinal studies of aggressive and antisocial behavior. Most likely to be lost are those individuals who are at greatest risk for dropping out of school and other deviant outcomes (Cairns & Cairns, 1991; Farrington & West, 1990). Maintenance of the sample also has an impact on data quality. The instruments used should take into account the cost to subjects (both perceived and real) as well as the information that the procedures will yield. Quantity of information should not be equated with quality. Subjects may be overwhelmed by the number of questions and the level of their intrusiveness. Further, researchers may be tyrannized by the amount of data that is yielded. Repeating exactly the same lengthy battery of inventories over multiple assessments may diminish, not enhance, the value of the study. If behavioral novelty and developmental changes are anticipated, the procedures should be age appropriate. Ongoing analyses are important to ensure that the information obtained is relevant to the constructs that are assessed.

Developmental Constructs and Statistics

It is a minor irony that many conceptual and statistical procedures introduced to study development in children reduce the impact of developmental change (Cairns, 1986; Wohlwill, 1973). For example, the product-moment correlation effectively eliminates real differences in performance associated with maturation. Similarly, statistical transformations that underlie the IQ ratio appear to have been introduced to eliminate age-related differences in cognitive functioning. Modern refinements of scaling have achieved the same outcome through standard scores, where same-age peers provide the reference group. These scaling techniques are not limited to the study of intelligence. They have become the strategies of choice for other domains of developmental assessment, including measures of aggressiveness, deviance, and unconventional actions.

The logic of the research task should be the criterion against which the adequacy of a given design or statistical analysis is judged. Accordingly, it has seemed reasonable to assume that because deviant phenomena are multidetermined and complex, the procedures and statistical analyses employed to study them should also be complex. However, this assumption demands critical scrutiny. Exactly the opposite conclusion can be reached if the principal task for developmental research is to understand and clarify. Reliance upon complexity in analysis to disentangle the network of multiple causes and outcomes may simply reflect shortcomings in other phases of the research. It is often the case that to clarify complex issues, the simpler the statistic, the better. Parsimony in analysis can be permitted because the major analytic problems have been solved earlier; namely, in the design created, in the methods adopted, and in the precision of the hypotheses.

Developmental researchers are usually confronted with networks of relationships, not single antecedent-consequent linkages. This state of affairs has yielded a cornucopia of positive findings and interpretations. The abundance of "significant" antecedent-consequent linkages in contemporary developmental research has also had a negative side, however, in that it shifts responsibility for understanding phenomena away from the data themselves. The findings have often become projective tests for the field, where the burden for interpretation shifts from data to a priori beliefs.

Beyond the usual challenges that face investigators who are confronted with complex data sets, developmental researchers have special problems. The first and more general difficulty confronting them is that available statistical models are inconsistent with developmental questions. For example, one question concerns novelty in development and how new adaptations emerge and lead to the reorganization of existing actions and dispositions. Virtually all "life-course" and "developmental" hypotheses presuppose that fresh influences and new opportunities arise either from within the individual or from the social context. Most theoretical constructs of personality and statistical models assume, however, that there is nothing new under the sun.

The assumption that there are stable factors or dimensions of personality seems implicit in many applications of structural equation models to longitudinal data sets. Presumably, the same latent variables are operative, despite changes in weights, configurations, and reliabilities of observed variables. This stable-dimension assumption is also implicit in the use of a single construct – "intelligence" or "aggression" or "deviancy" – to describe dispositions from early childhood to late maturity. On this score, it seems hazardous to assume at the outset that these dispositions are not themselves emergent over time.

Discovering Developmental Novelty

How might novel categories and dimensions that permit novelty be introduced into models that presuppose that the same latent variables are expressed in all developmental stages and in all persons? This factor- or dimensional-stability question can be clarified by employing concrete categories at the first level of data collection. Measures can be employed that preserve the concrete characteristics, functions, and features of the actions and interactions of subjects. This technique of data recording may be followed in direct observations, in interview reports, and in community reports. For example, our use of qualitative categories enabled us to determine whether across time some concrete phenomena would rise, others fall, and still others emerge anew or disappear. In addition, the information allowed us to use factor analysis and LISREL measurement models to determine whether new dimensions appeared over time. Using this strategy we proposed that a new dimension of "social aggression" appeared in girls in early adolescence that coexisted with confrontational "aggression" (Cairns, Cairns, Neckerman, Ferguson, & Gariépy, 1989).

Person-oriented and Variable-oriented Analysis

A related issue concerns the appropriate unit of analysis. Magnusson and Bergman (1984, 1990) observe that most analyses of behavior have been "variable oriented" rather than "person oriented." Because of the development of sophisticated statistical tools for data analysis, developmental research has been dominated, for decades, by a *variable approach* in which the focus is on the relations among variables. Problems are formulated and results interpreted using this approach. In *person-approach* analysis, the questions are asked and answered in terms of individuals. In operationalization, individuals are grouped in homogeneous categories with reference to similarities in their profiles based on values for variables relevant to the problem under consideration (e.g., Kagan, 1994; Magnusson, 1988). Of course, a person approach does not mean that the whole person can be investigated in a single study. Here the same rules that were discussed earlier apply. These rules emphasize the importance of identifying the proper level for the structures and processes under consideration, choosing the adequate data for that level, and interpreting the results with reference to a holistic theoretical framework. The development of effective methods for the analysis of data in a person approach is one of the most challenging tasks for the future (Bergman, 1988; Bergman & Magnusson, 1990).

Is this merely a new way to describe types, or another variation of the syndromes that are captured by the various psychiatric nosologies? Or is it simply equivalent to the use of cluster analysis rather than other parametric statistical models? It is an error to dismiss person orientation as merely a new name for old procedures. To the contrary, types presuppose stability, yet person analyses are a tool for studying developmental change. They are an alternative for the study of developmental pathways and trajectories as well as a method for identifying how configurations of characteristics affect individual functioning over time. Consider, for example, the effects of the early onset of menarche. In a person-oriented framework, homogeneous subsets of girls are identified in childhood, prior to the occurrence of menarche. The basis of homogeneity would be factors within the individual as well as those factors without (including social group membership, socioeconomic class, school performance) that are presumed to be relevant to particular life outcomes (such as teen parenthood or college graduation). Presumably, the relevant characteristics will be mutually constrained in such a way that a small number of such configurations could be identified. Such configurations are essential to any developmental analysis that attempts to plot the effects of novel events in ontogeny. Briefly, the effect – either for good or for ill – of maturational events such as the early onset of menarche upon individual developmental trajectories is presumed to depend upon the configurations in which events occur.

One strategy that we adopted has been to identify configurations of boys and girls who have common activity and demographic profiles in childhood. This configural strategy is based on the assumption that developmental trajectories of aggressive behavior reflect the operation of both personal and social factors over time. Therefore, the simultaneous employment of internal and external characteristics should be key to isolating commonalities in developmental pathways. This analytic procedure has proved to be most effective in identifying the developmental trajectories that lead to educational failure and dropping out of school (Cairns, Cairns, & Neckerman, 1989). The dropout rates in the 11th grade, given membership in 1 of 7 clusters identified 4 years earlier in the 7th grade, ranged from 0% to 82% for males and from 0% to 49% for females.

Homogeneous groupings also offered a way to identify persons who did not conform to the trajectory of other members of their group. Analysis of the developmental experiences of the 2% of the male cluster who dropped out versus the 98% who did not provided clues to the nature of emergent risks. Conversely, comparison of the 51% of the girls in the deviant cluster who did not drop out versus the 49% of the females who did drop out yielded information about protective factors. Such a strategy directs as much attention to the "failures" of prediction as to the "successes." The hazard with conventional models has been that developmental phenomena may themselves become distorted by the very operations designed to make them accessible to empirical analysis. This problem arises when standard multivariate analyses treat distinctive trajectories of individual development as error variance.

Time and Timing

A systems approach is not always developmental, but a developmental approach necessarily involves the study of systems over time. One obstacle to precise communication across areas occurs when there are differences in time units of measurement and analysis. In this regard, experimental psychology has historically had difficulty with time as an independent variable, and a great deal of effort has been expended in trying to eliminate its effects. Hence age is usually controlled in design by matching or covariance, in measurement by z-score transformations, and in statistics by the use of correctional analysis or regression equations. When age and developmental changes are eliminated empirically – by whatever procedure – one is invited to ignore them theoretically (Cairns, 1986, 1993).

Problems arise when the mechanisms grounded in different time intervals are pitted against each other. Hence social learning processes may be effective in the short run yet ineffective in the long run. The seemingly opposed set of outcomes is observed in multiple domains including, for example, the paradoxical effects of punishment on aggressive behavior of children (i.e., the same punitive event that is immediately effective can produce disastrous effects later on; see Patterson, 1982, and Cairns, 1979, for further discussion). In the classic paper on the "misbehavior of organisms," Breland and Breland (1961) invoked the concept of "instinctual drift" to account for their observation that the processes of maturation seemed to erode the processes of learning. Yet mechanisms that operate across different time frames do not have to be at odds with each other; they may collaborate rather than compete. To resolve disputes that arise because of differences in levels of analysis, such as nature and nurture, a first step may be to analyze the time-relativity of the mechanisms that have been implicated (see Turkewitz & Devenny, 1993).

"One Space of Phenomena" Rather than "Two Worlds of Scientific Psychology"

In a cogent analysis of what he designated the "two worlds of scientific psychology," Cronbach (1975) analyzed the separation between the interests, methods, and statistics of investigators who study individual differences mainly relying on a correlational research strategy on the one hand, and investigators who employ experimental methods on the other. Forerunners in the discipline had offered similar distinctions. For instance, G. Stanley Hall (1885) distinguished between the methods and concerns of experimental and comparative-historical approaches. The conclusion is that the nature of the questions addressed and the phenomena-to-be-studied demand quite different theoretical frameworks and research strategies.

Because each approach has produced its share of successes, one might argue for according them equal scientific status. There is a problem, however; when it comes to the study of persons over a significant portion of their life course, both approaches tend to downgrade the integrated nature of individual functioning. This omission shifts attention from processes that might explain certain puzzles of development, from the nature-nurture issue to the role of biological constraints on human activity and adaptation. Progress on these and related matters has therefore been slower than might be expected given the amount of research interest and activity that has been stimulated.

We believe part of the problem involves the limited goals that have been adopted for psychology and the ways in which the research task has been defined. Thus, Watson (1913) formulated the goal of psychology as "the prediction and control of behavior" and believed that this goal indicated that psychology was a "purely objective natural science." Even after they had rejected the restrictive assumptions of behaviorism per se, researchers still accepted prediction and control as the criteria for determining the scientific status of psychological research. And in those areas of study where control has not been feasible, prediction has by default become a primary measure of the success of the research enterprise.

We suggest, however, that a reasonable goal for psychological study is to enable researchers to understand and explain individual functioning and its organization over the life span, from conception to death. In this view, individual functioning is seen as a multidetermined, stochastic process in which genetic, biological, cognitive-emotional, and experiential factors interact in a probabilistic, often nonlinear fashion. The task for research is to identify order and lawfulness without denying the complexity of the phenomena-to-be-understood. Simplicity and parsimony in explanation are expected to be products of the research task, not imposed upon it by measures, designs, or transformations. In this regard, there has been a growing recognition in the physical and biological sciences that complex systems may have their own laws, and that these can be as simple and fundamental as any other law of nature (Gleick, 1987; Kadanoff, 1986; Lorentz, 1983; Thom, 1972). It seems reasonable to assume that a similar principle holds for the complex phenomena in individual psychological functioning, an insight adumbrated in psychology by Schneirla (1966). One must remain alert for avenues by which to integrate psychology's concerns and concepts with those of its sister sciences.

The perspective of the Nobel laureate Francis Crick is of special interest because Crick started his career in physics and later moved into biology. He writes:

> Physics is also different because its results can be expressed in powerful, deep, and often counterintuitive general laws. There is nothing in biology

that corresponds to special and general relativity, or quantum electrodynamics, or even such simple conservation laws as those of Newtonian mechanics; the conservation of energy, momentum and angular momentum. Biology has its "laws," such as those of Mendelian genetics, but they are often only rather broad generalizations, with significant exceptions to them . . . what is found in biology is mechanisms, mechanisms built with chemical components and that are often modified by other, later mechanisms added to the earlier ones. (Crick, 1988, p. 138)

Concluding Comment

Despite the theoretical and societal justifications for a developmental framework, there are formidable obstacles to be overcome. Some issues are technical, other problems are conceptual, and still other pitfalls concern the organization of the science. At the technical level, there is a danger when research designs and analytic procedures surge too far ahead of prior experience and successes. The recent publication of a series of volumes on longitudinal research design and analysis should help establish the guidelines for the boundaries of developmental research (e.g. Baltes & Baltes, 1990; Magnusson & Bergman, 1990; Rutter, 1988). These guidelines, coupled with recent theoretical reviews, mean headway is being made in the establishment and evaluation of the theoretical framework.

There are implications as well for the organization of the science. The boundaries of traditional disciplines are drawn so that interdisciplinary work is given lip service but only modest direct support. It remains risky to step outside one's recognized discipline, even in training. Yet an understanding of the phenomena under investigation might require the integration of information beyond that ordinarily employed in one's own discipline.

Intimately linked to training and support are the criteria employed by editorial and grant review boards to evaluate scientific contributions. There has been strong resistance to change when a shift has been made from traditional statistics, units of analysis, and research designs to alternative person-oriented analyses and other developmentally appropriate methods. Although such conservatism is understandable — in that the hard-won gains of the science should not be overlooked — one of its effects has been to stifle innovation. Such setbacks should be only temporary, however, as new criteria for rigor gain acceptance through the ultimate criteria of replication and validity over the long term.

An emergent body of information indicates that a shift in methods, analyses, and assumptions is required to enable researchers to understand personal integration in ontogeny. Accordingly, modern neurobiological and physiological studies have shown that a developmental perspective may clarify otherwise impenetrable issues of the brain-behavior relationship. Similarly, recent advances in microevolutionary study demonstrate that differences in the rate of development may be key to understanding genetic contributions to social behavior. Longitudinal studies indicate that puzzles of human development will be resolved only by multilevel, multidisciplinary study of persons over the life course. Does this constitute a paradigm shift, or is it better described as a paradigm push?

Further advances also require new standards for methodology in the study of behavioral ontogeny. Both longitudinal and cross-generational research designs are essential, and they should be yoked in the investigation of evolutionarily meaningful activity patterns. On the assumption that behavioral development is a leading edge for evolutionary adaptation, the search for mediational processes should be guided at all stages by studies of developmental processes. The challenge for contemporary theory is to establish a perspective that is systematic enough to integrate the multiple sub-processes of behavior, but precise enough to direct the drive for evidence.

We conclude that the investigation of developmental adaptation requires contribution from the interface of a number of traditional scientific disciplines: developmental biology, developmental psychology, physiology, neuropsychology, social psychology, sociology, and anthropology. Thus the total space of the phenomena of individual development forms a clearly defined and delimited domain for scientific discovery that must involve all of these disciplines. This domain constitutes a scientific discipline of its own, *developmental science.*

3   Human Lives in Changing Societies: Life Course and Developmental Insights

Glen H. Elder, Jr.

The study of lives and the life course represents an enduring interest of the social sciences and reflects important social changes over the twentieth century. Most notably, developments after World War II called for new ways of thinking about people's lives, about society, and about their connection. Pioneering longitudinal studies of American children, launched in the 1920s and 1930s (Eichorn, Clausen, Haan, Honzik, & Mussen, 1981), became studies of the young adult in postwar America, thereby focusing attention on social trajectories that extend across specific life stages. In addition, the rapidly changing demography of society assigned greater significance to the problems of aging and to their study. Insights regarding old age directed inquiry into earlier phases of life and into the process by which life patterns are shaped by a changing society.

This chapter presents the life course as a theoretical orientation for the study of human development that incorporates temporal, contextual, and processual distinctions. In concept, the life course refers to age-graded life patterns embedded in social structures and cultures that are subject to historical change. These structures vary from social ties with family and friends at the micro level to age-graded hierarchies in work organizations and to the policy dictates of the state. Change in the life course shapes the content, form, and process of individual development, and such change may be prompted in part by the maturation or aging of the individual as well as by social forces.

In the multidisciplinary field of developmental science, a theoretical orientation on the life course defines a common domain of inquiry with a framework that guides research in terms of problem identification and formulation, variable selection and rationales, and strategies of design and analysis. One unique feature of this approach is its usefulness in addressing questions that *begin* with the effect of macrosocial change, but it is by no means limited to such questions. Other primary entry points are employed by the chapters in this volume and by developmental psychologists in general.

A thorough account of macrosocial effects must at the very least begin with or include evidence on the status and current functioning of the environment as social structure, culture, and social process. Such an account typically crosses different levels of analysis, from the macroscopic level of society or the social order, to intermediate structures and localities (e.g., communities and neighborhoods), to the proximal world of school classes and families. Some analyses that begin with the behaving organism can, of course, be nested within this general framework, a perspective followed by *Children of the Great Depression* (Elder, 1974). Using such a framework on the life course, that Depression study assessed a wide range of the effects on children of family hardships, and it did so by taking into account *other* relevant influences as well.

The importance of research that begins with the larger society is underscored by Almond and Verba's classic study of the "civic culture" in five societies – the United Kingdom, West Germany, Italy, Mexico, and the United States (1963). The authors focus on the qualities of the self-confident citizen, who is likely to "follow politics, to discuss politics, to be a more active partisan" (pp. 206–207). The self-confident citizen not only thinks "he can participate, he thinks others ought to participate as well." Involvement in decision making within family, school, and workplace stands out along with formal education as a primary developmental factor in the life histories of self-confident citizens.

What about the underlying historical forces, however, and their influence on political behavior in these five societies? With an age range of 40 years or more in each of their national samples, the authors could have indexed exposure to major events and trends across the twentieth century – two world wars, a worldwide depression, post-1955 affluence, the growth of the nation-state, an increase in urban living – and assessed their effects on socialization and developmental processes. Unfortunately, they did not include these forces in the originating questions. Almond and Verba posed questions regarding the social origins of citizen competence rather than questions concerning societal change and its implications for the life course and development. But when one's aim is to illuminate the impact of social and cultural forces in lives and developmental experience, then one must inquire into these forces and their effects.

These issues involve one of four paradigmatic principles of life-course theory, the relation of human lives to variations in historical time and place. The first part of this chapter begins with a conceptual account of the paradigmatic principles: (1) historical and geographic variations in human lives, (2) human agency and its social constraints in shaping the life course and developmental trajectories, (3) the central role of timing in the structure and process of life-course development, and (4) linked or interdependent lives – the embeddedness of individual lives in a matrix of social relationships over time. The first three principles became prominent in life-course study through advances during the 1960s in the understanding of age and its temporal meanings – historical and social time and so on. I discuss these advances and their convergence with contributions (such as "interdependent lives") from the older "relationship" model of human lives in a general theory of the life course and human development. The closing part of this section clarifies concepts that are often used interchangeably, such as life cycle, life history, and life span.

I conclude the chapter by focusing on a distinguishing feature of life-course study, its sensitivity to the dynamic relation between lives and an ever changing society. One way to appreciate this perspective is to compare it to models or theories that neglect the institutions, structures, and ecologies of society. Such models are popular in sociological and population studies of cohorts. They typically explore categories of behavior change (e.g., the behavior of people born in a specific historical time) without considering the processes by which change occurs.

Another model views the environment from the vantage point of the developing organism and thus neglects the larger society. In this account, the social ecology of human development is a setting in which behavioral change and reorganization occur. Life-course studies seek to move beyond this limitation and articulate how societal and individual changes interact as social and developmental trajectories through specific mechanisms. I explore some of these mechanisms in this chapter.

Consistent with Gottlieb's definition of development (Chap. 4, this volume), life-course theory presupposes novelty and change in life patterns and their context. Social change may produce turning points in self-definition and social role. Life-course theory also attends to the differential timing and the interdependence of social and developmental pathways or trajectories, and it assumes that causal influences are potentially variable across the life course from birth to death. That is, social and developmental transitions are not likely to have the same correlates and influences over the life course. Widowhood is one example of such potential variation; the acquisition of a higher level of social mastery is another.

The task of linking social forces to individual development implies only a downward model of causation, though life-course theory also assumes that individuals function as agents that influence their own development. Within the social constraints and options established by a new regime, people make choices and take actions that shape their life course. This agentic perspective is underscored by the accumulating evidence on the role of selection effects (Cairns & Cairns, 1994). For example, highly aggressive girls are at risk of sexual involvement with boys of similar disposition, who, in turn, further jeopardize the girls' prospects of being part of a stable and nurturing family.

In the language of the life course, men and women bring their experiences, dispositions, knowledge, and beliefs to bear on new situations which, in turn, affects their subsequent adaptations. Beyond the individual, the social mobilization of people based on shared interests frequently affects the macrolevel of government or industry. Many examples come to mind, including the civil rights movement, which used political mobilization to achieve greater social equality and life opportunities for African-Americans. Button (1989) has documented this social transformation in the Deep South at the community level as manifested in better community services, education, and employment options for black citizens.

The Life-Course Paradigm and Conceptual Distinctions

Life-course theory represents a general change in how we think about and study human lives and development. From this perspective, the life course can be thought of as an emerging paradigm. Broadly speaking, the change is one element of a conceptual shift that has made time, context, and process more salient dimensions of theory and analysis in the social and behavioral sciences. Contemporary studies are more attentive to temporal distinctions in the historical and social world, to the social embeddedness of behavior and relationships, and to the process by which change occurs.

As a multidisciplinary field of ideas and empirical observations, the paradigm draws upon various conceptual streams, including the biographical tradition of Charlotte Bühler (1935), the generational tradition of life history studies (Thomas & Znaniecki, 1918–1920), the meanings of age in accounts of birth cohorts and age strata (Elder, 1974; Riley, Johnson, & Foner, 1972; Ryder, 1965), cultural and intergenerational models (Cole, 1992; Kertzer & Keith, 1984), and developmental (Baltes, 1987) and personality life-span psychology (Funder, Parke, Tomlinson-Keasey, & Widaman, 1993), a field that is flourishing with new ideas and initiatives.

My perspective is informed by all of these advances, though I tend to stress the social forces that shape the life course and its developmental consequences. This problem orientation, which I expressed initially in *Children of the Great Depression* (Elder, 1974), has since led me to conduct studies of wartime influences (Elder, 1987) and a longitudinal study of children in rapidly changing rural America (Elder, 1992a; Conger & Elder, 1994). Across these projects, the life course has evolved into an effective way to investigate the impact of social change on the developmental course of human lives.

The diversity of these conceptual streams is matched in part by some commonalities, such as those premises that regard the individual as a biological being. As David Magnusson (with Törestad, 1993, p. 430) points out, "an individual's way of functioning psychologically cannot be understood and explained (satisfactorily) without consideration of the fact that an individual has not only a mind but also a body." Biological events and their meaning are core elements of a person's life history: physical attributions and meanings inform cultural accounts of life patterns, and biological timing mechanisms have both social and developmental implications for trajectories of aging and health. Increasingly, biological factors are part of life-course models. Efforts to link processes within and across levels favor a view of behavior as an organized system.

There is coherence to the life course in the individual's total functioning and in crossing multiple levels. These levels range from structured pathways in whole societies (Buchmann, 1989; Mayer 1986), in social institutions, and in complex organizations to the social trajectories of individuals and their developmental paths. Interlocking trajectories, social and developmental, are nested in particular multilevel systems and acquire form and meaning from them.

Unfortunately, theories generally exist on either one level or another and consequently provide little guidance for life-course studies that cross levels, as in efforts to trace the impact of changing economic and political structures through particular locales and family processes to the developmental experience of individuals (Elder, 1974). Therefore, Bronfenbrenner's (1979) nested levels of social environment represent an important advance in linking macrochange and individual behavior.

The Life Course in Concept

In concept, the life course generally refers to the interdependence of age-graded trajectories, such as work and family, that are subject to changing conditions in the larger world, and to short-term transitions, ranging from birth to school entry to retirement (Elder, 1985). Each trajectory consists of a series of linked states, similar to linked jobs in a work history. A change in state thus marks a transition, as, for example, from one job to another.

Transitions are always embedded in trajectories that give them distinctive meaning.

Not restricted to the single histories or careers so widely studied in the past, the life-course paradigm orients analysis to the dynamics of multiple, interlocking pathways (Moen, Dempster-McClain, & Williams, 1992). Planning strategies are illustrated in the scheduling of marriage and parenthood and in the arrangement of family events according to the imperatives of a work career. Family careers also have profound implications for children's developmental courses, as when a family's economic misfortune interacts with an adolescent's maturational history to alter his or her appraisals of self (Elder, 1974, Chap. 5). Histories of family discord and ineffective parenting may also be part of this picture.

Greater breadth comes from a view of the full life course, its continuities and change. Analysis is sensitive to the impact of early transitions on later experience. Indeed, researchers now agree that the implications of early adult choices extend even into the later years of retirement and old age (Clausen, 1993), affecting everything from the adequacy of economic resources to adaptive skills. Quality of life of the aged adult cannot be understood in full without knowledge of the individual's prior life course. For example, the men who entered World War II right after they graduated from high school followed very different social and health pathways in the postwar era from those who did so more than a decade later (Elder, Shanahan, & Clipp, 1994). Late mobilization entailed lasting costs, including broken social ties, loss of income, and accelerated physical decline.

Paradigmatic Themes

Four themes are distinctive of life-course theory. They are (1) the interplay of human lives and changing historical times and places, (2) human agency in choice making and social constraints, (3) the timing of lives, and (4) linked, or interdependent, lives. The link between human lives and their contexts, both historical and cross-cultural, underscores the multiple levels, social embeddedness, and dynamism of the life course. Issues of timing, linked lives, and human agency identify key mechanisms by which environmental change and pathways influence the trajectory and substance of individual lives. Let us consider each of these central themes in more detail.

1. Human Lives in Historical Time and Place. Especially in rapidly changing societies, their varying years of birth expose individuals to different historical worlds, with distinctive priorities, constraints, and options. Differences in age mean differences in the potential effects of social change. One sociological study tested this notion by tracing the effects of drastic income loss in the 1930s on the families and individual experiences of two birth cohorts, one with birth dates at the beginning of the 1920s and the other with birth dates between 1928 and 1929 (Elder, 1974, 1979). The analysis found that the younger children were more strongly influenced by family hardship than were the older children, with impairment most evident in the lives of the younger boys. Though diminishing in strength over time, the difference persisted into the children's middle years in their work lives, family relationships, and psychological health.

This study illustrates a *cohort effect,* one of the ways in which lives can be influenced by social change. History is expressed as a cohort effect when social change and culture differentiate the life patterns of successive cohorts. History can also be expressed as a *period effect* when the influence of social change is relatively uniform across successive birth cohorts. Thus, families at different life stages became more labor intensive (e.g., members provided services) during the Great Depression.

Individual lives may well reflect historical influences (see also Tudge, Putnam, & Valsiner, Chap. 10, this volume), but for us to know this with certainty we must move beyond studying birth cohorts and their historical context to studying the environment. In exploring the implications for individuals of historical change, long term as well as short term, the analyst will necessarily address how these effects are expressed. What is the process by which population growth, economic decline, or rapid economic expansion is expressed in family experience and the lives of children? And, on the community level, what are the consequences of educational reform and new industry for families and children?

Historical influences are also expressed differentially in different places. A comparative study of Depression boys who grew up in the San Francisco area and those who grew up in Manchester, New Hampshire, shows that they had different life chances following their involvement in World War II (Elder, Modell, & Parke, 1993). The California boys managed to escape the limitations of their deprived households by joining the armed forces and, after the war, using the benefits of the GI Bill for higher education. College was less of an option for the working-class youth of Manchester, but their service experience did provide skill training through the GI Bill and enabled them to avoid prolonged hardship, for the most part. The particular social ecology of a locale, whether San Francisco or Manchester or anywhere else, gave shape to the Depression's imprint for this generation.

2. Human Agency and Social Constraints. Human agency and selection processes have become increasingly more important for understanding life-course development and aging. Within the constraints of their world, people often plan and choose among options that become the building blocks of their evolving life course. Their choices are influenced by a particular situation and by their interpretations of it, as well as by their life experiences and their dispositions. Individual differences and life histories interact with changing environments to produce behavioral outcomes and their correlated constraints.

An appreciation for human agency has always been expressed in biographical research, but conceptual trends in the behavioral sciences more generally affirm an agentic view of individuals in shaping development and the life course. These include the cognitive revolution and research on personal efficacy (Bandura, 1995), genetic influences on the selection of environments (Scarr & McCartney, 1983), and the extension of life studies beyond the early years.

Despite the social regulation of age-graded norms, the agency of individuals and their life choices ensure some degree of "loose coupling" between their actual social transitions and life stage (Elder & O'Rand, 1995). Contrary to the age-grading of cultures, people of the same age do not march in concert across the major events of the life course; rather, they vary in pace and sequencing, and this variation has real consequences for people and society (Hogan, 1981). Age at entry into a full-time job, at school leaving, at cohabitation and marriage, at childbearing, as well as at other events in the transition to adulthood, are not experienced by all members of a birth cohort, and those members who do experience them do so at widely varied times in their lives. Even in highly constrained societies (such as China during the Cultural Revolution), individual agency ensures a measure of loose coupling in lived experience.

3. The Timing of Lives. The social meanings of age deserve special mention because they have brought a temporal, age-graded perspective to social roles and events (Helson, Mitchell, & Moane, 1984). Social timing refers to the initiation of and departure from social roles, to the duration and sequence of social roles, and to relevant age expectations and beliefs. The social meanings of age give structure to the life course through age norms and sanctions, social timetables for the occurrence and order of events, generalized age grades (such as childhood and adolescence), and age hierarchies in organizational settings (i.e., the age structure of firms).

In theory, a normative concept of social time specifies appropriate times for marriage, childbearing, retirement, and death (Neugarten & Datan, 1973). Differential timing orders events (as when marriage occurs before the first child's birth) and determines the duration of the waiting time between one event and the next. Empirical findings (Hogan & Astone, 1986) are beginning to accumulate for event timing, sequences, and durations, although little is known about the causal processes in life transitions.

Social timing also applies to the scheduling of multiple transitions and to their synchrony or asynchrony. Young couples may schedule family and work events to minimize time and energy pressures. Disparities between social timing and biological timing frequently occur during the early years of development. Differential rates of physical maturation generate early and late maturers in an age group. Turkewitz and Devenny (1993) concede that an understanding of such differences is essential for theories that view development "as the outcome of interactions between a changing organism and changing context" (p. xii).

4. Linked Lives. Human lives are typically embedded in particular configurations of social relationships with kin, friends, and others across the life span. Social regulation, support, and patterning occur in part through these relationships and relationships with significant others. One example of this influence is apparent in historical and contemporary cultures in the timing of marriage among women (Hareven, 1982). The timing of marriage for a woman may be contingent on whether her older female siblings have married. Life-course regulation, support, and patterning through relationships are expressed across the family cycle of socialization and generational succession.

The misfortunes and opportunities of adult children become intergenerational as well as personal matters. Failures in marriage or work can lead children back to the parental household and have profound consequences for the parents' life plans and later years. When such misfortunes occur to families, they may impede the successful placement of offspring by limiting their options. As the historical record shows (Elder, 1985), "each generation is bound to fateful decisions and events in the other's life course" (p. 40).

The principle of linked lives extends beyond the notion of interdependent lives to the interlocking trajectories of individuals and their sequence of transitions, both social and developmental. On the social level the principle refers to the interdependent pathways of family and work, marriage and parenthood, work and leisure. Historically, family and the work careers of family members have become more interdependent in the Western world through the rising level of women's employment and the prevalence of adolescent work. At the same time, we have witnessed a diminution in the connections between marriage and childbearing. For an increasing proportion of American women, childbearing is occurring outside of marriage and even outside of the expectation of marriage (Cherlin, 1993).

Interlocking trajectories are characteristic of life-course dynamics across the life span, but they are especially prominent in the transition to adulthood. Frequently, within a span of 10 years, young people leave home, although they may return from time to time; they might also pursue higher education and, in some cases, complete degree requirements. Some young people might enter the military or vocational certification programs. Others enter the labor force, marry, and bear children. The challenge from a statistical standpoint is to create a model for these simultaneous, interlocking transitions. Upchurch, Lillard, and Panis (1994) are making significant headway in this area with their econometric models.

For developmental science, the methodological challenge centers on the relation between interacting social and developmental trajectories. Latent growth-curve analysis and hierarchical linear models (HLM) are especially promising for this line of research (Bryk & Raudenbusch, 1992), and for more holistic, person-centered approaches (see Magnusson & Cairns, this volume), because each study member has a growth curve or developmental trajectory on each variable. People with developmental trajectories can be grouped into categories and then compared systematically on antecedent and contemporary factors.

Two recent studies have modeled interlocking social and developmental trajectories with this methodology. McLeod and Shanahan (1994), in a nationwide longitudinal sample, found that a poverty trajectory over 6 years significantly increased depressed affect and acting-out behavior among boys and girls in elementary school, quite apart from prior (before $T1$ of study) exposure to poverty. Likewise, Ge and associates (1994) observed a course of negative life events from early to late adolescence that significantly increased the trajectory of depressed affect among girls in particular. This type of life-course research is a portent of things to come as more developmental studies model interlocking trajectories and their time-varying covariates and causal influences.

Converging Streams

According to its central themes, the life-course paradigm consists of well-established conceptual foci (e.g., linked lives), some new or reworked concepts (e.g., the timing of lives, and lives in time and place), and fresh theoretical integrations or syntheses. One important integration that has particular relevance is a merger between two conceptual streams of life-course study during the 1960s, the "social relations" tradition, which extends back to the 19th century, and a temporality perspective based on advances in the study of age in society and lives.

Generational studies are featured in the "social relations" tradition, from the pioneering study of Polish immigrants by Thomas and Znaniecki (1918–1920) to Kingsley Davis's (1940) comparative and historical study of parent-youth conflict to Alice and Peter Rossi's (1990) three-generation study. This line of research contributed to the popularity of socialization research in the 1960s and to the growth of intergenerational studies of social change. But the typical multigenerational study was uninformed by the social meanings of age and provided little sensitivity to issues of temporality and context. New work on age and society began to correct this limitation during the 1960s.

In particular, Norman Ryder (1965) and Matilda Riley's theory of age stratification (with others, 1972, 1988) brought a much-needed sociological understanding of age in the life course to life studies. Another pioneer, Bernice Neugarten (with Datan, 1973), fashioned a social psychology of age-grading across the life course, including a concept of the normative timetable with its system of expectations and informal sanctions. Contemporary studies of life transitions and their timing (Hogan, 1981; Modell, 1989) owe much to Neugarten's original work, first published in the 1950s.

Both analytical streams – social relations and age – informed a study of California children who grew up in the Great Depression (Elder, 1974). The basic model traced the effects of the economic collapse through family deprivation and intergenerational processes to the social experience of the children and their age-graded life course. Over the years, a large number of studies have joined the generation and age perspectives, including Hareven's (1982) historical study of the family and life course in the textile community of Manchester, New Hampshire; Rossi and Rossi's (1990) three-generation study of the relation between an individual's aging and kin-defined relationships across the life course; and Moen's two-generation study of women (with Dempster-McClain & Williams, 1992). Burton and Bengtson (1985) document the value of this conceptual integration by noting the consequences of a disparity between age and generational status among black mothers of teenagers who had just had a child. A majority of the young mothers refused to accept the child care burden of being a grandmother.

This newly emerging perspective on the life course called for appropriate data on people and social groups over time, as well as for statistical techniques for analyzing it. A similar call was made many years earlier in the 1920s by W. I. Thomas, a pioneer in the study of life histories. Thomas (Volkart, 1951) urged that research take full advantage of the "longitudinal approach to life history" (p. 593). Studies, he argued, should investigate "many types of individuals with regard to their experiences and various past periods of life in different situations" and follow "groups of individuals into the future, getting a continuous record of experiences as they occur" (p. 593). A number of longitudinal studies launched with children born in the 1920s or earlier seem to have followed Thomas's recommendation, but with applications that differed sharply from a life-course model.

Most prominent in this effort are both the Lewis Terman study of gifted Californians (born 1903–20) and the Oakland and Berkeley Longitudinal Studies of children (born 1920–21 and 1928–29 – see Eichorn et al., 1981; Elder, Pavalko, & Clipp, 1993, Chap. 2). These studies were not designed to track the developmental course of children into the adult years, but they eventually did so, with data collection continuing well into the 1990s. However, it is notable that early uses of the data did not examine the age-graded life course and its developmental effects, nor did this research explore the implications of historical change in this rapidly changing part of the 20th century. Indeed, the Terman study nearly succeeded in not collecting any systematic information at all on the Great Depression and World War II, two major crises and social disruptions in both national and personal experience. In the 1950 follow-up of the Terman men, a good many of the veterans expressed their disbelief that Terman had not asked them about their war experiences.

A historically based account of human lives emerged after 1960 and soon encouraged use of the older archival data that actually linked human development and lives to aspects of a changing society. Life patterns and the historical record were no longer unrelated fields in problem formulation and inquiry, as is evident from the unparalleled growth of longitudinal studies beginning in the 1960s (Young, Savola, & Phelps, 1991) as well as the development of statistical techniques and software to fit the analytic requirements of event sequences, person-centered analysis, and archival management. Prospective longitudinal data sets are no longer rare. Moreover, valuable data have also come from retrospective life histories, as collected by life calendars (Freedman, Thornton, Camburn, Alwin, & Young-DeMarco, 1988). Research questions about the life course have encouraged this change, and the developments themselves have generated new questions of this kind.

Some Conceptual Distinctions

Before turning to ways of linking social change and the life course, it is important to clarify concepts that have hitherto been used interchangeably, such as life cycles, life history, life span, and life course (Elder, 1992b). Each deserves notice, along with issues of continuity and change, in mapping the conceptual terrain.

The *life cycle* concept frequently describes a sequence of life events from birth to death, though it more precisely refers to a sequence of parenthood stages over the life course, from the birth of one's children to their departure from the home to their own childbearing (O'Rand & Krecker, 1990). This sequence, it should be noted, refers to a reproductive process in human populations. Within a life cycle of generational succession, the children as newborns are socialized until maturity, give birth to the next generation, grow old, and die. This cycle is repeated from one generation to the next, though *only* within the framework of a population. Some people do not have children and consequently are not part of an intergenerational life cycle.

The life cycle is commonly known in terms of the family cycle, a set of ordered stages of parenthood defined primarily by variations in family composition and size (Elder, 1978; Hill, 1970). Major transition points include marriage, births of the first and last child, the children's movement through school, departure of the eldest and youngest children from the home, and marital dissolution through the death of a spouse. The stages are not defined in terms of age, as a rule, and typically, they follow a preferred script of a marriage that bears children and survives to old age, an increasing rarity in contemporary society. Moreover, as Rindfuss, Swicegood, and Rosenfeld (1987) conclude, "understanding the nature and importance of sequence in the life course requires analyzing what the roles themselves mean and how they are causally linked" (p. 799). This meaning derives in large measure from knowledge of the timing and duration of events. Thus, in a family, a rapid sequence of births produces a very different dynamic of demands and pressures than does a sequence of widely dispersed births. A mother's life stage, whether she is in late adolescence or her mid-30s, also has obvious relevance to the meaning of a birth sequence.

Life history commonly refers either to a method of data collection or to a lifetime chronology of events and activities that typically and variably combine data records on education, work life, family, and residence. These records may be generated from information obtained either from archival materials or in interviews with a respondent, as in the use of a life calendar or age-event matrix (Freedman et al., 1988). Life calendars record the age (year and month) at which transitions occur in each activity domain and thus depict the unfolding life course in ways uniquely suited to event-history analyses and the assessment of time-varying causal influences (Featherman, 1986; Mayer & Tuma, 1990). Life history also refers to self-reported narrations of life, as in Thomas and Znaniecki's famous life history of Wladek in *The Polish Peasant in Europe and America* (1918–1920). Whether collected by a research staff or self-reported, life histories are products of data collected in time-ordered accounts of events.

Life span specifies the temporal scope of inquiry and specialization, as in life-span sociology or psychology. A life-span study extends across a substantial period of life and generally links behavior in two or more life stages. Instead of limiting research to social and developmental processes within a specific life stage, a life-span design favors studies of antecedents and consequences. Developmental trajectories across the life span are formed by linking states of psychological functioning in a temporal series. Examples include the emotional and physical health trajectories of adults from mid-life to the later years (Clipp, Pavalko, & Elder, 1992) and the intellectual trajectories of fluid and crystallized intelligence during this phase of the life course. Transitions, or changes in state, occur within trajectories of this kind. Increasingly, studies are investigating the transition mechanisms of developmental change (De Ribaupierre, 1989) as well as the processes linking social and developmental transitions. In terms of stage and rate of advance, developmental and social trajectories may show varying degrees of correspondence, such as in the case of a student's physical rate of maturation that does not match the athletic demands of a student's role. Life-span psychology, as a field of study, gained coherence and visibility through a series of conferences at the University of West Virginia beginning in the late 1960s (Baltes & Reese, 1984). The approach is defined by a concern with the description of and explanation for age-related biological and behavioral changes from birth to death.

Any coverage of life-span issues necessarily brings up the meanings of *life stage* and *life structure*. Sociologists tend to focus on the social life course in which life stage refers either to a socially defined position, such as the age of adolescence, or to an analytically defined position, such as the career stage of an individual at age 40. Men and women who differ in age when they encounter worklife misfortune may be said to occupy different life stages at the time.

Developmental stages and trajectories are also the foci of life-span psychology. Examples include Erik Erikson's (1963) psychosocial stages, such as the stage of generativity. In both sociology and psychology, stage-based characterizations of social and human development have lost favor to more dynamic models in developmental theory and research. In life-course theory, social stages retain their importance as a context for investigating the mechanisms of development and their explanations. However, they are seldom a focal point of study.

In addition to life stage and explanatory mechanisms, the concept of life organization or structure has proven useful since the early writings of W. I. Thomas and Florian Znaniecki (1918–1920). Life organization mainly refers to the subjective pattern and coherence of the constructed life history, although it also has an objective social reality in the records of society. Daniel Levinson, a personality psychologist, employed many of the same distinctions in his concept of life structure (1978) as a "tool for analyzing what is sometimes called 'the fabric of one's life'" (pp. 42–43). The self, social participation, and the sociocultural world pattern the life structure and its underlying process of choice making. In contemporary thinking on the life course, life structure depicts the individual's social life course (e.g., age-graded trajectories of work and family), the subjective account of this life pattern, its developmental trajectories, and their interrelations.

Continuity and change across the life course brings up the last set of conceptual distinctions. How can researchers account for processes of behavioral continuity and change in studies of the life course? The challenge in answering this question can be illustrated by research on veterans and their wartime legacy. Approximately half of all American men over the age of 60 have served in the military, and a good many served during periods of war. Large numbers of American veterans either were wounded in World War II, witnessed the death of their comrades, or endured inhumane periods of capture. For the majority of those veterans who survived such experiences, homecoming required major adjustments when they tried to reassemble their former lives in terms of work, marriage, and children. Some veterans made relatively smooth transitions to civilian life, whereas others struggled with emotional problems of various proportions. How are these veterans functioning in their later years when compared to nonveterans? To what extent have the emotional wounds of combat healed or become chronic sources of discomfort, or, perhaps, reopened after years of symptom-free living?

According to clinical observations, symptoms of war trauma show modest consistency across individuals, although courses of the disorder vary considerably. For example, symptoms of war stress might increase or decrease over time or might resurface in later life for some veterans. The challenge is to explain these different symptom trajectories, a task that requires knowledge of the processes, or *mechanisms,* that produce continuity and change. Three mechanisms have been useful in research on this problem (Clipp & Elder, 1996): interactional continuity, the situational activation of latent dispositions, and cumulative effects.

Interactional continuity refers to the persistence of the behavioral effects of wartime experience because a veteran's pattern of interacting with others tends to re-create the same conditions over and over again (Caspi, Bem, & Elder, 1989). Behaviors that are learned in one situation and that bring about certain rewards are likely to be evoked in subsequent situations with similar reward possibilities. Moreover, relational patterns that are carried into new situations often elicit responses from others that "support and validate" that pattern. Thus a veteran's hostile or isolate behavior may evoke a response from others (such as indifference) that maintains the behavior.

Situational activation refers to the experience of encountering situations that resemble wartime situations and tends to evoke similar behavioral and emotional responses. The risk of encountering such situations increases markedly across the later years of life. Formerly controllable situations become less manageable; for example, an individual's loss of structure and direction through retirement or the deaths of significant others might precipitate intrusive and even shattering memories of prior trauma experiences. Findings on veterans (Silva & Leiderman, 1986; van der Kolk, 1984) are consistent with this account.

Cumulative effects refers to behavioral continuity that is maintained through the progressive accumulation of the consequences of the behavior itself. Stress symptoms may persist in part through a life-course dynamic in which initial symptomatology is sustained by the progressive accumulation of its interpersonal or social consequences. For example, a veteran's explosiveness may threaten his marriage and thereby reinforce his irritability and ill temper. Such explosiveness could also lead to an erratic work history that undermines the family's stability and exacerbates the veteran's volatility and rage. Documentation of this sequence comes from a variety of life-history studies, including the Legacy of Vietnam project (Laufer, Yager, Frey-Wouters, & Donnellan, 1981). Dispositional tendencies can both affect the influence of interactional experiences and, potentially, drive the individual's selection of environments and experiences.

All of the concepts discussed to this point have a place in studies of the life course. Contemporary inquiry extends across the life span and frequently draws upon the life records and life cycles of successive generations. The life course takes the form of a multidimensional and intergenerational concept; a moving set of interlocking trajectories and transitions in areas of work, marriage, and parenthood. Developmental trajectories – intellectual functioning, academic and social competence, and so on – interact over time with this changing life course.

The concepts also reflect the intellectual foundation of life studies in the current scholarship on age and social relations. The age-graded life course, timetables, and birth cohorts are central to the study of age and the life course, whereas life cycle, generation, lineage, and family time are defining concepts of intergenerational studies in the "social relations" tradition. Both sets of concepts are needed. Consider a family timetable of four generations, in which the number and configuration of the generations varies sharply across a single life span. Thus, in the example that follows, an American born during World War I became one of several great-grandchildren of a woman in her 90s. Three higher stations in the generational series were occupied at this time (Hagestad, 1990): the parent, grandparent, and great-grandparent generations. This hierarchy continued until the great-grandmother died in the child's 6th year. By the time the child entered middle school, all grandparents on both sides of the family had died, producing a two-generation structure. Such dramatic changes in generational structure have consequences for personal identity, social obligations, and social support, but their full significance depends on the individual's life stage and historical context.

By the 1990s, the life course had become a general theoretical framework for the study of lives, human development, and aging in a changing society. Rapid social change drew attention to historical influences and prompted new sociological literature on age and relationships, which, in turn, fashioned concepts of a life course embedded in social institutions and subject to historical change.

Linking Social Change and Life Experience

The evolving field of life-course studies brings two formerly segregated lines of inquiry together: the study of life-course development and the study of social change. At present, efforts to link these domains are handicapped by perspectives that neglect the social institutions and ecologies of a changing society. Thus, one perspective, based on the study of cohorts, identifies broad categories of potential influences on life events yet provides no clear understanding of the effects and their explanatory mechanisms. The other approach views the social environment from the vantage point of the developing individual in context and, consequently, fails to extract the full implications of a changing social system for the individual. It is one thing to place a child in the Great Depression and quite another to show how the massive economic collapse drastically altered that child's social environment.

A view of the environment both as a behavior setting and from the perspective of the individual is prominent in life-span developmental psychology and in developmental psychology generally. Dannefer's (1984, p. 847) commentary on the "role of the social in life-span developmental psychology" correctly noted that the major question was whether the life-span model could incorporate "the range of social processes that organize the life courses of individuals and the collective life-course patterns of cohorts." He went on to say that definitional statements regarding the centrality of the social environment did not mean that "research will be designed, nor findings be interpreted, in a way that apprehends social structure as a constitutive force in development." This position is consistent with Vygotsky's (1987) cultural-historical perspective (see Tudge, Putnam, & Valsiner, Chap. 10).

The life-span model falls short of offering this mode of analysis and interpretation, but so too, for the most part, do models in contemporary psychology including the ecology of human development (see Bronfenbrenner, 1979). Theory in psychology cannot apprehend "social structure as a constitutive force in development" when it views the social environment from the perspective of the individual. Hetherington and Baltes (1988) observed that "child psychologists are likely to postulate a 'typical' course of ontogeny and to view non-normative and history-graded factors as modifiers, not as fundamental constituents, of development" (p. 9).

This perspective in child development and a cohort approach generally pose research questions that demonstrate lack of an informed knowledge of the workings of society, of social structure, and of social change relative to their human implications. As such, they do not contribute to a theory of how social factors and systemic changes influence the life course and developmental trajectories. The full meaning of this assertion can be seen by taking a closer look at the two approaches in the behavioral sciences, a cohort perspective and a developmental perspective based on the organism.

Birth Cohorts and Their Life Patterns

If birth cohorts represent a link between social change and life patterns, what do they tell us about this connection? Consider the dramatic change in women's lives over the last fifty years in Western societies (McLaughlin et al., 1988). A systematic comparison of birth cohorts from the 1920s to the 1960s shows major cohort differences in women's education and gainful employment as well as in the timing of family events. But what do these differences mean? Any comparison of cohorts involves at least three potential effects: cohort, period, and age (time of measurement).

Cohort and period effects can be thought of as historical in nature. Historical influence takes the form of a cohort effect when social change differentiates the life trajectories of successive cohorts. Thus, American men who were born just before the 1930s were affected by Depression hardships more adversely than were men who were born 10 years earlier (Elder, 1979). History takes the form of a period effect when the influence of social change or a social event is relatively uniform across successive cohorts. Secular trends in the scheduling of marriages and first births across the twentieth century are largely an expression of period effects, especially from the late 1920s to the early 1950s. A third type of effect occurs through maturation and aging. Chronological age indicates where the individual is located relative to aging. Much has been written about the methodological challenge posed by estimating the impact of these three effects (Glenn, 1977), but another issue is more central to our concerns.

What does a significant cohort or period effect tell us about social change in life experience? By itself, it tells very little. Either type of effect identifies a domain of potential influences, but cohort studies typically end by speculating about the prime influences. For example, studies of birth cohorts of American women (McLaughlin et al., 1988) since the Great Depression generally show a pattern of increasing life-course diversity with trends toward later marriage; delayed childbearing; more births outside of marriage in the preadult years; more paid employment, especially for mothers with young children; and higher rates of divorce. But why these trends? Cohort studies typically speculate about such forces without extending the analysis to their actual investigation. At most, we might get a plausible story of how twentieth-century change is linked to women's lives. But stories do not advance scientific understanding. They do not weigh specific forces or explicate the causal process.

A more specific example of the limitations of cohort studies for linking social change and the life course comes from a study by Rindfuss, Morgan, and Swicegood (1984) on the first birth transition of white, native-born women in the United States. Using birth years from 1915 to 1939, the study observed a strong period effect across the cohorts: "period factors increase or decrease childbearing at all ages and for all subgroups within society" (p.

368). But the researchers had no success in identifying the precise causal factors. Concerning the childbearing delay in the 1970s among educated women, they point to the plausible influence of the women's movement, rising interest rates, and soaring housing prices, but the data prevent any more conclusive statement. The range of potential influences under any "period" umbrella is so great that no conclusion can be drawn about specific effects.

Some guidance to the influence of history on cohort life patterns comes from the notion of historical settings as opportunity structures; the relative size, composition, and historical niche of a birth cohort have much to do with member access to life opportunities (Easterlin, 1980). Thus the large cohorts that reached maturity in the 1930s stand in contrast to the relatively small birth cohorts that came of age in the prosperous 1950s. The contrast is magnified by the economic depression of the 1930s and the greater prosperity of the 1950s. This contrast is dramatic in general outline but inconclusive as to the processes involved.

Likewise, although we might agree with the observation that as each cohort encounters a historical event or change (for example, a period of economic depression or prosperity) the cohort "is distinctively marked by the career stage it occupies" (Ryder, 1965, p. 846), we must conclude that much is left unspecified by this mode of analysis. Researchers, having shown the type of historical imprint by cohort, must also show how it occurred. They must explain what the process is by which successive birth cohorts are differentially influenced by particular historical forces.

The concept of cohort seems to offer a promising way of thinking about lives in a changing society, but its promise actually depends on the formulation of research questions that link specific changes to the life course. These questions are rare. To explore this influence of these changes, an alternative research design is needed, one that begins with the properties of a particular social change and traces their effects to life experience. This approach also represents an alternative to perspectives on the social environment that are based on the individual.

Representations of the Social and Historical

Some representations of the social and historical are selected in terms that are especially relevant for an understanding of the individual and life-span development. A study of factors that influence the meaning of adolescent status among young people might focus on social roles within the family and the community, such as the work responsibilities that children are expected to carry, their time pressures, and autonomy. Some factors might tap the social change taking place but do so only in part and not in terms of their implications for adolescents. These implications could be the focal point of study that asks, for instance, how historical developments between the 1930s and 1940s changed the nature of adolescence and thus the developmental experience of young Americans.

The difference between growing up in America in the depressed 1930s and in the war-mobilized early 1940s was a difference literally between two worlds of adolescence (Elder, 1980). Such differences had much to do with the experiences of a young person's significant others, including parents, siblings, friends, and acquaintances. Hard times in the Great Depression influenced the lives of adolescents through the economic and job losses of their parents, and also through the Depression's effects on their grandparents, who often had to move in with them for a time. For young people during World War II, the distinctive features of adolescence included the war-related employment of parents from sunup to sundown, the military service and war trauma of older brothers, and the mobilization of school children for civil defense and the war effort.

To understand historical forces, then, one needs an approach that begins with the transforming environment, not with the individual or other social factors. This approach is the framework of *Children of the Great Depression* (Elder, 1974), which traced the effects of drastic economic decline in the Great Depression to the lives of children as mediated by family adaptations and interactive processes, including a labor-intensive economy and altered family relationships. Each adaptation had developmental implications for the child; for example, a sense of industry and significance emerged from the family's increased demands for helpfulness. Other relevant influences in the research included rate of maturation and parent behavior. This type of analytic model was common throughout the project even though the study's general framework was organized around the economy's collapse.

If one's objective is to understand social change in lives and developmental processes, the most effective research strategy would be to begin by studying the particular environmental change and its human implications. Both cohort studies and social factors that predict individual behavior may provide useful first steps toward a more complete analysis of environmental influences over time. It is important to note again that a study framed in terms of the implications of social change is entirely consistent with the analytic perspective of developmental science. The objective is to nest the developmental analyses within a social-change framework.

Linking Mechanisms

Five conceptual mechanisms represent useful ways of thinking about the interaction between changing times and lives: the life-stage principle, the concept of interdependent lives, control cycles, situational imperatives, and the accentuation principle (Elder & Caspi, 1990).

The life-stage principle indicates that the personal implications of social or environmental change are contingent on where the person is located within the life course — whether older or younger. Age is an approximate index of developmental stage, social role, and status. No study can adequately relate lives to their changing world without taking the life stage of individuals into account. From this vantage point, the life-stage distinction represents a point of departure.

The concept of interdependent lives orients analysis to the web of social ties that relate all lives to each other, and therefore specifies interpersonal connections to particular social changes, from industrialization to economic decline to war mobilization. Much can be learned about the impact of social change from the implications of life stage and social ties or personal networks.

All life transitions place people in new situations that entail some loss of personal control over outcomes. In folk language, the initial phase is devoted to "learning the ropes." Whether normative or not, expected or unexpected, social transitions generally set in motion a "control cycle" in which control is lost and efforts are made to regain it. The task of regaining control has much to do with the behavioral imperatives of the new situation — the situation's requirements for behavior. Crisis situations are defined by a large contrast between the imperatives of successive situations. The effect of these imperatives on the individual depends on his or her life history of experiences and personal dispositions. This interaction or interplay makes up processes by which social change accentuates psychological dispositions.

1. The Life-Stage Principle. The life-stage principle assumes that the influence of a historical event on the life course depends on the stage at which individuals experience the event. This principle locates families and children within the life course and its age-graded tasks and experiences. It implies that the effects of social change should vary in type and relative influence across the life course, and it alerts the investigator to the complexity of interactions among historical, social, psychological, and biological factors.

Consider two families in 1930: Family A has two children born around 1920, and Family B has two children born between 1928 and 1930. On the basis of the life-stage principle, we would expect the meaning of Depression hardship to vary significantly for the two sets of children. At the height of the Depression, the older children were between 9 and 16 years old, too young to leave school and face a dismal employment situation and too old to be highly dependent on the family. By comparison, the younger children were between 1 and 8 years old, ages when they were most dependent on their families and thus at greatest risk of impaired development and life opportunities.

This contrast is actually represented by our comparison of two birth cohorts of Americans who grew up during the Great Depression: the Oakland Growth sample (birthdates of 1921–1922) and the Berkeley Guidance sample (birthdates of 1928–1929). The 167 men and women of the Oakland cohort were children during the prosperous 1920s, a time of unparalleled economic growth in California. Thus they entered the Depression after a relatively secure phase of early development. Later, they avoided the scars of joblessness after high school by virtue of wartime mobilization. By contrast, the 214 members of the Berkeley cohort entered hard times in the vulnerable years of early childhood and experienced the pressures of adolescence during the unsettled, although prosperous, years of World War II.

Members of the Oakland cohort, who were beyond the critical early stage of development and dependency when the Great Depression hit, left high school in the late 1930s, during economic recovery and the initial phase of wartime mobilization. They were old enough to play important roles in the household economy and to confront future prospects within the context of Depression realities. In contrast, for the younger Berkeley children family hardship came early and often became a prolonged deprivation experience. The causal link between economic deprivation in the 1930s and adolescent behavior included a pattern of socioeconomic instability with its distorting influence on family life – the emotional strain produced by resource exhaustion, loss of an effective, nurturant father, and marital discord.

Not surprisingly, the enduring adverse effects of Depression hardship turned out to be concentrated in the lives of the Berkeley boys, both in adolescence and in their early adult years. No such effects were observed in the lives of the Oakland boys. By comparison, the Berkeley girls were protected from the developmental risks of family hardship by their nurturant relation to mother; and they were exposed to living examples of maternal competence in hard times. Consequently, we find little evidence of adverse deprivational influences in the lives of these young women and in the lives of the Oakland women.

2. Interdependent Lives. Diverse life histories become the interweave of family ties, softening the edges of cohort uniqueness. Through interdependent lives, the family serves as a meeting ground for members of different cohorts (Hagestad, 1982). With each individual's actions a part of the social context of other family members, any change in one member's life constitutes a change in the lives and context of the other members.

The concept of interdependent lives represents a central theme of family systems theories (Minuchin, 1985) and life-course theory. Systems approaches assume that the family is a social group and that its functioning as a whole is different from the functioning of its parts. This assumption arises because the properties of the family as a whole are derived from the properties of the relationships between individuals in the family and not just from the characteristics of the individuals as separate persons. Effective social relations among people who are consequential for children represent "social capital," a resource that typically facilitates prosocial development. Capable adults do not ensure social capital for children, as demonstrated by a human development triangle (Coleman, 1990, p. 593). The resources of human capital (education, intellectual competence, adaptive skills, etc.) are located at the nodes of the triangle. The links between the nodes symbolize social capital. A facilitative pattern for human development requires substantial human capital at the nodes and social capital in the links. Weak connections between talented parents, such as in a conflicted marriage, represent a generalized loss of potential capital, both human and social.

The expansion of analytic models from a dyadic unit (e.g., mother-child) to a family system (e.g., mother-father-child) provides knowledge of how interactions between two people influence and are influenced by a third person. The response of each person to the other is conditioned by his or her joining relationship to a third person. Thus changes within any individual or relationship may affect all other persons and relationships.

Empirical examples of these social complexities are seen in research on the Berkeley Guidance sample of men and women who were born in 1928–1929 (Elder, Caspi, & Downey, 1986; Elder, Liker, & Cross, 1984). Families that suffered heavy income losses during the 1930s became more discordant in the marital relationship, owing largely to rising financial disputes and to the more irritable, tense, and volatile state of husbands. The latter change represented a primary determinant of the abusive parenting behavior of men. The more irritable men became under economic pressure, the more they tended to behave punitively and arbitrarily toward their offspring. Economic stress generally increased the explosive tendency of men, but it did so primarily when they initially ranked high on this characteristic. Yet even when irritable under economic stress, a father was less likely to abuse his children if their mother provided affectional support for the children. This maternal role also minimized continuation of a child's problem behavior.

The transmission of abusive behavior and its behavioral effects across the generations are another example of lives lived interdependently. Two aspects of this process are ordinarily studied in isolation. Multigeneration studies typically focus on the behavioral transmission process from parent to child, whereas life-span studies follow behavior patterns in childhood up to the adult years. These lines of analysis are complementary. They were brought together in a study of the proposition that unstable personalities (explosive, volatile) and unstable family relations (marital, parent-child) are mutually reinforcing dynamics across the life course (Elder, Caspi, & Downey, 1986). These dynamics persist from one generation to the next through a process of individual continuity and intergenerational transmission.

The four generations in this research come from the Berkeley Guidance archive: grandparents ($G1$), parents ($G2$), study children ($G3$), and great grandchildren ($G4$). All of the data on the grandparents were reported by the parents in 1929–1930. The parents in this analysis were linked to their own parents ($G1$) and to their children ($G3$) during the Great Depression. The study children were followed from childhood to their own parental years, and then their own children were studied. Overall, the intergenerational continuity of unstable problem behavior was most pronounced among the Berkeley females, and unstable family relationships played an important role in this persistence. Within all generations, the causal influence flowed from unstable personalities to unstable family relations. The association of hostility and discord linked unstable personalities in one generation to such personalities in the next generation. Empirical support for these linkages also comes from the Carolina Longitudinal Study under the direction of Robert and Beverly Cairns (1994) and from the Iowa Youth and Families Project (Whitbeck et al., 1992).

3. The Control Cycle. As elaborated from Thomas's early writings on crisis situations, social change creates a disparity between claims and resources, goals and accomplishments, and a corresponding loss of control prompts efforts to regain control. The entire process resembles a *control cycle*. This cyclical process has at its center the connection between a person's losing control and that person's efforts to restore control over life outcomes, a process documented by studies of reactance behavior.

Reactance feelings occur whenever one or more freedoms or expectations is eliminated or threatened. Such feelings motivate efforts to regain or to preserve control. The Brehms (1982) refer to the substantial evidence for such motivation and note that "it is the threat to control (which one already had) that motivates an attempt to deal with the environment. And the attempts to deal with the environment can be characterized as attempts to regain control" (p. 375). Bandura (1988, 1995) stresses the motivating effects of setting higher goals, of achieving them, and of setting even higher goals. The process entails the production *and* reduction of discrepancies, disequilibration, and equilibration.

The precipitating event for this process is one that substantially alters the balance between claims and resources. As the balance changes, the actor's control potential is threatened, and adaptive responses are called into play. Adaptive responses depend, of course, on the current conditions, the structured situation in history. Responses to historical transitions and the loss of personal control entail choices among given options, and this constraint illustrates how a social institution (e.g., the economy) might shape the life course.

4. Situational Imperatives. Among the most important considerations in the dynamic of control cycles are the behavioral requirements, or demands, of the new situation. I refer to these demands as *situational imperatives*. An example comes from a program of research on work and personality by Kohn (1977) and Kohn and Schooler (1983). This research showed that the behavioral imperatives of work shape how men and women think and function. The most powerful imperative is occupational self-direction; the greater their self-direction, the more the workers deal with substantively complex, nonroutinized tasks that entail minimal supervision. Job conditions that encourage self-direction are conducive to effective intellectual functioning and to an open, flexible approach toward others.

Both worker and situation must be part of a model in order to account for how aspects of the work setting and organization are linked to the personality of the worker. Consider, for example, the degree of control a person exercises over the work process. In Kohn and Schooler's research, self-directed men sought control over their work, and such control reinforced a self-directed orientation. When this match failed to occur, the mismatch set in motion a control-cycle dynamic like that described earlier.

5. The Accentuation Principle. Adaptive responses are shaped by the requirements of the new situation, but they also depend on the social and psychological resources people bring to the newly changed situation. Individual and relational attributes, such as coping styles and marital bonds, affect adaptation to new circumstances. The *accentuation principle* refers to the increase in emphasis or salience of these already prominent characteristics during social transitions in the life course.

One of the earliest documented cases of accentuation comes from the pioneering research of Theodore Newcomb on women students of then newly established Bennington College in rural Vermont, in the late 1930s (Newcomb, 1943). In the liberal environment of Bennington, entering students who were relatively independent of parental influences tended to shift their social and political attitudes more toward the college norm than did other students.

Over 30 years later, Newcomb returned to this problem of personal change in a survey of the college student literature. With Feldman (1969), he concluded that the distinguishing attributes of entering college students were likely to be "reinforced and extended by the experience incurred in those selected settings." Though Newcomb's emphasis changed from a shift in attitudes to the reinforcement of initial views, both studies show the accentuation of dispositions through the interaction of life history and the demands of the new situation.

A similar account comes from Allport, Bruner, and Jandorf (1941) in a neglected study of personality under social catastrophe. Analyzing personal documents that reported the experiences of 90 individuals during the Nazi revolution, they argue that "very rarely does catastrophic change produce catastrophic alterations in personality." On the contrary, the basic structure of personality persists despite the upset and upheaval in the total life space. Moreover, where change does take place, "it seems invariably to accentuate trends clearly present in the pre-crisis personality" (pp. 7–8).

Linking Contexts and Lives

Control cycles, situational imperatives, processes of accentuation, life-stage distinctions, and interdependent lives together provide an account of linkages between social change and life patterns. This connection occurs through individuals and social relationships and through their interplay over time in situations with varying requirements. The dynamic evolves through families – a meeting ground for interdependent lives – and through other primary environments, such as friendships. From this vantage point, the interaction between historical time and lifetime is a function of changes in the life courses of all significant others.

Each of these types of linking mechanisms may be thought of as an overlapping region of different conceptual systems, such as the individual and the family environment, the family unit and the neighborhood, and the neighborhood and a particular community and its social institutions. In relation to studies of lifetime influences from the Great Depression, "linkages provide answers to the question of why economic change has particular effects; they offer an interpretation of the relationship, an account of the process or mechanisms through which social change influences personality and behavior" (Elder, 1974, p. 13; Elder & Caspi, 1988). To illustrate this process, consider the relation between family hardship in the 1930s and the marital orientation of daughters, an example that adds greater detail to the global mechanisms already discussed, such as interdependent lives. In theory,

> economic deprivation fosters a relatively early interest in marriage among girls through interpersonal strains in the family and domestic socialization. Two questions are posed by this analytic mode; does family deprivation have such an effect on marital orientation, and is it mediated by the specified intervening variables? Another question concerns the relative importance of the two proposed linkages; does economic deprivation affect marital interest mainly through family strains or through domestic influences in the household? To identify the particular relevance of these global constructs for orientation to marriage, we convert each to more specific and concrete manifestations. Family strain is thus phrased as marital conflict and emotional estrangement from father; domestic socialization as mother's centrality in the family, the daughter's role in the household, and lack of parental support for the daughter's higher education. (Elder, 1974, p. 13)

The five linking mechanisms refer to the connection between social change and life course, but they are also useful in thinking about the social life course and its implications for development and aging. The control-cycle dynamic is set in motion as people move across life transitions from early childhood to later life. Each transition, even those embedded in a normative system of expectations (such as marriage and the first birth), entails some loss that initiates efforts to regain it. At the birth of the first child, assistance by the new mother's own mother can be viewed in terms of this equilibration process.

All new situations have their own behavioral imperatives and may entail stressors that accentuate personal dispositions, such as compliance with authority in hierarchical work settings. The life-stage principle alerts us to the age status and social roles people occupy when they enter new transitions. A case in point is the large difference in age among women who have a first child. Finally, the notion of interdependent lives underscores the social matrix in which lives are lived, a dynamic highlighted by the family life cycle of generational succession.

Studying Human Lives within and across Levels: A Concluding Note

Studies of human lives generally follow one of two tracks, the individual or the aggregate. The first approach includes case studies of individuals over a long segment of the life span as well as quantitative studies of behavioral continuity and change in the lives of people. Clues to behavioral change are provided by biological and maturational factors, and by the proximal situation itself. For the most part, however, accounts of individual change and continuity remain fixed on this level of analysis. They rarely venture into the larger environment and examine the transformations that take place within it.

A similar conclusion applies to studies of the life course in aggregates or social structures. Explanations for life-course change often draw upon a mix of cultural, demographic, and economic factors at the macrolevel, but they seldom relate patterns of individual behavior to large-scale structures and groups. In addition, studies of behavior settings are strangely out of step with the flow of human lives and life-span development. Developmentalists may be devoting more effort to the study of people over time, but we see little evidence of this in the temporal study of environments.

One of the more persuasive examples of this neglect comes from the overworked and underdeveloped application of socioeconomic status, or social class, in developmental studies. Single measures of this aspect of the environment are commonly used even when the study children or adults are followed across annual data points over a number of years. Moreover, correlations between social class and family or individual behavior are calculated without an explicit account of why social class matters. What is the mechanism by which class position influences behavior and values?

Over the last 25 years, Kohn and his colleagues (Kohn, 1977) have pursued questions of this sort, and their systematic efforts provide compelling answers and arguments for why the study of human lives in a changing society must relate the microexperience of lives and the macrolevel of institutions and structures. As Kohn has made clear, conditions of life influence how people think and believe, and both factors determine the choices people make regarding work, family, and education. Work influences personality, and personality influences work.

The flourishing area of life-course studies owes much to the general recognition that any effort to make sense of development should consider how lives are formed by a rapidly changing society. Initially, this recognition led to a methodological solution that simply provided a way to disentangle change within lives from change within society. Cohort sequential designs and the estimation of cohort, period, and age effects are part of this methodological approach. In the field of human development, much of this research is based on a theoretical model that views the environment from the vantage point of the individual rather than in terms of its own properties. This perspective minimizes the role of social environment's influence in human development and underestimates the impact of social change.

Research based on cohort sequential designs provides estimates of social change as indexed by cohort or period measurements, but it generally leaves the meaning of these estimates open to speculation. What is meant by a significant cohort or period effect? The imprecise meaning of these effects typically refers to uncertainty about the more potent aspects of the environment. What environmental effects are grouped under a significant cohort or period effect? This uncertainty also leaves open the *mechanism* by which an environmental change alters human lives. An uncertain antecedent is necessarily coupled with an imprecise knowledge of the intervening processes. The only certainty is the outcome of interest.

An alternative approach to studying the interplay of social change and lives focuses directly on such connections. This is the approach of our Life Course Studies program as it has evolved over the last 25 years, from initial studies of "children of the Great Depression" to investigations of the impact on human life of war mobilization, rural social change, and inner-city hardship. The Depression studies traced the effect of drastic income loss through the family environment to the lives of Americans who were born in the 1920s. Research on war mobilization assessed and explained the multi-faceted influence of war experience. Contemporary studies in the project have examined the impact of rural economic decline and dislocation on families and children in the Midwest (Conger & Elder, 1994; Elder, 1992a), and other research has been studying economic hardship in the lives of inner-city youth (Elder, Eccles, Ardelt, & Lord, 1995). By including a particular social change in the problem formulation, these studies inform our understanding of the life-course influences of dramatic social changes in 20th-century America. Cohort studies have been much less successful in this respect because aspects of social change are typically not an explicit part of the originating question.

The task of linking social change and lives is formidable because so little theory extends across levels. Theories are readily available on the micro and macro levels, but theoretical guidance for connecting the levels is generally lacking. How does the downward causation process work in relating macroevents and environments to individual life experience? The five theoretical orientations that have been discussed – the control cycle, situational imperatives, the accentuation principle, the life-stage principle, and interdependent lives – have proven useful as linking mechanisms.

The control cycle refers to a dynamic set in motion by a change in situation. Each change of situation entails some loss of control which motivates efforts to regain control. Some transitions, such as births, marriages, divorce, entry into and out of work, are an integral part of the normative life course. Other transitions stem from major historical change, such as the widespread hardship of the Depression era. Families in the Great Depression regained a measure of control over their situation through expenditure reductions and multiple earners.

The control-cycle dynamic varies according to the properties of the situation and the life history of experience and disposition that people bring to new environments. All situations have certain requirements for behavior. I have referred to these requirements as situational imperatives. Among children in the Great Depression, deprived households exposed them to a more demanding set of expectations than did households that avoided heavy losses. This change magnified a loss of control and set in motion the dynamic of a control cycle.

Each change of situation interacts with the life history of experience and disposition. Certain dispositions and experiences can enhance the discontinuity of a new situation. Thus explosive personalities have a low threshold for losing control. Strong economic stress during the 1930s increased the explosiveness of men who had been above average on this tendency before the Depression, and such behavior tended to increase the disorder of family life by undermining both parental and marital relations. This interaction between stress and disposition is central to an accentuation process. Initial dispositions are accentuated by stress. Accentuation, control cycles, and situational imperatives refer to elements in the fit between a person and the situation. The fourth linking mechanism, the life-stage principle, places all of this within the life course of the individual by noting when the person comes to a new situation or circumstance. At what age did the individual experience the Great Depression and World War II? According to the life-stage principle, the effect of social change varies according to the age of the person at the time. Age status is connected with competencies, social roles, and options that influence the meaning and adaptive possibilities of new situations. Thus the younger Berkeley boys were more vulnerable to family hardship than their older counterparts in the Oakland cohort, and they were more adversely influenced by economic deprivation.

All of the linking processes described to this point refer to the individual in a changing environment. The last mechanism, interdependent lives, places this actor within the social matrix of relationships and suggests that social change has powerful consequences for the individual through the lives of related others. The family unit provides some of the best examples of these indirect effects. Severe economic hardship during the 1930s disrupted the family by undermining the effectiveness of each person. Thus fathers became more unstable under economic loss, and this instability weakened the marriage.

In combination, the five mechanisms provide a way of thinking about the connection between lives and a changing society. Having established this connection, we still face the question of how or whether influences persist over the life span. Under what conditions do the behavior patterns of a child persist into his or her adult years? We have just begun to explore such questions in research that extends across lives and the generations.

4   Developmental Psychobiological Theory

Gilbert Gottlieb

In recent years, what might be called a "systems view" of individual development has been slowly catching on in both biology and psychology. The developmental psychobiological systems view sees individual development as hierarchically organized into multiple levels (e.g, genes, cytoplasm, cell, organ, organ system, organism, behavior, environment) that can influence each other. The traffic is bidirectional, exclusively neither bottom-up nor top-down. (A formal treatment of hierarchy theory can be found in Salthe, 1985, esp. Chap. 4.) Frances Degen Horowitz's (1987) review makes the systems case for developmental psychology, at least up to a point. (She still accepts some aspects of infant behavior as strictly genetically canalized, or "hard wired," and makes no mention of the possible prenatal experiential influences on infant behavior.) The geneticist Sewall Wright (1968) and the embryologists Ludwig von Bertalanffy (1933/1962) and Paul Weiss (1959) have long been championing such a systems view for developmental genetics and developmental biology. The systems view includes developmental approaches and theories that have been called ecological (Bronfenbrenner, 1979), transactional (Dewey & Bentley, 1949; Sameroff, 1983), contextual (Lerner & Kaufman, 1985), interactive (Cairns, 1979; Johnston, 1987; Magnusson, 1988), probabilistic epigenetic (Gottlieb, 1970), and individual-socioecological (Valsiner, 1987). For the present purposes, the metatheoretical developmental psychobiological systems view can be fairly represented by the schematic presented in Figure 1.

The most important feature of the developmental psychobiological systems view is the explicit recognition that the genes are an integral part of the system and their activity (i.e., genetic expression) is affected by events at other levels of the system, including the environment of the organism. It is a well-accepted fact, for example, that hormones circulating in the blood make their way into the cell and into the nucleus of the cell where they activate DNA that results in the production of protein (Gorbman, Dickhoff, Vigna, Clark, & Ralph, 1983, Fig. 1.13, p. 29). The flow of hormones

BIDIRECTIONAL INFLUENCES

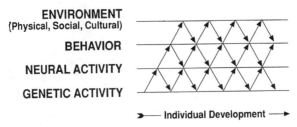

Figure 1. A developmental psychobiological systems framework: The traffic between levels is bidirectional.

themselves can be affected by environmental events such as light, day length, nutrition, and behavior, thereby completing the circle of mutually influential events from genes to environment. Another fact about genes that has not yet made its way into the psychological literature is that genetic activity does not by itself produce finished traits such as blue eyes, arms, legs, or neurons. The problem of anatomical and physiological differentiation remains unsolved, but it is unanimously recognized as requiring influences above the strictly cellular level (i.e., cell-to-cell interactions, positional influences, and so forth – Davidson, 1986; Edelman, 1988). Thus, the concept of the genetic determination of traits is truly outmoded, as is the concept of a genetically determined reaction range employed by Scarr-Salapatek (1976). (An insightful as well as witty critique of genetic determinism as applied to development is Oyama's [1985] *The Ontogeny of Information.*) The reaction-range concept is replaced by the concept of a norm of reaction, which is essentially nonpredictive because it utilizes the developmental systems view, where each new environment is expected to have a different influence on developmental outcomes that cannot be stated in advance of actual empirical investigation (Platt & Sanislow, 1988). Therefore, although the genes remain an essential part of any developmental system and plasticity cannot be regarded as infinite, a thoroughgoing application of the norm-of-reaction concept may make the genetic limitations on development in practice, if not in principle, unknowable (see critique in Gottlieb, 1995). Certainly, the appearance of mammalian dentition in birds (which otherwise never have teeth) under altered developmental circumstances provides striking testimony to the nonpredictability of genetic limitations on the phenotype (Kollar & Fisher, 1980).

The preceding considerations have led to a concern about the canalizing influence of events at other levels of the developmental system, because all levels of the system may be considered potentially coequal in this respect in the developmental systems view depicted in Figure 1.

Possible Experiential Canalization of Development

In the usual interpretative framework for thinking about the canalization of development, the developing organism's interaction with its environment is viewed as the source of perturbations to the system against which the genes must buffer the developing organism in order to bring about a species-typical phenotypic outcome. The following quotation makes that point:

> Ethologists have used various models of exactly how biological regulating mechanisms control the course of development, while allowing for the modification of development by the environment. One model, proposed by Waddington (1957), represents development as a ball rolling down an "epigenetic landscape." As the ball descends, this landscape becomes increasingly furrowed by valleys that greatly restrict the sideways movement of the ball. Slight perturbations from the developmental pathway can be corrected later through a "self-righting tendency," and the ball returns to its earlier groove. Thus, the general course of development is set, but some variation is possible because of particular environmental events. (Miller, 1989)

Consider the possibility that the developing organism's usual or typical experience can play a canalizing role that not only brings about species-specific behavior but also prevents the developing organism from being susceptible to non-species-typical forms of stimulation. Thus, normal experience helps to achieve species-specific behavioral development, and part of that process may involve making the developing organism unresponsive to extraspecific experiential influences.[7]

---

[7] Although Waddington was a rather surprisingly strict genetic determinist, he was one of the few major thinkers working in the field of evolutionary biology who believed that it was necessary to take into account developmental and organismic considerations, whereas most of the major figures in the making of modern synthesis (neo-Darwinism) consider only natural selection and genetic variation to be the prime factors of importance in evolution.

Experiential Canalization of Species-specific Perceptual Development

The concept of species-specific perception means that individuals of a given species respond in a characteristic way to certain objects; that is, they respond only to certain patterns of sensory stimulation and not to others. Usually, these patterns of stimulation are provided by other members of the species. For example, young mallard ducklings and wood ducklings that have been hatched in incubators and never before exposed to maternal stimulation will selectively approach their own species maternal assembly call in a simultaneous auditory choice test with the mallard and wood duck maternal calls. These calls differ on critical acoustic dimensions that mallard and wood ducklings find attractive. For the mallard ducklings that feature is a call repetition rate of 4 notes/sec (±.5), and for the wood ducklings the feature is a descending frequency (Hz) modulation around 1,200 Hz (±200 Hz). It turns out that the ducklings' own vocalizations contain those features in an abstract way, so when the ducklings are prevented from hearing their own or sib vocalizations they do not show their usual highly selective response to the maternal call of their own species (summarized in Gottlieb, 1981).

The fact that the ducklings have to hear their own (or sib) vocalizations to show the species-specific responsiveness to their respective maternal calls raises the possibility that exposure to such vocalizations is also playing a canalizing role in development. That is, in the absence of exposure to their own vocalizations the ducklings may become susceptible to extra-specific maternal calls, whereas exposure to their own vocalizations may render them unsusceptible to extraspecific maternal stimulation. If this hypothesis were to be supported, it would demonstrate that normally occurring *experience* can canalize species-specific development. It is widely believed in biology and psychology that genes or the gene-directed maturation of the sense organs and nervous system are responsible for the canalization of species-specific development in humans and animals (e.g., Fishbein, 1976; Kovach & Wilson, 1988; Lumsden & Wilson, 1980; Marler, Zoloth, & Dooling, 1981; Parker & Gibson, 1979; Scarr-Salapatek, 1976; Waddington, 1942, 1957).

In sum, the developmental systems view gives rise to the idea that canalization can take place not only at the genetic level but at all levels of the developing system (Figure 1), including the developing organism's usually occurring experiences. The experiential canalization of species-specific behavioral development has only rarely been experimentally demonstrated, although it is almost certainly a ubiquitous event in the life of all individuals.

To briefly summarize the main findings of one of my own studies on the experiential canalization of species-specific behavior, exposure of mallard ducklings (*Anas platyrhynchos*) to their variable-rate embryonic contact call not only fosters species-specific perceptual development (i.e., ensuring selective responsiveness to the maternal call of the species), it buffers the duckling from becoming responsive to social signals from other species (Gottlieb, 1991a). In the absence of exposure to the contact call, the duckling is capable of becoming attached to the maternal call of another species even in the presence of its own species call (in simultaneous auditory choice tests). A previous demonstration of malleability in devocalized mallard ducklings (Gottlieb, 1987) involved the induction of a preference for either a chicken (*Gallus gallus*) maternal call or a wood duck (*Aix sponsa*) maternal call, in which case the birds were tested with the chicken versus wood duck calls, not the mallard maternal call. At the beginning, it did not seem possible to demonstrate malleability in the presence of the species-specific maternal call. It was only when the possible canalizing effect of experience was considered that it became apparent that devocalization might permit such a degree of malleability that exposure to an extraspecific maternal call would override the "innate" attractiveness of the species maternal call.

Clearer thinking about what genes do and do not do in individual development gave rise to the idea that canalization must take place not only at the genetic level but at all levels of the developing system (Figure 1), including the developing organism's usually occurring experiences. That canalizing influences are potentially present at all levels of the developing system has not been widely appreciated. Rather, the widespread tendency has been to ascribe canalization exclusively to genetic activity, thereby short-circuiting developmental analysis and completely overlooking the various levels in the hierarchy of developmental systems that are necessary to produce a normal organism and species-typical behavior and psychological functioning. It is all too common to read statements such as "the vertebrate brain is fully capable of encoding stimulus information by genetic instruction" (Kovach & Wilson, 1988, p. 659), which is merely a verbal way to close the tremendous gap between molecular biology and behavioral development. It also shows a lack of appreciation of what genes do and do not do during individual development. As it becomes more widely understood that differentiation of the nervous system (and of *all* organ systems) takes place via influences above the level of the cell (Davidson,

1986; Edelman, 1987, 1988; Pritchard, 1986), a more thoroughgoing attitude or appreciation of developmental analysis will eventually supplant the
verbalism of "genetic determination" and the empty metaphor of the "epigenetic landscape." These ideas have been obstacles to thinking clearly
about the need for conceptual and empirical analysis at all levels of the
developmental systems hierarchy.

The remainder of this chapter is devoted to a detailed description of a
developmental psychobiological systems view. The application of this view
to human development is made in Gottlieb, Wahlsten, & Lickliter (in press)
and Shanahan, Valsiner, and Gottlieb (in press). The principal ideas concern
the epigenetic characterization of individual development as an emergent,
coactional, hierarchical system.

The Developing Individual as an Emergent, Coactional, Hierarchical System

The historically correct definition of "epigenesis" – the emergence of new
structures and functions during the course of individual development – did
not specify, even in a general way, how the emergent properties come into
existence (Needham, 1959). Thus, there was still room for the
preformation-like thinking about development that Gottlieb (1970) had
earlier labeled the predetermined conception of epigenesis, in contrast to a
probabilistic conception. That epigenetic development is probabilistically
determined by active interactions among its constituent parts is now so well
accepted that epigenesis is sometimes defined as the interactionist approach
to the study of individual development (e.g., Dewsbury, 1978; Johnston,
1987). That is a fitting tribute to the career-long labors of Zing-Yang Kuo
(1976), T. C. Schneirla (1961), and Daniel S. Lehrman (1970), the principal
champions of the interaction idea in the field of psychology, particularly as
it applies to the study of behavioral and psychological development. Thus,
it seems appropriate to offer a new definition of epigenesis that includes not
only the idea of the emergence of new properties but also the idea that the
emergent properties arise through reciprocal interactions (coactions)
among already existing constituents. Somewhat more formally expressed,
the new definition of epigenesis would say that *individual development is
characterized by an increase of complexity of organization – that is, the
emergence of new structural and functional properties and competencies –
at all levels of analysis* (molecular, subcellular, cellular, organismic) *as a
consequence of horizontal and vertical coactions among its parts, including organism-environment coactions.* Horizontal coactions are those that

occur at the same level (gene-gene, cell-cell, tissue-tissue, organism-organism), whereas vertical coactions occur at different levels (gene-cytoplasm, cell-tissue, behavioral activity–nervous system) and are reciprocal, meaning that they can influence each other in either direction, from lower to higher, or from higher to lower, levels of the developing system. For example, the sensory experience of a developing organism affects the differentiation of its nerve cells, such that the more experience the more differentiation and the less experience the less differentiation (e.g., enhanced activity or experience during individual development causes more elaborate branching of dendrites and more synaptic contacts among nerve cells in the brain [Greenough & Juraska, 1979]).[8] Reciprocally, the more highly differentiated nervous system permits a greater degree of behavioral competency and the less differentiated nervous system permits a lesser degree of behavioral competency. Thus, the essence of the probabilistic conception of epigenesis is the bidirectionality of structure-function relationships, as depicted in Figure 1.

Developmental Causality (Coaction)

Behavioral (or organic or neural) outcomes of development are a consequence of *at least* (at minimum) *two* specific components of coaction (e.g., person-person, organism-organism, organism-environment, cell-cell, nucleus-cytoplasm, sensory stimulation–sensory system, activity-motor behavior). The cause of development – what makes development happen – is the relationship of the two components, not the components themselves. Genes in themselves cannot cause development any more than stimulation in itself can cause development. When we speak of coaction as being at the heart of developmental analysis or causality what we mean is that we need to specify some relationship between at least two components of the developmental system. The concept used most frequently to designate coactions at the organismic level of functioning is *experience;* thus experience is a relational term. As documented earlier (Gottlieb, 1976), experience can play at least three different roles in anatomical, physiological, and behavioral development. It can be necessary to sustain already achieved states of affairs (*maintenance function*), it can temporally regulate when a feature appears during development (*facilitative function*), and it can be

---

[8] More recent research indicates that not only the amount of neural differentiation but the *direction* of such differentiation is influenced by sensory input to the cortex (Greenough & Chang, 1988).

necessary to bring about a state of affairs that would not appear unless the experience occurred (*inductive function*).

Developing systems are by definition always changing in some way. Therefore, statements of developmental causality must also include a *temporal* dimension describing when the experience or organic coactions occurred. For example, one of the earliest findings of experimental embryology had to do with the differences in outcome according to the time during early development when tissue was transplanted. When tissue from the head region of the embryo was transplanted to the embryo's back, if the transplantation occurred early in development, the tissue differentiated according to its new surround (i.e., it differentiated into back tissue), whereas, if the transplant occurred later in development, the tissue differentiated according to its previous surround so that, for example, a third eye might appear on the back of the embryo. These transplantation experiments not only demonstrated the import of time but also showed the essentially coactional nature of embryonic development.

Significance of Coaction for Individual Development

The early formulation by August Weismann (1894) of the role of hereditary material (what came to be called genes) in individual development held that different parts of the genome or genic system caused the differentiation of the different parts of the developing organism, so there were thought to be genes for eyes, genes for legs, genes for toes, and so forth. Hans Driesch's experiment (1908/1929), in which he separated the first two cells of a sea urchin's development and obtained a fully formed sea urchin from each of the cells, showed that each cell contained a complete complement of genes. This means that each cell is capable of developing into any part of the body, a competency that was called *equipotentiality* or *pluripotency* in the jargon of the early history of experimental embryology and *totipotency* and *multipotentiality* in today's terms (e.g., DiBerardino, 1988). Each cell does not develop into just any part of the body even though it has the capability of doing so. Each cell develops in accordance with its surround, so cells at the anterior pole of the embryo develop into parts of the head, cells at the posterior pole develop into parts of the tail end of the body, cells in the foremost lateral region of the embryo develop into forelimbs and those in the hindmost lateral region develop into hindlimbs, the dorsal area of the embryo develops into the back, and so on. Although we do not know what actually causes cells to differentiate appropriately according to their surround, we do know that it is the cell's interaction with its surround, including other cells in that same area, that causes the cell to differentiate appropriately. The actual role of genes (DNA) is not to produce an arm or a leg or fingers, but to produce protein. The protein produced by the DNA-RNA-cytoplasm coaction is influenced by coactions *above the level of DNA-RNA coaction.*

In sum, when certain scientists refer to behavior or to any other aspect of organismic structure or function as being "genetically determined," they are not mindful of the fact that genes synthesize protein in the context of a developmental system of higher influences. Thus, for example, as experiments on the early development of the nervous system have demonstrated, the amount of protein synthesis is regulated by neural activity, once again demonstrating the bidirectionality and coaction of influences during individual development (e.g., Born & Rubel, 1988; summaries in Changeux & Konishi, 1987). More recently, immediate early gene expression has been shown to be influenced by sensory stimulation (Mack & Mack, 1992). Since this research was performed on adult rats, that suggests the bidirectional influences in Figure 1 go across the life span, not just during early formative periods of development.

The Hierarchical Systems View

Much has been written about the holistic or systems nature of individual development, beginning as early as Smuts (1926) and continuing to the present (e.g., Sameroff, 1983; Butterworth & Bryant, 1990; Ford & Lerner, 1992). In fact, there is no other way to envisage the manner in which development must occur if a harmoniously functioning, fully integrated organism is to be its product. The writings of the geneticist Sewall Wright (1968) and the embryologist Paul Weiss (1959) very well portray the major components of the developing individual as an emergent, coactional, hierarchical system. So far we have dealt with the concepts of emergence and coaction as they pertain to the development of individuals. The notion of hierarchy, as it applies to individual development, simply means that coactions occur vertically as well as horizontally in all developmental systems. All the parts of the system are capable of influencing all the other parts of the system, however indirectly that influence may manifest itself. Consonant with Wright's and Weiss's depiction of the developmental system, the organismic hierarchy proceeds from the lowest level, that of the genome or DNA in the nucleus, to the nucleus in the cytoplasm in the cell, to the cell in a tissue, to the tissue in an organ, the organ in an organ system, the organ system in an organism, the organism in an environment of other organisms and physical features, the environment in an ecosystem, and so on back down through the hierarchical developmental system (review by Grene, 1987; Salthe, 1985). A dramatic developmental effect traversing the many levels from the environment back to the cytoplasm of the cell is shown by the experiments of Victor Jollos in the 1930s and Mae-Wan Ho in the 1980s. In Ho's experiment (1984), an extraorganismic environmental event such as a brief period of exposure to ether occurring at a particular time in embryonic development can alter the cytoplasm of the cell in such a way that the protein produced by DNA-RNA-cytoplasm coaction eventually becomes a second set of wings (an abnormal "bithorax" condition) in place of the halteres (balancing organs) on the body of an otherwise normal fruitfly. Obviously, it is very likely that "signals" have been altered at various levels of the developmental hierarchy to achieve such an outcome. (Excellent texts that describe the many different kinds of coactions that are a necessary and normal part of embryonic development are N. K. Wessells's [1977] *Tissue Interactions and Development* and, more recently, for the nervous system, Gerald Edelman's [1987] *Neural Darwinism.*)

It happens that when the cytoplasm of the cell is altered, as in the experiments of Jollos and Ho, the effect is transgenerational such that the untreated daughters of the treated mothers continue for a number of generations to produce bithorax offspring and do so even when mated with males from untreated lines. Such a result has evolutionary as well as developmental significance that, to this date, has been little exploited because the neo-Darwinian, modern synthesis does not yet have a role in evolution for anything but changes in genes and gene frequencies in evolution. Epigenetic development above the level of genes has not yet been incorporated into the modern synthesis (Futuyma, 1988; Gottlieb, 1992; Løvtrup, 1987).

Another remarkable organism-environment coaction occurs routinely in coral reef fish. These fish live in spatially well-defined, social groups in which there are many females and few males. When a male dies or is otherwise removed from the group, one of the females initiates a sex reversal over a period of about two days in which she develops the coloration, behavior, and gonadal physiology and anatomy of a fully functioning male (Shapiro, 1980). Such sex reversals keep the sex ratios about the same in social groups of coral reef fish. Apparently, it is the higher-ranking females that are the first to change their sex and that inhibits sex reversal in lower-ranking females in the group. Sex reversal in coral reef fish provides an excellent example of the vertical dimension of developmental causality.

The completely reciprocal or bidirectional nature of the vertical or hierarchical organization of individual development is nowhere more apparent than in the responsiveness of cellular or nuclear DNA itself to behaviorally mediated events originating in the external environment of the organism (e.g., Hydén & Egyházi, 1962, 1964). The major theoretical point is that the genes are part of the developmental system in the same sense as other components (cell, tissue, organism), so genes must be susceptible to influence from other levels during the process of individual development. DNA produces protein, cells are composed of protein, so, from a comparative-evolutionary perspective, there must be a high correlation between the *size* of cells, amount of protein, and quantity of DNA, and there must also be a high correlation between the *number* of cells, amount of protein, and quantity of DNA, and so there is (Cavalier-Smith, 1985; Mirsky & Ris, 1951). For our developmental-behavioral/psychological purposes, it is most interesting to focus on the developing brain, and we find there is the expected correlation between the number of brain cells and the quantity of DNA (Zamenhof & van Marthens, 1978, 1979). From the present point of view, it is significant that the amount of protein in the developing brains of rodents and chicks is influenced by two sorts of environmental input: nutrition and sensorimotor experience. Undernutrition and "supernutrition" produce newborn rats and chicks with lower and higher quantities of cerebral protein respectively (op. cit.). Similar cerebral consequences are produced by extreme variations (social isolation, environmental enrichment) in sensorimotor experience during the postnatal period (Renner & Rosenzweig, 1987).

Because the route from DNA to protein is through the mediation of RNA (DNA-> RNA-> protein), it is significant for the present theoretical viewpoint that social isolation and environmental enrichment produce alterations in the complexity (or diversity) of RNA sequences in the brains of rodents. (RNA complexity or diversity refers to the total number of nucleotides of individual RNA molecules.) Environmental enrichment produces an increase in the diversity of RNA sequences whereas social isolation results in a significantly reduced degree of RNA diversity (Grouse, Schrier, Lefendre, & Nelson, 1980; Uphouse & Bonner, 1975). Because the diversity of RNA sequences (or lack of it) is a direct consequence of DNA activity, the enriched and deprived environments are affecting DNA activity. These experientially produced alterations in RNA diversity are specific to the brain. When other organs are examined (e.g., the liver), no such changes are found.

Nonlinear Causality

Because of the emergent nature of epigenetic development, another important feature of developmental systems is that causality is often not "linear"
or straightforward. In developmental systems, the coaction of X and Y often
produces W rather than more of X or Y, or some variant of X or Y. Another,
perhaps clearer, way to express this idea is to say that developmental
causality is often not obvious. For example, in Gottlieb's research described
earlier, mallard duck embryos had to hear their own vocalizations prior to
hatching if they were to show their usual highly specific behavioral response to the mallard maternal assembly call after hatching. If the mallard
duck embryo was deprived of hearing its own or sib vocalizations, it lost its
species-specific perceptual specificity and became as responsive to the
maternal assembly calls of other species as to the mallard hen's call. To the
human ear, the embryo's vocalizations sound nothing like the maternal call.
It turned out, however, that there are certain rather abstract acoustic ingredients in the embryonic vocalizations that correspond to critical acoustic
features that identify the mallard hen's assembly call. In the absence of
experiencing those ingredients, the mallard duckling's auditory perceptual
system is not completely "tuned" to those features in the mallard hen's call,
and they respond to the calls of other species that resemble the mallard in
these acoustic dimensions. The intricacy of the developmental causal network revealed in these experiments proved to be striking. Not only must the
duckling experience the vocalizations as an embryo (the experience is
ineffective after hatching), the embryo must experience *embryonic* vocalizations. That is, the embryonic vocalizations change after hatching and no
longer contain the proper ingredients to tune the embryo to the maternal call
(Gottlieb, 1985).

   Prenatal nonlinear causality is also nonobvious because the information,
outside of experimental laboratory contexts, is usually not available to
researchers. For example, the rate of adult sexual development is retarded
in female gerbils that were adjacent to a male fetus during gestation (Clark
& Galef, 1988). To further compound the nonobvious, the daughters of late-
maturing females are themselves retarded in that respect – a transgenerational effect!

   In a very different example of nonobvious and nonlinear developmental
causality, Cierpial and McCarty (1987) found that the so-called spontaneously hypertensive (SHR) rat strain employed as an animal model of
human hypertension is made hypertensive by coacting with their mothers
after birth. When SHR rat pups are suckled and reared by normal rat

mothers after birth they do not develop hypertension. It appears that there is a "hyperactive" component in SHR mothers' maternal behavior that causes SHR pups to develop hypertension (Myers, Brunelli, Shair, Squire, & Hofer, 1989; Myers, Brunelli, Squire, Shindeldecker, & Hofer, 1989). The highly specific coactional nature of the development of hypertension in SHR rats is shown by the fact that normotensive rats do not develop hypertension when they are suckled and reared by SHR mothers. Thus, although SHR rat pups differ in some way from normal rat pups, the development of hypertension in them nonetheless requires an interaction with their mother; it is not an inevitable outcome of the fact that they are genetically, physiologically, and/or anatomically different from normal rat pups. This is a good example of the *relational* aspect of the definition of experience and developmental causality offered earlier. The cause of the hypertension in the SHR rat strain is not in the SHR rat pups or in the SHR mothers but in the nursing relationship between the SHR rat pups and their mother.

Another example of a nonlinear and nonobvious developmental experience undergirding species-typical behavioral development is Wallman's (1979) demonstration that if chicks are not permitted to see their toes during the first two days after hatching, they do not eat or pick up mealworms as chicks normally do. Instead, the chicks stare at the mealworms. Wallman suggests that many features of the usual rearing environment of infants may offer experiences that are necessary for the expression of species-typical behavior.

The Unresolved Problem of Differentiation

The nonlinear, emergent, coactional nature of individual development is well exemplified by the phenomenon of *differentiation,* whereby a new kind of organization comes into being by the coaction of preexisting parts. If genes directly caused parts of the embryo, then there would be less of a problem in understanding differentiation. Because the route from gene to mature structure or organism is not straightforward, differentiation poses a significant intellectual puzzle. The problem of differentiation also involves our limited understanding of the role of genes in development.

It has been recognized since the time of Driesch's (1908/1929) earth-shaking experiments demonstrating the genetic equipotentiality of all cells of the organism that the chief problem of understanding development is that of understanding why originally equipotential cells actually do become different in the course of development (i.e., how is it they differentiate into cells that form the tissues of very different organ systems). The problem of understanding development thus has become the problem of understanding cellular differentiation. We still do not understand differentiation, and it is quite telling of the immense difficulty of the problem that today's theory of differentiation is very much like the necessarily vaguer theories put forth by E. B. Wilson in 1896 and T. H. Morgan in 1934 (reviewed in Davidson, 1986), namely, that ultimate or eventual cellular differentiation is influenced by an earlier coaction between the genetic material in the nucleus of the cell with particular regions of the cytoplasm of the cell. Some of the vagueness has been removed in recent years by the determination of actual regional differences in the cytoplasm (extensively reviewed by Davidson, 1986). Thus, the protein resulting from locale or regional differences of nucleo-cytoplasmic coaction is biochemically distinct, which, in some as yet unknown way, influences or biases its future course of development. For example, proteins with the same or similar biochemical makeups may stay together during cellular migration during early development and thus eventually come to form a certain part of the organism by the three-dimensional spatial field considerations of the embryo mentioned earlier. Although the actual means or mechanisms by which some cells become one part of the organism and others become another part are still unresolved, we do have a name for the essential coactions that cause cells to differentiate: They are called embryonic *inductions* (recent review in Hamburger, 1988). The nonlinear hallmark of developmental causality is well exemplified by embryonic induction, in which one kind of cell (A) coacting with a second kind of cell (B) produces a third kind of cell (C). For example, if they are left in place, cells in the upper one-third of an early frog embryo differentiate into nerve cells: If removed from that region, those same cells can become skin cells. Equipotentiality and the critical role of spatial position in determining differentiation in the embryo is well captured in a quotation from the autobiography of Hans Spemann, the principal discoverer of the phenomenon of embryonic induction: "We are standing and walking with parts of our body which could have been used for thinking if they had been developed in another position in the embryo" (translated by B. K. Hall, 1988, p. 174). It might have been even more striking – and equally correct – if Spemann had elected to say, "We are sitting with parts of our body which could have been used for thinking. . . ."

Even if we do not yet have a complete understanding of differentiation, the facts at our disposal show us that epigenesis is correctly characterized as an emergent, coactional, hierarchical system that results in increasingly complex biological, behavioral, and psychological organization during the course of individual development.

In sum, the genes are part of the developmental system and are not inviolate or immune to influences from other levels of the system, in contrast to what one sometimes reads in the biological literature from the time of August Weismann to the present day. For example, the eminent evolutionary biologist Ernst Mayr has written "the DNA of the genotype does not itself enter into the developmental pathway but simply serves as a set of instructions" (Mayr, 1982, p. 824). Rather to the contrary, as has been demonstrated repeatedly since Hydén and Egyházi's behavioral research in the early 1960s, individual experience alters gene expression during ontogenetic development. It would seem of great importance for developmental psychologists (one wants to say for *all* psychologists) to be fully aware of this momentous change in our knowledge of genetic activity during individual development, along with the fact that genes do not by themselves produce differentiated phenotypic traits. One can hope that the immense gap between molecular biology and developmental psychology will one day be filled with facts as well as valid concepts. Although still very much a minority viewpoint, the epigenetic, coactional, developmental systems way of thinking is becoming evident in other areas of science, for example, in cell biology (Rubin, 1995) and in evolutionary biology (Kitchell, 1990). Gottlieb (1992) describes the developmental genesis of novel behavior and its implications for evolution.

5   The Question of Continuity and Change in Development

Jean-Louis Gariépy

A major endeavor in modern developmental psychobiology is to elucidate the origins of novel adaptive capacities in the individual and the species. On the premise that epigenesis proceeds through progressive differentiation and functional integration, the goal is to uncover mechanisms common to both the attainment of normative endpoints within the species and the occurrence of deviations from these universals during development (Gottlieb, 1992; Kuo, 1976; Lehrman, 1953; Schneirla, 1966). Because this question is often regarded as the central concern of developmental research, it is rarely distinguished from another one requiring us to explain how psychological and behavioral capacities, once established, support malleable and reversible adaptations during ontogeny. An analysis of functional integration from the standpoint of interactive processes may be sufficient to explain how development reaches specific endpoints. But the second problem, the issue of continuity and change, requires in addition an analysis of how the organism establishes, maintains, and reorganizes its relationship with the environment over ontogeny (Cairns, 1979; Piaget, 1967).

With a specific reference to social behaviors, Magnusson and Cairns (this volume) propose that these actions "have distinctive properties in adaptation because they organize the space between the organism and the environment, and thereby promote rapid, selective, and novel adaptations." More broadly, they suggest that behavior plays an integrative role at the interface of intra- and extraorganismic activity. While recognizing the interdependence of activity within the organism and activity within the organism's natural ecology, their perspective also postulates a necessary boundary between the two domains of activity. The organismic concept of hierarchical interaction, by contrast, assumes a functional integration between all levels of organization, from the genes to the environment, so that the system as a whole must be viewed as a unit. Although this is entirely appropriate for several areas of investigation, the same model may impose unnecessary limits to the study of continuity and change in development.

Specifically, it might be misleading to assume that behavior is a *product* of interactions between levels. In the following sections, an alternative model is examined where behavioral activity is defined as the *origin* of a process that brings intra- and extraorganismic conditions into functional alignment. This model postulates two hierarchical domains instead of one: the organism itself, and its natural ecology.

In keeping with the Magnusson and Cairns proposal, it is suggested that behavior is the leading edge of continuity and change in adaptive patterns over the life span. To better appreciate this proposal, it will be useful to discuss the concepts of "psychological levels" and "anagenesis" introduced respectively by Schneirla (1949) and Rensch (1959). These concepts emphasize the major "leaps" that took place over macroevolutionary time in psychological capacities and control of environmental factors. The evolutionary trends captured in both cases indicate that these capacities are most advanced in social species where the control of interactions with others is an essential aspect of adaptive activity (Cairns, 1973, 1979; Cairns, Gariépy & Hood, 1990; Magnusson, 1988). The study of this activity over time raises three basic questions: (a) what constitutes a state of adaptation, (b) by what mechanisms are functional relationships with the environment established, maintained, and changed, and (c) how do the different systems of the organism and the environment support new adaptive directions and provide for their consolidation? The first part of this essay outlines a theoretical framework for addressing these questions. Concrete applications are presented in the second part with reference to research conducted by Robert B. Cairns, Jean-Louis Gariépy, and the neurobiologist Mark H. Lewis on the flexibility and reversibility of social adaptations in mice.

1. The Psychological Mediation of Adaptive Behaviors. Most evolutionary biologists agree that evolution from the first unicellular organisms to the primate order gave rise to substantial improvements in adaptive capacities. To stress the importance of this progression, Huxley (1957) and Rensch (1959) enlarged the concepts of evolution and phylogenesis to encompass at least two different (but not exclusive) processes. The first, which they termed "cladogenesis," is the well-known Darwinian process of diversification and augmentation of species variety obtained from the splitting of lineages. For the second process, they introduced the term "anagenesis" to designate the improvements in structures, functions, and adaptive modes observed over macroevolutionary time. A classic example of structural anagenesis is the increase in brain-body ratio observed independently in the evolution of birds and mammals from the reptilian ancestors to the modern descendants. Correlated to these structural changes in the two groups is a graded series of improvements in psychological capacities and adaptive modes.

In spite of its relevance for the study of behavioral adaptation, research on the nature and origin of species differences in psychological capacities has not been a favored enterprise in the behavioral science. On at least two occasions over the last hundred years, efforts were deployed to establish a systematic research program on this question. The first was that of the early school of comparative psychology that emerged at the instigation of Romanes (1884). As an enthusiastic follower of Darwin's (1872) ideas on the subject, Romanes envisioned the possibility of applying his concept of phyletic continuity and the comparative method to reconstruct the origins of intelligence and higher human psychological capacities. The basic assumptions that guided this research were clearly stated by Harlow (1958a), who wrote: "Simple as well as complex problems might be arranged into an orderly classification in terms of difficulty, and the capabilities of animals on these tasks would correspond roughly to their position on the phylogenetic scale" (p. 283). Long before Harlow, however, this approach was already criticized for its misuse of the evolutionary taxonomy and the comparative method. In addition, the realization was growing that unitary definitions of intelligence and simple performance scores capture very little of the natural diversity in psychological capacities (Scott, 1967). With a few exceptions, this line of research basically stopped after 1947, when the APA voted to merge comparative psychology with its experimental division. By this decision, animal psychology was purified of its last vestiges of "mentalism" and lack of "experimental rigor" (see Beach, 1950, and Scott, 1967, for a review).

The second wave was primarily associated with the comparative work of T. C. Schneirla on the evolutionary and developmental origins of graded differences in adaptive capacities. The objects of the comparative work no longer were the finished products – the differential capacities to perform specified tasks – but were the developmental processes giving rise to these differences. In this endeavor, Schneirla explicitly rejected the earlier notion of directed progress in evolution, or teleological finality. The idea of improvement itself was not abandoned, however – for it was taken as a basic fact of macroevolution – except that now it was clearly spelled out. Schneirla (1949) used the term "level," which had been coined by Needham (1929) to describe what Huxley (1957) later called anagenetic "grades." Although Schneirla never used the second term himself, his "doctrine of psychological levels" emphasizes the same evolutionary trend toward greater flexibility and control in modes of adaptation. According to the theory, the most important change across levels is obtained through a qualitative shift from the primacy of stimulus intensity in behavioral organization to the primacy of the configurational properties of stimulative events (Turkewitz, Gardner, & Lewkowicz, 1984). Rensch (1959) described the same trend as follows: (a) an increase in complexity and differentiation *due to development,* (b) a progressive *centralization* of structures and functions in a central nervous system, (c) a correlated increase in the *plasticity* of the functions in a central nervous system, and (d) an enhanced *command* and independence *of environmental factors.* The end of this second phase in the comparative study of psychological capacities was quieter than the first phase. It was not precipitated by a public debate on the question: It simply vanished when its own focus on the early stages of development was redefined as the psychobiological study of developmental processes.

The concept of anagenesis figured importantly in Gottlieb's (1992) recent discussion of behavioral plasticity and neophenogenesis. His main point was that a larger brain and a longer developmental basis for differentiation and integration, coupled with a greater tendency to explore the environment, create a situation where interactive processes multiply the chances of producing novelties in adaptive patterns. What he emphasized in relation to anagenesis were the multiple avenues for change that are generated through the interactions between increasingly more complex systems, their development, and the timing of stimulative events. But the specific advantages of possessing higher psychological capacities for flexible adaptation on a day-to-day basis were not discussed, except for their role in fostering exploratory behavior.

2. Bidirectionality and Changes in Adapted States. The success of modern developmental psychobiology resides in the formulation of an interactive-organismic framework capable of explaining both the recurrence of universal outcomes within the species and the constant variability observed around these normative endpoints. With regard to our original question, let us examine whether the mechanisms postulated to account for the origin of this variability may be sufficient to account for the reorganization of adaptive systems over ontogeny. These mechanisms were recently illustrated by Gottlieb (1992) in his reference to a study by Cooper and Zubek (1958) that compared the learning performance of maze-bright and maze-dull rat strains. When tested after being raised under the same conditions as those used for selective breeding, these two strains showed the expected difference in maze-learning ability. However, when rearing conditions were significantly altered (by enrichment or impoverishment) no strain difference was observed. Gottlieb (1992) interpreted these results using the concept of norm-of-reaction, which "presupposes no practical limits on the phenotypical variability that may result from exposure to all possible environments" (p. 178). In other words, plasticity in developmental outcomes is a natural product of the cumulative effects of interactions taking place between all levels of organismic activity.

Under the assumption of equivalent processes, reorganization in adaptive patterns, just like variability in the development of structures and functions, could be explained by the novel interactions observed between a modified environment and the structures laid down by previous developmental history. Cases do exist where this generalization applies. To illustrate, consider the temporal changes observed in amoebae in the tendency to approach or withdraw from the same chemical source over time. Whether one or the other orientation is observed depends on some threshold value established as a joint function of the stimulative properties of the chemical itself and the intracellular state induced by previous encounters with it. Clearly, this kind of behavioral reorganization can be accounted for entirely in terms of bidirectional interactions between intra- and extra-organismic factors over time. Now consider a more evolved organism, as, for example, a mouse or a monkey. The same analytic framework would recognize in these cases higher organismic levels and depict a far more complex environment for the analysis of interactive processes. In this light, what limits the range of adaptive variability in the amoeba is the confinement of interactive activity at the lowest levels of organization. But to the extent that one views adaptive changes as endpoints to be explained, the task remains the same for all species: to understand its determinants through an analysis of relevant interactive processes.

The question being raised here is: How far can one go in explaining adaptive behavior within a framework that does not incorporate species differences in psychological mediation? Consider, for instance, how primates achieve an enhanced command and independence of environmental factors through communication and social organization. A knowledge of individual histories and their interactions is necessary to understand group functioning at any given point in time. This was well illustrated in F. B. M. de Waal's (1982) analysis of three dominance "takeovers" in a group of chimpanzees. In all cases, these takeovers were supported by coalitions formed long in advance of the actual events. At the time the insurrections took place, the patterning of social approaches and avoidances reflected the *anticipation* of specific responses by the participants, and was clearly organized with respect to the structural features of the group as a whole (e.g., affiliative networks, kinship, dominance hierarchy, see de Waal, 1982, 1989). In his retrospective construction of these events, de Waal (1982) emphasized the necessity to postulate that the participants behaved according to planned strategies that consisted in both shared and conflicting attempts to exploit the social structure of the group in a goal-directed manner.

3. Behavior as the Leading Edge of Adaptation. The modern approach to the question of continuity and change in behavior is still largely oriented by the goal of identifying its causal factors. In the transition from the mechanistic approach that dominated the first part of the century to the more recent organismic-interactionist framework, one assumption remained unchanged: It is the notion that behavior is a dependent variable, an outcome to be explained in terms of its determinants. There is a growing consensus that this epistemological stance may impair rather than facilitate appraisal of behavioral phenomena. Commenting upon the distinction that Schneirla (1959) made between the tonic and the phasic aspects of approach-withdrawal systems, Ethel Tobach (1969) concluded that it is through their activity that organisms "define their own integrity-promoting tonicity" (p. 227). In a critique of the "lens model" of Egon Brunswick (1952), Powers (1973) offered a very similar view of behavioral activity. He wrote: "If an organism is seen to be altering its behavior in an environment that is full of disturbances in such a way as to keep producing the same final result, one may be tempted to think that the organism produces that final result and it is simply varying its outputs as necessary so as to keep that final result happening over and over" (p. 7). Cairns (1993) took a further step by describing behavioral activity as capable of inducing change not only in the environment but also in the structures of the organism and the species. (See also Baldwin, 1894b, and Preyer, 1888–1889.)

The transition from a passive to an active mode of adaptation is regarded by Schneirla (1949) as the most fundamental dimension of change across psychological levels. For organisms where the mediation of behavior does not advance beyond the "principle of differential organic thresholds" (Schneirla, 1949, p. 259), adaptive orientations are best described as basic approaches or withdrawals. However, for organisms where the development of psychological capacities advances beyond this level, approaches eventually become *seeking* behaviors and withdrawals, *avoidances.* Behavior of this kind is goal directed. This goal generally remains the same: to establish or maintain conditions that favor the recurrence of vital stimulations. How such conditions are realized, however, is infinitely variable, as the means must change to fit the changing context for action. As pointed out by Schneirla (1949), variability in lower organisms is considerably reduced by perceptual abilities that limit the range of relevant stimulative conditions and the actions that bring about these conditions. In higher species, by contrast, these conditions are actively constructed through cognitive-representational activity, memory, learning, and, certainly among the great apes and humans, through a capacity to reflect upon these conditions and to anticipate the effects of action.

I do not mean to imply that the existence of higher adaptive capacities is simply ignored in human psychology. In fact, investigators have learned a great deal about the nature of these capacities through research on symbolic function, self-concepts, metacognition, and dialectical thinking, among other areas. However, with a few exceptions (e.g., Cairns, 1979; Sells, 1966), the significance of these capacities for biological adaptation has been poorly appreciated. On this point, it seems important to recognize a transition from a primitive form, in which adaptive behavior is a true product of systemic interactions, to a more advanced form, where the interactive context is controlled and defined through individual actions and cognitions. Evolution and development bring behavior (and its cognitive aspects) to the forefront of the adaptive process. This view was clearly expressed by Magnusson (1988), who wrote: "The individual's ability to predict and take control of the environment forms the fundamental basis for goal-directed activity and for the experience of meaningfulness" (p. 29).

4. Adapted States over Ontogeny. To address the basic question how functional relationships with the environment are established, maintained, and changed through behavioral processes, it may be useful first to define what is meant by adaptation or, more specifically, by the general state of an adapted system. A definition may be established by examining some implications of the concept of bidirectionality introduced by Gottlieb (1983, 1992). This concept specifies that the functional relationship between components – the interaction taking place between them – promotes the structural-functional changes within living systems. At the gene-cell level, for example, this bidirectionality implies that the set of genes being turned on or off at any point in time depends on the existing conditions within the cell, and reciprocally, that these conditions are themselves linked to genetic activity. A logical consequence of bidirectionality between these two structures is that their organizational states – the patterning of on-off genes on the one hand, and the chemical composition of the cell on the other – are strongly correlated. At a higher level of organization, cellular activity and tissue activity are similarly interdependent. Because bidirectional influences are exerted between all organismic levels, what applies to lower levels also applies to systemic organization as a whole, so that over time a strong network of correlations is created among all constituent structures.

The same processes that operate within to bring into functional alignment the different systems of the organism also operate without. An example was recently provided by Cairns, McGuire, and Gariépy (1993):

> It should not be surprising to find hot-tempered, impulsive children growing up with family members who themselves exhibit and reward these traits, or subcultures of aggressive adolescents in which aggressive behavior is viewed as an asset rather than a liability. More broadly, social systems are usually formed in ways that are correlated with and support bio-behavioral dispositions. The biological forces that operate to enhance adaptation should typically operate in the same direction as the environmental experiences so that nature-nurture competition should be the exception rather than the rule. (p. 110)

From this perspective, a state of adaptation can be defined as one in which correlations within and correlations without are themselves correlated. The tendency to maintain such an organizational state over time would explain the strong stabilities so often reported in the human literature for various adaptive patterns, ranging from the quality of infant-mother attachment to personality styles and forms of social adjustment. The developmental emergence of systemic correlations, or functional alignment of activity between all systemic levels, creates a homeostatic equilibrium that tends to perpetuate itself and to favor conservatism in structures and functions.

A related perspective on conservatism is provided by proposals of Hegmann and DeFries (1970) that correlations between genetic influences and correlations between features of the environment often tend to be themselves correlated and that a correlation between genetic and environmental effects can enhance the biological efficiency of the adaptational process because both forces "push" behavior in the same direction. Their observations suggest a linkage between developmental accommodations and evolutionary modifications.

Extending this proposal further, Cairns et al. (1990) observed that "in periods of severe challenges, parallel and mutually supportive behavioral modifications may be rapidly mobilized in ontogeny and evolution by separate routes that act jointly to consolidate the same forms of adaptations" (p. 56). They illustrated this proposal by comparing the developmental functions observed for relevant features of social adaptation across successive generations of mice at the time the mice were being selected for high and low levels of aggression. This comparison showed that features of social interactions most susceptible to accommodation in the course of development were the same ones that were susceptible to modification in the course of microevolution. Specifically, it was observed that changes in the propensity to freeze and to become immobile when exposed to novel social stimuli mediated both the effects of experience over development and those of selective breeding over generations. In the second case, the effects consisted in progressive changes in the rates of development of social inhibition in the low-aggressive line, such that ancestral prepubertal levels were retained progressively longer in the ontogeny of the descendant generations (i.e., neoteny). Although different mechanisms of change were involved, it is the same feature of social adaptation that appeared to be open to rapid change and reorganization over both development and microevolution. At this juncture, the obvious questions are: How could episodic behavioral accommodations trigger the changes in biosocial (internal-external systems) that are necessary to support new adaptive directions, and how are they consolidated?

5. Revising the Organismic Model. In the current organismic model, individual behavior is depicted as a third level of activity, above the neurological and below the environmental. Cognitions and adaptive behaviors arise as the interactive activity that takes place between these levels. Under the assumption of complete bidirectionality, this activity is necessarily isomorphic with its interactive context. A full description of the organizational states and activity within the hierarchical system would permit one to fully predict its course. If, in this model, behavior remains a probabilistic outcome, it is only with regard to the fact that the interactive context created by the joint states of activity at the neurological and environmental levels is itself a probabilistic event.

The preceding discussion clearly indicates the need for a systemic model that adequately reflects the special properties of evolved behavior. These are easily forgotten when behavioral activity is situated as part of a single hierarchical system that encompasses every level of activity from the genetic to the environmental. A model is needed that places behavioral activity at the *origin* of the process of adaptation. To do so, it is necessary to recognize a boundary between the organism and its environment, an interface where the integrative functions of behavior can be specified. This is presented in Figure 1, where, instead of a single domain, two hierarchical domains of development are depicted: the individual organism and the social-ecological domains. The first domain, here called the intra-organismic, is defined as in Gottlieb's (1983, 1992) model, as a hierarchy of structures and functions that, from the genes to the nervous system, may be represented by any number of relevant and specifiable levels of organiza-tion. The second domain, the extraorganismic, consists of those physical and social aspects within the environment that have relevance from the standpoint of individual adaptation. For monkeys, apes, and humans, which are primarily social species, a useful depiction of the extraorganismic do-main may consist in the different levels of their social organization, as suggested in the primate literature by Hinde and Stevenson-Hinde (1976) and by Bronfenbrenner (1979) in the human literature. For the sake of clarity, these levels are considerably simplified in Figure 2.

The arrows in the center of the figure depict a reciprocal relationship between behavioral activity and the intra- and extraorganismic domains. This is a special case of bidirectionality, however, in that the relationship specified here takes the form of a recursive induction-support loop. On the premise that this relationship is actively established by the organism itself, processes of induction temporally precede those of support. In this se-quence, behavioral activity recursively supports (or validates) itself through the alignment that it induces between biological and environmental features. An interesting consequence of this special relationship is that behavior is never completely isomorphic with the objective conditions observed punctually within the two domains.

With respect to continuity and change in adaptive patterns, organization within and without the organism may either play a supportive role or impose constraints. Support is provided when conditions within and outside the organism are functionally aligned. In this case, behavioral activity is correlated to these conditions and current adaptive patterns are maintained. In the second case, adaptive challenges occur that compromise this align-ment, and those same conditions now impose limits on how the interactive context may be redefined. To illustrate, consider a situation in which an individual is threatened by another group member. How this situation is eventually controlled by the recipient is necessarily constrained by a host of factors, ranging all the way from the social status of the protagonists and their associated physiological states to the specific circumstances of their interaction. Within these constraints, however, cognitive activity may bring to the forefront configural aspects of the situation that create a "limited window of opportunity" for stimulus control. For example, this may consist

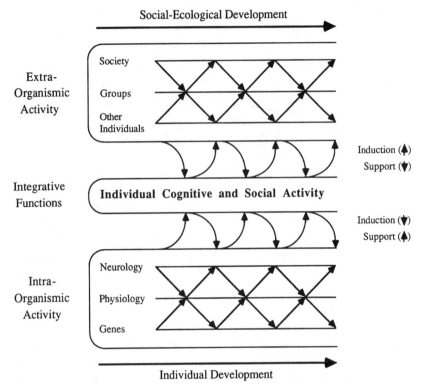

Figure 2. The revised systemic framework postulates two hierarchical domains of development instead of one: individual and social-ecological. This model specifies a boundary between these two domains of activity and situates higher cognitive and behavioral functions at their interface. The arrows in the center of the figure depict a reciprocal induction-support loop between the intra- and extraorganismic domains. In this sequence, behavioral activity recursively supports and validates itself through the alignment that it induces between biological and environmental features. In this process, those aspects of intra- and extraorganismic organization that are most vulnerable to change in the short term provide support for the new adaptive directions. If the conditions whereby this partial alignment was initiated are maintained, by virtue of bidirectionality, other systems within the two hierarchical domains eventually become correlated and further consolidate the new adaptive directions.

in enlisting the support of a nearby individual to manipulate the social signals given to the aggressor or to take advantage of some change in its interactive behavior. Depending on its outcome, a single interaction of this sort may have long-term effects for the participants, including a change in motivational states, self and social perceptions, and the physiological substrates of these functions. To the extent that these correlated effects would be validated and supported by parallel changes in the social ecology of the group, their behavioral equivalent may also tend to resist modification.

As pointed out by Cairns (1973, 1979), the social-interactive context affords unique opportunities for both continuity and change in behavioral adaptation. Unlike activities directed at the physical world, social actions involve other individuals that share the same psychological and behavioral capacities. Accordingly, the basis for the organization of action in this context may be rapidly transformed as new constraints and opportunities emerge in the temporal flow of social interchanges. In the light of the constant flux in social interactions, relationships, and social structures, maintaining and establishing new organism-environment relationships requires that activity within the different systems of the organism – genetic, hormonal, or neurological – be in the service of establishing them. Any behavior that would become stereotyped or frozen (i.e., determined) by those same systems would lose its most vital function of promoting flexible and reversible adaptations (Cairns, 1993). To examine the processes leading to the consolidation of new adaptive directions, it is necessary to examine the dynamic interplay that exists between different systemic levels and their respective time frames for reorganization.

6. Time Frames, Levels, and Systemic Change. A direct consequence of the emergence of correlations between systemic components is that adapted systems exhibit a good deal of inertia in which certain forms of equilibrium tend to perpetuate themselves. But circumstances also occur when this equilibrium is threatened. Although the construction of functional relationships with the environment is necessarily constrained by the trace effects created internally and externally by previous adaptations, in the new systemic model, it is the activity of the organism that sets the stage for systemic changes by inducing new functional relationships between the constituent levels. To make sense of the process of adaptation, from the initial phase of behavioral accommodation to the systemic consolidation of new adaptive directions, it is necessary to examine the dynamic interplay that exists between different systemic levels and their time frames for reorganization.

It is well documented that the different systems of the organism (neurobiological, endocrinological, or genetic) are not forever fixed in a given state of activity, but are eminently responsive to changes in stimulative conditions. The analysis of the adaptive process requires attention to the fact that functional changes within these different systems do not occur all at once, but may take place over vastly different time frames. For instance, depending on which level of neurological activity is being investigated, the relevant time frame for the study of change may be fractions of a second (e.g., neurotransmitter release), hours or days (receptor densities), or the entire lifetime of the organism (synaptic connections within neural nets). Finally, to capture reorganization at the level of the genome as a whole, our time frame must encompass successive generations.

That the various systems of the organism are differentially open for change over different periods of time provides for both conservatism and the possibility of fail-safe, innovative, and reversible changes in adaptive patterns (Cairns, 1993). In this way, when new adaptive challenges arise, those systems open for change over the short term may minimize the constraints imposed by other systems that change over longer periods of time. If those conditions represent only transient changes from the normative context, the overall systemic support for adjustment to the norm is not lost, and a return to the previous adaptation is equally facilitated. However, if those same conditions endure, by virtue of bidirectionality activity within other systems eventually becomes aligned with the changed adaptive directions, and new correlations are established in which a new systemic equilibrium is created. Over generations, it is this same process that forces reorganization at the genetic level and its eventual alignment with adaptive directions, which, in their initial stage of behavioral accommodation, appeared as punctual adjustments.

The different systems within the intra- and extraorganismic domains do impose constraints on how much variability is possible in adaptive patterns, but they do not determine them in the causal sense normally attributed to this term. On this point, I want to emphasize that even the degree of constraint imposed on behavioral reorganization by these systems diminishes in direct proportion to the complexity of hierarchical organization. This results from the fact that multiplying the number of systems and their complexity creates additional avenues for systemic change and that this addition is generally correlated with greater psychological capacities for initiating these changes. As a rule, however, when conditions remain the same across the short term and the long term, typically these systems collaborate rather than compete, because their action is normally correlated and supports the same forms of adaptation.

7. Flexibility and Reversibility in the Social Behaviors of Mice. Over the last 50 years, selective breeding programs have become a method of choice for studying various mechanisms of behavior regulation, including its genetic, hormonal, and neurological basis. In one such program, implemented some 20 years ago by Robert B. Cairns at the University of North Carolina at Chapel Hill, mice were selected for high and low levels of aggression. Selective breeding resulted in the rapid establishment (four generations) of lines of mice that, following isolation rearing, differed markedly in their propensity to attack when exposed for the first time to an unfamiliar mouse (Cairns, MacCombie, & Hood, 1983). In a short dyadic test conducted when the animals reached puberty, males in the high-aggressive line lunged in fierce attacks on the partner mouse, generally within the first minute of the test. By contrast, instead of attacking, low-aggressive mice exhibited a strong tendency to freeze and to become immobile upon social contact (Gariépy, Hood, & Cairns, 1988). It has been established in repeated measurements that dopamine concentrations have been significantly lower in the low-aggressive line in areas of the brain — the caudate nucleus and the nucleus accumbens — that are associated with the regulation of emotional responding, motivational states, and the initiation of action (Lewis, Gariépy, Southerland, Mailman, & Cairns, 1988). I must say that 10 years ago, when I was a fervent ethologist, I would have been perfectly satisfied with the demonstration that individual differences in aggressive behavior are heritable and that these differences are expressed in terms of a difference in central dopaminergic functions.

Fortunately, this was not the whole story. In the generations following line differentiation, Cairns attempted to determine if the genetic effects could be attenuated or magnified through social experience. The results were very conclusive: Four short 10-minute exposures to a conspecific, even with long intertest intervals, were sufficient to wipe out completely the line differences. Upon a fourth test, the experienced low-aggressive animals attacked as rapidly and as fiercely as did the high-aggressive ones (Cairns et al., 1983). Although the lines were firmly established at this point, the phenotypic differences disappeared when the animals were tested under conditions that differed from those under which selective breeding had taken place. Preliminary research suggested that the experiential effects were supported, at least in part, by an increase in dopaminergic activity (as measured by higher turnover rates; Milko, 1992). Research by Liljequist et al. (1993) also suggested a possible role for an increase in the density and/or affinity of N-methyl-D-asparate (NMDA) receptors in the cortex, the amygdala, and the hyppocampus, as these receptors are involved in the formation of memory traces.

Further research was conducted with the goal of determining whether the same experiential effects could take place over intervals of hours or days instead of weeks and months. To this end, extended tests (8 to 24 hr) were conducted that involved placing together in a large enclosure a female mouse and a high- and a low-aggressive male mouse. As expected, high-aggressive subjects were invariably the first to attack in every test. However, in 22 out of 54 of these tests, low-aggressive subjects achieved full dominance − generally within 2 hours − over their high-aggressive opponent (Gariépy, Lewis, & Cairns, in press). In these cases of line reversal, the initial inhibition and avoidance typical of the low-aggressive animals was gradually replaced by more frequent approaches, and attacks were initiated at a higher rate when some of the high-aggressive partners, because they were counterattacked, decreased their own rate of aggressive initiation and became more reactive.

By placing these animals together, my colleagues and I created for the low-aggressive subjects conditions that were uncorrelated with those that, over the generations, had served to consolidate their genetic and neurological biases toward inhibition and low aggression. Similarly, a defeat may be viewed as demanding a form of social adjustment for which the high-aggressive animals were "unprepared." Nonetheless, by the end of the tests, the animals of both lines seemed perfectly adjusted to their new social statuses; the dominant member was generally found in close proximity to the female, often assisting her in the building of a nest, whereas the submissive male was found digging, eating, or sleeping at some distance from the pair.

There was no a priori basis for predicting the outcome of the social interactions involving these high- and low-aggressive animals. All subjects had been socially isolated since weaning, and in the tests they were matched by age and weight. With other factors kept constant, had we made such predictions on the basis of the genetic and neurobiological biases with which the subjects initially entered the test situation, we would have been proven wrong 40% of the time. Rather, a behavioral analysis of these transitions suggested that as the initial set of interactive constraints was changed, so did the perception of stimulus intensity and opportunities for control, the motivation to attack or flee, in sum, the basis for the organization of action. In the process, a new context was constituted within which the natural synchrony of social interactions took over in the shaping of adaptive patterns that were true novelties compared to those displayed in the first minutes of interactions.

In an attempt to identify possible mechanisms supporting the new adaptive directions adopted by the two animals, levels of circulating testosterone and corticosterone were measured for all male dyads immediately after the test. Large differences were found between the males that had achieved a dominant or a submissive status. Specifically, the corticosterone levels for the submissive member of each pair were twice as high as that of the dominant member. Exactly the same pattern of difference was observed for testosterone, except that in this case, higher levels were measured for the dominant members of the pairs. The differences were particularly impressive in that no line differences had been observed for the same steroids in previous analyses conducted for inexperienced, isolated subjects (Gariépy, 1995; Gariépy, Lewis, & Cairns, in press). Such a process would be entirely consistent with the proposal that activity at the organism-environment boundary is at the forefront of the adaptive process and that points of systemic vulnerability exist for fail-safe reorganization in adaptive patterns. The findings also supported the view that otherwise strong and well-established differences in genetic background and neurochemistry can be easily overridden when circumstances are encountered that are uncorrelated with those that favored their consolidation over generations and development.

As described earlier, we have established that compared to high-aggressive animals, low-aggressive mice have lower dopamine concentrations in nucleus accumbens and caudate nucleus, with increased dopamine receptor densities in these same regions. Thus we wished to determine the effects of administration of a dopamine receptor agonist on social behavior. Mice of both lines were administered either saline, 1.0, 3.0, or 10 mg/kg (sc) of the selective, full efficacy D_1 receptor agonist dihydrexidine and their behavior assessed in the social interaction test. The results of this study were both surprising and striking. Dihydrexidine dose dependently reduced aggression in high-aggressive mice and similarly reduced non-agonistic approaches in the low-aggressive line, without affecting its characteristic freezing behavior. In both cases, the effects were related to a marked increase in reactivity to the mild social stimulation provided by the partner mouse, as measured by increases in behaviors such as escape, reflexive kicking, and vocalization. In independent experiments, mice of both lines were pretreated with the selective D_1 antagonist SCH23390 (0.1 mg/kg) or the selective D_2 antagonist remoxipride (1.0 mg/kg), after which they received dihydrexidine (10 mg/kg) and were tested as before. The effects of dihydrexidine on social reactivity were significantly antagonized in both lines by SCH23390 but were not attenuated by remoxipride. These experiments confirmed further the role that D_1 dopamine receptors play in the mediation of social reactivity (Lewis, Gariépy, Gendreau, Nichols, & Mailman, 1994).

The mechanism by which social isolation induces marked differences in social behavior in selectively bred lines has been a major question for this research. On this issue, our hypothesis was that social isolation causes a significant increase in the sensitivity of postsynaptic dopamine receptors. We tested this hypothesis by examining the effects of the same D_1 receptor agonist on the social behavior of both isolated and group-housed mice of each line. The effects of dihydrexidine on social behaviors essentially replicated those previously observed by Lewis et al. (1994). The "supersensitivity" to the D_1 dopamine agonist observed among isolated mice confirmed the role of this receptor in the mediation of the isolation effects. Finally, the fact that NC900 mice were the most sensitive to the pharmacological challenge suggested that social isolation has a differential effect on the two lines (Gariépy et al., 1995).

Because both social isolation and administration of a D_1 dopamine agonist can induce social reactivity in mice, we hypothesized that isolation rearing must exert its effects, at least in part, by up regulation of D_1 dopamine receptors. To test this hypothesis, we have conducted homogenate binding experiments using striatal tissue taken from mice of both lines. Half of the animals were socially reared from weaning until sacrifice (Day 45), and half were group reared for the same period of time. Relative to the group condition, homogenate binding data revealed a substantial increase in striatal densities of D_1 dopamine receptors among isolated animals. That such an increase was observed in the striatum is entirely consistent with the known functions of this area in the integration of affective, emotional, and motivational states and would explain the strong propensity of isolated animals to react strongly to novel social stimulation. Moreover, the significantly greater increase in D_1 receptor density observed in high-aggressive mice was consistent with their known tendency to be more reactive to social stimuli following isolation than low-aggressive mice (Gariépy et al., 1995). Future experiments will include further tests of the effects of social isolation on specific dopamine receptor subtypes and examining the behavioral effects of pharmacologically down regulating these receptors during the period of social isolation.

The previous experiments on the linkages between social reactivity, rearing conditions, and the D_1 dopamine receptor indicated that both genetic differences and differential rearing conditions can alter the sensitivity of this receptor. To examine further the influence of experiential input on D_1 receptor function we verified the possibility of altering its sensitivity by having our animals undergo a dramatic change in social experience over their lifetime. Accordingly, we initially isolated both high- and low-aggressive mice at weaning. At Day 45, half of the animals from each line were placed into social groups. At Day 64, about 12 mice per line per housing condition were tested in a social-interaction test. A second set of animals representing both lines and housing conditions was challenged, as before, with dihydrexidine prior to the social test. A final set of animals was sacrificed for receptor studies at Day 64. We hypothesized that returning animals to social groups would reduce social reactivity, attenuate the dihydrexidine-induced social reactivity, and reduce D_1 dopamine receptor sensitivity. Our results supported these hypotheses. Mice of both lines that experienced a change in rearing condition exhibited significantly less reactivity, a reduced response to dihydrexidine, and a decreased density of D_1 receptors when compared to animals that remained singly caged. This experiment constituted a striking demonstration of the plasticity of the neurobiological system supporting reactive responses, and confirmed the view that its functional organization is eminently open to experiential input (Gariépy, Lewis, & Cairns, in press).

There are important similarities between the social conditions created in this experiment and those that prevailed over the extended test described earlier. In both cases, the animals were challenged to adjust to social conditions for which they were psychologically and biologically unprepared. Here, upon introduction to a group situation, the previously isolated high-aggressive subjects carried the psychological characteristics of an established territory holder, and they were supported in this status by enhanced dopaminergic functions and a corresponding tendency to react violently to the presence of conspecifics. Accordingly, interactions during the first half hour of group formation were characteristically intense, and violent attacks and withdrawals among the four animals predominated. However, the frequency of these behaviors diminished when one of the participants eventually established its dominance over the other males. As the new social order precluded the expression of highly reactive behaviors, these responses to social approaches became less frequent and were gradually replaced by the less provocative and more submissive upright posture.

Summary and Conclusions

The systemic approach presented here is necessarily based upon the modern organismic viewpoint except for an essential difference: The highest level of organismic activity – cognitive and behavioral activity – figures not as an interactive product, but as the interface between the intra- and the extraorganismic domains. As suggested in Chapter 2, by Magnusson and Cairns, the function of activity at this interface is to establish through time a dynamic coordination between internal and external structures in ways that support preservation, development, and novel adaptive patterns. Accordingly, the study of change in adaptive patterns begins with a systematic analysis of the cognitive-behavioral accommodations observed in the short term, along with appropriately time-framed analyses of the supportive changes taking place in the other systems of the organism and the environment. In this framework, the systemic changes that are necessary to support and consolidate new adaptive directions are examined with respect to the dynamic interplay that exists between different systemic levels and their respective time frames for reorganization.

The elucidation of how new functional alignments between environmental and organismic systems are achieved requires a systemic analysis of how, through behavior, novelties are introduced in the organization and coordination of the two systems over time. An important property of the hierarchical organization of living systems, both within and without the organism, appears to be the existence of multiple points of entry whereby rapid and fail-safe adaptive reorganizations may be initiated. Those aspects of behavioral regulation that have a direct impact on the outcome of social interactions, seem to be the same ones that are addressed over multiple windows of time. A remarkable aspect of the behavioral function in evolved species is its capacity to force reorganization between these different systems such that activity within and activity without are kept in alignment in the service of continued adaptation. It is in this role that behavior serves as an adaptive device in a system that otherwise tends to conservation and continuity in structure and function.

6   Primates and Persons: A Comparative Developmental Understanding of Social Organization

Arnold J. Sameroff and Stephen J. Suomi

A rhesus monkey mother hearing the cry of her infant interrupts whatever she is doing and hurries to comfort the baby. A chimpanzee mother sees her baby in distress and rushes to soothe her distraught offspring. A human mother hears the cry of her infant and also hurries to ease the child, *but* suddenly stops. She remembers reading that if she quickly responds to her crying baby she will reinforce the crying and produce in the future a whiny brat. This reflective overlay on human behavior is a major distinguishing feature of our species that transcends the here-and-now reality of emotional impulses and extends the range of influences on current action far into both the past and the future.

The embeddedness of each contemporary human in a system of representations, both cognitive and cultural, is the basis for the richness and diversity in patterns of human socialization. For nonhuman primates this variation is far more limited, and differences in social organization are more closely tied to differences in species. In this presentation, we hope to illuminate the determinants of the *diversity* in the social organization of apes and monkeys and the *uniformities* in the social organization of humans. From this investigation, we hope to gain a better perspective on the processes by which human culture regulates development as well as on the processes by which human culture is regulated by development. Where biological reductionists and contextual antireductionists have emphasized their differences, we plan to focus on the intersections where culture acts to transcend the limits of individual biology and biological constraints shape the organization of culture.

The theme of this volume is that behavior develops in a context and cannot be separated from that context. At any and every level of analysis, a unit of activity cannot be understood apart from the system in which it participates and the systems of which it is composed. These processes of coaction (Gottlieb, this volume) or transaction (Sameroff, 1995; Sameroff & Chandler, 1975) are the fundamental characteristics of any activity.

97

Despite lip service to the futility of the nature-nurture controversy, behavioral geneticists continue to debate the separate proportions of variance contributed by biology and environment, and advocates of contextualism continue to ignore the biological differences among humans. We hope to reinforce the dynamic unifying perspective of this volume that only by understanding the inseparability of organism and context can one understand the determinants of behavior (Magnusson & Cairns, this volume).

An understanding of primate behavior and especially the development of that behavior requires that individuals be viewed in transaction with the social world in which they live as well as with the biological world of which they are composed. Unfortunately, the ability to think about two things or levels at the same time, much less three, seems to elude many humans, whereas the demonstration that subhuman primates can consider more than one thing at a time is a constant surprise.

Determinants of Development

Developmental understanding of the genotype (Gottlieb, this volume; Oyama, 1989) has emphasized an epigenetic perspective denying any determining influence of genes on the individual. The coaction perspective requires that every living event be interpreted as the outcome of a relation between individual and environment, between unit and context. The genotype in each cell is identical, but the particular set of genes that are active at any point in time is regulated by the state of the phenotype. Depending on the current chemical environment, certain genes are activated that alter the phenotype. The altered phenotype may then act reciprocally to deactivate the original genes and to activate another set that will produce further developmental changes in the phenotype. These transactions between genotype and phenotype exemplify the bidirectional determinism that characterizes all of life, from the biological to the social.

As evolution progressed, the development of offspring came to require a behavioral contribution from parents in addition to their biological contribution. Where there may be some question about this role for lower orders, for primates it is clear that without an interactive environment there can be no offspring survival. A caregiver is required to feed, protect, and socialize the young of a species until the offspring are ready to function independently in these domains. Given this parental role the next question is where the organization of this caregiving behavior resides. Is there a plan, either in the genes or in the culture, that guides the actions of parents, or is parental behavior an emergent property that arises from the here-and-now interactions of offspring and their caregivers? Many human parents would argue that they have a plan for raising their children to fulfill societal goals of productive work and family life. The question remains, however, whether such a plan is a purely social construction (Berger & Luckman, 1966) or is determined more by behavior that children elicit from their parents.

In examining what determines individual development, we will be focusing on a distinction between local and distal influences on parental behavior, between the reactions that children elicit from their parents and a planned developmental agenda that guides parental action. A biological analogy would be in the changes in embryological theorizing that followed Spemann's (1927) induction experiments. Before such experiments, it was believed that cells were fated to become specific tissues in specific adult organs, that there was a predetermined plan. Spemann demonstrated that when similar cells were moved into different locations in the embryo where they would be in contact with different types of cells, they became something quite different. After Spemann, development was reinterpreted as the result of local relationships rather than as the consequence of a deterministic plan.

During the growth of the nervous system, underlying tissue in the early embryo induces the development of a neural plate in the outer cell layer. The cells at the front end of the neural plate induce the cells further forward to form a nose and then the cells on the side to form eyes. In each case, there is no central organizer regulating that the spinal cord should be in one place and the nose and eyes in another. It is the cells of the neural plate that *locally* organize the development of the next phase. The destiny of a particular set of cells does not appear to be an exclusive property of that set of cells, nor of the genetic material within those cells, but rather of the interaction between cells and their environment (Ebert & Sussex, 1970). Virtually every vertebrate tissue and organ is formed by induction from neighboring tissues (Kessler & Melton, 1994). In a reversal of the typical use of biological metaphors to explain psychological functioning, a recent review of developmental biology summarized the issue by stating that most development works through "peer pressure" from neighboring cells (Schmidt, 1994).

This differentiation between distal interactions with a master plan and local interactions with neighbors is what we are trying to examine in the analysis of culture. Stimulated by elements of chaos theory (Gleick, 1987), modern dynamic systems theory is engaged in examining how order and pattern can emerge in a number of domains through the interaction of component processes without the need of hierarchical instructions (Thelen, 1989). It may be that we are misled by the dynamics of development to believe that the processes are so complicated that they are beyond understanding, yet in a number of instances such complexity arises from the activity of a few simple subprocesses (Bateson, 1996). So our question is, do humans develop according to a scheme characterized by a cognized socialization agenda or does behavioral organization represent the outcome of local reactions between a growing child and a dynamic environment that build on each other to produce the complexity we see in contemporary humans?

Environtype

Before engaging the dynamic processes of development, we will begin with a description of the preorganized ingredients of human growth. Such patterning has typically been restricted to the genotype with a belief that the pattern is a plan (Wolpert, 1994). However, another pattern can be identified in the developmental agenda of families and cultures. Just as there is a biological organization, the genotype, that regulates the physical outcome of each individual, there is a social organization that regulates the way human beings fit into their society. This organization operates through family and cultural socialization patterns and has been postulated to compose an "environtype," analogous to the biological genotype (Sameroff, 1985; Sameroff & Fiese, 1990).

The child's behavior at any point in time is a product of the transactions between the phenotype, or the child; the environtype, or a regulator of external experience; and the genotype, or a regulator of biological organization. (See Figure 3.) This system is reciprocally determined at each point in development. On the environmental side, the environtype contains a range of possible reactions to the child, but the particular regulating experiences that are active at any point in time are in response to the behavioral status of the child's phenotype. Once the child changes as a consequence of one set of experiences, that set of experiences may be inhibited and another set activated in response to the changed status of the child. The most explicit form of such regulation is in educational curricula. A set of lessons is given until the child reaches a criterion of knowledge, which triggers a shift to the next set of lessons. In turn, when the child reaches the next criterion the lessons are again shifted. Training in addition is followed by training in subtraction, which is followed by training in multiplication and then division.

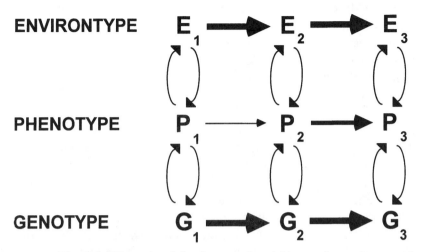

Figure 3. Transactional-developmental model integrating environmental, genetic, and individual regulating systems.

Traditional psychological research on child development has empha-sized both the child's utilization of biological capacities to gain experience and the role of experience in shaping a child's competencies. Far less attention has been paid to how that experience is organized. We have already mentioned the organization of experience that is explicit in educa-tional curricula, but the implicit organization of experience found in the family and social context that compose the environtype has so far been neglected. A corollary of this point is a growing research emphasis on family management strategies (Furstenberg, Eccles, Elder, Cook, & Sameroff, in press). Whereas most psychological research on parenting has focused on dimensions such as control and warmth, in parent-child interac-tions most parenting does not involve such proximal interactions. Although parents spend only a small part of the day with their children, they can make arrangements for the rest of the children's time. They can choose the schools their children attend, arrange alternative caregiving arrangements, and enlist their children in a variety of extracurricular activities. The extent to which parents engage in such management can have a dramatic impact on the developmental course and progress of their offspring. Parental man-agement is a major part of a child's environtype.

The environtype is composed of subsystems that not only transact with the child but also transact with each other. Bronfenbrenner (1977) has provided the most detailed descriptions of environmental organizations that influence developmental processes within categories of microsystems, mesosystems, exosystems, and macrosystems. The microsystem is the immediate setting of a child in an environment with particular features, activities, and roles, for example, the home or the school. The mesosystem comprises the relationships between the major settings at a particular point in an individual's development, for example, between home and school. The exosystem is an extension of the mesosystem that includes settings that the child may not be a part of but that affect the settings in which the child does participate, for example, the parent's world of work. Finally, the macrosystem includes the overarching institutional patterns of the culture, including the economic, social, and political systems of which the microsystems, mesosystems, and exosystems are concrete expressions.

Bronfenbrenner (1986) went on to review the research paradigms that examined the influence of the environment on development. These paradigms vary in the detail in which the dimensions of external systems are examined. The simplest is the social-address model, in which family process is not considered at all. Here the focus is on such variables as ethnicity or social status with no attention to the activities within these addresses that could affect the child. More complex are process-context models, in which there is an examination of the impact of external environment on particular family processes. Here the more complex focus is on the interaction between context and family variables. Bronfenbrenner cited, as an example, studies by Tulkin and his colleagues (Tulkin & Cohler, 1973; Tulkin & Covitz, 1975) in which the pattern of correlations between parenting behavior and child behavior in one social address, middle-class families, was different from that in another social address, lower-class families.

At the most complex level are person-process-context models, which add a third term to the predictive equation. Interactions between process and context were studied in interaction with the specific characteristics of the individuals in the family. Crockenberg's (1981) study of the relations among mother's social support, child attachment, and child temperament served as an example. She found that when the infant had a difficult temperament, there was a stronger relation between social support and secure attachment than when the infant had an easy temperament. When such interactions are found among variables in the person-process-context model, there is a great similarity to what would be expected from transactional processes.

Bronfenbrenner's (1977) original ecological model provided a perceptive organization for an analysis of synchronic processes, a cross-sectional slice of life that incorporated the multiple contexts that could influence development. He stressed the importance of moving beyond the mother-child relationship to a concern for the effects of other relationships in which the child participates without the parent and the parent participates without the child. The mesosystem level of analysis integrated the multiple child contexts of family, school, and peer group. The exosystem analysis integrated the multiple parental contexts of the workplace, social networks, and community influences. To this synchronic approach Bronfenbrenner (1986) added a diachronic dimension in a chronosystem level of analysis for examining the effects of environmental changes on individual development over time. The necessity for examining the life-long coherence of environmental influences has become a more common theme in developmentalist thinking, especially through increasing attention to analyses of the life course (Elder, this volume). The environtype is an organizational framework for capturing the quality of this coherence.

Although there is an endless range of environmental factors involved in any given developmental ecology, most attention has been devoted to levels of environmental factors contained within the culture, the family, and the individual parent. Developmental regulations at each of these levels can be conceptualized as being carried within codes: a cultural code, a family code, and an individual code for each parent. The developmental consequence of interpreting these codes is to produce an adult member of society who can play a role in reproducing society. Regulation during childhood is aimed at cognitive behavior and social-emotional adaptation so that the child ultimately will be able to occupy a cultural role. The codes are hierarchically related in their evolution and in their current influence on the child. The experience of the developing child is partially determined by the beliefs, values, and personalities of the parents, partially by the family's interaction patterns and transgenerational history, and partially by the socialization beliefs, controls, and supports of the culture.

Representation and Practice

There is a distinction that must be recognized between codes and behaviors. The environtype is no more a description of the experiential environment than the genotype is a description of the child, but it may be no less. In each case, the code must be actualized through active processes at either the behavioral or biological level. The codes of the environtype may have an organizational and regulatory influence on parent behavior, but the behavior is not the same as the codes. Moreover, developmental goals are not necessarily recognized by all members of society nor, perhaps, by any member of a particular society. They are the result of ultimate causes in the evolution of human cultures. If a culture is not successful in producing new adults to carry on roles it will no longer exist. The proximate causes of why any particular set of parents is engaged in child rearing will have a wide range of variability as well as a wide range of coherence. For some parents there is a clear philosophy of child rearing and clearly desired goals for their children. For other parents there is far less reflection on these issues. Reiss (1989) implicitly focused on this contrast in conceptualizing family behavior in terms of representation and practice. The representational level is where the family conceptualizes its behavior. The practicing level is where the behavior actually takes place. This distinction will become clearer in the following discussion.

The environtype can be conceptualized independent of the child: School systems can describe their curricula, and some parents can describe their child-rearing systems. Expected increases in the abilities of the growing child are major triggers for regulatory changes wherein teacher or parent alters behavior and most likely were major contributors to the evolution of the developmental agenda. In an analysis of the developmental transitions that trigger regulatory shifts, a distinction is generally made between normative transitions, that is, the milestones, and nonnormative transitions, that is, accidents, societal changes, and historical events. This distinction is important when examining any individual life course, but for a general exposition the focus will be on normative events.

Although developmental milestones have always been thought to be a property of the child, their significance is much reduced unless there is a triggered regulation from the environtype. Different parents, different families, different cultures, and different historical epochs may be sensitive to different behavior of the child as a regulatory trigger (deVries & Sameroff, 1984). For example, in the United States it was not until the major changes in the educational system stimulated by evidence of advanced Soviet technology (the first satellite in space, Sputnik) that newborn intellectual competence, that is, the ability to perceive and learn, became an important milestone. Adolescence is characterized by major biological changes, yet different cultures can define it independent of the pubertal status of the child (Worthman, 1993). In some cultures adolescence is closely tied to biological changes, in others it precedes or follows these changes, and in still others it is independent of these changes.

The ingredients of the cultural code are the complex of characteristics that organize a society's child-rearing system and that incorporate elements of socialization and education. These processes are embedded in sets of social controls and social supports. They are based on beliefs that differ in the amount of community consensus ranging from mores and norms to fads and fashions. The content of such a cultural code is a core concern of both sociology and anthropology. Human societies vary greatly in the experiences they provide their children (Worthman, 1993). Infancy is a time period when these differences are first apparent in birthing practices (Lozoff, 1983), feeding and sleeping arrangements (Whiting, 1981), and the size of the family unit (Draper, 1976).

The biological characteristics of the child played a role in the evolution of the cultural code but did not determine it, just as the chemical characteristics of molecules played a role in the evolution of the genetic code but did not determine it. Many common biological characteristics of the human species have acted to produce similar developmental agendas in most societies. For example, in most cultures formal education begins between the ages of 6 and 8, when most children have reached the cognitive ability to learn from such structured experiences (Rogoff, 1981). However, there are historical and cross-cultural differences where changes in child behavior are emphasized or ignored. Informal education can begin at many different ages, depending on the culture's attributions to the child. Some middle-class parents have been convinced that prenatal experiences will enhance the cognitive development of their children and consequently begin stimulation programs during pregnancy, whereas others believe it best to wait until the first grade before beginning formal learning experiences. In Kenya, Gusii mothers believe that infants should be soothed and protected from excitement; in the United States, mothers believe that babies should be verbally stimulated and excited when awake; and in Japan, mothers emphasize empathy and sensitivity to others in interactions (LeVine et al., 1994). Such examples demonstrate the variability of human developmental contexts and the openness of the regulatory system to modification.

Regulation of Human Development: Child Contributions

What are the developmental milestones that can act as triggers to the environtype, and are they universal for all humans? The word *can* is especially important here because a major question that we will ask of the primate literature is whether there are alternative pathways that can result from an offspring-initiated transaction. In response to similar child behavior, will some parents respond one way, others another, and still others not at all? With humans the answer is clearly yes at both the cultural and the family level. Cultures either respond or do not to a variety of developmental steps depending on the step's meaning in that culture's developmental agenda. Within a culture, different families may respond differently, and within a family, different parents may respond differently depending on individual familial and parental experiences and agendas.

Universal milestones arise on the child side as the product of transactions between the genotype and phenotype. Species characteristics that are tightly regulated become defining biological characteristics of humanity. Given this uniformity of child characteristics is there a matching uniformity of environmental response? In terms used by behavioral geneticists, is there a high level of organism-environment covariation? At the lower bound of human culture, we can ask whether there are any universals in the transactions between the child and the social surround. At the upper bound of nonhuman primate culture, we can ask whether there are any nonuniversals in the transactions between offspring and their caregivers.

In human cultures, there are a number of candidates for the status of universals. These include attachment, separation, exploration, play, aggression, and social behavior. There is also a set of universals in the responses of caregivers. Papousek and Papousek (1987) have labeled these "intuitive parenting." Their list includes tactual, visual, and auditory reactions and communications that are frequently outside the awareness of the responding parent. Yet these seeming universals are often given different meanings and responded to differently depending on the multiple transactions between the child, the culture, and the ecological niche in which they find themselves.

Parent Contributions: Local versus Distal Interactions

In our attempts to understand the developmental significance of culture, we have been struck by parental behavior that may appear to result from represented systems of child-rearing beliefs but, under closer analysis, seem to be directly elicited by the behavior of the offspring. In such instances, we are interested in distinguishing what might be called local interactions from those that may be more distally determined. We do not mean here the distinction between proximal and ultimate causation important to evolutionary explanations of behavior (Mayr, 1961). Both the local and distal aspects we are examining can be considered as proximal causes. Parent belief systems about socialization can be just as much in the here-and-now as their child-rearing behavior can.

One indication that distal influences are at work is the group differences that are found within the same species in response to the same stimulus. There would be no need to seek an explanation in the realm of culture if such differences did not exist. The culture question arises again when we examine the societal responses to the changing characteristics of the child. Is there a common response, or is there a range of reaction? Many of the parental responses are directly related to the characteristics of the stimulus. A mother's withdrawal of the breast can be directly related to painful biting behavior of the infant. On the other hand, other mothers may have much more distal reasons for stopping breastfeeding, such as a child-rearing strategy designed to avoid spoiling the child. In still other circumstances, a cultural overlay designed to increase the interval between births may lead to a continuance of breastfeeding into the third or fourth year, as in many nomadic cultures (Erikson, 1950; Whiting, 1981).

Separation is another area of human universality (Bowlby, 1973) for which weaning is a major determinant on the parent side and exploration a major determinant on the infant side. Here again there is a universal stimulus in the child's increasing capacity at locomotion, first through crawling and then through walking and running. At the parental level, the local response is to provide greater freedom as the effort to constrain the increasingly stronger and heavier infant becomes more and more difficult. But at the same time there is a represented awareness of potential dangers to the still immature human, and thus the parent must take protective measures so that the infant does not fall prey to predators or physical dangers. This representation can take on a life of its own within a cultural code that defines infants as being incompetent until well into the second year of life so that they must be swaddled and constrained on a cradle board. Such is the case with the Kikuyu who live in highland areas of West Africa where it would be quite easy for a child to have dangerous falls (deVries & Sameroff, 1984). At the intracultural family level, there can be different attributions placed on the burgeoning motor skills of the child. Sports-minded families may actively stimulate and foster athletic behavior, whereas more sedentary parents may inhibit the same infant behavior in the service of maintaining a tranquil home life. Again, different ecologies promote different parenting practices, which can be represented at different levels of the environtype, in the cultural code, the family code, or the representations of the individual parent.

Adolescence is another universal milestone characterized by a young person's increasing size and maturity of sexual behavior. Is there a uniformity in the environmental reaction to this developmental transition? Although there has been significant debate about adolescence as a period of turmoil, the argument has shifted from the earlier interpretations of *Sturm und Drang* as a characteristic of the adolescent to viewing it as a manifestation of the changing relationship between parent and child (Steinberg, 1987). Again the parent is required to let go of some degree of regulation of the youth because of physical inability to control someone with the strength if not the wisdom of an adult, but the timing, form, and process of this letting go is extremely varied. Adolescence is a developmental stage that provides a clear example of how cultural codes produce a variety of meanings and behaviors as different developmental agendas are played out. Although biologists can define adolescence in terms of the maturation of the reproductive system and its hormonal changes, few cultures are so medically minded. Among these are the Kikuyu, for whom the adolescent transition, marked by circumcision for boys and clitoridectomy for girls, is closely tied to the maturational appearance of the children as evidenced by the status of their sexual characteristics. Worthman (1993) described these variations in cultural definitions that range from the nonexistent to the highly elaborated and prolonged. In the latter category are the Masai who transitioned a cohort of children into adolescence every 7 years. Thus the range of ages was from 7 to 14 at the start and 14 to 21 at the end. In Western culture adolescence as a stage was not recognized until the 19th century (Ariès, 1962) and has continued to evolve through the middle of the 20th. Even within this stage there has been a dramatic change in the social responsibilities of 14- to 18-year-olds over the last century in the United States (Elder, 1980). Where a century ago nearly all these children were working, now nearly all these children are in school.

The role of culture is easy to envision when the concern is with the human species but seems relatively absent in the life of lower orders of vertebrates. Complex parental behaviors have been found that are dependent on elicitation by offspring behavior. Moreover, these elicitations are part of a chain of reciprocal interactions between parent and young that are necessary not only to produce competent adults but also to ensure the survival of the offspring (Blass, 1990; Hofer, 1994; Rosenblatt, 1965). But what of those species that are the closest to humans? Nonhuman primates exhibit a range of complexity in their social interactions that approximate what are believed to be the culture of the earliest humans. What is the source of such complexity? To what extent can it be explained as the manifestation of the interaction of simple behavioral subsystems, and to what extent is there something that transcends the here and now, that exists in the mind of individuals and is behaviorally transmitted as a developmental agenda from one generation to another? To answer these questions, we will have to engage in a more detailed description of the lives of apes and monkeys.

Primate Universals

Apes and Old World monkeys are humans' closest phylogenetic relatives, and humans share most of their genetic heritage – as much as 94% for rhesus monkeys and 98% for chimpanzees in terms of common unreplicated DNA (Lovejoy, 1981). Although monkeys are clearly not furry little humans with tails, most aspects of their embryology, anatomy, and physiology are homologous with those of human beings. Moreover, monkeys, apes, and humans exhibit surprisingly similar patterns and sequences of early infant emotional, social, and cognitive development. Such development inevitably transpires in and transacts with a complex and dynamic social environment in virtually all advanced nonhuman primate species, as it clearly does in virtually all human cultures. Indeed, although no nonhuman primate species shares human language or culture, many aspects of their own complex environtypes seem hauntingly familiar.

Consider the case of rhesus monkeys (*Macaca mulatta*). Members of this highly successful species of Old World monkeys live in large social groups (termed "troops") that range in size from several dozen to more than a hundred individuals. Each troop consists of several multigenerational matrilineal families of females and prepubertal males, as well as adult males born outside of their resident troop. This form of social group organization derives from the fact that females remain in their natal troop throughout their entire lives, whereas males typically emigrate from their natal troop around puberty and eventually join other established troops. Each rhesus monkey troop thus represents a distinctive social entity, with its own unique history and blend of matrilines and immigrant males. Although different troops may have overlapping ranges and even daily exposure to one another, each troop is a cohesive social unit that can become remarkably tight knit when challenged (Lindburg, 1971).

Every rhesus monkey troop is characterized by several distinct dominance hierarchies. For example, there is a clear-cut linear hierarchy between the troop's different multigenerational matrilines, such that all members of the highest-ranking matriline (including infants) outrank all members of the second-ranked matriline (including adults), who in turn outrank all members of the third-ranked matriline, and so forth. There is also a clear-cut hierarchy among females *within* each matriline, following the surprising general rule that younger sisters outrank older sisters. In addition, there is a separate hierarchy for the immigrant adult males (roughly related to relative tenure in their resident troop), as well as a hierarchy among like-aged infants born in the troop matching exactly that of their mothers (cf. Sade, 1967). These complex social relationships seem to require any fully functioning troop member to have some knowledge of most if not all of other members' specific kinship and dominance status in order to survive, let alone thrive in troop life. How are such capabilities developed and maintained in generation after generation of monkeys born into each troop?

Rhesus monkey infants spend all of their first weeks of life in physical contact with or within arm's reach of their biological mothers, who provide them with nourishment, psychological warmth, and protection. In their second month of life, these infants begin to leave their mothers for brief exploratory forays. By this time each infant has already established a strong bond with its mother, and it uses her as a "secure base" from which to organize the exploration of its immediate environment. In the course of such exploration the infant encounters other members of its troop, and in the succeeding weeks and months it spends increasing amounts of time away from its mother, engaging in extensive interactions with others, especially peers (Harlow & Harlow, 1965). In this respect the mother's influence on the infant clearly shifts from exclusively proximal to primarily distal.

For young rhesus monkeys from 6 months of age onward, play with peers becomes the predominant social activity. These play interactions become increasingly complex and involve specific sequences and patterns of behavior that appear to simulate virtually all adult social activities, including reproductive behavior and dominance-aggression interactions. In other words, play with peers provides a medium through which specific behavior patterns crucial to normal adult functioning can be developed, practiced, and perfected long before they must become functional in adult life (Suomi & Harlow, 1975).

The onset of puberty in rhesus monkeys occurs near the end of the third year of life (for females) and the beginning of the fourth year (for males), and it is clearly associated with major life transitions for both genders. Although females remain in their natal troop throughout this period and after, their interactions with peers decline dramatically, and they redirect much of their social activities toward other members of their own matriline, including the infants that they subsequently bear. Pubertal males, by contrast, leave their natal troop. The few individual males that refuse to leave voluntarily are eventually expelled physically, usually by members of unrelated matrilines. In either case, these young males typically join all-male gangs for varying periods before they attempt to enter a new troop (Suomi, 1991). It should be noted that the time of adolescence and young adulthood is clearly the most dangerous period of life for a male rhesus monkey – in the wild, the mortality rate for males from the time they leave their natal troop until they are successfully integrated into a new troop approaches 50% (Dittus, 1979). It is also clear that individual males employ different "strategies" in their efforts to join a new troop, and that each strategy entails a different set of potential risks and benefits (Suomi, Rasmussen, & Higley, 1992).

The just-described sequences of behavioral ontogeny and patterns of social troop organization have been observed not only in rhesus monkey troops living in the wild but also in groups maintained in captivity. These species-normative developmental sequences and group social structures are typical for many species of Old World monkeys, and they are similar in many respects to those seen in other nonhuman primate taxa (Lindburg, 1971).

It can be argued that Bronfenbrenner's (1977) characterization of environmental organizations that influence human developmental processes generalize at least in part to rhesus monkey environtypes. A rhesus monkey baby is born into a microsystem initially restricted to the mother, but with increasing age it expands to include sibs, other close relatives, other members of the troop, and members of other troops interacting with the infant. The organization of these microsystems is influenced by the higher-order mesosystem that defines the relationships between members of the family, families in the troop, and troops. Mesosystems influence rhesus monkey infants largely via indirect means, but juveniles become increasingly involved directly with their mesosystems not only through their playful interactions with peers but also in their observation of and participation in interactions with adolescents, adult females from other matrilines, and resident and immigrating adult males. To the extent that the infants do not interact with other troops, their interaction might be considered an exosystem. Exosystem interactions determine which is the dominant troop at any point in time and may result in a shift that would alter the behavior of all members of the infant's troop should there be a change in the troop hierarchy. The generality of Bronfenbrenner's model perhaps breaks down somewhat for rhesus monkeys at the level of macrosystems, where over-arching cultural patterns are organized, although there do appear to be systematic differences in both individual and social group characteristics between rhesus monkeys living in urban versus rural settings in India (Singh, 1969) and between rhesus monkeys of Chinese origin and those of Indian heritage (Champoux, Suomi, & Schneider, 1994).

Regulation of Rhesus Monkey Social Development

What factors regulate the processes by which rhesus monkeys born with an active but limited behavioral repertoire and a restricted social sphere develop into contributing members of clearly defined families residing within large and stable complex social groups? How is an infant rhesus monkey influenced by various aspects of its environtype – parental, family (matriline), or community (troop) – and how does it influence each of these in the process of its own development? Data from both laboratory and field studies suggest that for rhesus monkeys these regulating factors are multiple, reciprocal, and developmentally dynamic in their influence.

Infant Contributions

Rhesus monkey infants are hardly passive recipients of whatever stimuli their mothers and others happen to provide. Instead, they are born with strong behavioral propensities, clear-cut perceptual biases, and numerous physical and social features that make them highly attractive to any caregiver, especially their mothers. For example, newborn rhesus monkeys have several physical features that clearly distinguish them from older conspecifics and appear to serve as releasing stimuli for potential caregivers. They share many of the "babylike" physical and physiognomic characteristics of human neonates that elicit "intuitive parenting" in most cultures (Papousek et al., 1981). In addition, they are born with an un-usually dark coat and bright red facial coloration that are highly attractive to adult females (Higley et al., 1987). The importance of these features for eliciting maternal bonding is emphasized when the coat and facial col-orations begin to fade – around the time of weaning (4 to 5 months of age). During this period rhesus monkey infants begin to be treated quite differently (and generally less tolerantly) not only by their mothers but also by older siblings and both kin and nonkin adults of both sexes (Suomi, 1979).

Infant monkeys, thus, have shown clear evidence of influencing the microsystem level (and beyond) of their environtype through their appearance, as well as by differential behavior patterns and temperamental characteristics (e.g., Suomi, 1987). However, such influences are not permanent, and when their physical appearance and behavioral repertoires change, rhesus monkey infants elicit different reactions from all aspects of their environtypes – they are no longer treated like infants. Later in development, changes in physical appearance and behavioral repertoires that accompany the onset of puberty are similarly associated with major changes in how both male and female adolescents are treated by the rest of their family and troop (Suomi et al., 1992).

Maternal and Matrilineal Contributions

Just as rhesus monkey infants influence their mothers and others through universal (e.g., facial coloration) and individual (e.g., temperament) characteristics, so too do mothers and others in the social group have both universal and individual influences on their infants. A wealth of laboratory and field data have consistently demonstrated that maternal behavior varies as a function of differences in rank, parity, and style. High-ranking mothers are consistently more "laissez-faire" in their oversight of offspring than are low-ranking mothers, who are considerably more socially restricted in their ability to "rescue" their infants should they get into trouble and hence are typically more reluctant to let them explore at will. Multiparous rhesus monkey mothers rear their infants in different fashion than do primiparous mothers, in terms of developmental changes in both physical contact and punishment patterns. Still other laboratory and field studies have shown that within the same social group individual mothers consistently differ in their maternal "style," and their offspring consistently differ in many aspects of their attachment and subsequent social behavior, as well as in their hormonal, neurochemical, and immunological reactivity (Suomi, 1995).

The behavioral and physiological developmental profiles of rhesus monkey infants are also influenced to an increasing degree by intra- and interfamilial social factors as the infants get older. For example, from the outset female infants outrank their older sisters within their family's dominance hierarchy, initially as a direct consequence of their mother's interventions on their behalf during sibling squabbles. This preferential treatment by their mothers is soon reinforced by other members of the matriline, such that these young females are permitted priority of access to preferred foods, objects, and places over their older sisters, even though the older sisters are bigger, stronger, and more advanced cognitively and socially. Thus, although the older sisters may clearly be capable of dominating their younger siblings both physically and socially in any one-on-one encounter, in reality the younger siblings consistently have the backing of both their mother and the rest of the matriline, and with that help they are able to dominate their older sisters (Berman, 1992). In time both younger and older siblings come to accept their differential social status, which usually is sustained for the rest of their respective lives, even after their mother is no longer around to reinforce the relationship herself. Here, perceptions of differential social status by other family and group members, initially based on differential social reinforcement by the mother, eventually become essentially self-sustaining, maintained in part by selective reinforcement by other family and troop members.

In parallel fashion, the dominance status of a mother within the rest of her troop (i.e., outside her matriline) also has definite social and perhaps physiological consequences for her offspring during their juvenile years. Rhesus monkey infants share their mother's relative position within the troop hierarchy, and this perceived relationship clearly influences the ways in which they are treated throughout development by other troop members.

Infants of high-ranking mothers, for example, are dominant over juveniles, adolescents, and adults in low-ranking matrilines from the time of their very first interactions. As they are growing up these high-ranking infants "get used to" prevailing in conflicts with older and physically stronger conspecifics when in the presence of their mother and other matriline relatives. Offspring of high-ranking mothers also outrank their same-aged peers from other matrilines, with whom they spend a great deal of time in complex play interactions throughout their juvenile years. Many of these play interactions are essentially "dominance neutral" or, alternatively, involve frequent and rapid shifts of partnerships and coalitions. However, some peer play bouts result in intervention by older monkeys, at which point relative social dominance quickly comes back as a factor. All in all, offspring of high-ranking females generally and consistently experience greater control over and choice in their social interactions with those outside their family than do their peers from low-ranking families. Put another way, offspring of high- and low-ranking families are likely to have quite different social experiences throughout development even though they are all growing up in the same physical environment and social troop.

Transactions during Adolescence

The complex and developmentally dynamic nature of transactions between individual monkeys and their respective environtypes becomes obvious when one considers processes that serve to regulate adolescent behavior, especially in males. Virtually all rhesus males emigrate from their natal troops around the time of puberty, and most of these males spend some time associated with all-male "gangs" prior to joining another full-fledged rhesus monkey troop. However, there are marked differences among these males in the specific timing of and strategy underlying their emigration activities, as well as clear differences in the way they are treated by others in their natal troop during this process.

For example, most rhesus monkey males leave their natal troops for brief periods during their second year and for increasing portions of the day at the beginning of their third year, prior to the major physical and hormonal changes associated with puberty. These males usually leave their natal troop permanently sometime during their fourth year (most often during the breeding season), typically joining an all-male gang for at least several months before attempting to move into a new troop. However, approximately 20% of the males remain in their natal troop throughout their fourth and sometimes fifth year, whereas a few males leave before the start of their third year, long before any physical features of pubertal change are apparent (Suomi, 1991).

It is noteworthy that male monkeys who differ in the developmental timing of their natal troop emigration also appear to differ consistently in several behavioral and physiological characteristics. For example, males who wait until their fifth year to emigrate are in general more fearful and anxious in both their social and exploratory behavior than their earlier-emigrating peers, and they seem less aggressive in their play interactions, particularly those involving younger play partners. These late-emigrating males also tend to be more physiologically reactive, exhibiting significantly higher and more stable heart rates and greater adrenocortical responsiveness to environmental challenges than their earlier-emigrating peers (Rasmussen & Suomi, 1989). On the other hand, the few males that emigrate very early, during their second year, tend to be impulsive, socially inept, and prone to become involved in aggressive interchanges. They also consistently show significantly lower cerebrospinal fluid levels of the serotonin metabolite 5-HIAA, along with higher adrenocortical reactivity, than do monkeys who emigrate in their third or fourth year (Mehlman et al., in press). These behavioral and physiological individual differences appear to be essentially independent of the dominance status of the different males.

The differences in timing of male emigration, and their behavioral and physiological correlates, do not emerge in a social vacuum. To the contrary, other troop members almost certainly are actively contributing to these different patterns. For example, the males who permanently leave their natal troop prior to 3 years of age do not do so voluntarily. Instead, they are literally driven out of the troop by members of other matrilines, who apparently cannot tolerate these young males' general social incompetence, impulsivity, and propensity for involvement in aggressive interactions. Most of these early-expelled males are unable (or unwilling) to join the all-male adolescent gangs, let alone another troop, and so they become basically solitary, with exceedingly high subsequent mortality rates (Mehlman et al., in press).

In contrast, the modal group of males who emigrate during their fourth year largely do so voluntarily, essentially extending their earlier daytime exploratory forays away from their natal troop. Much of this exploration involves following and occasionally interacting with members of other troops and the all-male gangs. During those times each day when they are physically within their natal troop these males' interactions with most troop members become increasingly negative. In particular, nonmatrilinear adult females become progressively more hostile toward these juvenile males, especially when they try to play with the females' yearling offspring. It is noteworthy that this change in "attitude" toward these juvenile males essentially coincides with their pubertal growth spurt and increasing capacity to inflict injury on those females' young offspring. At any rate, the modal pattern for these males is to join all-male gangs as soon as they stop spending nights in their natal troop (Rasmussen & Suomi, in preparation).

A third emigration pattern is shown by males who "wait" until their fifth year to emigrate. These males typically have nonthreatening dispositions and nonaggressive play interactions with younger juveniles. The juveniles' mothers usually tolerate such interactions with their offspring, in contrast to those involving the modal males, even after these males have begun their physical growth spurt. Eventually, however, these males are also forced out of their natal troop, usually by the same nonmatrilineal females. In contrast to the modal male pattern, however, these late-emigrating males often bypass the all-male gangs and instead go more or less directly into new troops.

In sum, there is considerable variability in the timing and pattern of adolescent male emigration from rhesus monkey troops, and this variability is clearly a product of different phenotype-environtype transactions. Specific adolescent male behavioral and physiological phenotypes are strongly associated with specific emigration strategies. However, these strategies do not emerge in a social vacuum, but instead reflect in large part the differential treatment of these different males throughout their development by the rest of the troop.

Other Environtypic Regulating Influences

An increasing body of data suggests that environtypic influences may actually affect the timing of pubertal process itself in individual male and female monkeys. Data from laboratory studies of other primate species have clearly demonstrated that the onset of puberty can be significantly accelerated or delayed by a variety of social factors, including the dominance status of the individual, demographic characteristics of the social group, and the presence or absence of environmental stressors. For example, Snowdon and his colleagues (Savage, Ziegler, & Snowdon, 1988) have shown that the onset of puberty in cotton-top tamarin females can be delayed by over a year by keeping them in their nuclear families (once removed, they typically begin ovulation within days), while Levin and colleagues have found that squirrel monkey males with a history of brief social separations during childhood enter puberty significantly earlier than do squirrel monkey males with no early separation experience (Levine, Wiener, & Coe, 1993).

Social environmental influences on physical development and physiological processes are not limited to pubertal phenomena in rhesus monkeys and other nonhuman primate species but instead can transpire during many different developmental periods or phases, including adulthood. For example, studies of capuchin monkeys, macaques, and baboons have shown that recent acquisition of high dominance status in some males is associated with major increases in testosterone levels, as well as dramatic changes in physical appearance, including significant weight gain and increases in size and musculature. These physical changes clearly follow, rather than precede, the males' rise in dominance status. On the other hand, dramatic drops in dominance status are often followed by obvious weight loss and deterioration in physical health, especially in elderly males (Suomi, in press). Although the actual mechanisms underlying these physical and physiological changes are not fully understood at present, it is clear that they are precipitated by transactions with the environtype that ultimately may involve changes in the genotype itself, for example, by selectively "turning on" or "turning off" specific genes or gene complexes.

The preceding discussion provides ample evidence that rhesus monkeys and other nonhuman primate species are subject to numerous environmental influences throughout development. These influences transpire at every stage of development and appear to operate at multiple levels of analysis, including complex social behavioral patterns, neurochemical and psychophysiological functioning, and perhaps even activity at the level of the genome. On the other hand, it is also clear that each individual is capable of influencing, if not actually transforming, various aspects of its environment at virtually all developmental stages or phases. Thus, development is continuously characterized by dynamic phenotype-environtype transactions.

Although the precise pattern of transactions is probably unique for each and every rhesus monkey, there are clearly some general species-normative patterns that transpire for virtually every individual during the process of development, as well as some features that are common to every rhesus monkey troop in the wild, for example, a social structure based on multigenerational matrilines, with males emigrating around the time of puberty. These general patterns of biobehavioral ontogeny and social organization, complex as they may be, have probably been the norm for millions of generations of rhesus monkeys. As far as we know such patterns have evolved without recourse to a written historical record or even a series of oral traditions. Indeed, it is highly likely that rhesus monkeys lack the cognitive capabilities to reflect on past events or to plan very far in the future (Suomi, 1995). Yet generation after generation of rhesus monkeys have grown up in the same basic type of social environment and have followed common general developmental trajectories.

Studies of other advanced species of nonhuman primates have provided comparable pictures of clearly identifiable species-normative patterns of biobehavioral ontogeny and social group organization, although the precise patterns of development and social group organization can differ substantially from species to species, even among closely related taxa. For example, all apes (gibbons, orangutans, gorillas, and chimpanzees) mature much more slowly than do rhesus monkeys, and each species has its own normative pattern of social group organization that differs substantially from that characteristic of rhesus monkeys and other macaques (Smuts et al., 1987). These patterns have also been in place for countless generations, again without the benefit of any obvious oral or written cultural traditions.

Is Development Regulated?

The idea of developmental regulation presented a teleological dilemma to early behaviorists, who sought to deny intention to material phenomena. Development has inherited much of its conceptualization from the study of evolution where directionality seemed obvious to all. Life began with the simple and moved toward the complex. Although the idea of progress in evolution was effectively undercut by Darwinian theory (Simpson, 1970), there remained the idea for most people that humans represented some, perhaps intended, endpoint of a historical progression. Darwin's explanation of evolution as not progress but selection from existing variety may not yet be fully appreciated despite the scores of years since its formulation (Kessen, 1979, 1993). But regulation conceived as a probabilistic function of organism-environment interactions remains a viable alternative without vitalistic baggage.

If one seeks a direction for development, one can still look to evolutionary concepts for guidance. The simplest formulation is based on the fundamental property of life to conserve itself. In the course of such conservation, there is a need to be responsive to environmental perturbations that threaten conservation. To the extent that this responsiveness is self-stabilizing, it will tend to be maintained in the organism or any other level of living organization. Major discontinuities in evolution are generally tied to major discontinuities in the environment and are the result of improved and extended capacities for self-regulation. The shift from cold- to self-regulating warm-blooded species extended the range of temperatures in which individuals could survive. The shift from no-shelled eggs of fish, to hard-shelled eggs of reptiles, to eggs retained within the mother in placental mammals is another progression in which the prenatal organism is insulated from greater and greater levels of environmental variation.

Culture is another step in the evolution of adaptive systems to buffer environmental perturbations by increasing internal complexity of organization. What culture provides is a stepping back from here-and-now experiences into a historical stream that summarizes a group's adaptive experiences across time. The human mother who steps back from her crying infant because of a representation is inhibiting the here-and-now for the sake of the future. This idea of a future may be part of the crucial distinction we find between monkey and human existence.

The developmental principle that is demonstrated is one of conservation. Species, cultures, families, and individuals seem to encode in some form of representation and repeat in some form of practice what has been adaptive for them in buffering internal organization from environmental perturbation. These representations range from the fully biological as found in the genotype to the fully social as found in legal systems. In between are multiple transactions that alter the expression of genes and laws in practice. But inherent in all living systems is the dialectic that promotes transformation in the service of conservation. This transformational aspect is the motor for evolution at the phylogenetic level and for development at the ontogenetic.

A Perspective on the Future

Our discussion of primates has been devoted to a contrast between humans and other species in an effort to understand both the limits imposed by our biological heritage and the possibilities for transcending those limits proposed by modern societies. The recent evolution of the environtype, containing the external familial and cultural regulators of development, has progressed at a much greater rate than the evolution of the genotype, the internal biological regulator. Wilson (1975), a leading sociobiologist, described human society as autocatalytic. He saw civilization as fueled by positive feedback from its own social products, operating independently of the typical constraints that influenced all other evolutionary progressions. At the social level recent changes are found in modifications of women's roles and in the changing organization of the family. At the individual level intelligence scores have risen dramatically in the last generation in a wide variety of countries around the world (Flynn, 1984, 1987). Whereas some of these changes are thought to have positive consequences for society, there are negative signs associated with historical change that should not be ignored. In the near term, rates of cancer, environmental devastation, and poverty have increased despite major advances in our understanding of molecular biology, ecological systems, and economic processes. The judgment of progress will be found in the development of future generations, the ultimate test of evolutionary adaptation.

The exposition here is to emphasize the middle ground in the relation of biology and society. Development is not as open a system as some environmentalists would hope nor is it as closed as some biologists maintain. The question we have been addressing is whether we can specify which developmental phenomena in which systems are regulated more by proximal interactions and which by more distal representations. The local interactions of parents and their offspring are ingredients in the cultural complexity that will follow. The study of nonhuman primates offers an opportunity to examine a developmental system that may be on the threshold of culture that enlightens the understanding of our own society that for now stands on the other side of that achievement.

7   Cognitive Development

Frederick J. Morrison and Peter A. Ornstein

The study of cognitive development has been at the core of research in developmental psychology for more than 20 years. During this time, the field has witnessed the outlines of some major transformations in the conceptualization and study of cognition. Ironically, the most recent trends in research harken back to an earlier era of cognitive developmental science dating as far back as the late 19th century. In this chapter, we trace the evolution of theory and research on cognitive development, describing the forces that have shaped current thinking. We highlight this progression by drawing examples from the domain of memory because research on children's memory dates back a full century (e.g., Binet & Henri, 1894a, 1894b) and has generated an extensive data base from which to view the historical evolution of the field (Kail, 1990; Ornstein, 1978a; Schneider & Pressley, 1989). Moreover, recent trends in cognitive research are most dramatically highlighted by the changing nature of work on memory development (see, e.g., Fivush & Hudson, 1990; Morrison, 1987; Ornstein, Gordon, & Larus, 1992; Trabasso & Nickels, 1992).

Cognition and Development: A Historical Sketch

Approximately 100 years ago, two early giants in the field, James Mark Baldwin and Alfred Binet, laid the foundations for theory and research in cognitive development. Baldwin's structural theory constituted a very rich and dynamic framework for viewing children's cognition and development, a perspective that anticipated the Piagetian enterprise and in some ways was appropriated by it (Cairns, 1983, 1992; Cairns & Ornstein, 1979). In particular, Baldwin's emphasis on an invariant sequence of stages in mental development, coupled with his insistence on the dynamic interplay between social forces and the developing self, yielded a theory that seems remarkably consistent with the themes of modern developmental science. Moreover, Binet's (e.g., Binet & Henri, 1894a, 1894b) early research on children's memory for sets of words and for prose passages was quite indistinguishable from major studies of memory published in the mid-1970s, in terms of the underlying conceptualization and sophistication of analysis (Cairns & Ornstein, 1979; Siegler, 1992; Thieman & Brewer, 1978). In particular, these studies of constructive memory, as well as Binet's pioneering investigations of children's eyewitness testimony, the development of number concepts, and the nature of expertise in chess, read like a modern list of central themes in cognitive developmental research.

Both Baldwin and Binet paved the way for a modern science of development, and their publications could have been watershed events in the evolution of the discipline. Unfortunately, their insights were not pursued systematically by others in subsequent years, in part because scandal resulted in Baldwin leaving the field abruptly and because Binet's followers focused mostly on intelligence testing and not on fundamental work in cognitive development (Cairns, 1983; Cairns & Ornstein, 1979). But there were two other reasons for the failure of Baldwin's and Binet's ideas to take hold, both of which involved clashes between assumptions underlying major theoretical perspectives. First, there was a fundamental conflict between the dynamic framework of Baldwin and Binet and the structuralist perspective of Wundt and Tichener, who held especially strong beliefs that a serious scientific study of development was not possible (Parke, Ornstein, Reiser, & Zahn-Waxler, 1994).

Second, a parallel conflict between paradigms erupted with the rise of the behaviorist movement. Watson's behaviorism could have led to a flourishing study of children, albeit one based on quite different principles (e.g., conditioning) than those employed by Baldwin and Binet. Nonetheless, with the exception of the early studies of the acquisition of fear (e.g., Jones, 1924; Watson & Rayner, 1920), a learning-based developmental psychology did not flower. Indeed, behaviorism, with its delegitimization of the study of mental processes, hardly represented an intellectual environment conducive to the exploration of the development of memory and cognition. As a consequence of these trends in the early decades of the 20th century, developmental psychology parted company with mainstream experimental psychology, and developmentalists followed in the traditions of G. S. Hall and others who spearheaded the child study movement (see Cairns, 1983).

The influence of behaviorism was felt for many years, and it was only after World War II that researchers working within the context of Hull's (e.g., 1943) neobehaviorist framework began to attack problems in the general domain of unobservable events such as thinking and its development. For example, Kuenne (1946), Kendler and Kendler (1962), and Zeaman and House (1963) pioneered the exploration of discrimination learning, concept formation, and transfer, employing acceptable cognitive modifications of the Hullian concept of the fractional anticipatory goal response (Hull, 1939).

Of course, parallel changes were afoot in the general field of experimental psychology. By the late 1960s, even the neobehaviorist efforts to accommodate cognitive phenomena began to crumble under their own weight. Their explanatory frameworks came to be recognized as being so convoluted that they no longer represented fruitful theoretical approaches (Lachman, Lachman, & Butterfield, 1979). Ironically, the attempt to explain aspects of thinking, such as concept formation and utilization in discrimination learning terms that make use of constructs such as implicit verbal mediating stimulus-response complexes (e.g., Kendler & Kendler, 1962), was turned upside down by the growing realization that age changes, even in simple discrimination learning, were based upon fundamental developmental changes in conceptual structure (see, e.g., Kendler & Kendler, 1975).

At the same time, the successful application of experimental techniques to the study of attention (Broadbent, 1958), memory (Peterson & Peterson, 1959), and information processing in general (Sperling, 1960), laid the foundation for a new science of the mind. The resulting cognitive revolution was characterized by an explicit emphasis on subject-controlled processes that could direct the flow of information within a limited capacity mental system. Cognitive psychology was born (Neisser, 1967) with the explicit mandate to study these important mental processes that had been excluded by the behaviorists. The fortuitous rise of interest in computer technology and artificial intelligence provided a usable theoretical vocabulary for conceptualizing mental phenomena. Theoretical notions such as hardware versus software, parallel versus serial processing, and the general flow-diagram approach to the mind came to shape the conceptual and research strategies of the new breed of cognitive and cognitive-developmental scientists.

The Rise of Modern Cognitive Developmental Psychology

The rebirth of cognitive development during the mid-1960s directly reflected the changes taking place in the experimental study of adult cognition. By the end of the 1950s, a growing number of researchers became convinced that the application of experimental methodologies could yield substantial dividends in the study of children. Thus, an experimental child psychology emerged, although this movement was fueled initially by a methodological fervor that lacked an integrative conceptual framework. Examples of the kinds of problems tackled in this era included (a) the social conditioning of vocalizations (Reingold, Gewirtz, & Ross, 1959); (b) the nature and determinants of infant attention (Fantz, 1958; Salapatek & Kessen, 1966; Super, Kagan, Morrison, Haith, & Wieffenbach, 1972); (c) the use of traditional learning tasks (e.g., central vs. incidental learning) to examine the development of attention (e.g., Hagen & Hale, 1973); (d) the importance of changing modes of representation (enactive, ikonic, symbolic) on the course of cognitive growth (Bruner, 1964); and (e) the use of verbal mediation in learning and memory (Keeney, Canizzo, & Flavell, 1967; Reese, 1962). Finally, efforts were made to directly adapt some of the fledgling conceptualizations of attentional mechanisms to the study of attentional development (e.g., Doyle, 1973; Maccoby & Konrad, 1966).

Although this period was characterized by considerable productivity, the efforts of these developmental researchers were linked predominantly by a shared commitment to methodological rigor. Real theoretical integration would come a number of years later with the widespread application of the information-processing perspective. Consistent with the "parent" discipline, the science of cognitive development that emerged during this period took on a clearly discernible shape and focus. There was a fundamental emphasis on universal properties of mind, such as sensation and perception, attention and memory, thinking and reasoning, the development of which could be characterized precisely in information-processing terms (see, e.g., Kail & Bisanz, 1982; Siegler, 1983). The new approach reflected the predominant, though not exclusive, use of laboratory experimentation and the belief that such methods yielded clearer statements of cause-effect relations than could be derived from observations of cognition in external contexts. Further, results from laboratory experimentation were presumed to yield more "basic" findings, upon which an understanding of more "complex" phenomena, such as culture and schooling, would be based.

Equally important in the rise of modern cognitive development was the discovery and importation of the developmental psychology of Jean Piaget, as Flavell's (1963) influential book was titled. Representing a link with the earlier thinking of Baldwin, the theory of Piaget provided researchers with a biological metaphor for the study of mental development that contrasted sharply with that of the information-processing approach. Within this organismic perspective, children's adaptation required the reciprocal balance of the underlying processes of assimilation and accommodation, resulting in their active construction and modification of knowledge and understanding. This conceptualization differed from the competing information-processing perspective in the dominant metaphors and vocabulary used to describe cognition and development, in the research strategies adopted, and in the perceived priority of methodology.

Concerning methodology, Piaget (1951, 1952, 1954) elected to examine cognitive development in relatively naturalistic settings using detailed case study assessments of small numbers of children. Oftentimes, he developed ingenious paradigms for the observation of children's behavior (e.g., their patterns of searching for hidden objects) and for the discovery of their thinking about a range of physical phenomena (e.g., their understanding of the concept of the conservation of liquids). A fundamental tenet of the Piagetian approach was the importance of systematic observations for characterizing a wide range of children's skills and the value of longitudinal analysis for probing the mechanisms of developmental change. This approach led to a very rich descriptive data base on children's thinking, closely tied to the contexts in which cognition naturally occurs. Nonetheless, Piaget's methodology was criticized on other grounds (see, e.g., Siegel & Brainerd, 1978). For example, the small samples often used by Piaget were thought to be problematic, as was the lack of experimental control inherent in his observational techniques. Although this set of criticisms could not be leveled at research emanating from the information-processing perspective (with its emphasis on controlled laboratory experimentation and measurement and the random sampling of subjects), the methodologically rigorous studies that were crafted lost sight of the real-world relevance of the phenomena being explored.

The Piagetian approach represented the intellectual road that was taken by influential scholars such as Beilin (1964), Bruner (1964), Smedslund (1964), and Wohlwill (1973). Apart from its theoretical utility, Piaget's work also generated an impressive array of cognitive phenomena in children (e.g., object permanence, egocentrism, conservation, transitive inferences) that needed to be understood. Dissatisfaction with the Piagetian explanations of these phenomena, however, eventually led several psychologists to construct competing interpretations based on information processing models. Thus, for example, these models were used to analyze the nature and determinants of developmental change in conservation (e.g., Gelman, 1969), class inclusion (e.g., Klahr & Wallace, 1972), transitive inference (e.g., Trabasso, 1977), and combinatorial reasoning (Siegler,

1976). This cross-fertilization continues to the present day in the form of developmental theories that can be viewed as neo-Piagetian in character (Case, 1978, 1985; Fischer, 1980).

Memory Development in Children: A Case Study

As a way of making concrete some of the trends discussed in the preceding sections, it would be instructive to examine the evolution of one particular area within cognitive development. During the late 1960s and early 1970s, the study of the development of memory in children became a central focus of research in cognitive development. A number of factors contributed to this trend (Ornstein, 1978a). The most salient influences included (a) the groundbreaking studies of Flavell (e.g., Flavell, Beach, & Chinsky, 1966), extending earlier conceptualizations of "mediators" to account for what would come to be called "strategies," and (b) efforts to apply multistore models of memory (e.g., Atkinson & Shiffrin, 1968) to questions of development (e.g., Morrison, Holmes, & Haith, 1974; Ornstein, Naus, & Liberty, 1975).

For example, in a series of studies, Ornstein and his colleagues explored age-related trends in memory, focusing on children's changing utilization of rehearsal as a deliberately employed strategy for remembering. Findings from this research program revealed consistent and dramatic increases over the elementary school years in children's use of active, cumulative rehearsal techniques. The theoretical framework informing this program of research was derived directly from memory models that differentiated between the "hardware" (e.g., specific memory stores) and "software" (e.g., subject-controlled processes) of mind. This work, as well as the research of Morrison and his collaborators on early sensory memory, contributed to a consensus that, to a considerable extent, cognitive development reflected software as opposed to hardware changes (Morrison, Holmes, & Haith, 1974).

Both of these research programs examined memory in the laboratory and emphasized processing operations that transferred information from one stage (or store) to the next. Thus, for example, the growth of active rehearsal techniques over the course of the elementary school years was viewed as affecting the transfer of information from short- to long-term memory or the organization of transferred information so as to facilitate subsequent retrieval (Ornstein & Naus, 1978). In addition, the capacity of immediate memory was viewed as being age-invariant. Similarly, Morrison and his colleagues (e.g., Morrison, Holmes, & Haith, 1974) demonstrated that the capacity of initial sensory memory was essentially constant across a wide age range (e.g., 5 to 20), with major developmental changes occurring in the facility with which information was moved from the sensory to the short-term store (see Siegler, 1983).

As the preceding examples illustrate, the dominant characteristics of research in this genre reflected certain underlying assumptions about the practices and standards of scientific investigation:

1. The focus of inquiry was squarely placed on memory qua memory, one of the supposed universal properties of mind. These were not explorations of memory as it may function as a means to the solution of some problem or the achievement of a larger goal (see Paris [1978] for a discussion of these issues). Rather, memory was viewed as an end in itself.

2. The models employed to conceptualize and understand memory were basically mechanistic and therefore silent with regard to the important roles played by context and experience (see Brown & DeLoache, 1978). Neither could the theoretical language of the extant models easily accommodate mechanisms of change that should be central to developmental accounts of cognition. Moreover, the dominant multistore model appeared to give equal weight to all individual components in the processing system. Little consideration was given to the hypothesis that one or a subset of components, for example, the nature and organization of long-term memory (i.e., the knowledge base), might play a disproportionally powerful role in guiding the processing of information and shaping the course of cognitive development.

3. Consonant with such attitudes, the methodologies employed to understand memory development were basically reductionistic and analytic. These largely laboratory-based procedures were readily translated into a set of corresponding statistical techniques that reflected commonly held assumptions about the nature of data and analysis.

4. On a broader scale, the need to emphasize technological, statistical, and analytical methods strengthened the ties with other experimentally oriented scientists within psychology, especially cognitive psychologists. At the same time, however, these alliances reinforced a form of insularity that discouraged interaction between cognitive developmentalists and other psychologists interested in children's social behavior and personality, as well as other scientists (e.g., sociologists, anthropologists, pediatricians) concerned with broader questions of development (see Morrison, Lord, & Keating, 1984).

5. As testimony to this trend, the establishment of graduate programs in developmental psychology in the context of traditional psychology depart-

ments increased steadily. The scientists of development who graduated from these programs were accomplished foremost in technical and laboratory skills.

Emerging Concerns

At this point it is important to state that clear advances in understanding memory and cognitive development were achieved within the paradigm outlined here. Examples include significant increases in our understanding of perceptual development in infancy (Haith & Campos, 1983) and the documentation of the role of strategies in remembering (Flavell & Markman, 1983), as well as the systematic hypothesis testing that was applied to Piaget's theory of intellectual growth (Brainerd, 1978). These substantial accomplishments notwithstanding, a number of quite serious questions were raised about the completeness and adequacy of the account of children's cognition emerging from this view. Two of the most serious concerns centered on demonstrations of the importance of context and knowledge in diagnosing cognitive skill and characterizing its growth.

The Primacy of Knowledge

Research over the last decade has conclusively demonstrated that developmental changes in memory and other cognitive processes reflect to a considerable extent underlying changes in children's representation and knowledge of the world (Chi & Ceci, 1987). Thus, in contrast to the traditional information-processing framework as originally conceptualized, not all elements in the information-processing system carry equal weight in both controlling current performance and shaping developmental change. For example, children's strategies for remembering cannot be examined in isolation of children's knowledge of the domain to which the strategies are to be applied (Ornstein & Naus, 1985). The very ability to use a "simple" clustering strategy to remember categorizable items requires a richly articulated set of associations among exemplars of the categories represented in the to-be-remembered materials.

The importance of underlying knowledge was perhaps signaled most dramatically by Chi's (1978) demonstration that children who were experts in chess would outperform adult novices in the game in tasks that required remembering the position of the pieces taken from standard chess game configurations. The superiority of the chess experts was confined to the domain of chess, however, as the adults surpassed the children in more traditional digit span memory. This finding and others to follow (e.g., Bjorklund & Zeman, 1982; Ceci & Liker, 1986; Chi & Koeske, 1983) led to a growing appreciation that changes in knowledge and processing can be domain specific, with individuals evidencing cognitive skill in some areas but not others. Moreover, this work began to raise anew fundamental questions about the meaning and measurement of deliberate mnemonic strategies, because phenomena thought to involve complex strategic operations could more parsimoniously be attributed to automatic consequences of the nature and organization of information in the knowledge base (see, e.g., Bjorklund, 1985, 1987). Although this extreme position has generated considerable debate (Bjorklund, 1985; Ornstein & Naus, 1985), there is no doubt that memorization is now viewed as involving a very complex interaction between strategic efforts and the status of the representations that underlie the materials to be remembered. One larger implication of this emerging conceptualization is that traditional descriptions of universal changes in memory across age need to be modified so as to account for the early expression of skill in some domains and its later emergence in other domains, possibly through transfer or generalization mechanisms (Ornstein, Baker-Ward, & Naus, 1988).

The Roles of Context

Context became important in two distinct but complementary ways, one focusing on the origins of the skills under investigation and the other on the basic diagnosis and characterization of these skills. Concerning the matter of origins, the well-documented sequence of memory strategy emergence now seems likely to depend upon children's participation in formalized, Western-style educational settings (Cole & Scribner, 1974; Rogoff, 1981; Wagner, 1978). Concerning the question of diagnosis, it is now clear that even within the Western context, variations in the characteristics of the setting in which cognitive assessments are made have a profound influence on the nature of our accounts of skill development (Flavell, 1985; Folds, Footo, Guttentag, & Ornstein, 1990; Kagan, 1989). Thus, combining across these two senses of context, it became apparent that universalist accounts of memory changes across age were inaccurate or at least incomplete.

Current Orientation

Gradually, over the last decade, scientific and professional attitudes have begun to show signs of change, in part because of the concerns already expressed. Ironically, the emerging attitude toward the study of cognitive development returns us to an earlier era, characterized by flexibility in the approaches adopted to examine the complexities of human development. The outline of this evolving perspective – which is consistent with many of the themes of developmental science, as articulated in this volume – can be readily seen by comparing it with the orientation illustrated earlier.

1. In contrast to the earlier exclusive emphasis on the universal characterization of memory and its study in relative isolation, there is an increasing interest in the exploration of memory in context and in the service of other cognitive and social goals. Not only is the context specificity of mnemonic expression recognized (Folds, Footo, Guttentag, & Ornstein, 1990), but the role of memory in the growth of complex cognitive skills, such as story comprehension (Trabasso & Nickels, 1992) and quantitative reasoning (Siegler & Shrager, 1984), is being actively explored.

2. There is growing recognition of the limitations of mechanistic models of information processing (Brown & DeLoache, 1978; see also Kail & Bisanz, 1982), and at least an awareness of the need to include context, knowledge, and mechanisms of change in a full account of cognitive development. Admittedly, in contrast to the clear evidence of an increasingly sensitive characterization of children's abilities, less progress is discernible on the central developmental questions in the study of cognition. Nonetheless, progress is evident in terms of both macro- and microanalyses of development. Thus, developmental psychologists are now focusing on the critical family (Okagaki & Sternberg, 1991; Sigel, Stinson, & Flaugher, 1991), school and day care (Darlington, 1991; Stevenson & Lee, 1990), societal (Stevenson, Chen, & Uttal, 1990), and cultural (Gordon & Armour-Thomas, 1991) contexts that shape and support intellectual growth. In parallel, progress is being made in characterizing underlying mechanisms of developmental change. Some prominent candidates for these mechanisms have recently been proposed by theorists working within contrasting perspectives. For example, developmental changes in memory and cognition have been viewed as reflecting the progressive automization of elementary cognitive operations (Bjorklund, 1987; Case, 1985; Guttentag, 1984; Manis, Keating, & Morrison, 1980; Ornstein, Baker-Ward, & Naus, 1988). Corresponding changes in basic quantitative reasoning, moreover, have been taken to reflect shifts in simple arithmetic strategies, which in turn seem to stem from the underlying strength of problem-to-solution associations (Siegler & Shrager, 1984).

3. Corresponding changes are observed at the methodological level. Current approaches to the study of memory are characterized by their

variety and flexibility, with increasing awareness that there is no one exclusively correct method for understanding development. Thus, it is felt that the problems under investigation should dictate the methods and analytic procedures, and not vice versa. Laboratory assessments of memory and other cognitive skills continue to flourish, although there is an increasing interest in microgenetic (e.g., Siegler & Crowley, 1991) and longitudinal methods (Weinert & Schneider, 1993). However, laboratory-based methodologies by no means represent the only strategies currently available to working scientists. Salient examples of a more flexible approach can be found in the extensive body of research on the mnemonic underpinnings of children's eyewitness testimony (see, e.g., Ceci, Toglia, & Ross, 1987; Doris, 1991), in the explorations of everyday thinking in naturalistic contexts (Rogoff & Lave, 1984), and in the contributions of school to the emergence of mnemonic and cognitive skill (Morrison, Griffith, & Frazier, in press).

4. Parallel changes are visible in the reference groups of cognitive developmentalists. The once relatively exclusive ties with cognitive psychology, though still evident, have been broadened considerably, as students of cognitive development now find common ground with other developmentalists, both within psychology and in other disciplines. It is now apparent that a more complete understanding of cognitive growth will benefit from knowledge and insights from anthropology, education, and pediatrics, and as such, cognitive developmentalists frequently find themselves in collaboration with professionals from these fields. In parallel, candidates for the mechanisms of developmental change are increasingly coming from areas such as neurophysiology and computer modeling (Siegler, 1989).

5. Finally, although graduate training in developmental research continues to reflect the assumptions of the field of psychology, efforts are being made to provide students with a greater appreciation of the perspectives of other disciplines concerned with development. Ongoing interactions and, in some cases, collaborative research across disciplinary boundaries are being actively explored, as seen in work carried out by members of the Carolina Consortium on Human Development described in this volume.

Memory Development in Children Revisited

Consistent with many of the developments already sketched, research on children's memory has been transformed in the last decade. Although laboratory-based research enjoys continued popularity, there has been a dramatic increase in attention paid to the exploration of memory in "every-day" contexts. Admittedly, there is considerable debate among cognitive psychologists about the merits of "laboratory" versus "everyday" memory research (see, e.g., Banaji & Crowder, 1989; Loftus, 1991; Neisser, 1978; Tulving, 1991). Nonetheless, it is certainly the case that developmental studies of memory carried out beyond the confines of the laboratory have yielded characterizations of children's skills that stand in marked contrast to earlier accounts of their competencies (cf. Fivush & Hudson, 1990; Ornstein, 1978b). Indeed, when remembering is embedded in activities that are of inherent meaning and importance to children, their performance can be surprisingly impressive (Baker-Ward, Ornstein, & Gordon, 1993).

To illustrate briefly the changing focus of research, consider a set of studies exploring the impact of young children's growing knowledge of the world on their abilities to remember. Research by Nelson and her col-leagues (e.g., Nelson, 1986; Nelson, Fivush, Hudson, & Lucariello, 1983; Nelson & Hudson, 1988), for example, has indicated that preschoolers can be quite sensitive to regularly occurring events, readily forming "scripts" for routines such as getting ready for bed and eating in a fast food restau-rant. This developing understanding of familiar activities, moreover, seems to contribute to young children's impressive memory for salient, personally experienced events (e.g., Fivush, Gray, & Fromhoff, 1987; Hudson & Fivush, 1991; Ratner, Smith, & Dion, 1986). Scripted knowledge certainly assists children in the interpretation of ongoing events, and experiences that deviate moderately from existing scripts may be especially well remem-bered. For example, the details of a kindergarten class's visit to what was an unusual museum from the children's perspective – one in which they were permitted to dig (in a sand table) for "archeological artifacts" – were well remembered after one year (Fivush, Hudson, & Nelson, 1984) and, to some extent, after six years (Hudson & Fivush, 1991).

An additional theme of current work on children's memory is that it is increasingly being inspired by concerns that extend far beyond the tradi-tional scope of laboratory studies. For example, the pressing need to gather information concerning young children's abilities to provide testimony in legal situations led Ornstein and his colleagues (e.g., Baker-Ward, Gordon, Ornstein, Larus, & Clubb, 1993; Ornstein, Gordon, & Larus, 1992; Orns-tein, Gordon, Baker-Ward, & Merritt, in press) to carry out an integrated series of studies on children's long-term retention of the details of physical examinations and other medical procedures. This work was predicated on the assumption that accurate testimony is based upon effective memory, and, hence, that it is essential to gather fundamental information concerning what children of different ages can be expected to remember about a variety of salient and somewhat stressful experiences. In general, this research program demonstrated that children between 3 and 7 years of age evidenced quite good recall of the component features of medical check-ups, although there were clear age differences both in terms of the amount remembered and the degree of forgetting over time. Moreover, 3-year-olds were shown to be much more dependent upon specific forms of questions (e.g., yes-no probes) than older children, who could generate a considerable amount of detail in response to general, open-ended questions about visits to the doctor. These findings have implications for understanding memory development as well as for practical concerns about how to best obtain testimony from children of different ages (see Gordon, Schroeder, Ornstein, & Baker-Ward, 1995).

Similarly, other current work on memory was inspired by classic concerns about the mechanisms of children's cognitive development. For example, by comparing the performance of children whose birth dates are close together, but yet are on either side of the cutoff date for school entry, Morrison and his colleagues (e.g., Bisanz, Morrison, & Dunn, 1995; Ferreira & Morrison, 1994; Morrison, Griffith, & Frazier, in press; Morrison, Smith, & Dow-Ehrensberger, 1995; Varnhagen, Morrison, & Everall, 1994) were able to examine in a systematic manner the cognitive consequences of exposure to school. In essence, this "natural experiment" has been used to answer some very significant questions about the relative contributions of both experience and maturation to the development of important memory and cognitive skills. In a series of studies, Morrison and his colleagues have discovered a surprising degree of specificity in the nature and timing of developmental changes in these skills. For example, Bisanz, Morrison, and Dunn (1995) found significant schooling influences on the growth of elementary addition skills in both kindergarten and first grade, but found only age-related changes in the same children in conservation of number. Moreover, Morrison, Smith, and Dow-Ehrensberger (1995) observed substantial schooling influences on the growth of memory skills in the first grade. These findings have implications not only for understanding the sources of cognitive growth but also for revealing the kinds of cognitive skills that are uniquely enhanced by the schooling experience.

Final Thoughts

As illustrated in this historical analysis of the study of children's memory, the field of cognitive development has matured substantially in recent years. Although current research reflects considerable conceptual and methodological diversity, a unifying theme is found in the underlying emphasis on the dynamic and adaptive nature of cognitive processing. Implicit in this emerging theme is a reconceptualization of the classic dichotomy between basic and applied research. Whereas the traditional approach was essentially unidirectional, with basic research on processes presumed to be fundamental and universal eventually leading to application, recent developments in the field emphasize a bidirectional relation between basic and applied approaches. As suggested here, theory and research developed in the laboratory have made clear contributions to understanding eyewitness testimony and the influences of schooling. However, these "applied" research programs have also yielded novel insights into the nature, magnitude, and timing of changes in children's cognitive skills. This reciprocal interplay between basic and applied research in current work highlights the artificiality of earlier distinctions between these two approaches to developmental issues. This broadened perspective, combined with methodological flexibility and a renewed focus on the sources and mechanisms of cognitive growth, reflects the spirit and style of the pioneers in the study of development a century ago.

8 Early Social-Communicative Development: Illustrative Developmental Analyses

Carol O. Eckerman

How young children come to seek out other human beings and how they communicate effectively with them have been topics of considerable import for philosophers, scientists, and parents from at least the mid-19th century. Dramatic changes take place in these domains during the first 3 years of life, changes that provide both clear opportunities and challenges for our understanding of developmental processes. Sociability is seldom attributed to human newborns, who although they are selectively responsive to forms of stimulation that other humans provide par excellence, appear not to understand that this stimulation comes from another, separate being. Yet, as early as 1 year of age, infants clearly recognize the many familiar human beings of their world, seek out interactions with one or more of these familiar humans, and actively protest and seek to redress forced separations from them. Further, even though newborns are engaged in communication and cooperative interactions with other human beings from birth, the forms of cooperative action, infants' roles in generating them, and the forms of communication employed change markedly over the first 3 years. In the Western industrialized societies most intensively studied, the forms of cooperative action change from the suckling bouts and *en face* exchanges of affective signals characteristic of the first months after birth to the 3-year-old's newly generated games, collaborative pretend play, and verbal conversations and arguments. The infant's role changes from selective responsiveness to another's sights, sounds, and touches, to anticipation of parents' actions in such well-practiced rituals of cooperative action as peek-a-boo, to the gradual taking over of more responsibility for generating familiar rituals, to the generation of new forms of cooperative action even with new partners. Communication changes from the nonintentional communicative acts of the newborn, to intentional communication through nonconventional acts, to the use of conventional gestures and words. Thus, in 3 short years, newborns become transformed into truly

135

sociable children who employ effectively the basic forms of communication characteristic of their culture.

This chapter focuses upon how these developmental changes in sociability and interpersonal communication come about and presents illustrative developmental analyses that are congruent with the developmental science principles espoused in this volume. First, brief historical reviews are presented of some of the changing answers to the focal question of how developing humans come to seek out and effectively communicate with other humans. Second, the commonalities in these histories of early social development and language acquisition are noted. Third, four illustrative developmental analyses are detailed. Finally, the relations between these illustrations and the principles of developmental science are examined, and some further research challenges are posed.

A Brief History of Research on the Origins of Human Sociability

Our first empirical accounts of early human social behavior came from the diaries kept by men and women of science during the latter half of the 19th century and into the early 20th. Charles Darwin (1877), for example, kept a diary of the emotional expressions of one of his children. By 1936, Wayne Dennis was able to find and integrate some 48 diary accounts. These diaries typically focused upon the first appearance of new forms of behavior – for example, the first smile, the first appearance of crying upon separation from the parent, the first expression of anger, the first use of a conventional gesture, the first word (see Kessen, Haith, & Salapatek, 1970, for a thoughtful analysis of these diary accounts).

Subsequently, normative studies appeared in which a single investigator, or a team of investigators, charted the appearance of behavioral novelties for a sizable group of children. Arnold Gesell's (1925) first scale of infant development and Mary Shirley's (1931, 1933a, 1933b) detailed observations of the motor, social, and personality development of 25 children are prime examples of this approach. Common to both the diary accounts and the early normative studies were (a) a focus upon the capabilities of the individual child, (b) an emphasis upon the age of occurrence of new forms of behavior, and (c) the expectation of massive regularities in the timing of these new forms of behavior as a result of strong biological or genetic regulation of the developmental process.

Later, attention focused upon the role of the developing child's social environment, especially parents' child-rearing practices, in accounting for the individual differences that became apparent in children's early social behavior (e.g., Sears, Maccoby, & Levin, 1957; Sears, Rau, & Alpert, 1965). Typically, measures of parental characteristics were obtained with little attention to how the child's behavior or characteristics might have influenced these measures, and these parental measures were used to predict differences in children's social behavior (see Bell, 1968, for an excellent review and critique of this approach). The measures of children's social behavior, too, typically did not take the parents' current behavior or the social context into account. Thus, although the focus had broadened to include both parent and young child, the individual characteristics of each were the focus, and it was generally assumed that it was the differences in parental characteristics that produced the differences in children's social behavior. Little of this research was done initially with very young children, and most assessed children at only one age. Nevertheless, the findings often were assumed to apply to younger children and across broad spans of development.

During the 1940s and 1950s, also, secondary-drive and secondary-reinforcer explanations of the origins of human sociability predominated. These explanations borrowed concepts from the general learning theories of that time (from Hullian drive-reduction theory and Skinnerian operant learning) in an attempt to explain the developmental emergence of the propensity by young infants to seek out proximity to and interactions with their parents (see Maccoby & Masters's 1970 review). These explanations moved beyond descriptions of the time of emergence of behavior novelties and demonstrations of parental impact on children's social behavior to a more detailed explanation of how one particular behavioral novelty (seeking out specific human beings) developed. In these explanations, human sociability was viewed as a fortuitous by-product of other more basic, or primary, aspects of human functioning. According to the drive-reduction explanations, the sights, sounds, and touches of parents were repeatedly paired with the reduction of such primary drives of the child as those for food and the reduction of painful stimuli, because human infants required parental intervention in order to meet these needs. As a result of these repetitive pairings, obtaining access to the sights, sounds, and touches of parents became a learned, or secondary, drive; and hence the child came to seek out access to people and to act distressed upon forcible removal from them.

The secondary-reinforcer explanations were similar in form but stressed how the sights, sounds, and touches of parents became secondary reinforcers through their pairing with such primary reinforcers as food and

water. Thus, behaviors of the infant that produced these secondary reinforcers (such as crawling toward the mother and crying upon separation)
became strengthened. It should be emphasized that these explanations of
the origins of sociability were largely armchair explanations, explanations
developed from the learning theory of the time with little empirical inquiry
into the early sociability of the infant beyond that provided by the earlier
diaries and normative studies. These explanations fit well, too, with much
of the psychoanalytic theory of the time that also emphasized the secondary
nature of human sociability. Parents satisfied their infants' basic instinctual
drives and thus across time became the objects of those instincts.

In the late 1950s, several forces converged to produce a reexamination
of secondary explanations of the origins of human sociability. Some of the
most influential were Harlow's studies of "mother surrogates," the imprinting studies of the European ethologists, and some new developments that
made direct study of the human infant more feasible. Harlow's studies (e.g.,
1958b; Harlow & Zimmerman, 1959) were interpreted as showing that very
young rhesus monkeys sought out contact with objects possessing certain
tactile properties (e.g., a wire cylinder covered with a terry cloth towel) and
that this perceptual preference was the basis of their seeking out proximity
to and contact with their mothers, their use of them as a secure base in new
environments, and their distress when separated from them. The infant
rhesus monkey showed sociability to a "surrogate mother" who provided
this appropriate tactile stimulation even when this "mother" never fed the
infant; whereas, the infant showed little sociability to a surrogate who
provided food but did not provide the appropriate tactile stimulation. Thus,
rhesus sociability seemed to be built upon the *primary* basis of attraction to
the particular forms of tactile stimulation provided par excellence by the
rhesus mother. Similarly, in imprinting studies (see Immelmann's 1975
review), precocial birds from hatching followed objects possessing certain
perceptual characteristics even when these objects had never been paired
with food, and the experience of following these objects led to strong
attraction to them of the kind we might call "sociability."

These studies of nonhumans pushed researchers to reexamine their ideas
about the origins of human sociability. If such "lower" organisms as rhesus
monkeys, ducklings, and chickens came into the world with specific perceptual preferences that aided in connecting them with members of their
own species and if these preferences did not depend upon some other class
of "more basic" needs or reinforcers, why not consider this possibility for
the human? Fortunately, this willingness to reexamine explanations was
met with important conceptual and empirical advances that made the direct

study of perceptual preferences in human infants more feasible and more likely to yield orderly, interpretable results. One critical conceptual advance was the introduction of the concept of different states of arousal or consciousness for the human newborn and infant (e.g., see Prechtl's 1974 review). This concept enabled the researcher to divide the time spent with a given infant into at least five states (e.g., deep sleep, light sleep, drowsy, alert, fussing/crying) and to search for systematic patterns of responsiveness to stimuli within each of these states. Soon it was discovered that the same infant responded quite differently to the same stimulus in different states, showing how critical the concept of state was for bringing order to and understanding of infant responsiveness.

Near the same time, too, an important new research technique for studying human infants' preferences among visual stimuli was introduced: Fantz's looking chamber (1958). The empirical study of the perceptual preferences of the human infant quickly gathered steam, leading to the discovery of a wide variety of sensory and perceptual preferences in the young human that would seem to provide an important basis for the infant's development of sociability (see Schaffer, 1984, and Sherrod, 1981, for reviews).

Thus, views of human sociability as a secondary phenomenon receded, and in their place came explanations stressing the evolution of some primary bases for human sociability. John Bowlby's classic paper on human attachment (1958) and his subsequent volumes (1969, 1973) provided a landmark reconceptualization of the origins of human sociability (or attachment) that blended concepts of European ethology, psychoanalytic theory, and systems theory and that set the stage for much of the research on human sociability during the 1960s and 1970s. Among the most important changes stimulated by Bowlby's work was the move from focusing either upon the infant or upon the mother in isolation to viewing the mother-infant dyad as the important unit for study. The mother and infant were viewed as having coevolved a series of adaptations to one another over evolutionary time that led to infant sociability and a progressive series of changes in the nature of the infant's attachment to his or her mother. The infant, for example, was equipped with certain instinctual behaviors (e.g., rooting, crying, smiling) that served to promote proximity to and contact with the mother; and the mother showed certain characteristic responses to these instinctual behaviors that served to fulfill their function and to provide the infant with the interactive experiences leading to various developments in his or her attachment to the mother. Attempts to measure attachment followed (e.g., Ainsworth, 1963; Schaffer & Emerson, 1964), as did attempts to understand individual differences in attachment (Ainsworth, Bell, & Stayton, 1971). Curiously, however, much of the research aimed at measuring infant attachment and individual differences in attachment during the 1960s and 1970s was adevelopmental in focus. By adevelopmental, I mean that the research did not attempt to understand the continuously changing interplay between mother and child as the infant developed, but rather focused upon one particular point in this developmental sequence (the attachment charac-teristic of the 1-year-old) and sought to capture important individual differences in attachment at this age, predict these individual differences from earlier measures of the mother's behavior, and show the importance of these individual differences in the prediction of later valued aspects of social functioning (see Ainsworth, Blehar, Waters, & Wall, 1978, for a review of this work and Lamb, Thompson, Gardner, Charnov, & Estes, 1984, for a critique).

In the mid-1970s, however, another line of research, stimulated by Bowlby's views and those of others who focused upon the reciprocal influ-ences exerted by mothers and offspring (e.g., Bell, 1968; Rheingold, 1963, 1969), gathered steam. This line of research (e.g., Brazelton, Koslowski, & Main, 1974; Schaffer, 1977; Stern, 1974a, 1974b) attempted to capture the actual moment-by-moment dynamics of interactions of mothers and in-fants, stressed that both mothers and infants were influencing one another in these interactions, and sought to understand the developmental course of these interactions. It is this line of research (excellently reviewed by Kaye, 1982, and Schaffer, 1984), that led to the conceptualization of early social-communicative development to be detailed as the initial illustrative developmental analysis. First, however, a brief account of related develop-ments in a historically separate domain of inquiry, language development, is required.

A Brief History of Research on Language Development

This history focuses upon developments within the study of young chil-dren's language acquisition that most clearly relate to how children come to effectively communicate with others. It begins, like that for early social development, with the diary accounts and early normative studies of behav-ioral novelties (e.g., Gesell, 1925; Leopold, 1939, 1947, 1949a, 1949b). Behavioral novelties such as the first use of conventional gestures and first words were of great interest, perhaps because of the widespread view that the developing child's mastery of human language was a critical hallmark of the child's integration into human society most generally, and into the child's own specific language community more specifically. By the 1930s and 1940s, descriptions of children's language productions also had become more formalized with the so-called count studies. These studies (see McCarthy's 1954 review) reviewed young children's verbal productions and produced numerical counts of various words and parts of speech. They shared with the diary accounts and normative studies a near exclusive focus upon the child's verbal productions, a focus upon the formal aspects of these productions, and the expectation of widespread regularities in developmental change in these productions.

A distinctively different approach to early language development appeared in the 1950s and 1960s when learning theorists attempted to explain language acquisition as a subset of other learned behaviors (e.g., Mowrer, 1954; Osgood, 1963; Skinner, 1957). Perhaps the most important such attempt was that by B. F. Skinner in his book *Verbal Behavior* (1957). Skinner used the principles of operant conditioning to generate an account of how children learn language. In doing so, he produced an early functional account of language development – that is, one that stressed the uses of language in a child's life. This account emphasized that language was no different from any other learned behavior and that an understanding of language development was to be found in the detailing of how others selectively reinforced classes of sounds in specific contexts.

At first, "relatively unpatterned vocalizations, selectively reinforced, gradually assume forms which produce appropriate consequences in a given verbal community" (Skinner, 1957, p. 31). Word learning occurred when a given sound (e.g., "mama") was selectively reinforced in the presence of the mother; in other words, the presence of the mother became a discriminative stimulus for the word "mama." Sentences were learned through reinforcement of successive approximations to meaningful strings of words. And so on. As with the secondary accounts of sociability discussed earlier, this account of language acquisition was largely an "armchair" account – a persuasive account of language development using general principles of learning theory in the absence of relevant empirical studies of the language-learning child.

Problems with such learning accounts quickly surfaced. For example, parents seldom seemed to correct their children's syntax, responding more to the truthfulness of their utterances. Too, children were found to produce verbal utterances (e.g., "foots") that they seldom, if ever, heard and were unlikely to be encouraged to produce. Further, the psycholinguistic theorists of the time were strongly critical of these learning approaches because they did not take into account what were thought to be the unique characteristics of the language system (e.g., Chomsky's 1959 review of *Verbal Behavior*). These psycholinguists focused upon language form, rather than language use, and attempted to specify the underlying mental processes that the formal syntactical structures of language represented. In 1957, with the publication of *Syntactic Structures,* Chomsky introduced generative transformational grammar to account for the regularities in adult syntactic structures and revolutionized the study of children's language development as others applied his model of language to children's early two- and three-word utterances (e.g., Braine, 1963; Brown & Bellugi, 1964; McNeill, 1966; Miller & Ervin, 1964).

Not only did the early psycholinguists focus upon regularities in syntactical structures, but they also postulated innate mechanisms to account for these regularities. Chomsky, for example, postulated an innate Language Acquisition Device (LAD) that contained universal linguistic principles. The LAD provided the child with a primitive theory applicable to any natural language. It enabled the child to process language input in terms of this theory and form hypotheses based on the regularities found in that input. Across time, with repeated hypothesis testing, the child derived the syntactic rules of the language community in which he or she was reared. Such innate explanations of language acquisition were bolstered further in 1967 with Lenneberg's publication of a book detailing the biological and evolutionary evidence for viewing language as an innate species-specific system. Thus, as noted by George Miller, there were now two theories of language: "one of them, empiricist associationism, was impossible; the other, nativism, was miraculous" (Miller in Bruner, 1983, p. 34).

Meanwhile, the work on children's early language productions, stimulated by linguists such as Chomsky, uncovered problems with focusing solely upon the syntactic structure of these productions, problems that led to a "semantic revolution" (see Golinkoff & Gordon, 1983, for a more complete account of changes within psycholinguistic approaches to children's language from the 1960s to the 1980s). Not only the form but also the content, or meaning, of children's early utterances became the focus of study, as it became clear that the same form could express diverse meanings. Children's utterances began to be "richly interpreted" in terms of the understandings of the world they represented. With the new emphasis upon meanings, inquiry was expanded from the earlier focus on two- and three-word utterances to single-word utterances and even to preverbal forms of expressing meaning. The new focus upon meanings also shifted interest away from innate explanations of language acquisition. Utterances reflected children's world knowledge, and this knowledge was seen as slowly developing out of the child's experiences with the world. Thus, cognitive development and all the environmental influences contributing to cognitive development were increasingly seen as critical to the process of language acquisition.

Still another change within psycholinguistic approaches occurred in the 1970s when researchers increasingly became convinced of the need to study the child's verbal utterances in relation to their immediate social context. Language acquisition was now seen as embedded in social interaction processes to which both the child and the parent contributed. The functional aspects of language addressed earlier by Skinner began to be addressed again. Children were viewed as learning a social system of communication, and language was one component of this system. How children used language to communicate during social interaction became an area of study, as did analyses of how parents and others facilitated the learning of the appropriate uses of language.

In the 1970s Bruner provided detailed case studies of the social interaction rituals, or games, that mothers and infants engaged in, documenting how mothers mapped their language onto the nonverbal understandings children could be expected to have about the various steps of the games, and how children began to use words in these games (e.g., Ratner & Bruner, 1978; Ninio & Bruner, 1978). Others showed that parents systematically altered (simplified) their speech when talking to their children (e.g., Snow & Ferguson, 1977) and that these alterations changed in tandem with the developmental achievements of their children. Others studied infants' abilities to preverbally accomplish some of the same communicative functions later accomplished by speech (e.g., Bates, Camaioni, & Volterra, 1975; Harding & Golinkoff, 1979) and puzzled about the continuities that might exist between nonverbal and verbal forms of communication. Linguists such as Halliday (1975) provided categorizations of the different functions of children's language. Philosophers such as Austin (1962) and Searle (1969) elaborated speech act theory and others (e.g., Dore, 1973, 1974) adopted speech act theory in understanding children's early preverbal and verbal communication.

Some Commonalities between the Two Histories

In both domains reviewed, empirical inquiry began with a focus upon children's overt behavior and with analyses that paid little if any attention to the social-cultural context in which the behavior occurred. There were exceptions (e.g., in the writings of Baldwin, 1902), but these exceptions have become more influential in present-day thinking about early social development than they appear to have been in their own time, at least as influences upon the American empirical psychological tradition. There followed, in both domains, refinements of research techniques that nevertheless retained this focus on decontextualized infant behavior – the normative studies, the counting studies, and the studies of language centering upon its syntactic structure.

Only more recently has the realization emerged broadly, again in both domains, that infant behavior needs to be studied in relation to the broader context in which it is embedded. In psycholinguistic studies, this realization came first with respect to the broad animate and inanimate contexts in which children's utterances occurred, as researchers attempted to infer the meaning of these utterances from all the contextual cues available. Later, this realization was expanded to include detailed sequential analyses of social interaction processes and even the embedding of these processes within different cultural contexts (e.g., Schieffelin, 1990; Schieffelin & Ochs, 1983). In the domain of social development, the concentration upon the parent-infant system emerged with Bowlby's landmark conceptualization of the development of attachment; but it was not until later that the details of parent-infant interaction processes became a central focus of human infancy research.

Thus, by the 1970s and 1980s, many researchers of both social development and language acquisition were intent upon understanding the dynamics of parent-infant interaction processes; the contributions of both partners to these processes; the continuously changing nature of these interactions across time; and such important contributors to and products of these interactions as attachment, communication skills, and verbal language. It is their combined efforts that have led to the conceptualization of early social-communicative development to be detailed as our first illustration.

There were some broad commonalities, too, in the changing theoretical accounts for early social development and language acquisition. Sharply conflicting learning and innate accounts of development emerged in both domains, reflecting the widespread nature-nurture debates of earlier decades. These polarized accounts have been supplemented in both domains by multicausal models that attempt to explain the complex interplay in development among "experiential" and "biological or organismic" factors. Bowlby's emphasis upon an interplay among the infants' instinctual responses, mothers' evolved responses to these instinctual behaviors, infants' changing cognitions, and individual patterns of interactive experience is one example of a step in this direction. Schaffer's conceptualization, to be presented next, is a further step. Within the domain of language development too, current researchers struggle to provide an integrated account of the role of perceptual predispositions, learning biases, cognitive development, social-interactive development, parental alterations of speech input, and cultural processes in children's acquisition of their native language.

Illustration 1: Schaffer's Conceptualization of
Early Social-Communicative Development

In the 1980s, Rudolph Schaffer reviewed existing research on both early sociability and early language development and presented a conceptual framework for thinking about early social-communicative development that emphasized several themes related to the present developmental principles (Schaffer, 1984). A close look at this conceptualization is warranted because it is arguably the most detailed modern conceptualization of the *developmental progression* of early social-communicative development and because it provides a useful framework for the illustrative empirical analyses that follow.

Schaffer's first main claim is that the child's integration into her or his social world is a *joint enterprise* of child and parent. As had been for Bowlby, the unit of analysis for understanding early social-communicative development is the parent-infant dyad, rather than either individual alone. Schaffer, however, proceeds to a second main claim—that the parent-infant dyad works together to accomplish five successive interactive tasks that are critical for the child's social-communicative development during the first 3 years of life.

1. From birth to around 2 months of life, parent-infant interactions center on the task of regulating the infant's basic physiological processes.
2. From roughly 2 to 5 months of age, the interactions between infant and parent focus upon maintaining the infant's attentiveness and positive affect in *en face* exchanges.
3. Beginning around 5 months and proceeding for much of the first 2 years, the interactions between infant and parent address the task of achieving joint attention to objects and events beyond the dyad.
4. Starting somewhat later, around 8 months of age, Schaffer postulated for the dyad an overlapping interactive task of achieving

interactions in which the infant is a fully competent partner (i.e., interactions marked by both an understanding of reciprocity and the capacity for intentionality).

5. Still later, around 18 months of age, the dyad's interactions increasingly address the task of integrating the child's emerging productive language abilities into the existing nonverbal modes of effective communication.

These five interactive tasks thus emerge in a sequential order and dominate parent-infant interactions during different developmental periods.

Schaffer chose to concentrate on these five interactive tasks because they seemed to him to characterize well the descriptions of parent-infant interaction to be found in the by-then voluminous literature on such interactions among largely white, middle-class mother-infant dyads in Western industrialized societies. In this sense, his tasks were inductively derived conceptualizations of tasks for a particular set of cultural contexts. But these five tasks were emphasized by Schaffer because he viewed them as likely "species-typical" tasks, that is, tasks that seemed widely applicable to social-communicative development within any human culture.

This belief resulted in part because each later task could be viewed as building upon a certain degree of mastery of the prior tasks; that is, there was some logical ordering of the tasks. For example, working on maintaining attention in *en face* interaction would seem to require prior mastery of a certain degree of regularization of the infant's states so that a state of quiet alertness could characterize periods of *en face* exchange. Or, achieving verbal means of communicating about a distant object would seem to demand prior mastery of joint attention to that object. Although Schaffer acknowledged that the number of interactive tasks occurring within a given developmental period and the conceptualization of what these specific tasks were depended in part upon the researcher's level of analysis and the specific questions being asked about development, he nevertheless proceeded with his review of the literature, believing that the five interactive tasks he emphasized would be found to be widely applicable.

Schaffer's third main claim is that parent and infant are engaged in continuously changing patterns of interactions marked by bidirectional influence. Periodic changes (or reorganizations) in the infant's behavioral organization or cognitive capabilities prompt the dyad's change in focus from one interactive task to another. For example, changes in eye-hand coordination set the stage for the task of achieving joint attention to objects external to the dyad, and changes in symbolic representation set the stage for working on integrated verbal and nonverbal communication. Changes in the infant acted as the "pacer" for each new developmental task, but these changes in the infant were the result in part of parent-infant interactions involved in the mastery of the prior interactive tasks.

Once a new interactive task was engaged, a mentor-apprenticeship metaphor was used to describe the continuously changing ways in which parent and infant worked together on that task. Initially, the parent bore most of the responsibility for accomplishing the task and would adjust his or her behavior to the infant's, structuring the interactions to achieve the desired end. In so doing, the parent helped create interactive experiences for the infant that enabled the infant to gradually acquire the means to play a more equal role in achieving the task. As the infant acquired such means, the parent progressively asked the infant to perform those aspects of the interactive task within the infant's capabilities and thus aided the infant in becoming a more adept partner in accomplishing the developmental task. In Schaffer's own words:

> The impetus that sets periodic reorganization into motion may well stem from the child's inner program, establishing new goals; the pursuit of those goals, however, is a *joint* enterprise. . . . he acts as pacer but the parent is required to organize the child's world in such a way as to help him successfully to accomplish the tasks of that period. In time the parent's involvement becomes less direct as she is able increasingly to hand over responsibility to the child for tasks previously tackled jointly; at all stages, however, the nature of her interactive behavior must change in tandem with his. (pp. 14–15)

Schaffer's use of the mentor-apprentice metaphor closely resembles the "frames" of Kaye (1982), the concept of "scaffolding" as used by Bruner (1983) and others (e.g., Hodapp, Goldfield, & Boyatzis, 1984), the one-step-ahead model of Heckhausen (1987), and the concepts of the zone of proximal development and collaborative learning as articulated by Vygotsky (1978), Rogoff (1990), and Tudge, Putnam, and Valsiner (Chapter 9) among others. What Schaffer contributed beyond an articulation of the mentor-apprentice metaphor, however, was a detailed accounting, based on the extensive literature of that time, of just how this metaphor seemed to work for each of the interactive tasks he emphasized.

Schaffer also foreshadowed two more recent conceptual emphases – the study of the joint enterprise between parent and infant in cultural context and the integration of dyadic processes (mother-infant interaction processes) into the broader context of group interactional dynamics. In the first case, Schaffer clearly acknowledged how most of the existing interactive literature he reviewed was based on a quite limited sample of human beings – predominately white, middle-class, well-educated parents and healthy full-term infants developing in current-day industrialized societies. He raised the question of whether the postulated interactive tasks for the first 3 years of life and the mentor-apprentice metaphor might not be widely applicable – even perhaps across all human societies – whereas the specific means a given parent and infant employ for accomplishing each task might vary widely depending upon the infant's specific characteristics, the parents' characteristics, family circumstances, and cultural context. With respect to moving from dyadic interactional dynamics to group interactional dynamics, Schaffer recounted a series of beginning studies that attempted to relate interactional dynamics within a dyad to the group context in which they occur.

Schaffer's conceptualization of the process of early social-communicative development published in 1984 needs to be updated to include the vast amount of new data gathered during the past decade on dyadic interactive processes, language development viewed in a social-communicative context, cross-cultural studies of early social-communicative behavior, polyadric interactions, and social networks. Still, it stands as a detailed conceptualization of the processes of early social-communicative development that promises much as a guide to future research. Most especially, this conceptualization is of sufficient detail to guide inquiry about (a) the generality of the tasks proposed, (b) the specific dyadic processes used in accomplishing each task, (c) whether each new task does build upon the accomplishments of earlier tasks, and (d) the specific ways infant biological variation and social contextual variation influence early social-communicative development. In short, it details a specific developmental pathway that can now be used as a guide for addressing many of the issues surrounding the study of developmental process. The next illustration is one example.

Illustration 2: A Comparative Study of
Early Social-Communicative Development

The next illustration is an ongoing longitudinal study of the parent-infant interaction processes that facilitate normative social-communicative and intellectual development among very prematurely born infants. In this study, Jerri Oehler, Hui-Chin Hsu, Ricki Goldstein, and I use a conceptualization of social-communicative development similar to Schaffer's and conduct a comparative study aimed at addressing the general utility of this conceptualization for different populations of developing humans. Our comparisons are made not among societies or cultures, but among three groups of infants that vary in perinatal biological risk and early behavioral characteristics. We also compare Schaffer's conceptualization, based largely on studies of white middle-class infants and parents, with that arising from the study of all three of our groups, which include many African-American children and children being reared in families marked by low economic and educational levels.

Specifically, we compare the early social-communicative development of two groups of very-low-birthweight infants (a lower- and a higher-biological-risk group) and a group of healthy, full-term infants. Infants of all three groups are developing within contemporary U.S. culture in families of comparable racial, educational, and economic variation. The very-low-birthweight (VLBW) infants were born weighing less than 1,250 grams. All were born at least 8 weeks early, and some as early as 16 weeks. As a group, these VLBW infants are at risk for behavioral and cognitive delays, language delays, persistent neurological abnormalities, growth retardation, and learning disabilities (e.g., Eckerman, Sturm, & Gross, 1985; Fitzhardinge, 1980; Hack & Breslau, 1986; Hack, Breslau, Weissman, Aram, Klein, & Borawski, 1991). Yet the same studies that document these developmental problems also show that the full range of developmental potential is compatible with births so early and at such low weights. The challenge is to understand why some VLBW infants show markedly abnormal paths of development, whereas others show normative paths that may even be indistinguishable from those of healthy, full-term infants.

One necessary element for this understanding is the variations among VLBW newborns in perinatal biological risk. Many suffer serious medical complications during their intensive-care nursery stay that place their rapidly developing central nervous systems at risk. Recently, we have developed a way to assess variations among VLBW infants in their degree of likely damage to the central nervous system – the Neurobiologic Risk Score (NBRS; Brazy, Eckerman, Oehler, Goldstein, & O'Rand, 1991). The NBRS summarizes the occurrence and severity of 13 medical complications with known potential for damage to the central nervous system through the mechanisms of hypoxemia, insufficient blood flow, inadequate substrate for cellular metabolism, or direct tissue damage. The NBRS shows moderate correlations (.48 - .61) with the MDI and PDI scores of the Bayley Scales of Infant Development (Bayley, 1969) and with the incidence of neurological abnormalities throughout at least the first 2 years of life (Brazy et al., 1991). Still, the range of developmental outcomes at 2 years of age is considerable, even among those VLBW infants with higher NBRSs. Clearly, the developmental pathway between a high perinatal biological risk score and subsequent outcome is not fixed. The multiple developmental processes translating perinatal biological risk into more or less normative pathways of development demand study.

We began our study of these developmental processes by examining the early behavioral characteristics associated with variations in perinatal biological risk and assessing the impact of these biological-behavioral differences upon parent-infant interaction processes. This focus follows from the view (1) that much of early development is a joint enterprise between parents and infants that is played out in their continuously changing patterns of interaction and (2) that these interactions are affected by the characteristics of each partner. We first sought to understand what VLBW infants were like as early social partners for their parents (Eckerman & Oehler, 1992).

We found that higher-biological-risk versus lower-biological-risk VLBW newborns, before term age, responded quite differently to simple forms of social stimulation like those that parents provide in early interactions. The higher-risk infants responded with even more visual attention to an examiner talking to them in the higher-pitch, exaggerated intonation contours characteristic of mothers' talk to their newborn infants. In contrast, they responded with less visual attention and more facial grimacing suggestive of negative affect when the examiner added such simple forms of tactile stimulation to her talking as holding the infant's wrists or stroking an arm with continuous moderate pressure (Eckerman, Oehler, Hannan, & Molitor, 1995; Eckerman, Oehler, Medvin, & Hannan, 1994). These findings suggest that the higher-biological-risk VLBW newborns are more reactive to social stimulation (both more positively responsive and more negatively responsive) than lower-biological-risk VLBW newborns and that they show more problems of self-regulation (i.e., they switch more rapidly from higher positive responsiveness to higher negative responsiveness as tactile stimulation is added to talking). Thus, at least the higher-risk VLBW newborns would appear to be more difficult early social partners for their parents.

The ongoing study assesses the impact of these early variations in biological risk and their attendant differences in early behavioral characteristics upon parent-infant interaction processes. Two groups of VLBW infant-parent dyads (a higher-biological-risk and a lower-biological-risk group as based on the NBRS) and a group of healthy full-term infants are being studied longitudinally from their birth through 2 years adjusted age. We focus on three interactive tasks thought to be critical to early social-communicative development and thought likely to pose special problems for VLBW newborns and their parents: (1) the task of arousal regulation in social exchanges during the first 4 months after term age; (2) the task of achieving and maintaining joint attention to objects and events beyond the dyad from 9 months through 2 years; and (3) the task of integrating newly developing verbal skills into the prior nonverbal forms of communication beginning around the middle of the 2nd year of life. Each of these tasks is conceptualized in a way similar to Schaffer's, although we stress arousal regulation in *en face* exchanges, rather than the maintenance of attention and positive affect. This slight shift in emphasis is in line with recent work emphasizing the centrality of arousal or affect regulation for influencing how much mutual gazing and positive affect occurs in *en face* interactions (e.g., Field, 1981; Tronick, 1989).

Prior work suggests that each of our three tasks is more difficult for prematurely born infants and their parents. Our prior studies relating perinatal biological risk to newborn reactivity and self-regulation abilities suggest that parents and their higher-biological-risk VLBW infants may face substantial difficulties as they work on the task of arousal regulation in *en face* exchanges. Landry's research program has demonstrated differences in attentional processes for higher- versus lower-biological-risk premature infants and associated differences in how their mothers negotiate joint attention with them (e.g., Garner, Landry, & Richardson, 1990; Landry & Chapieski, 1988). Finally, although we know little about how premature infants move from nonverbal to verbal communication, language seems to pose special problems for prematurely born children, especially VLBW infants (Largo, Molinari, Comenale Pinto, Weber, & Duc, 1986; Vohr, Garcia-Coll, & Oh, 1989), and some of these difficulties have been linked to specific nervous system damage (e.g., intraventricular hemorrhage resulting in left lateral ventricular dilatation and later expressive language deficits; Bendersky & Lewis, 1990).

To study how mothers and infants jointly negotiate each of the focal interactive tasks, we have created contexts for interaction within the home environment that set the stage for each hypothesized task, and we repeatedly assess across developmental time how the mothers and infants engage in this task. To assess how dyads go about the task of arousal regulation, we repeatedly videotape mothers and infants in two types of *en face* encounters that our mothers report are fairly natural for them during the earliest months – holding their infants on their laps in an *en face* position and "talking to or messing with them" and placing their infant on a table and changing their clothes. To assess how mothers and infants go about the task of achieving joint attention, we repeatedly videotaped mothers and their infants between 9 and 21 months of age as they play together on the floor with a set of toys we bring to the home. To assess how mothers and infants go about the task of achieving integrated verbal and nonverbal communication, we repeatedly ask mothers to look at two picture books with their children between 9 and 21 months of age, and we follow the progression from the infants' treating the books much as they do any other toy to the dyad's use of the books as a context for engaging in rituals of communication that appear to be excellent settings for integrating toddlers' rapidly developing productive language abilities into the existing patterns of nonverbal communication (cf. Ninio & Bruner, 1978). This emphasis upon repeated longitudinal assessments of each dyad as it engages in each task reflects our interest in how dyads *jointly negotiate* each task. Joint negotiation is a process of changing interactions marked by bidirectional influence and as such can be assessed only by examining changes in interaction processes across time. Key questions concern the changing role of each partner – how earlier patterns of interaction seem to facilitate infants' taking on more or different roles later, and whether and how parents alter their strategies across time in response to their infants' behavior. Too, in a comparative study, repeatedly assessing the skills at issue across a sizable span of developmental time enables one to address whether any differences in interactive processes seen between groups at a given age reflect qualitative differences in their interactions or whether the differences between groups reflect their being at different points along a common developmental progression. Answering this question is critical for assessing the generality of any proposed path of development.

We also assess the infants' skills in accomplishing each interactive task outside the mother-infant interactive context so that we can (1) compare the skills of different children under comparable interactive conditions and (2) relate earlier mother-infant interactive processes to a common outcome measure of infant skill. For example, with infants at 4 months of age, we use a scripted, playful encounter with a new adult female to assess the infants' abilities in arousal regulation (Eckerman, Oehler, Molitor, Hsu, & Smith, 1994). The adult greets the infant and engages the child in a game of peek-a-boo in which she repeatedly covers and uncovers her face to reveal a smiling face talking to the infant in an animated form of "motherese." The amount of physical contact the adult makes with the infant's body increases across successive rounds of the game to progressively place more demands upon the infant for arousal regulation. Using other standardized procedures, we assess the abilities of infants at 15 months of age to engage in joint attention and at 24 months of age to engage in integrated nonverbal and verbal communication. We also do a broad assessment of each child's developmental status at 24 months – motor and cognitive developmental level, productive and receptive language abilities, physical growth, health, neurological status, and temperament.

Several other measures are included in the study (e.g., repeated neurobehavioral assessments, medical histories, mothers' reports of social support and the stresses associated with parenting, family composition and economic resources, and maternal psychopathology). The measures detailed, however, are sufficient for illustrating the research strategy of this comparative study of a specific hypothesized developmental pathway of early social-communicative development. Our most general hypothesis is that all three groups of subjects focus their interactions sequentially around the tasks of arousal regulation, joint attention, and integrated verbal and nonverbal communication. However, the details of how these tasks are mastered, the specific interactive processes conducive to the mastery of these tasks, and the levels of mastery are expected to differ among our groups, reflecting the impact of early differences in infants' central nervous system development and associated behavioral characteristics on the processes of early social-communicative development.

Planned analyses first address selected pieces of this developmental story and only later contribute to an assessment of our general hypothesis. First, there are analyses comparing the developmental course of mother-infant interaction within each of our interactive contexts for our three groups of dyads, using both dyadic measures of their "success" with respect to the hypothesized task (e.g., the amount of mutual gaze or joint attention) and measures of specific interactive processes (e.g., mothers' reduction of stimulation when their infant begins to grimace or show high limb activity). Second, the differences among the groups highlighted in these analyses become the outcome measures we attempt to predict using the measures of earlier infant biological and behavioral differences as well as confounded perinatal status variables (e.g., gestational age, length of hospitalization) and social contextual variables (e.g., mother's age, race, economic circumstances, degree of social support, and psychopathology). Third, we can attempt to predict our targeted outcomes for infants at 4, 15, and 24 months of age using our early biological-behavioral measures as well as the interactive processes looked at in prior analyses as differing among our groups and the interaction between these two sets of predictor variables.

Armed with the results of these analyses of each interactive task considered separately, we hope to be in a position to examine specific hypothesized paths of influence between infant perinatal biological risk and social-communicative outcome at 2 years of age. For example, we can assess hypotheses about how specific interactive processes related to each developmental task – both independent of and in interaction with the infant's early biological-behavioral status – increase our ability to understand variations in language competence of children at 2 years of age beyond that achieved from knowing perinatal biological status and such global measures of family environment as socioeconomic status (SES), mother's education level, race, and psychopathology. Other analyses can address the issue of continuity versus discontinuity in task mastery or general infant behavioral characteristics. How well, for example, do the levels of mastery of Tasks 1 and 2 predict that for Task 3, and does this prediction vary for higher-biological-risk infants versus full-term infants? Do the interactive processes hypothesized to facilitate infants' arousal regulation and joint attention increase our ability to predict reactivity at 24 months above that achieved by assessments of reactivity around term age? And so on. The degree of perceived support for our conceptualized pathway of social-communicative development will depend greatly on how clearly all our findings converge in supporting this conceptualization.

The results of this study are yet to be fully assessed, as it will be at least 3 years before data collection is complete. Nevertheless, the study illustrates one way of translating the conceptualization offered by Schaffer and some of the developmental principles articulated in this volume into an actual research endeavor. Although this design compares developmental processes and pathways for three groups of infants growing up in contemporary American society, its logic would seem applicable to comparisons across cultures. Sometimes, observations of a seldom-studied culture are presented as a challenge to the details of the conceptualization of social-communicative development derived from the extensive study of one or a few cultures. Such challenges are useful, but we also need to assess whether there are some commonalities in developmental pathways across diverse cultures although many of the details of how these pathways are traversed may differ culture to culture (cf. Fogel, Toda, & Kawai, 1988).

For example, Schieffelin and Ochs's observations of the social interactions of Kahlui infants (1983) are cited widely for the doubt they throw upon the importance of *en face* interactions in early social-communicative development. In Kahlui culture, young infants are rarely talked to directly, and infants are positioned by their mothers to look outward toward others rather than in *en face* positions. Such observations clearly challenge any general pathway of development that focuses upon *en face* interactions per se. And yet, as I read reports such as these, I find myself wishing for much more information. Are the first 4 or so months of life in Kahlui culture marked by distinctive interaction patterns of some form that seem to deal with the issue of infant-arousal regulation? If so, how is this accomplished, and is a mentor-apprentice model appropriate? In short, I wish for detailed information about early social-communicative development in other cultures that is presented not only "in its own terms" but also in relation to the conceptualizations of development that have been worked out through the long-term study by many individuals of development within a few cultures.

Illustration 3: A Developmental Analysis of One Developmental Transition in a Proposed Pathway

The third example of a developmental analysis takes place at a more microanalytic level of analysis than the prior two. The focus now is upon one specific developmental transition along a proposed pathway of social-communicative development. The developmental transition at issue is the emergence around 2 years of age of a new way of behaving in social encounters – what I call the imitative pattern (Eckerman, 1993a, 1993b). The focal questions for the developmental analysis are two: (1) Why and how does this new behavior pattern emerge in development? and (2) What are the consequences of this new behavior pattern for the child's continuing development?

The interactive task at issue is how children first become full partners in generating cooperative forms of interaction with others, beyond the well-practiced specific rituals of coordinated action they engage in with parents and other very familiar partners. Parents in Western industrialized societies regularly engage their children in rituals of cooperative action, and their children first become equal partners in generating cooperative action with others within the context of these well-practiced rituals. For example, parents repeatedly engage their infants in such familiar games of childhood as pat-a-cake, peek-a-boo, and give-and-take. At first, parents set the stage for their child to make a behavioral contribution (perhaps only a responsive laugh or smile), time their own behavior to coordinate with their child's, and supply any actions defining the ritual that their child fails to produce. Across time, parents gradually reduce these supports and demand more participation of their child as the child develops each new skill involved in conducting the rituals (e.g., Bruner, 1983; Heckhausen, 1987; Hodapp et al., 1984). By 1 year of age, infants are fully competent participants in some of these rituals of cooperative action (e.g., peek-a-boo and give-and-take; Bruner, 1983), whereas they remain apprentices in others (e.g., picture-book reading; Ninio & Bruner, 1978). But how do infants become fully competent partners in generating cooperative forms of action with others when they cannot depend upon such rituals of cooperative action? The emergence of the imitative pattern seems to play an important role here.

I and several colleagues (Claudia Davis, Sherry Didow, and Mark Stein) first became aware of the imitative pattern and its importance in a longitudinal study of the abilities of dyads of unfamiliar peers to construct cooperative interactions (e.g., a game or a rudimentary conversation). In this initial study (Eckerman, Davis, & Didow, 1989), 14 dyads of unacquainted peers were observed longitudinally at 16, 20, 24, 28, and 32 months of age in a standardized play setting conducive to cooperative play. The play materials used and the unfamiliarity of the peer partner minimized the possibilities for engaging in familiar rituals of cooperative action. To assess whether and how children cooperated with one another, each child's actions with objects, movements in space, vocalizations, and gestures were coded independently from videotaped records and later integrated along the same time line. Next, each child's actions were coded for their relationship to the ongoing or immediately preceding actions of the other child – as coordinated (or cooperative), tangential, interfering, or unrelated. Cooperative acts were those acts thematically related to the specifics of the peer's acts that allowed the peer to continue in her or his own activity while expanding that activity to include both participants. A wide variety of such acts were coded (e.g., imitative acts, complementary role acts such as "finding" a "hiding" peer, complementary gestural or verbal directives, and appropriate responses to such directives). Very few actions of the toddlers at 16 months were cooperative acts, but, across the next 12 months, the incidence of cooperative acts increased dramatically.

Two findings about how this increase came about were striking: (1) Imitation of the peer's nonverbal actions accounted for almost all the cooperative acts throughout this entire age period; and (2) The increase in imitative acts occurred in a marked stepwise fashion. At one age, the toddlers were rarely imitating one another, and yet 4 months later they imitated a wide variety of actions as frequently as once every 12 seconds when they were playing together with similar play material. This stepwise increase in imitative acts occurred at an average age of 20 to 24 months, but the age of emergence varied widely across the dyads. Also, this new readiness to imitate (the imitative pattern) functioned to generate a wide variety of extended forms of cooperative action (reciprocal imitation games, follow-the-leader games, and more complex patterns formed by embedding follow-the-leader sequences within an overall pattern of reciprocal imitation; see Eckerman, 1993a, 1993b).

These findings were replicated with a programmed adult partner who behaved in several ways thought more conducive than a peer's behavior to enabling toddlers to respond cooperatively (Eckerman & Didow, 1989). Unlike toddler peers who rarely explicitly invite another child's participation in their play and often jump at a rapid pace from one activity to another without leaving space for another's cooperative response, the adult performed well-formed play overtures, left space and time for the child to respond, and repeated the same overture several times before moving on to a new activity. Although toddlers from 16 to 32 months of age readily approached the adult and played near her, cooperative responses to her overtures were rare from toddlers at 16 months and increased markedly across the next 12 months. Again, almost all the cooperative actions were imitations of the adult's nonverbal actions, and these imitations functioned to generate sustained reciprocal imitation games with the adult.

Thus, the emergence of the imitative pattern around 20 to 24 months of age reflects a new competence in generating cooperative action with others. Toddlers now generate a wide variety of new forms of cooperative action with others, and even with others no more skillful than themselves. Our attention has turned to understanding why and how the imitative pattern emerges in development. Several findings (detailed in Eckerman, 1993b) led us to explore its developmental emergence from a dynamic-systems perspective (Fogel & Thelen, 1987; Smith & Thelen, 1993; Thelen, 1989). Briefly, the imitative pattern shows at least three characteristics stressed within the dynamic-systems perspective: (1) It is a qualitatively new form of behavior that emerges relatively suddenly in development (a "phase shift"), (2) its emergence seems to await development in one or more later-appearing contributing elements ("control parameters") because toddlers show many of the elements of this behavior pattern long before the imitative pattern appears (e.g., the ability to imitate the play actions at issue and to engage in intentional communication), and (3) the imitative pattern occurs under specific task demands (e.g., when rituals of interaction cannot be relied upon, there is no scaffolding social partner, and a variety of actions are possible).

These considerations led us to study one possible late-developing element that might trigger the emergence of the imitative pattern (toddlers' awareness of being imitated) and to ask how the awareness of being imitated might constrain subsequent actions by toddlers so as to give rise to the imitative pattern. This was an attempt to assess the claim of the dynamic-systems perspective that stable forms of behavior are the result of locally acting constraints among the diverse elements of a multicausal system, rather than the result of some central plan or program. We constructed a play setting in which only eight play actions were likely and used an unfamiliar programmed adult to manipulate 24-month-old toddlers' awareness of being imitated (Eckerman & Stein, 1990).

For one group, every time the toddler performed one of these eight actions, the adult immediately performed the same action on the same play material, smoothly inserting her action before the child could act again and making it quite likely that the toddlers would see her action and be aware of being imitated. For a second group, the adult behaved in exactly the same way except that she responded to each action by performing a different play action on the same material that had no more meaningful connection to the child's action than that characterizing the parallel play of toddlers. The effects of this manipulation were striking. When the adult deftly imitated the toddlers, the imitative pattern appeared at once and characterized the entire session; whereas there was little order to the social exchange when the adult performed a different action. The adult's imitation of the toddlers' actions constrained the toddlers' next actions in at least two ways conducive to the appearance of the imitative pattern. First, when imitated, toddlers were significantly more likely to continue acting upon the same play material and thus maintain a state of joint attention. Second, given that they continued to act on the same play material, they were significantly more likely to repeat their specific action on that object from one turn to the next. Thus, their awareness of being imitated begat answering imitative acts and prolonged gamelike bouts of reciprocal imitation (a key feature of the imitative pattern).

These findings both illustrate the productiveness of assessing locally acting constraints to understand the emergence of an orderly pattern of behavior and lend support to viewing the awareness of being imitated as one later-developing element critical to the developmental emergence of the imitative pattern (a control parameter). It cannot, however, be the only control parameter for the imitative pattern, because it cannot account for the marked increase in the *initiation* of imitative acts, another key feature of the imitative pattern (Eckerman, 1993b). Our inquiry has turned now to exploring developments in toddlers' understandings of themselves and others in our search for other control parameters. Numerous important changes in children's cognitions occur during the general developmental period in which the imitative pattern emerges (e.g., Brownell, 1986, 1988; Bullock & Lutkenhaus, 1988; Frye, 1991; Pipp, Fisher, & Jennings, 1987), and toddlers' understandings of themselves and others appear to be most pertinent for cooperative behavior. To cooperate in a mature manner with others seems to demand an understanding of both self and others as active independent agents; an understanding of both one's own and another's goals; an ability to negotiate to arrive at a common goal; an ability to monitor another's actions in relation to one's own actions; and an ability to monitor one's own and another's actions with respect to a joint goal in order to make corrections, to develop new means, and so forth (cf. Asendorpf & Baudonnière, 1993; Brownell & Carriger, 1991).

We plan to trace the development of at least five aspects of these understandings that are not known to be in place long before the emergence of the imitative pattern in order to discover which of these elements emerge just prior to or concurrent with the imitative pattern. We then will try to manipulate these later-developing understandings in order to specify which seem to trigger the developmental switch from a nonimitative mode of behavior to the imitative pattern and how they exert locally acting constraints that result in the imitative pattern of behavior. As Thelen (1989) has argued tellingly, when such manipulative strategies are doable and yield clear evidence of phase shifts in behavioral organization, we are able to achieve a clarity of understanding of developmental process in humans seldom achieved through the more usual correlative strategies.

There is, however, another key question about the emergence of the imitative pattern – that of its consequences for subsequent developmental processes. We propose that the cooperative action generated through nonverbal imitative acts provides interactive experiences conducive to toddlers' development of verbal means of achieving and supporting cooperative action. We have tested this idea in two preliminary ways. First, we analyzed all the peer-directed talk occurring in the prior longitudinal study of peer dyads and asked about developmental changes in this talk relative to the time of emergence of the imitative pattern, the social contexts in which this talk occurred, and the functions apparently served by the talk (for related findings see Didow & Eckerman, 1991; Eckerman, 1993a). Peer-directed verbalizations remained infrequent and roughly constant in frequency prior to the emergence of the imitative pattern; but after its emergence, they increased markedly in a linear fashion. Furthermore, verbalizations serving different interactive functions emerged at different times relative to the imitative pattern. For example, children's verbalizations claiming ownership or possession of objects began to increase in frequency at the same age as the emergence of the imitative pattern, whereas verbalizations directing the partner in how to act began to increase in frequency 4 months later.

Further, when data were collapsed across all ages after the emergence of the imitative pattern, peer-directed verbalizations were much more apt to occur when the two children were engaged in sustained bouts of nonverbal cooperative activity constructed through nonverbal imitative acts than when they were simply close together in space playing with the same toy. Too, verbalizations directing the other peer's actions and verbal responses to the peer's talk that were well-connected topically to that talk occurred most often during these bouts of nonverbal coordinated action. Thus, the understandings of what the children were doing together, created through their imitative acts, seemed to create a supportive frame for their directing verbalizations to one another that could aid the cooperative action and for their answering each other's talk in a topically relevant manner and thus generating a new form of cooperative action – cooperative talk.

A second study exploring our claims about how the experiences created by the imitative pattern facilitate toddlers' development of verbal means of achieving cooperative action used a manipulative strategy (Didow, 1993). A programmed adult partner created three different social contexts surrounding her use of speech with 24-month-old toddlers. For one context (Imitation-Self), the adult involved the toddler in reciprocal imitation games like those regularly generated by toddler peers after the emergence of the imitative pattern, and the adult verbally described her own nonverbal play actions. For another (Parallel-Self), the adult involved the child in playing together side by side with the same play material but without imitative activity or any other more meaningful connection between the toddler's actions and her own, and the adult verbally described her own actions. The final context (Parallel-Child) involved the same kind of parallel play, but the adult verbally described the child's play actions rather than her own actions. The primary question was whether the Imitation-Self context aided the toddler in responding verbally to the adult's speech with a relevant, topically connected utterance. The findings were very clear: The Imitation-Self condition led to many more topically connected verbal responses by the toddler (and hence cooperative conversations) than did either of the other conditions, which were indistinguishable in their effects upon the child's use of language.

The studies described reflect a general mode of inquiry that potentially is widely applicable to any number of specific developmental transitions within a hypothesized pathway of development. Among its key features are

(1) a detailed examination of new forms of behavioral organization important in children's development and the use of that new behavioral organization as the anchor point for inquiry, (2) an examination of developmental changes in the several elements contributing to that new behavioral organization to determine possible heterochronicity in the development of the separate elements, (3) attempts to isolate late-developing elements that may trigger the emergence of the new behavioral organization of interest, (4) the use of manipulative strategies to confirm that a hypothesized element can in fact trigger the new organization and to assess the locally acting constraints among the different contributing elements that help explain the new form of behavioral organization, and (5) an examination of the new experiences resulting from the new form of behavioral organization and how they contribute to subsequent developmental processes.

Illustration 4: Heterochronicity of Development and
Individual Differences in Developmental Transitions

The final illustration is a report by Alan Fogel and his coworkers (Fogel, Nwokah, Hsu, Dedo, & Walker, 1993) of individual differences among mother-infant dyads in how a specific developmental transition comes about – the transition from assuming *en face* positions to looking away from one another to the broader environment. It too was guided by a dynamic-systems perspective on development. In this report, Fogel explicitly addresses individual differences in the relative timing of developmental changes in multiple elements contributing to a new dyadic behavioral organization, and he attempts to trace the impact of these differences upon both the timing of the emergence of the new form of behavioral organization and the elements that function as control parameters in triggering its emergence.

Specifically, the study examined changes in mothers' positioning of their children with respect to themselves – changes from positioning their infants faced toward themselves in ways that facilitate *en face* interactions to placing their infants facing away from themselves. Thirteen mother-infant dyads were observed at weekly intervals throughout the infants' first 5 months of life. Mothers held their infants in their laps and were asked to "play and talk to your baby as you would at home." Transitions in the mothers' positioning of their infants were examined as a function of three specific elements hypothesized to contribute to dyadic positioning and their changes across development (infant gazing away from mother, infant positive facial expressions, and infant visually guided reaching). All three elements contributed to an understanding of when mothers changed their infants' position from facing toward them to facing away. Across all ages and dyads, more position changes occurred when infants looked away from their mothers with either a neutral or a positive facial expression. With development, too, all dyads moved from a predominance of *en face* positions to mothers positioning their infants away from themselves in line with their infants' gazing away from them.

The time at which this transition to "gaze away/position away" occurred in development, however, appeared to depend upon the individual differences among dyads in the relative timing of changes in infant gazing away, infant postural self-support, and the onset of visually guided reaching. For roughly half the dyads, mothers tended to move to positioning their infants away from themselves as soon as their infants began to spend sizable periods of time gazing away from them. For other dyads, however, this transition did not occur then, but only later, when the infants began to show visually guided reaching. For these latter dyads, there were between 2 and 5 weeks of interaction in which the infants looked away from their mothers a good deal, but their mothers showed high frequencies of repositioning their infants toward them or in supine positions.

Fogel suggests that these differences among dyads in the timing of matching infant gaze away with maternal positioning of the infant away from herself are explained by differences in developmental timing between the interacting elements of the mother-infant system. When increased gazing away from the mother co-occurs developmentally with postural self-control, then this combination triggers the transition to the mother's positioning her infant away from herself when her infant gazes away. When, however, postural self-control is more delayed, then the onset of visually directed reaching triggers the same transition.

The results of this single study obviously need to be treated with caution, given the exploratory and descriptive nature of the research, the relatively small sample of dyads, the absence of direct measures of postural self-control, and the many other contributing elements not yet examined. Nevertheless, this work serves to demonstrate the potential fruitfulness of explicitly studying the specific forms of developmental heterochronicity to be found among the multiple elements contributing to any specific developmental transition. Once pivotal heterochronicities are hypothesized based on studies such as this, manipulative strategies can be undertaken to more explicitly confirm the importance of these differences in timing in triggering developmental transitions.

Relating the Illustrations to
the Principles of Developmental Science

The developmental analyses detailed here are the result of intellectual traditions and lines of inquiry somewhat different from those most influential in Magnusson's and Cairns's thinking; nevertheless, the four analyses provide specific illustrations of how the developmental principles articulated by Magnusson and Cairns (this volume) can be translated into productive research endeavors. It is time now to more carefully examine these links between the illustrative analyses and each developmental principle considered in turn.

The first developmental principle reflects a holistic view of an organism's development: "An individual develops and functions psychologically as an integrated organism." Schaffer's conceptualization of early social-communicative development explicitly addressed aspects of this integration (1) by detailing how social-interaction processes and language acquisition are interrelated, (2) by relating changes in "maturational" processes (such as changes in visual scanning and fixation patterns, in eye-hand coordination in reaching, and in representational abilities) to changes in the interactive tasks mastered through mother-child interaction processes, and (3) by attempting to integrate the child's changing cognitions with changing social interaction patterns. Throughout, bidirectional paths of influence were stressed between different facets of an organism's functioning (between language and social interaction, between cognitions and social behavior, between new infant behavioral abilities and parent-infant interaction processes), reflecting the integrated nature of the young child's functioning. The comparative study (Illustration 2), too, stressed the integration of infants' central nervous system functioning, such behavioral characteristics as reactivity and self-regulation, social and communicative development, and motor and intellectual functioning. The studies of toddlers' abilities to construct cooperative action with others increasingly stressed the integration of social behavior and cognitive understandings of self and others, and Fogel's study explicitly addressed how visual-motor coordination, attention regulation, affective facial expressions, and postural self-control act together to produce a specific transition in mother-infant interaction processes. Finally, the orientation of all four analyses around the concept of dyadic-interactive tasks enables the exploration of what happens when one or several elements thought critical to the mastery of a task in typically developing children "fail" or take a markedly different form (as, for example, among very-high-biological-risk infants). How does the integrated system reorganize itself so as to still accomplish the interactive task, and what are the consequences upon development of such reorganizations?

The second principle stresses the bidirectional nature of the influence continuously exerted between the developing organism and its environment: "An individual develops and functions in a dynamic, continuous, and reciprocal process of interaction with his or her environment, including relations with other individuals, groups, and the subculture." All four illustrations emphasize the continuing and changing patterns of bidirectional influence between mother and infant during early social-communicative development. Development is conceptualized as a joint endeavor of parent and child, and the specific roles of each and the processes of influence are viewed as continuously changing as they work together on a sequence of interactive tasks. Even the tasks are conceptualized as tasks of the dyad, not of the individual organism. Further, the ongoing study of very prematurely born infants seeks to assess the impact of early biological-behavioral differences among infants on this entire pathway of development – of mother and child jointly negotiating three sequential developmental tasks – and compares the pathways negotiated by white, middle-class infants with those of African-American infants, and those of infants living in poverty. The toddler studies of cooperative action expand the study of bidirectional influence processes to those occurring between toddlers and their agemates and between toddlers and unfamiliar adults.

The third principle is a corollary of the first about the holistic nature of development: "Individual functioning depends upon and influences the reciprocal interaction among subsystems within the individual." The relevance of the present illustrations already has been discussed with respect to the first principle.

The fourth principle emphasizes that novel patterns of individual functioning arise during development. The appearance of such novel forms has been stressed throughout the illustrative analyses. For example, Schaffer emphasizes the periodic appearance of new forms of behavioral or cognitive organization in the infant and their role as "pacers" for new interactive tasks to be jointly negotiated by mother and infant. The studies of toddlers' abilities to generate cooperative activity are oriented around the appearance of a behavioral novelty – the imitative pattern – and the questions of how this novelty arises in development and what are its immediate consequences and its influence upon subsequent processes of development. In addition, Fogel's study focuses upon the timing of the appearance of new forms of infant behavior and the impact of that timing on a new form of maternal responsiveness to infant behavior.

The fifth principle – that the individual's development "reflects a mosaic of ontogenetic trajectories" and "differences in the rate of development may produce major differences in the organization and configuration of psychological functions" – is explicitly addressed in the fourth illustration. Individual differences in how the ontogenetic trajectories of three elements were related to one another were used to explain individual differences in how the transition away from *en face* interactions with mothers occurred. Also, implicit in the study of the impact of very early births upon social-communicative development (the second illustration) is the realization that these early births are a major deviation in the timing of new modes of organism-environment interaction. Births at 24 to 32 weeks' postconceptional age mean that the prematurely born newborn's relatively immature organs and neural and behavioral systems interact with a quite different environment (all the distinctive features of the customary postnatal environment and the special features of intensive-care nurseries) well before the time that these interactions usually take place. These "mistimed" or "unusually timed" interactions may well be expected to have differential effects on individual developmental trajectories, resulting in different patterns of heterochronicity among elements for premature infants versus full-term infants and for premature infants varying in the earliness of their birth and all the attendant medical complications.

The sixth principle stresses the sensitivity of patterns of behavioral or psychological organization to the conditions under which they are formed. This sensitivity, of course, is stressed within the dynamic-systems perspective on development that guided Illustrations 3 and 4. This sensitivity is clearly demonstrated in the study manipulating toddlers' awareness of being imitated by a partner. When a partner behaved in a way facilitating this awareness, toddlers clearly and consistently showed the form of behavioral organization called the imitative pattern; when the partner changed only one element, however, this pattern did not emerge at all. Similarly, the role of context in the emergence of skilled verbal behavior is seen in the studies of toddlers engaged in nonverbal cooperative action generated by means of the imitative pattern. In the context of nonverbal imitative behavior, toddlers talked more often to agemates and topically connected their verbalizations to their partners, generating rudimentary verbal conversations. In other contexts, coexisting in the same play session, toddlers showed much less skillful verbal behavior.

The final principle, about conservation in development despite continuous change, is illustrated in all four research examples. Schaffer's conceptualization of five sequential tasks that he expects virtually all parent-infant dyads to jointly negotiate is a claim that these aspects of early social-communicative development are conserved despite the continuously changing process of social interaction and communication and individual variations in these processes. Similarly, the ongoing comparative study of very prematurely born and full-term infants is based on the expectation of conservatism in the nature of the interactive tasks negotiated by individual dyads despite the expected major impact of infants' early biological-behavioral characteristics on how these tasks are negotiated and the level of mastery achieved in given developmental periods. Fogel's study, too, focuses upon a transition common to all his mother-infant dyads despite individual variation in its timing relative to other aspects of the infant's development and relative to the infant's age. Finally, the series of studies on toddlers' skills in generating cooperative action emphasizes the emergence of the same new behavior pattern, the imitative pattern, across different dyads of peers although the age of emergence varies. Furthermore, common constraints on development thought to contribute to the conservatism of development are stressed – both the common "control parameters" that trigger the emergence of the imitative behavior through locally acting constraints on the moment-by-moment flow of social interaction and the common consequences of the emergence of the imitative pattern in terms of the experiences created by this new mode of behavior that facilitate the development of still more mature, verbal commonalities in how toddlers generate cooperative action with others.

Some Future Challenges

The several correspondences noted between the illustrative developmental analyses and the principles of a developmental science are not meant to minimize the challenges ahead for realizing these principles in empirical inquiry. The challenges are immense. I would especially note two for the domain of early social-communicative development. First, there is the need to place interactive tasks and processes of joint negotiation within a broader cultural context and in so doing to place the dyadic-interaction processes stressed here within the context of group processes and the broader social environment of the developing child. Second, there is a need to find more compelling ways to relate biological factors and biological development to the behavioral-social-cognitive aspects of development stressed currently in early social-communicative development. A major issue here is how to move beyond simply studying the impact of early biological differences or "predispositions" on subsequent paths of development (such as the comparative study of very prematurely born and full-term infants) to integrating the study of continuously changing biological characteristics into this story at the same level of detail as is now achievable for social, behavioral, and cognitive aspects. Animal-model work may prove especially helpful here, both for pointing to specific points of profitable inquiry in the human and for documenting the plausibility of hypotheses generated from human data with all its necessary confounds.

There exists also one overarching challenge for implementing these principles of developmental science in empirical inquiry – that posed by the necessary tension existing between the general, more summary accounts of developmental process and the more detailed analysis of the component pieces of the developmental story. I use the analogy of the hawk and the mole in describing this challenge and the differences in research style among developmental investigators. The hawk flies over the landscape of development and experiences its broadness and how its major features, or landmarks, relate to one another as seen from a distance. The mole experiences development in burrowing under the landscape and examining in great detail the specific features that interest it most, often discovering phenomena not readily apparent. Ideally, the mole periodically will find itself above ground, enabling it to experience the landscape more broadly, and the hawk periodically will dive toward a target of inquiry to explore it more thoroughly. Both hawk and mole are exploring and trying to understand the same landscape, but from very different perspectives.

A major challenge, as I see it, is to connect the approaches of the hawk and the mole in ways in which they can enrich one another. This chapter recounts the efforts of one investigator who tries to use the mole's strengths in inquiry without sacrificing the hawk's-eye view of the broad developmental landscape. For me much of the excitement of the attempt to combine the many developmental domains of inquiry into a self-conscious entity called "developmental science" is in its promise of making salient the tension between mole and hawk and of meeting the challenge to develop productive modes of integration.

9   Developmental Psychopathology

E. Jane Costello and Adrian Angold

One stimulus to the growth of developmental science has been the hope that understanding the patterns of "normal" human development will help us understand, and perhaps treat, abnormal developmental patterns. For example, in a report (1990) to the U.S. Congress, *National Plan for Research on Child and Adolescent Mental Disorders,* the National Advisory Mental Health Council stated that "the different rates of development of various brain systems may be related to the ages at which the symptoms of major mental disorders appear, and may offer clues to the causes of these disorders." This finding is put forward as a reason for the National Institute of Mental Health to support basic developmental research. It is equally possible, however, to argue the converse: that studying abnormal development may help us understand the basic principles of human development. For example, one result of Binet's efforts to find a way of identifying children in need of special education was to refine the concept of intelligence, and much basic research in anatomy and physiology was the work of physicians intent on learning how the body functioned so that they could cure its ills. For many developmentalists, the need to understand so as to intervene is at least part of what drives them on.

Thus a chapter on psychopathology is not out of place in a volume on developmental science. It provides an opportunity to examine the usefulness of developmental science's taking a developmental approach to the causes, the course, and the care of psychiatric problems. It also provides a setting in which to evaluate the usefulness of developmental science to child psychopathology. We begin this chapter by discussing how ideas about development and mental illness in children have been intertwined since the mid-19th century, when observations and ideas about these topics began to be published in any numbers. From this background, we go on to discuss ways in which the two disciplines most closely involved in working with disturbed children, child psychiatry and clinical child psychology, have drawn from their parent disciplines those ideas and methods that in

168

many respects assume a developmental viewpoint, although they sometimes focus on the development of different things. We then examine some of the specific theoretical and methodological issues that child psychopathology is currently struggling with and discuss how current attempts to solve them are affected by taking a developmental stance. Finally, we suggest that epidemiology, the study of patterns of disease distribution in time and space, provides a useful frame of reference for many aspects of research on developmental psychopathology.

Development and Childhood Psychopathology: A Historical Overview

Child psychiatry and clinical child psychology, as they have developed during the past century, have been faced with two sets of practical problems: (1) how to identify, classify, and care for the severely disturbed or dysfunctional child, and (2) how to distinguish minor aberrations in the course of normal development from behaviors or emotional states that predict serious disorders or deficits over time (Kanner, 1972). These practical, clinical problems of necessity forced practitioners to take theoretical positions on issues of causality and development. Anyone who believed, as Alexander Crichton (1763–1865) did, that a child could be born "raving mad," with "superhuman, demonic qualities . . . stronger than four women," with "an indescribable laughter, for which no reason could be found, and [with] an uncontrollable destructiveness" that included climbing walls and tearing its clothes (quoted respectfully in Maudsley, 1879, p. 258), necessarily had a theory of developmental psychopathology different from that of a disciple of John Locke, who regarded the infant mind as a blank page that only perception and experience could fill, a mind that could not be insane because it had no "reason" to be. Similarly, the treatment by clinicians and parents of masturbation by a child differed depending on whether the activity was seen as a statistically "normal" behavior of little significance for the development of the child or as the first step on the pathway to idiocy, epilepsy, paralysis, and "masturbatory insanity" (Skae, 1874). Thus ideas about human development and ideas about the developmental trajectory of disease were intertwined from the first. One of the problems for the clinician faced with a particular child at a particular moment was to decide whether the symptom observed was the first, mild sign of a degenerative condition or was a phenomenon that, however alarming at the time, held little prognostic significance.

Identification and Classification of Severe Disorders

1. Distinguishing between Mental Retardation and Psychiatric Disorder. At the most severe end of the spectrum of mental disorders, an important and basic distinction was the one that was made between "imbeciles" and "lunatics." As universal education spread across Europe and America in the second half of the 19th century, children who could not handle the demands of the educational system became a visible and troubling group. In her historical overview of child psychiatry, Stella Chess points out that the distinction between, and division of responsibility for, developmentally retarded "idiots" and psychiatrically disordered "lunatics" was far from clear throughout the 19th century. In the United States, in 1876 all of the charter members of the American Association on Mental Deficiency were psychiatrists, and the child-guidance movement began in 1894 at the University of Pennsylvania in a clinic set up to care primarily for the feebleminded (Chess & Hassibi, 1986). The distinction between the psychiatrically ill child and the severely mentally retarded child emerged slowly over the second half of the 19th century.

The distinction was far from clear also in the aims and methods of the first institutions for children opened in England: a school was set up in Bath in 1846 by the Misses White, and an asylum for idiots was founded in 1848 by a distinguished psychiatrist, John Conolly. Both institutions were inspired by the French and German educational traditions for the mentally retarded, but both were equally concerned with "moral culture . . . control of temper, obedience, order, kindness to each other" (von Gontard, 1988, p. 576). Gradually, specific groups of children were described and causes for their disabilities identified: John Langdon Down, a psychiatrist and superintendent of a large asylum for idiots, described Down syndrome in 1867, and William Ireland, superintendent of the Scottish National Institution for Imbecile Children, developed a classification system with categories such as epileptic, microcephalic, and inflammatory idiocy, demonstrating that the same phenomenon of idiocy could result from many different causes (Ireland, 1877).

In the late 19th century, psychiatrists began to recognize mental retardation as a problem to be treated separately from "insanity." At the same time, psychologists and those responsible for the new public education systems began to recognize a continuum of cognitive ability among children, which included some of the most dysfunctional children previously treated by psychiatry as well as children who were struggling to survive in the new compulsory education system. Throughout the industrialized world, as universal education spread, the right of *all* children to be educated was acknowledged. For example, special classes for the "feebleminded" were mandated in England by the Elementary Education Act (Defective and Epileptic Children) of 1899. The care of mentally retarded children was largely removed from the sphere of psychiatry, unless the child's emotional or behavioral problems were also severe. Psychologists, however, continued to be actively involved in this area of developmental psychopathology. Causal theories focused on genetics, perinatal insults, and early environmental adversity and treatment centered on pinpointing the children's precise deficits and maximizing their potential rather than on "curing" them as the European pioneers in the treatment of idiocy had hoped to do.

2. Distinguishing among Psychiatric Disorders. Descriptions can also be found of children during the same period whose behavioral problems were not primarily those of intellectual development. James Prichard (1786–1848), senior physician to the Bristol Infirmary, was definite that the distinction was real, writing that "idiotism and imbecility are observed in childhood, but insanity, properly so termed, is rare before the age of puberty" (Prichard, 1837, p. 127). He defined *moral insanity* as "madness consisting in a morbid perversion of the natural feelings, affections, inclinations, temper, habits, moral dispositions, and natural impulses, without any remarkable disorder or defect of the intellect or knowing and reasoning faculties, and particularly without any insane illusion or hallucination" (ibid., p. 16). Prichard was a great admirer of Philippe Pinel, who had first described "madness without delirium." Prichard distinguished moral insanity from, on the one hand, "mania, or raving madness . . . in which the mind is totally deranged" (ibid.), and which he attributed to physical causes such as convulsions, and, on the other hand, imbecility or mental retardation.

Prichard thus used *moral* in its 18th-century sense of pertaining to personality or character. Henry Maudsley (1879), writing 40 years later, used the term in its 19th-century sense, referring to ethics and norms. He distinguished between *instinctive insanity,* which was "an aberration and exaggeration of instincts and passions," and *moral insanity,* which was a defect of the moral qualities along a dimension of "viciousness to those extreme manifestations which pass far beyond what anyone would call wickedness" (ibid., p. 289). In the process, he broadened the realm of child psychiatry to include problems of conduct previously considered the responsibility of religion and the law. Maudsley preferred to use the term *affective* where Prichard used *moral,* "as being a more general term and expressing more truly the fundamental condition of nerve-element, which shows itself in affections of the mode of feeling generally, not of the special mode of moral feeling only" (ibid., p. 280).

When writing about etiology rather than classification, however, both Prichard and Maudsley followed the French tradition in distinguishing between *moral* and *physical* causes of mental disorder, using *moral* in the sense of what came to be called exogenous causes. (Prichard [1837], quoting Georget, lists among the moral causes of insanity domestic grief, disappointment in love, political events, fanaticism, jealousy, poverty or reversal of fortune, reading romances, and excessive study.). Mental retardation was seen as stemming exclusively from physical causes: either convulsions of some type in the early years or some defect transmitted from a parent. This defect might be inherited or it might be "traceable to parental intemperance and excess" (Maudsley, 1879, p. 44). The dominant causal theory of psychopathology in the second half of the 19th century was a genetic one: Heredity and degeneration caused disease, which started with scarcely perceptible signs in early childhood but took a progressive and irreversible course and would probably be transmitted to future generations if the affected individual were permitted to breed. Even when the proximal cause of insanity was a moral one, "the different forms of insanity that occur in young children . . . are almost always traceable to nervous disease in the preceding generation" (Maudsley, 1879, p. 68). Prichard was following the European tradition of Etienne Esquirol and Pinel in adopting what might today be called a vulnerability-stress model of causation. "A certain peculiarity of natural temperament or habit of body is a necessary condition for the development of insanity: without the previous existence of this condition the causes which give rise to the disease will either act upon the individual without any noxious effect, or they will call forth some other train of morbid phenomena" (Prichard, 1837, p. 121). Both genetic vulnerability and a hostile environment or damaging lifestyle were necessary for the onset of disease; but once the disease process began, there was little that could be done to reverse it.

Psychiatrists in the 19th century thus had a developmental causal theory about psychopathology. Nevertheless, it was a narrow form of developmental theory, in which the course of the disease was progressive and irreversible, tied into the development of the child in that it manifested itself differently as the child grew but was impervious to other influences, such as treatment or learning. "All one could do was to prevent the most extreme manifestations by strict punishment and to protect those not affected" (von Gontard, 1988, p. 579). The most effective defense for society was to prevent the procreation of the insane, and eugenics and life-long segregation in asylums were seen as more effective intervention strategies than attempting to treat or cure the person. Although a continuum of severity was documented in child psychiatric disorders, as it was in mental retardation, the psychiatric continuum was interpreted quite differently. It took the form of a disease continuum within the individual across time, rather than a distribution of severity that would remain fairly constant across individuals over time, as was the case for mental retardation. Very few children received any form of psychiatric treatment, and the prognosis, even for children who presented with mild symptoms, was believed to be a gloomy one.

3. Psychoanalytic Theory and Developmental Psychopathology. One of the strengths of the psychoanalytic approach to psychopathology, as its theory and treatment methods developed around the turn of the century, was that it rejected the therapeutic pessimism of much contemporary child psychiatry. Although Sigmund Freud himself accepted that individuals had innate or constitutional characteristics, he developed what his daughter, Anna Freud, described as an "etiological formula of a sliding scale of internal and external influences: that there are people whose 'sexual constitution would not have led them into a neurosis if they had not had [certain] experiences, and these experiences would not have had a traumatic effect on them if their libido had been otherwise disposed' (S. Freud, 1916–1917, p. 347)" (A. Freud, 1965, p. 520). "Hereditary factors depend for their pathogenic impact on the accidental influences with which they interact" (ibid., p. 138). Children whose libido "disposed" them to pathology could be saved by the right environment, or therapy, or both. Thus although even mild symptoms could be ominous, the course was not inevitable. Psychoanalytic theory was fundamentally developmental at a time when the term had no place in mainline child psychiatry; for example, whereas the entries under the heading "Development" in Anna Freud's *Normality and Pathology in Childhood* (1965) take up two columns, there is not a single entry under that heading in two of the classics of mid-20th-century American child psychiatry, Kanner (1972) and Chess & Hassibi (1978, 1986). Psychoanalytic theory was also developmental in the multiple senses discussed later in this chapter and throughout this volume; that is, it emphasized multiple determination of outcomes, the transformation and hierarchical integration of behavior, and the emergence of novelty. In the words of Anna Freud:

> According to our psychoanalytic conceptions, the final achievement of social adaptation is the result of a number and variety of developmental advances. To enumerate these in detail is useful, because in this way we create the prerequisites for predicting future massive disturbance at a time when only the merest indications of disharmony, unevenness in growth, or faulty response to the environment are present. This endeavor also disposes effectively of the conception of dissociality as a nosological entity which is based on one specific cause, whether this is thought to be internal (such as "mental deficiency" or "moral insanity") or external (such as broken homes, parental discord, parental neglect, separations, etc.). As we abandon thinking in terms of specific *causes* of dissociality, we become able to think increasingly in terms of successful or unsuccessful *transformations* of the self-indulgent and asocial trends and attitudes which normally are part of the original nature of the child. This helps to construct developmental lines which lead to pathological results, although these are more complex, less well defined, and contain a wider range of possibilities than the lines of normal development." (A. Freud, 1965, pp. 166–167)

In the last two decades, the influence of Freudian developmental psychopathology on clinical teaching and practice has declined, as a more phenomenological approach to describing psychopathology has gained popularity, particularly in the United States. The nosologies currently in use for describing psychiatric problems, such as the *International Classification of Diseases* (World Health Organization, 1977) and the *Diagnostic and Statistical Manual* (American Psychiatric Association, 1994), are essentially nondevelopmental in their approaches, searching for common denominators that describe the manifestations of a disorder at every age, rather than attempting, as the Freudian approach does, to describe the development of the disease in the context of the development of the individual. In this they follow the examples of medicine, which looks for diseases that have a standard etiology and set of manifestations, and of some branches of psychology, which seek to pin down concepts like intelligence in forms that are deliberately designed to transcend differences that are a function of developmental factors. Although the *content* of psychodynamic theories as an explanation of child psychopathology has not stood up to empirical research, the *form*, with its emphasis on how the development of the child and of the disease are intertwined, retains attraction as a model for developmental psychopathology.

Distinguishing Normal from Abnormal

Meanwhile, at the other end of the spectrum of severity, work began in the 1940s to differentiate between what Lapouse and Monk (1958, p. 1136) called "deviations from the usual pattern" and behavior that could be seen (at least in hindsight) to be part of the picture of normal development. As Lapouse and Monk stated the problem in the 1950s:

> One of the great psychiatric dilemmas of our time is the decision as to what is normal and what is abnormal in human behavior. Lacking specific tests to make the distinction, the diagnostician has recourse mainly to his clinical judgment which rests on his training, experience, perceptiveness, and theoretical persuasion. . . . In child psychiatry, Leo Kanner points out that recorded symptoms "are of necessity those of selected groups and not of the total population of children"; and, he continues, "This selectiveness, in the absence of 'normal controls,' has often resulted in a tendency to attribute to single behavior items an exaggerated 'seriousness' with regard to their intrinsic psychopathologic significance. The seriousness becomes attached to the signal regardless of what it announces and who announces it. The high annoyance threshold of many fond and fondly resourceful parents keeps away from clinics and out of reach of statistics a multitude of early breath holders, nail biters, nose pickers and casual masturbators who, largely because of this kind of parental attitude, develop into reasonably happy and well-adjusted adults" (Kanner, 1945). (Lapouse & Monk, 1958, p. 1136)

One of the achievements of the early child psychiatric epidemiologists, such as Lapouse and Monk (1958) and Shepherd, Oppenheim, and Mitchell (1971), has been to document just how common *individual* "abnormal" behaviors are in the general population of children. For example, in their survey of a random sample of 6- to 12-year-olds in Buffalo, New York, Lapouse and Monk found that, as reported by their mothers, 43% of the children had seven or more fears or worries, 49% were overactive, and 48% lost their tempers twice a week or more (1958). Similarly, Shepherd et al. found that on their scale of 25 "deviant" behaviors only 40% of a population sample of elementary school children were *not* deviant (1971). However, only 2.6% of the children were deviant in seven or more areas.

The idea of scales of deviance, distinguishing among children by degree of symptomatology rather than pattern or classification, became popular in the mid-20th century. Such scales were often given a name, such as "maladjustment" or "maladaptation," that implied that the problem was one of how a child fit with the demands of the environment, in contrast to the "disease" or "degenerative" models implicit in early child psychiatry. This had the welcome effect of opening up psychopathology to the research paradigms that were proving so powerful in the exploration of "normal" psychological characteristics such as intelligence. By the mid-1970s, when they were ably reviewed by Gould et al. for President Carter's Commission on Mental Health, hundreds of studies had been published documenting the kinds of maladjusted behavior observed by parents, teachers, and others in children of every age and social class in the United States and Britain (Gould, Wunsch-Hitzig, & Dohrenwend, 1980).

A problem with this approach to understanding the development of mental health problems, as Gould et al. pointed out, was the huge variability in the proportion of children identified as having significant levels of "maladjustment," depending on which scale was used. In their survey, they found that the percentage of various nonclinical samples of children judged to be maladjusted varied from 6.6% to 22.0% when teachers were the informants, and from 10.9% to 37.0% when mothers were the informants. A second problem with the attempt to develop global maladjustment scales was that, in following the model of concepts like intelligence, scales were deliberately constructed so as to "correct for" effects of age, sex, and ethnicity. For the developmentalist, this meant that they could not be used to study the interrelationship of development and psychopathology (Cairns, 1983). They also begged the question of what behavior is or is not "maladjusted" at different developmental stages or in different contexts. In addition, the early scales did not address clinicians' awareness that there were patterns to the ways that deviant behaviors clustered. Recent "behavior problem scales" have paid much more attention to such patterns, as we will discuss later. But so far the emphasis has still been on producing scales that can be used over a wide age range (e.g., Achenbach & Edelbrock, 1983). Work has barely begun to map the significance of patterns of symptoms in time and space as they occur in the population.

As a final note to this section on the background of developmental psychopathology, it is interesting to note that the intertwining of developmental psychology and developmental psychopathology was characteristic of several pioneers of developmental psychology around the turn of the century. For example, in Cairns's account of the emergence of developmental psychology (Cairns, 1983), of the five "pioneers" of developmental science whose contributions he discusses – Preyer, Binet, Hall, Baldwin, and Sigmund Freud – three are still recognized for their contributions to psychopathologic knowledge. Although the two streams of investigation have diverged during the 20th century, one of the themes of this chapter is that they can and should come together again to shape the future.

From Past to Present: The Current Role of Developmental Issues in Child Psychopathology

Clinicians dealing with psychopathology in the young are still struggling to navigate confusing and sometimes conflicting currents of theory and practice. At one extreme, developmental psychology has focused, as Anna Freud put it, on "whether the child under examination has reached developmental levels which are adequate for his age" in various areas of competence: emotional, cognitive, motor, and so on (1965, p. 151). Some of the first papers to describe the domain of developmental psychopathology have adopted this approach, postulating a relationship between the "developmental tasks" of the growing child and the different types of psychological disorder that failure to master these tasks would entail (Garber, 1984; Sroufe & Rutter, 1984). At the other extreme, the attempt is being made, particularly in the diagnostic system of American psychiatry (American Psychiatric Association, 1987), to define mental illnesses as if they were as age-independent as a broken leg. There are currently strong pressures, especially from agencies that provide or pay for mental health services, to formulate children's problems in categorical, nondevelopmental language, so that a "case" of depression is defined in the same terms whether the patient is 7 or 70.

Yet both clinicians and researchers are aware that the current taxonomies are a poor fit for many children's problems, and that at some developmental stages – infancy, for example – they are clearly inappropriate. In the next section we argue that the developmental view and the medical view of psychopathology are in fact conceptually much more similar than might at first appear. Where they differ, this is often because they either have chosen or have been forced to concentrate on particular aspects of developmental psychopathology that magnify their differences. We then consider some of the theoretical and methodological implications for child psychopathology of taking a developmental approach to the emotional and behavioral problems of today's children.

What Do We Mean by "Development"?

Central to the view of development taken in this chapter is Gottlieb's definition of epigenesis, discussed earlier in this volume. Gottlieb argues:

> Individual development is characterized by an increase of complexity of organization (i.e., the emergence of new structural and functional properties and competencies) at all levels of analysis (molecular, subcellular, cellular, organismic) as a consequence of horizontal and vertical coactions among the organisms' parts, including organism-environment coactions. Horizontal coactions are those that occur at the same level (gene-gene . . . organism-organism), whereas vertical coactions occur at different levels (cell-tissue, . . . behavioral activity-nervous system) and are reciprocal, meaning that they can influence each other in either direction, from lower to higher or from higher to lower levels of the developing system. (Gottlieb, 1991a, p. 7)

This concept of development (a) presupposes change and novelty, (b) underscores the importance of timing in behavioral establishment and organization, (c) emphasizes multiple determination, and (d) leads us *not* to expect invariant relationships between causes and outcomes across the span of development (Cappiocco & Tassinary, 1990). For heuristic purposes we distinguish five broad system areas that involve the developing child, and with which developmental psychopathology has to be concerned:

(I) The intraorganismic or neurobiological area. This area includes anatomical, physiological, and neurocognitive systems. It also includes measures of cognitive performance, such as reading and math ability and general intelligence.

(II) The phenomenological-behavioral area. This area includes observable or reportable behavior or emotional states. In operational terms it is represented by a series of developmental trajectories, some of which are regarded as being "unsatisfactory" or "deviant."

(III) The family-genetic area. The most proximal part of the social environment for most children is the family, which serves to transmit both genetic material and an environment within which that inheritance is manifested.

(IV and V) The sociocultural areas of school and community. These areas include a variety of demographic variables (such as social class), and more specific measures of relatedness to the community, including peer network measures, and measures of the community's definitions of, and attitudes toward, deviance. The child's community changes with development, embracing larger neighborhoods and schools, which transmit different, and often conflicting, sets of expectations. Children also change the community as they move through it, meeting or conflicting with its expectations for them. Different academic disciplines have traditionally concentrated on pathology identified in these different system areas: medicine and neuropsychology in the first, psychiatry and clinical psychology in the second, and so on. Recently, developmental science has begun to challenge these disciplines to examine ways in which pathology might be affected by, and affect, coaction across these system areas (Cicchetti, 1984).

A Developmental View of Pathology

Nagel noted that "The concept of *development* . . . involves two essential components: The notion of a system possessing a definite structure and a definite set of pre-existing capacities; and the notion of a sequential set of changes in the system, yielding relatively permanent but novel increments not only in its structure but in its modes of operation as well" (Nagel, 1957, p. 17). Thus, Nagel was concerned to distinguish development from other sorts of change; it is not disorganized, and both form and function may be different at later stages from those observed in earlier stages, though only within a certain framework. Furthermore, as Mayr (1982) has pointed out, the idea of organized change implies a "teleonomic" view of change; that is, change that follows a program leading to some appropriate endpoint. This endpoint is not a mystical notion, but simply the result of the process of natural selection.

Developmental Psychopathology and the Medical Model

In all these respects, as Hay and Angold have pointed out (1993), disease as thought of within the "medical model" of pathology is a developmental concept.

> As an example, consider the processes of tumorigenesis in the case of carcinoma of the cervix. Investigations of the process began from the observation that there was a class of cancers that appeared to arise from the cervix and spread both locally and sometimes to other regions of the body. In other words, an endpoint was first observed. The question then became: How is this endpoint reached? We now know that certain factors are associated with the appearance of premalignant atypical cells in the cervix, which may progress through further degrees of cellular transfor-

mation to "malignant" lesions that are capable of invading and damaging normal tissues. The continuance of this process is dependent upon the tumor achieving an adequate blood supply, and surviving the inflammatory response that such an invasion will often precipitate. At a later stage, distant metastasis (spread) may occur, with the appearance of independent tumors in other parts of the body. Thus, the process of disease progression has much in common with development: It is "programmed" by the nature of cellular transformation that begins the process, and in general follows a reasonably regular course, though with wide variations in rate. Furthermore, there is a hierarchial integration involved in the progression. Cell transformation is required before local invasion occurs, and metastasis is usually a feature of an advanced invasive tumor. Each step, therefore, builds on the preceding stage, and the "achievements" of the preceding stage are "integrated" into that which succeeds it. Thus, metastatic tumors consist of invasive groups of transformed cells, which may, in turn, metastasize themselves. (Hay & Angold, 1993, pp. 10–12)

It may seem strange at first to consider tumorigenesis as an example of epigenesis, but it fits the definition. Development and pathology are not as far apart conceptually as they might at first appear to be.

The "medical model" of disease uses a set of terms or concepts to discuss the development of disease that have close parallels in the language or concepts of developmental science. *Etiology, pathogenesis, risk,* and *prevention,* all terms widely used in both clinical and epidemiological medicine, describe ideas familiar to developmental science.

Etiology and Pathogenesis. The etiology of a disease is the cluster of factors that lead to and promote the development of the disease. These factors may exist at a number of levels, ranging from the nature of social organizations to the structure of individual molecules. Scientists may understand the *etiology* of a disease, that is, the factors that determine its presence, long before they fully understand its pathogenesis, the *process* by which the disease is generated. In the 1950s it was observed that mesothelioma was much more common than expected downwind of a particular asbestos plant in London. This led to the hypothesis, later confirmed, that asbestos is an etiological factor for mesothelioma. However, the mechanism by which asbestos leads to this particular tumor remains uncertain to this day. In the pathogenesis of phenylketonuria, failure to produce the enzyme phenylalanine hydroxylase, for whatever reason, leads phenylalanine to build up in the body. This part of the pathogenesis of phenylketonuria is clear. It is still unclear, however, exactly how this buildup results in the mental retardation typical of the disease.

Risk. Risk is a statistical concept expressing in quantitative terms the likelihood of an event given the presence of some other circumstance.

> For an individual, the risk for disease properly defined takes on only two values: zero and unity. The application of some intermediate value for risk to an individual is only a means of estimating the individual's risk by the mean risk of many other presumably similar individuals. The actual risk for an individual is a matter of whether or not a sufficient cause has been or will be formed, whereas the mean risk for a group indicates the proportion of individuals for whom sufficient causes are formed. (Rothman, 1976, p. 589)

Thus a risk estimate expresses the likelihood that a pathological process will move from one developmental stage to the next. In the development of our understanding of the pathogenesis of a disease, a factor that increases the risk of a disease in a population may move into the category of an etiologic factor, necessary to pathogenesis on its own or in conjunction with other factors, or it may be seen as one of a number of factors, any one or group of which will serve the same function in the process of pathogenesis. Thus smoking is a risk factor for lung cancer, but it is neither necessary nor sufficient to pathogenesis, because lung cancer can occur in nonsmokers, and most smokers do not get lung cancer.

Prevention. A disease can be prevented if the individual avoids exposure to any of the risk factors for that disease or its precursors, or if, on exposure to a potential cause of disease, some protective factor cancels out the risk of disease. That is, one can work to prevent risk factors for the disease or to prevent the disease once exposure has occurred. In medicine, preventive activities are divided into three broad categories, which follow the developmental course of a disease. *Primary prevention* is aimed at removing risk factors; for example, clean water supplies prevent access to cholera and typhoid germs, seat belts keep heads away from windscreens, and antenatal care reduces a host of risk factors to the developing fetus. *Secondary prevention* operates at a level at which a risk factor is present but has not yet caused overt disease. It is sometimes extended to include early, reversible stages of disease. Medication to lower blood pressure and reduce the risk of stroke is an example of secondary prevention. *Tertiary prevention* is invoked when overt disease is present, as a means of minimizing residual impairment to the individual or of preventing the diseased individual from acting as a risk factor for disease in others. As we discussed earlier, isolation was for centuries the strategy adopted for tertiary prevention of many severe diseases with a lengthy course, such as leprosy and tuberculosis, as communities sought to protect their members from contagion. In the case of mental illness, the aim may have been to prevent the mentally ill from having children.

These aspects of pathology – etiology, pathogenesis, risk, and prevention – are easily compatible with a developmental view of both the individual and the disease. They all fit the description given earlier of development in terms of vertical and horizontal coaction among parts of the organism, or between the organism and the external environment. They make specific reference to the importance of timing and interaction; for example, a secondary prevention only functions to prevent onset in the presence of a relevant risk factor. They are consistent with multiple determination of some diseases, though for others a single risk factor may be both necessary and sufficient. They certainly lead us not to expect invariant relationships between causes and outcomes across the span of development of a disease. They point out that pathology is constrained by context, as is development. All possible abnormalities do not occur, and there are tremendous differences in the frequencies of occurrence of different disorders. Thus, just as development leads to a particular set of species-typical, system-related endpoints, so pathological changes are often species typical and organ specific, though every cell in the body contains the same genetic code.

In sum, the medical model of disease has a great deal in common, in both its theoretical concerns and its practical applications, with current thinking about how biological organisms develop. There should be no communication problems for developmental psychopathologists in integrating the two approaches – should they choose to do so. The next question is whether developmental psychopathology should make the attempt, whether it should look elsewhere for its model of psychopathology, or whether only a whole new way of looking at psychopathology will be adequate to the challenge of understanding the causes and cures of emotional and behavioral problems.

Developmental Psychology and Developmental Psychopathology

In the past century, both religion and law have lost ground as the languages in which we discuss problems of childhood deviance; the chief contender with the disease model has become the model based on the psychology of human development. Psychology sets out to describe principles governing the regularities and commonalities of human development; these may, however, disguise themselves in a hundred variations on a common theme. Against this background, there has been intense debate about the best way in which to think about the behavior and affect that are at the extremes of observed distributions of behavior or that cause pain to the individual or to society. Many people are hostile to equating such states with "diseases," given the standard view of disease as caused by pathogens somehow external to the individual, and given also the social impact of defining deviant affect or behavior as the mark of a "mental illness." There are also objections to an approach that leads to categorizing psychopathology as either present or not present; defining people as either depressed or not depressed, for instance, flies in the face of both common sense and research evidence that many affective states and behavioral patterns can be described on a continuum (Achenbach, 1991). There is the problem, too, that many people view a disease-based approach as inherently nondevelopmental. Although the disease itself may have a developmental course, along the lines sketched earlier, a "disease" has, according to this view, the same etiology, pathogenesis, risk factors, presentation, and treatment at any stage in the development of the individual. Measles is measles is measles. Thus there are ethical, theoretical, and methodological objections to a disease-based view of psychopathology.

Can developmental science help in this debate? Setting the ethical issue about labeling aside for the moment, empirical research should be able to address such questions as whether a categorical approach makes sense for developmental psychopathology, or under what developmental circumstances one can usefully talk about a "disease."

Categories versus Continua. The debate about whether or not psychopathology should be described in terms of disease categories has generated more heat than light for many decades. The battle lines are drawn roughly speaking between medicine and psychology, with psychiatrists arguing that disease categories are necessary as a means of communication among professionals and as a focus for decision making and treatment (American Psychiatric Association, 1994), whereas child psychologists have been reluctant to use categorical "labels," perhaps in part because they have been particularly aware of how rapidly children change as they grow. Without going into the minutiae of the argument, it is important to point out that there is nothing in developmental science that argues *against* the usefulness or validity of disease categories in principle. A medical condition may have very different presentation, risk factors, and implications for treatment and prevention at different developmental stages and yet still be usefully and validly given the same name. Consider a broken leg as an example. Most people would call a broken leg a broken leg in whomever they saw it. Yet in a 6-month-old baby and a 60-year-old woman there may be considerable differences in the proximal cause (child abuse, falling over), risk factors (drug-addict parent, osteoporosis), and implications for treatment and prevention. Even in adulthood treatment is not impervious to developmental considerations: The treatment of prostate cancer or renal failure may be very different depending on whether the patient is 40 or 80. But these differences are consistent with using the same classification for the condition because of underlying continuities that serve a useful function in guiding decision making and research.

The most powerful argument against the use of disease categories for psychopathology is their inaccuracy and inability to mirror what clinicians and researchers see. These are cogent criticisms. They are made more so when we ask how it is possible to track the development of a disorder across the development of the child. If a child lies at age 6 and steals at age 10, what justification to we have for calling both of these behaviors part of the same syndrome "Conduct Disorder"? Figure 4 organizes some of the main patterns of association that would strengthen the belief in an underlying disease. It is important to note that none of these patterns is in itself conclusive and also that they require a strong etiological theory to bind the data into a convincing story.

The work needed to apply this set of rules to child and adolescent psychopathology has hardly begun. Conduct disorder is the sole exception to this; a series of careful developmental studies has begun to map out the connections between symptom patterns across developmental phases (Figure 4). But a great deal still remains to be done.

Another version of the argument against forcing psychopathology into the Procrustean beds of diagnostic categories is that saying that someone has a diagnosis tells the clinician little about its prognostic significance or how to manage it. It may be more important for the treating clinician to know that an adolescent is suicidal than to know than he or she meets criteria for a DSM-IV (American Psychiatric Association, 1994) diagnosis of major depressive episode. And if all the points made earlier about the variability of presentation across developmental phases are true of a particular disorder, perhaps it is not worth the effort involved to develop methods for making reliable diagnoses that carry across the age range.

It is certainly true that for many management decisions in all branches of medicine, other factors than diagnosis are vitally important. Level of functioning, family circumstances, availability of support services, and pres-

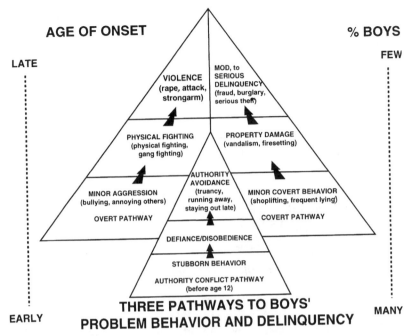

Figure 4. (Reproduced from Loeber, R., Hay, D. F. [1994] Developmental approaches to aggression and conduct problems. In M. Rutter and D. F. Hay [Eds.], *Development through life: A handbook for clinicians.* Oxford: Blackwell Scientific Publications, pp. 488–515. By permission of the publisher.)

ence of other comorbid problems are all factors that can have a major impact on treatment. Current attempts to classify psychiatric disorders into a coherent taxonomy have adopted a "multiaxial" system by which a clinician is encouraged to describe the patient from several points of view, of which psychiatric diagnosis is only one (American Psychiatric Association, 1994; Rutter, Lebovici, & Eisenberg, 1969). For developmental science, the argument about categories versus dimensions is not a useful one. Categories are needed when decisions have to be made and resources allocated to one person rather than another, and for that reason they will always be used in clinical contexts. It is clearly a good idea to have categories available that describe reality as closely as possible. Robins and Guze (1970) have provided a useful approach to evaluating the validity of diagnostic categories in psychiatry, and by these criteria few childhood diagnoses can be said to be well validated (e.g., Hay & Angold, 1993). Lack of validation and disproof are different things, and for the most part it is information that is lacking. However, categories will continue to be used in contexts where decisions have to be made about which child needs which kind of care.

For scientific, rather than administrative, purposes the issues have to do with how most accurately to describe phenomena that are both constant and changing, channeled and variable. It would be premature to conclude that dimensional approaches are necessarily superior for all, or even most, purposes. However, it is clear that a nondevelopmental approach to psychiatric diagnosis has failed. There is too much evidence that patterns of symptomatology and impairment change with age for age-invariant diagnostic criteria to be a reasonable goal. The task ahead is to begin the process of deriving developmentally appropriate criteria, and the reality is that there is as much work to be done using dimensional approaches as there is to define categorical taxa.

The Theory and Methods of Developmental Psychopathology

Given the breadth of scope claimed in this chapter for developmental science and its areas of concern, it is clear that no grand unified theory is yet available for developmental psychopathology. Nor is any one research strategy the answer to all questions. However, there are some general principles that can be recommended, and we review these very briefly in this final section.

Theory. We have developed the argument here that theories guiding developmental psychopathology will be capable of handling both constancy and change, and will be consistent with the notion of goal-directed change (Cicchetti, 1984; Overton & Horowitz, 1991). They will also integrate theory and knowledge about normal and abnormal development into a coherent picture. As an example, Garber (1984) and Sroufe and Rutter (1984) have drawn up outlines linking the developmental "tasks" of various stages of childhood to putative developmental problems. (See Table 1.) In Garber's words: "A child experiencing separation anxiety may not have successfully negotiated the developmental tasks of attachment and dependency during infancy and may have an inadequately developed notion of object permanence. Another child diagnosed as having an aggressive subtype of conduct disorder may be delayed developmentally in his or her perspective-taking ability (Chandler, 1973) and/or capacity for empathy (Ellis, 1982)" (Garber, 1984, p. 38). From this perspective, it should be possible to use a hundred years' worth of knowledge about development to

Table 1. Salient Development Issues

Age (Years)	Issues
0–1	Biological regulation; harmonious didactic interaction; formation of an effective attachment relationship
1–2.5	Exploration, experimentation, and mastery of the object world (care-giver as secure base); individualization and autonomy; responding to external control of impulses
3–5	Flexible self-control; self-reliance; initiative; identification and gender concept; establishing effective peer contact (empathy)
6–12	Social understanding (equity, fairness); gender constancy; same-sex chumships; sense of "industry" (competence); social adjustment
13+	"Formal operations" (flexible perspective taking; "as if" thinking); loyal friendships (same sex); beginning heterosexual relationships; emancipation; identity

Source: "The Domain of Developmental Psychopathology," by L. A. Sroufe and M. Rutter, 1984, *Child Development,* 55, p. 22. By permission of the authors.

set out a series of questions about what abnormal development would look like, and to compare these predictions with clinical experience about the phenomenology of emotional and behavioral deviance at different ages and stages. This would enable us to see, for different areas of symptomatology, what kind of model best fits the data.

Such studies, however, will need to state clearly the developmental theories behind their questions and be explicit (and daring) in their hypotheses about the developmental processes leading to the phenomena observed. Most importantly, they will have to be designed to expect and be capable of assessing changes in psychopathology, rather than try to pin down static patterns of association.

Methods. Historically, the method of developmental psychopathology has been the case study; fine examples can be found in the work of Anna Freud (1965). In the future, we believe that other methods will prove more powerful to tease out the issues laid out earlier. First of all, longitudinal studies will be needed, using within-subject designs to trace the characteristics, and patterns of characteristics, of individual children or groups of children, controlling for specified risk and protective factors, over appropriate developmental phases. Second, these studies will be largely prospective. The anamnestic strategy of psychiatry and clinical psychology has serious limitations as a way of testing developmental hypotheses, above all because of the fallibility and malleability of human memory. (See Morrison & Ornstein, this volume.) Third, studies will be much more careful than they have generally been to specify who is in the sample and to whom the findings generalize. Given the predicted coaction among the various system areas outlined earlier in this chapter, it will be important to describe, and possibly control through sample selection, the family and sociocultural characteristics of subjects. And whether one adopts diagnoses or symptom scales as the method for describing psychopathology, it will be critical to make a careful assessment of comorbidity with symptom areas other than the one under study. The developmental progression identified could be linked to quite a different pathological process. For example, a study investigating the mood variability believed to be characteristic of adolescent depression suggested that, at least in hospitalized adolescents, a high degree of lability typified depressed patients with a comorbid "acting out" diagnosis, but not patients who were only depressed (Costello, Benjamin, Angold, & Silver, 1991). The high rate of comorbidity among psychiatric diagnoses using current diagnostic methods indicates that individual areas of psychopathology need to be studied in relation to one another. If depressed children are also often anxious and conduct disordered (see Angold & Costello, 1992), to focus solely on depression is to ignore the phenomenology.

In this context, we have found epidemiology, the study of patterns of disease distribution in time and place (Lilienfeld & Lilienfeld, 1980), to provide an extremely useful framework within which to think about the theoretical and methodological problems of developmental psychopathology. Epidemiologists have been grappling for over one hundred years with issues of generalizability, validity of diagnostic categories, stability and change in the manifestation of pathology across time, and the relationships among risk, protection, and pathology. They have been quick to adapt advances in statistical methods to the problems of tracking continuity and change. Of particular importance to developmental psychopathology has been the work by psychiatric epidemiologists in the past two decades to improve the assessment of psychopathology across the age range, in the service of reliable case identification. They are currently turning their attention to the assessment of functional impairment and risk factors and to extending our capacity to make reliable assessments in difficult age ranges, such as early childhood and the transition from adolescence to adulthood. With these tools to hand, we shall be able to get on with the task of mapping the developmental pathways to pathology across the various developmental system areas. The goal of this effort was defined for us almost a decade ago:

Developmental psychopathology . . . should bridge fields of study, span the life cycle, and aid in the discovery of important new truths about the processes underlying adaptation and maladaptation, as well as the best means of preventing or ameliorating psychopathology. Moreover, this discipline should contribute greatly to reducing the dualisms that exist between the clinical study of and research into childhood and adult disorders, between the behavioral and biological sciences, between developmental psychology and psychopathology, and between basic and applied science. (Cicchetti, 1990, p. 20)

10 Culture and Cognition in Developmental Perspective

Jonathan Tudge, Sarah Putnam, and Jaan Valsiner

In this chapter we focus on the relation between culture and cognition from a developmental perspective, emphasizing learning to read as a way of illustrating the co-constructive nature of development. The ideas expressed in the previous chapters have provided the perfect context within which to provide a developmental approach to this issue. Magnusson and Cairns's first proposition stated, "An individual develops and functions psychologically as an integrated organism. Maturational, experiential, and cultural contributions are fused in ontogeny. Single aspects do not develop and function in isolation, and they should not be divorced from the totality in analysis" (Magnusson & Cairns, Chap. 2). This proposition was illustrated nicely by Gottlieb (Chap. 4), who focused primarily on interactions (or coactions) at the genetic level, but persuasively argued that human functioning cannot be understood without consideration of the complexity of interactions at all levels, from the cellular to the cultural.

In fact, many of the points raised by Gottlieb with reference to genetic-organismic interaction would apply equally to the relation between individuals and culture. For example, his statements, "Genetic activity (expression) can be influenced by events inside and outside the cell, including the environment of the organism" and "Considerable morphological and behavioral 'evolution' can occur without changing the genetic composition of an interbreeding population," could with little difficulty be rewritten to account for the development of individuals in cultures, including change from within the culture and without. As Magnusson and Cairns's second proposition put it: "An individual develops and functions in a dynamic, continuous, and reciprocal process of interaction with his or her environment, including relations with other individuals, groups, and the subculture," while, at the same time, "novel patterns of individual functioning arise during individual ontogeny" (fourth proposition). Gottlieb's perspective, namely that "the developing organism's usual or typical experience can play a canalizing role that not only brings about species-specific behavior but also prevents the developing organism from being susceptible to non-species-typical forms of stimulation" (1991b, p. 6), also applies to the sociocultural levels of his model.

A Systemic Approach to Development

The systemic approach to development views culture as one part of a system in dynamic relation with all other parts. If we accept the validity of the previously mentioned propositions, it becomes clear that human development can be no more explained by focusing solely on the genetic, biological, or biochemical properties of developing organisms, or on the phenotypic expression of these properties, than it can be by considering solely the social, cultural, or historical contexts within which those organisms exist. We may choose to shed light on only one part of the system, but to ignore the system as a whole is to provide a relatively impoverished account of developmental processes. Moreover, as the authors of previous chapters in this volume have argued, developmental systems are by their very nature not static; to study them therefore requires the use of research strategies that allow examination of development both in context and in process.

To take this systemic view of development means that dichotomies are instantly forsworn; just as genes and environments exist in dynamic interaction so that one cannot sensibly describe their separate influences on development, so too is the relation between culture and cognition one of intricate, dynamic transaction in the course of development. This is not the way in which most scholars within the fields of human development, psychology, and cultural anthropology have viewed the relation between culture and cognition, however. As Cole (1985) pointed out, Wilhelm Wundt divided psychology into two primary categories – psychological functions that may be thought of as belonging to the individual on the one hand, and those that may be viewed as social or cultural on the other. The latter represent "mental products which are created by a community of human life and are, therefore, inexplicable in terms merely of individual consciousness, since they presuppose the reciprocal action of many" (Wundt, 1916, p. 3).

This division into individual and sociocultural factors has introduced into 20th-century psychology a basic distinction that is constantly used to segregate different streams of knowledge from one another (Danziger, 1990; Kroger & Scheibe, 1990), thereby hindering understanding of human development. Different contemporary directions in psychology – cognitive, social, cross-cultural, and cultural-contextual – have been taken, separate from one another. Thus the role of culture in human cognitive and social development has been viewed differently by psychologists who pledge allegiance to one or another of those domains of discourse.

Perspectives on the Relation between Culture and Cognition

Cognitive Pychologists

Most cognitive psychologists share a view of cognition as being "in the head" (a "person" variable) and of contexts (race, class, ethnicity, culture) as variables that exert an influence on cognitive performance but whose impact may be controlled for. The traditional belief among cognitive developmental psychologists is that one goal of the field should be to uncover "basic" cognitive processes that are impervious to cultural influence and that reflect, instead, developmental (age-related) factors. According to Shweder, "the aim [of general psychology] is to get behind superficial appearances, local manifestations, and external resources to isolate the intrinsic central processing mechanism of the mental life and describe the invariant laws of its operation" (1990, p. 5).

As Morrison and Ornstein (this volume) point out, contemporary cognitive psychologists do not ignore such contextual factors as race, ethnicity, gender, and the local contexts within which experiments are run (home or laboratory, for example). However, these factors are treated, in Whiting's (1976) terms, as "packaged" independent variables that in some fashion have an impact upon performance and may serve to differentiate the subjects of the experiment. Instead, cognitive psychologists may examine the speed or depth of processing in subjects from specified backgrounds, or they may focus on memory performance under different conditions (contexts). All too rarely do mainstream cognitive psychologists "unpackage" these backgrounds or contexts, that is, examine the processes that may help us to understand the relation between race or socioeconomic status and whatever performance characteristics are being assessed.

Cross-cultural Psychologists

Some cognitive psychologists are more interested than others in the contextual (particularly cultural) variables that have an impact on cognition. For the most part, however, cross-cultural psychologists, although more interested in cultural variation in performance, accept the prevailing opinion of their mainstream colleagues that cognition resides "in the head." Their view is that the content (though not the nature) of cognition is highly affected by culture and that performance (though not competence) is likely to be greatly influenced by test familiarity, and so on. Nevertheless, underlying structures are there to be uncovered. One way in which efforts have been made to achieve this has been to translate the test materials into forms that are more meaningful to the participants, so as to allow children's "true" competence to be expressed (Glick, 1975; Irvine, 1978; Laboratory of Comparative Human Cognition, 1983; Nyiti, 1982).

Plenty of group differences in performance have been identified by cross-cultural cognitive-developmental psychologists (the age at which children attain concrete operational thinking, children's abilities to classify objects, performance on tests of memory, and so on), but these differences tend to be set within one of two frameworks, both of which presuppose the existence of a central-processing mechanism. The first is that this mechanism has developed less fully in certain groups, due to experiential limitations, and the second is that the mechanism is the same in all groups but that tests developed for use with one group do not adequately tap the abilities of another and that "culture-free" or "culture-fair" tests are required (Laboratory of Comparative Human Cognition, 1983; Shweder, 1990).

Cultural Anthropologists

Cultural anthropologists have traditionally been more interested in cultural practices than have the psychologists, focusing their attention on kinship classifications, initiation rites, group processes, and so on, which vary from culture to culture (Cole, 1985; Shweder, 1990). They have tended to leave consideration of cognition to the psychologists. Cultural anthropologists and psychologists (whether general, developmental, or cross-cultural) have thereby tended to reinforce Wundt's dualistic approach to mind and society, cognition and culture. (A recent exception to this tendency is provided by Shore [1991], who calls for cultural anthropologists to be as much interested in the "how" as in the "what" of meaning making and takes a perspective very similar to one that we espouse.)

The perspectives just outlined tend to view contextual factors, including culture, as variables that allow examination of differences in performance as a function of membership in one or another social group. Variables can be controlled for, or manipulated in interesting ways, in order to examine their impact upon cognitive performance. Interaction effects are fairly common, but are treated at a statistical level. They do not influence the prevailing belief that independent and dependent variables are separate entities, with the former exerting sometimes unidirectional, sometimes bidirectional, sometimes insignificant effects on the latter.

Cultural-Contextual Psychologists

By comparison, proponents of what we are calling the cultural-contextual perspective believe that culture and cognition are not variables but constitute dynamic processes, continually in development and continually transforming one another. A simple unidirectional model (culture directs cognition) is unlikely to aid understanding the processes whereby cultures (including cultural institutions, skills, tools, values, and beliefs) are passed on from generation to generation while at the same time undergoing dynamic flux, altering as a result of the changing needs, beliefs, and technological advances of their members. From a bidirectional perspective on the relation between individuals and the contexts and cultures in which they develop, active developing people construct their own selves using cultural means and in the process construct their cultures anew. In so doing they always go beyond the state of culture that existed in the lives of the parental generation (Valsiner, 1987, 1989).

The lack of success that mainstream cognitive-developmental psychologists have had in "unpacking" the complex package of "variables" is a logical consequence of their general methodological assumptions, including the historical "behavioristic" version and the new "cognitivist" reincarnation (Valsiner, 1991a). The perspective of developmental science as we understand it requires the use of basic assumptions that lead to the replacement of the person-based "variable"-oriented approach by one that is systemic. This approach has been termed "co-constructionist" (Wozniak, 1986), "persons-in-contexts" (Valsiner, 1987), "individuals-acting-with-mediational-means" (Wertsch, 1991), and "person-process-context" (Bronfenbrenner & Crouter, 1983).

The co-constructionist perspective adopted by cultural-contextual psychologists in developmental psychology entails analysis of the processes by which developing individuals actively relate to the culturally organized context and create their own new forms of conduct that depend on the nature of the context (Valsiner, 1988b). Our view is therefore that a dualistic approach to culture and cognition should be abandoned and that their interrelations or co-constructions need to become the focus of theoretical and empirical attention. As Rogoff argued, "Rather than viewing individuals, their social partners, and the sociocultural context as independent 'influences' or factors of development, I argue that they represent differing angles of analysis of an integrated process" (1990, p. 26). From this perspective, it therefore makes more sense to think of cognizing rather than cognition; thinking *about* something rather than thought in the abstract, solving a problem rather than ability to problem solve, remembering something rather than memory. In this sense, thinking cannot be considered a "person-variable" but a "person-in-context" ongoing process, that incorporates simultaneously individual characteristics, the context of the activity the individual is engaged in, and developmental processes. In other words, and borrowing from Bateson (1972), Geertz (1973), and Wertsch (1991), mind is viewed in the co-constructionist perspective as not being "in the head" or the simple product of things "outside the head" but stretching "beyond the head" in such a way that internal and external are enmeshed.

From "Variables" to Adequate Units of Analysis

The co-constructionist perspective sets clear expectations for rethinking our methodology of research on human development. That is, culture and cognition cannot be thought of as variables, independent or dependent, that allow separate examination, just as nature and nurture are no longer thought of as exerting separate influences on development. Interaction thus should not be thought of in its statistical sense, but thought of rather as a whole that is more than the sum of its separate parts. As Bronfenbrenner playfully expressed it: "Interactions are the main effects" (U. Bronfenbrenner, personal communication, 1985). Or, in Rogoff's words: "In the contextual perspective, meaning and context are not elements that can be handled separately or derived from adding elements together. Context is not so much a set of stimuli that impinge upon a person as it is a web of relations interwoven to form the fabric of meaning" (1982, p. 149).

This approach carries with it the notion that what occurs on any single level of analysis (biological, cognitive, cultural) influences what happens on all others; this is not to say that meaningful research must always consider all levels, but that a cultural-contextualist perspective requires units of analysis that cross these levels. This perspective also has clear implications for the way in which development is conceptualized. Overton (1984) and with Horowitz (1991), for example, wrote in favor of a teleonomic approach to development, one that stresses an ideal endpoint that is the standard against which to judge the extent of development (see also Angold & Costello, 1991; Costello & Angold, this volume). A contextualist perspective is unlikely to focus on ideal endpoints, however, which led

Overton to argue that contextualism "cannot form the basis for scientifically viable research programs" (1984, p. 218). A more complete understanding of the culture-contextualist perspective requires a better-differentiated notion of development. Gottlieb (1970, 1983), for example, has distinguished between "predetermined" and "probabilistic" epigenesis. The former refers to an organismic (Overton, 1984; Pepper, 1942) view of development in which an ideal endpoint will be reached as long as nothing interferes with the biological-maturational unfolding of the organism's orthogenetic potential. By contrast, a probabilistic epigenetic viewpoint (or that of "limited indeterminacy" [Valsiner, 1987]) captures the view that development is essentially plastic, designating, according to Gottlieb, "the view that the behavioral development of individuals within a species does not follow an invariant or inevitable course, and, more specifically, that the sequence or outcome of individual behavioral development is probable (with respect to norms) rather than certain" (1970, p. 123).

However, plasticity of development by no means implies a lack of constraints. As Gollin (1981) has argued, organisms are organized and have internal coherence – and so, for the most part, are the contexts within which they exist. "The quality of the organization provides opportunities for change as well as constraints upon the extent and direction of change. Thus, while the determination of change is probabilistic, it is not chaotic" (p. 232). Development, in a probabilistic universe, is thus not simply random change, but follows a path that can best be understood by focusing on the multiple levels of organization that constitute individuals living in a social world.

From the perspective of developmental psychology, it might be worth viewing the culture-cognition relation as akin to the parent-child relation; having a child makes one a parent, and one cannot have a child without becoming a parent. In other words, the two are enmeshed, and although the relationship between them indeed changes over time, and eventually death separates them, it is not possible to understand one without considering the other. Nevertheless, the two are separate entities, with different ways of making sense of themselves, each other, the world, and so on. Similarly, culture and the individuals within cultures and individual cognitive processes are not one and the same, just as the various parts of the human organism (gene, cytoplasm) are not one and the same.

In the terms introduced by one of us (Valsiner, 1987, 1989), we can use the perspective of "inclusive separation" to study the development of cognitive functions and their social context. Cognitive functions come into existence and differentiate due to the constant challenges and adaptation tasks that the social world entails. The cognitive and social facets of human development are differentiated but yet mutually interdependent, and it is this process that holds the key to the mystery of human development. Cognitive functioning and the social and cultural contexts in which they express themselves can, of course, be examined separately. Cognitive psychologists do indeed study cognitive processes with little or no attention paid to the social and cultural world in which those processes are expressed, just as geneticists may study genes without being overly concerned with the ways in which they are expressed. However, the central challenge that the authors in this volume have extended to developmentalists is to study development in a way that deals with the interrelation of various parts of the developing system (this position is discussed in more detail in Tudge, Shanahan, & Valsiner, in press).

The core methodological issue is how to learn about this interrelation as a continually developing process. This issue requires researchers to address the issue of appropriate units of analysis and to re-think whether the methodological canons of nondevelopmental psychology are of use in developmental science (Asendorpf & Valsiner, 1992; Cairns, 1986; Gigerenzer, Swijtink, Porter, Daston, Beatty, & Kruger, 1989; Winegar & Valsiner, 1992). It is clear that the unit of analysis that would retain the developmental nature of the cultural co-construction process has extensions in three directions:

1. It has to entail a sequence of events that takes place in real time.
2. It has to include both the intrapersonal (cognitive, affective, temperamental, biological, maturational) and interpersonal facets of individual activity.
3. The unit of analysis has to include both the person's activity and the context in which it takes place. That context necessarily includes both the physical objects (and/or persons) and their cultural meanings, as well as the understanding of the context that the acting person has constructed.

Such a unit of analysis constitutes a Gestalt-like process, within which both the person and the environment are shown to be meaningfully related to one another. In other words, developmental science operates with the notion of systemic organization not only at the level of theorizing but also at the level of the actual analysis of the processes of development.

Historical Foundations of the Co-constructionist Approach

This co-constructionist position is far from new. A number of theorists have, albeit in different ways, focused attention primarily on mutually constituting and constructing systems. For example, Jean Piaget viewed the developing organism in continuous interaction (interactivity) with the surrounding environment, both physical and social. Because most commentaries on Piaget stress the child's interaction with the physical and logico-mathematical worlds, it is worth emphasizing Piaget's statement, "Social life is a necessary condition for the development of logic. We thus believe that social life transforms the individual's very nature" (1977, p. 239). He believed that developing mental structures develop only as a function of experience, activity over time, with the physical and social world. Piaget's mechanisms of development (assimilation and accommodation, which, as equilibration is achieved, bring about a developmental synthesis) were derived from James M. Baldwin's concepts of circular reaction and persistent imitation (1892, 1894a, 1906).

Baldwin's perspective is one of the roots of the co-constructionist approach to human development. The processes of persistent imitation of other persons (who are both variable and intrapersonally inconsistent [Baldwin, 1894b]) in ontogeny constitute the basis of children's constructions of their cognitive functions and meanings, according to Baldwin. The development of the self is mediated through experience, including both inter- and intrapersonal experience. Baldwin coined the term "sembled meanings" (a translation of Theodor Lipps's *Einfühlung*) as a way of expressing what contemporary psychologists term "empathy" (Baldwin, 1906). For Baldwin, this term involved the unity of personal and social development. He explicitly viewed the developing person's experience as always consisting of meaningful experience of the world, with language as an appropriate mediator, being both social and individual (1908). Baldwin claimed, furthermore, that experiencing is both an event and a vehicle of development: "*All experience as such is . . . a sembled meaning; it is not only context, it is also developing inner life.* It follows that . . . the subject having the experience intends *any process of constituting this experience as well as this experience as constituted by his own process*" (1908, p. 63). In other words, persons in activity relate to the world (experiencing it in terms of subjective meanings) and create the world by experiencing it. Baldwin's evolution to the basic process involved in this active construction of self–world relations (persistent imitation) was later adopted by Lev Vygotsky in his emphasis on the semiotic reconstruction of the social world (implied in his cultural-historical theory) and in his discussion of the "zone of proximal development" (Kozulin, 1990; Tudge, 1990; Tudge & Winterhoff, 1993; Valsiner & van der Veer, 1993; Wertsch, 1985, 1991).

Vygotsky's cultural-historical theory carried Baldwin's pioneering ideas further and brought them closer to child development per se. Vygotsky's consistent emphasis on units of analysis in sociogenetic investigation that encapsulated the individual and social simultaneously (see Valsiner, 1988b) was paired with the constant insistence that human development is a process of semiotically mediated construction of people's experiences (Wertsch, 1991). The core of his cultural-historical theory ("sociocultural theory" in Wertsch's [1991] terms) involves the emergence (in both phylogenesis and ontogenesis) of tool- and sign-construction activities and the use of tools and signs first in extrapersonal (interpersonal and in individual play with objects) and then in intrapersonal domains (Luria, 1928; Vygotsky, 1929). In ontogenetic development, the resources of sign construction are made available to children by social others but, particularly in the case of speech, in ways that allow great variability. These constructed signs subsequently become internalized in novel forms, through the "growing-in" of children's previously external speech inward into the mind, and turn into thinking processes (Vygotsky, 1987; Vygotsky & Luria, 1930/1984).

This process of internalization links Vygotsky's sociogenetic views directly with those of Pierre Janet (van der Veer & Valsiner, 1988). In fact, Vygotsky's sociogenetic postulate – that psychological functions appear first at the interpersonal level and only subsequently at the intrapersonal level – followed quite directly from Janet. According to Janet, the social origins of psychological functions gradually become unrecognizable in the course of individual activity, as the speech component and action become increasingly separate from one another (except for cases of psychopathology – see Janet, 1921, 1925).

This linkage between social and individual factors in development was also a feature of John Dewey's thinking. For example, Dewey declared:

> Every individual has grown up, and always must grow up, in a social medium. His responses grow intelligent, or gain meaning, simply because he lives and acts in a medium of accepted meanings and values. . . . Through social intercourse, through sharing of the activities embodying beliefs, he gradually acquires a mind of his own. The conception of mind as a purely isolated possession of the self is at the very antipodes of the truth. The self achieves mind in the degree in which knowledge of things

is incarnate in the life about him; the self is not a separate mind building up knowledge anew on its own account. (1916, p. 344)

Dewey argued, echoing Vygotsky, that joint activity with others who are more competent in the social group into which children are growing is essential for individual development. For example, in Dewey's discussion of the way in which a child comes to understand the meaning of the word "hat" he stated:

> In short, the sound h-a-t gains meaning in precisely the same way that the thing "hat" gains it, by being used in a given way. And they acquire the same meaning with the child which they have with the adult because they are used in a common experience by both. The guarantee for the same manner of use is found in the fact that the thing and the sound are first employed in a joint activity, as a means of setting up an active connection between the child and a grown-up. (ibid., p. 18)

The historical roots of the co-constructionist perspective also include the work of George Herbert Mead, whose ideas developed in conjunction with the work of Baldwin and Janet (Valsiner & van der Veer, 1988). Mead posited a dialectical relation between the developing "I" who is active, and takes on social roles (thus becoming "me") or "the organized set of attitudes of others which one . . . assumes" (1934, p. 175). As was the case for the other proponents of this perspective, the ongoing dynamic relation between the two parts of the self ("I" and "me") is based on the individual's ongoing social experience. Mead stated:

> Our contention is that mind can never find expression, and could never have come into existence at all, except in terms of a social environment; that an organized set or pattern of social relations and interactions (especially those of communication by means of gestures functioning as significant symbols and thus creating a universe of discourse) is necessarily presupposed by it and involved in its nature. (1956, pp. 256–257)

It is important to recognize that these various foundations of what we are calling the co-constructionist approach have had some impact on developmental psychology, particularly in the last decade or so. Urie Bronfenbrenner's stress upon an ecological approach to human development, in which he called for "person-process-context" models to be employed in psychological research (1993; Bronfenbrenner & Crouter, 1983) is just one example of recent formulations of this perspective. Barbara Rogoff's (1990) focus on the need to examine the ways in which young children, in the course of guided participation, come to appropriate (make sense of, while at the same time transforming) their social world is another. Michael Cole (1985; Newman, Griffin, & Cole, 1989), Jim Wertsch (1985, 1991), and Peeter Tulviste (1989, 1991) are others who are recent proponents of the perspective. Perhaps not surprisingly, they have all been influenced by Vygotsky and the cultural-historical school. We shall therefore provide a little more detail of Vygotsky's theoretical position.

The cultural-historical school, of which Vygotsky was the principal formulator, emphasizes that individual and social factors are not separate but instead are mutually constitutive or co-constructive processes. The appropriate unit of analysis, therefore, cannot be something at either the individual or social level but something that captures both. Goal-directed activity satisfies that requirement, according to a number of scholars whose ideas were influenced by the cultural-historical school (Cole, 1985; Davydov & Radzikhovskii, 1985; Leontyev, 1981; Wertsch, 1985, 1991; Zinchenko, 1985). Leontyev argued, "Human psychology is concerned with the activity of concrete individuals, which takes place either in a collective – i.e., jointly with other people – or in a situation in which the subject deals directly with the surrounding world of objects – e.g., at the potter's wheel or the writer's desk" (1981, p. 47). Objects are not viewed in this formulation as separate from human creation or intentionality. Even when considering objects in the "natural" world, the social world is ever present; one person's flower is another's weed.

Objects also have particular significance in the sociohistorical perspective insofar as they are tools that allow greater control over the world. Vygotsky (1981) distinguished between technical and psychological tools, with the former referring to those that help humans control aspects of their external world (an ax to chop wood, for example) and the latter referring to control over their internal world. A mnemonic device to aid memory or a word ("stop" or "press") to help control motor responses would both be examples of psychological tools. For Vygotsky, words constitute a prime example of such a psychological tool; they have a phenomenal impact upon children's development, being used not only to control oneself and those around but serving as the main means for learning about one's world and one's culture.

Semiotic activity, of which language use is a primary component, thus is simultaneously an individual and a cultural activity. Speech is at the same time internal and external, linking an individual to the social world that he or she currently inhabits and to the history of that world, its culture, its meanings, and its values. Thus to understand speech requires knowing the varying contexts that help provide support for the construction of meaning. These contexts can be conceptualized as a set of levels, from the most proximal to the most distal. Speech, or language activity to serve a particular goal, can be considered at the level of *microgenesis* (the development of an utterance or dialogue), *ontogenesis* (the development of the individual's ability to use the tool over time), *history and culture* (the development of modes of using the tool that are considered appropriate in that culture at that time), and *phylogenesis* (the evolutionary development of language and literacy). This interlocking set of levels with which to make sense of a child's activity constitutes an approach to cognition that does not seek to separate it from the contexts that give it meaning.

Culture and Cognition in Context: The Example of Reading

To provide a more concrete focus for this chapter we shall examine one activity, reading, in order to illustrate both the cultural-historical perspective and the central arguments – that processes of thinking cannot be divorced from the social, historical, and cultural contexts within which they are taking place, and that any activity, reading included, is co-constructed by individuals and the contexts in which they are active. From this perspective, reading, like any goal-directed activity, can be only partially understood if only one of these four levels is considered in isolation. For example, the steps or processes of performing the activity (solving specific reading or writing tasks at home or in school, including any assistance being given) constitute the microgenetic level. To give meaning to these microgenetic processes, however, requires knowing the individual's age and his or her current independent ability to perform the activity (the ontogenetic level). The type of assistance provided for a 3-year-old beginning reader is likely to differ from that provided a 9-year-old beginning reader, whereas the help provided a child who is almost fluent is likely to be very different from that provided one who is struggling to learn.

An ontogenetic focus, therefore, provides meaning for the microgenetic processes themselves. But complete understanding of learning to read (when considered ontogenetically) can be elucidated by awareness of the third level – that of history and culture, in particular the emergence and development of writing systems and the available tools and institutional supports (or hindrances) for its use. Availability of materials that can be read, supports for reading, expectations about who should learn to read, and the age at which reading is considered an appropriate activity differ widely both across cultures and over time in any one culture. Finally, these historical and cultural differences are likely to be understood to the fullest by placing them at the level of phylogeny, the emergence and development of semiotic systems in evolution as well as the current species-typical means for being literate.

Moreover, reading is necessarily a co-constructive activity and allows us to focus on a specific activity to illustrate the ways in which culture and cognition are intrinsically and necessarily related. On the one hand, there is cultural support for reading in highly literate societies, partly in that written symbols are ever present and partly in that those who are more competent try hard to help children learn to read and thus to learn about their culture. At the same time, children actively try to make sense of the symbols that they see around them, both in books and in other contexts. Moreover, while children are learning to read they are simultaneously producing their own text.

Literacy in Phylogeny

In cultural-historical theory, the development of tool use, of which symbols are the most important, is quite critical (Leontyev, 1981). As Gelb expressed it: "As language distinguishes man from animal, so writing distinguishes civilized man from barbarian" (Gelb, 1952, p. 221). The development of the first tokens, to serve as tools to remember the identity and quantity of different objects, was probably in the Middle East around 10,000 years ago (Schmandt-Besserat, 1978) and has been viewed as the precursor to literacy (Damerow, 1988). The next known development of this type of semiotically mediated form was approximately 6,000 years later with the introduction of cuneiform ("wedge-shaped") writing, pictographic representations etched in clay (Damerow, 1988; Schmandt-Besserat, 1978). Whereas the tablets had literally "stood for" the object being represented, the clay pictures symbolized them – a critical step in the development of literacy, and one that had profound cognitive consequences (Damerow, 1988; Donald, 1991). This semiotic and technological change constituted a giant step for humankind for many reasons, among them that people needed to be able to understand this new technology. "The invention of writing and of a convenient system of records on paper has had a greater influence in uplifting the human race than any other intellectual achievement in the career of man" (Breasted, 1926, quoted in Gelb, 1952, p. 221).

This view implies that the causal direction is from writing to civilization. In fact, as would be argued from a co-constructionist perspective, the development of a new technology is simultaneously responsible for new modes of organization and thought while at the same time dependent on new forms of thinking. This point is made well by Gelb:

> Everywhere in the Ancient World writing appears first at a time which is characterized by a simultaneous growth of all those various elements which together make for what we usually call civilization. Whenever writing appears it is accompanied by a remarkable development of government, arts, commerce, industry, metallurgy, extensive means of transportation, full agriculture and domestication of animals, in contrast to which all the previous periods, without writing, make the impression of cultures of a rather primitive make-up. There is no need, however, to urge that the introduction of writing was the factor which was responsible for the birth of original civilizations. It seems rather that all the factors – geographic, social, economic – leading towards a full civilization simultaneously created a complex of conditions which could not function without writing. Or, to put it in other words: Writing exists only in a civilization and a civilization cannot exist without writing. (ibid., pp. 221–222)

To express this view in ontogenetic time, rather than phylogenetic, one can refer to Piaget, who argued that children cannot truly discuss matters with others until they have attained concrete operational thought because until then their thinking is highly egocentric. On the other hand, Piaget also believed that peer discussion was highly influential in bringing about a decline in egocentric thinking (Tudge & Rogoff, 1989). This apparent paradox can be understood only when viewing development in dynamic, dialectical flux.

Reading in Historical and Cultural Terms

At this level, the question of interest relates to the reasons for literacy coming to be viewed as important and the particular forms of literacy developed. Religion appears to have played a key role in many societies, for one impetus to read has been to be able to read religious texts (Akinnaso, 1991; Duranti & Ochs, 1986; Goody, 1987; Heubner, 1987; Schieffelin & Cochran-Smith, 1984). The growth of technology, both in terms of requirements to make sense of that technology (considerably helped by being able to read) and in terms of the ability to make text widely available, once printing presses had developed (Eisenstein, 1979; Wagner, 1991), appears critical to understanding the growth of literacy.

The link between technological complexity and reading is complicated, however, with clear implications for cognition stemming from the developing practice of helping children learn via books rather than in the course of participation in activity. Literal apprenticeship, participation, and observation give way in literate societies to "symbolized" (if not "decontextualized") learning. Learning increasingly becomes tied to reading (a tool to make sense of tools) and becomes decreasingly tied to the contexts of the activities and skills that children have to understand to become economically self-sufficient in their society.

Reading, over historical time, increasingly has become an essential means of economic and political advance. Control over this technology (being able to master its use) provides enormous power, as revolutionaries from Luther to Lenin have been aware. Governments have long feared providing the poor with opportunities for learning to read, as late as the last century. For example, in England the president of the Royal Society argued successfully against a bill to establish a national system of elementary education because "it would in effect be found to be prejudicial to their morals and happiness; it would teach them to despise their lot in life" (quoted in Turman, 1987). American slaveowners made precisely the same argument in relation to their slaves (Turman, 1987), and the Russian minister of public education under Alexander I and Nicholas I declared: "To instruct all the people, or even a disproportionate number of them, in literacy would do more harm than good" (quoted in Johnson, 1950, p. 88). By contrast, Marx, Engels, and Lenin believed that the education of the masses was essential for the development of communism (Tudge, 1973), and the ability to read was a cornerstone in the assault on oppression by Paulo Freire, the radical Brazilian educator (Freire, 1972).

Heath and Thomas (1984) argued, however, that just as Gelb stated with regard to the development of literacy in phylogenetic development, it is not possible to make simple causal statements about the "consequences" of literacy:

> In spite of all the claims about the consequences of literacy, recent research has shown that the changes which have come with literacy across societies and historical periods have been neither consistent nor predictable. We cannot yet make generalizations about literacy as a causal factor, nor indeed as a necessary accompaniment of specific features of society. The prior conditions and co-occurring contexts of literacy in each society determine its forms, values, and functions. (p. 68)

Culture, with its role in defining the value, form, and function of written language, also defines the ways in which literacy develops for its members. The emergence of reading and writing for individuals in different cultures, cultures both within a society and between societies, appears to vary widely in relationship with the co-occurring contexts of literacy. These contexts of literacy form a pattern that gives a specific character to the processes of learning to read, a pattern made up of whether and to what degree written materials are present or pervasive in culture, how written materials are used, the attitudes and expectations of members of the culture toward learning to read and write, and the functions written language serves for members of the culture. Without understanding of this cultural pattern, the processes of learning to read in ontogenesis can only be poorly comprehended.

Cultural-contextual researchers, focusing on nonliterate communities in which adults and children have fairly recently been introduced to reading, provide evidence that the patterns of early reading that in the West are viewed as the norm are far from being universal. Schieffelin and Cochran-Smith (1984), for example, described approaches to literacy among the Kaluli of New Guinea. Literacy was introduced by missionaries, with Bible reading the prime (often sole) reason both for its introduction and for its use by individual Kaluli. In general the Kaluli viewed reading's utility as highly limited, of no relevance for their everyday lives, and as too difficult to be taught to children. Printed material was never made easily available to children, and parents (even those who themselves were learning to read) considered reading to their children as *ba madali* (to no purpose). Moreover, the form of interaction when reading occurred was quite unlike that found in all other contexts. Duranti and Ochs (1986) found a similar discontinuity from typical adult-child interactions when children were learning to read in school in Western Samoa.

The cognitive consequences of reading, as with literacy in general, are difficult to assess – primarily because literacy almost always occurs within schooled populations. Difficulties abound, also, in definitions of literacy, which can range from being able to read and write one's own name to undergoing a set number of years of schooling to being conceived of as literate within one's own group (an "emic" approach to literacy) to competent performance on standardized tests (Langer, 1987; Wagner, 1991). These definitional differences notwithstanding, it is widely held (see, for example, reviews by Laboratory of Comparative Human Cognition, 1983; Rogoff, 1981) that literacy has general and widespread effects upon cognition. However, disentangling the confound of literacy and schooling has not been easy. Scribner and Cole's research (1981) among the Vai of Liberia is thus particularly interesting, in that it provided the opportunity of teasing apart literacy from schooling. The Vai use four different writing systems, each associated with a different activity; thus the indigenous language is used for family and community matters, Arabic for religious purposes (reading the Koran), Arabic for record keeping, and English for communicating with teachers and other government officials. Various cognitive tests (found to differentiate schooled from nonschooled individuals in other cultures) revealed that those who had attended school (in English) performed better on many tests (though not all) compared to the nonschooled Vai and Arabic literates, who did not differ from nonliterates on logical and classifications tasks. However, most importantly, function-specific cognitive change was found – people literate in Vai and English (the two literacies used widely for letter writing) performed better at the communication tasks than Arabic literates and nonliterates, Arabic literates performed better than other groups on certain types of memory task (remembering strings of words), and the Vai literates performed better on tests in which the graphic units were syllabic (rather than words), the form most familiar to them.

Even in a literate society, cultural variations are to be found. For example, Heath (1983, 1986a, 1986b) found that the way in which the white middle-class children in her study learned to read was likely to serve them well in school, whereas this was not the case for the working-class white and black children she studied. Each of the cultural communities in which Heath gathered her data developed a distinct pattern for the use of reading and writing, a pattern that appeared to achieve the different cognitive and social goals of each culture. The question arises, however, as to why it should be that the black families studied by Heath had different perspectives to books and print. It is necessary, as always, to move between levels – to understand the interpersonal relation to language, one must understand the cultural and historical, as well as the individual, levels. Thus Ogbu (1987) emphasized the impact of approaches to literacy that have developed over generations among blacks. McLane's study of inner-city parents and children (reported in McLane & McNamee, 1990) provides support for the notion that the more didactic approaches to reading adopted by poor parents might reflect a lack of confidence in the schools their children attended.

Reading in Ontogenesis

To understand the process of learning oral language requires consideration, at the very minimum, of biological and maturational developments, on the one hand, and input from the social world, on the other. Even though deaf children have particular problems (especially those born to hearing parents; see, for example, Marschark, 1993), in all but the most exceptional circumstances, children learn to talk. The same is not true of learning to read, even for children who grow up in a literate society. Reading, in fact, constitutes a particularly interesting activity because whereas the same interaction of maturational and social factors is necessary for reading to occur, they are even less sufficient than is the case with oral language.

Experience with books is not the only source of literacy experience for children (Anderson & Stokes, 1984; Heath, 1986b; Wells, 1981). Children's first exposure to print, at least in literate technologically complex societies, is less likely to come in the form of books, than from the text that is ubiquitous in signs, on packaged food items, in advertising, on television (both in programming designed for children and "adult" programming), and in all the "ambient print" that is such a feature of the environment in literate societies. Adults may draw attention to those signs, but children are as likely to do it themselves. Unlike oral language, which is so embedded in communication that children are able to learn it without ever being aware that they could not talk at some earlier stage, written language is a puzzle that children become acutely aware surrounds them, a powerful tool used by more competent others who, for example, can find out what is on television by reading the newspaper. Children quickly learn the meaning of symbols that are important to them, the "M" for McDonald's being only one of the many examples (Anderson & Stokes, 1984; Leichter, 1984).

Attitudes and expectations of members of the culture toward learning to read and write are particularly apparent for children who do not learn to read at an age considered to be "on time" within a particular culture. In a culture in which age norms are widely available for reading, the implications of being a nonreader are strikingly different for those younger than the norm, at the norm, and older than the norm. Almost from the start, the discrepancy between the poorer readers and their more accomplished classmates is made obvious to all by the written material they have access to: "Are you still on the blue reader?" marks the discrepancy immediately. Problems are often compounded by the fact that those who are slower to learn are likely to be kept longer on the "basal" readers and to spend more time on phonics than reading for enjoyment (Roberts, 1969). Initial slowness in learning to read may easily become compounded with a sense of failure and frustration resulting in a downward spiral of increasingly poor performance and increasing lack of belief in one's ability to learn (Kemp, 1985). The relation between nonreaders and cultural expectations is also apparent when focusing on adult illiteracy, which is a very different phenomenon in a literate culture than in one in which many adults are nonreaders (Hagell & Tudge, in press).

Surprisingly, although it is true that children who do not learn to read as fast or as well as many of their peers have continued difficulties in school, children who learn to read early appear to cause some embarrassment to their parents, particularly in those cases in which parents believe that it is the school's responsibility to teach reading. The early fluent readers in Clark's (1976) study, for example, did not have parents who tried to teach them to read early; some parents, in fact, were bothered by their children's fluency, believing that the teaching of reading was the school's prerogative. Of the 32 parents in Clark's study, no fewer than 25 "insisted that the initial interest [in learning to read] was from the child and that they gradually or reluctantly responded to requests for help" (p. 53).

Reading in Microgenesis

It is at the microgenetic level that it is possible to examine reading in process, the moment-by-moment interactions between a reader (including beginning readers), the material being read (or looked at or listened to), and at least one other person (the writer of the material) and, often, another person – the person either listening to or assisting with the reading. In cases in which an adult is helping a child to read, it is easy to think of the former as teaching, the latter as learning, and the two as engaged in separate processes. This distinction, however, does not adequately capture either the co-constructionist perspective or the reality in which what one member of this dyad does is inextricably linked to what the other is doing. The Russian word *obuchenie* means neither teaching nor learning, but conceptualizes both as a single process (Valsiner, 1988a; Wertsch & Rogoff, 1984). This nicely captures our perspective on reading. As a developmental phenomenon (at least in some cultures), it is both taught and learned, but the process is in essence transactional.

From the perspective of teaching children to read, innumerable materials are available, many of which are expressly designed to help teachers to teach and learners to learn. For example, often the first reading activities that children engage in require them to do little more than listen – stories are told, often (in some cultures at least) from brightly colored attractive books that tell stories designed to be interesting to children. From the perspective of learning to read, listening to stories read by a reader may go hand in hand with "reading" first books, books that very often have no words, simply pictures, to allow children to tell a story or talk about the objects displayed in the picture. Being read to and this type of early reading are both activities that are designed to encourage the notion that books tell a story, that there is a beginning, middle, and end, and that reading is a fun activity to do with a more competent adult. Many children, in fact, do not distinguish between the pictures and the words when first they look at books; "reading" simply signifies the process of looking at books and recounting a story, or naming the objects that are depicted (Ferreiro & Teberosky, 1983).

Even in the context of book-reading cultures, however, there are differences in the ways in which children and adults deal with books, differences related to language skill (DeBaryshe, Caulfield, Witty, & Holt, 1991). In one home, a parent may read through a story from beginning to end, but in another, the book may feature only pictures, and the "reading" may consist of talking about the pictures, about what they represent and what the child knows about them. In still another home, however, the adults may see reading as a necessary skill for their children to learn, but also as an activity that requires hard work. The child must repeat back the words on a page, and little effort is made to link what is on the page to anything in the child's life (Heath, 1983). Reading may then come to be regarded primarily as a chore, as something to be mastered, as a skill that one needs to have (unfortunate but true), and "you're going to have to master it." The great differences in "social interactional and language features of book-reading episodes involving children of the same age . . . indicate that being read to is not the seamless whole that it has been considered in much previous research" (Teale, 1984).

Even when adults have no belief that reading is appropriate, let alone necessary, for children's development, the child's role cannot be ignored — the essence of the co-constructionist position. For example, Fitzgerald and Needlman (1991), describing a study in which books were made available to parents who had no books at home, reported that one mother asked for a replacement copy of her book: "My daughter insists on reading it every night; by now it's in tatters" (p. 18). Similarly, Schieffelin and Cochran-Smith (1984), studying reading among the typically nonliterate Kaluli of New Guinea, described one child who worked to ensure that she was able to engage in reading with her mother even though in this culture children were not expected to learn to read (in fact, it was not considered desirable). The result was a mother-child dyadic interaction in reading that was quite similar to those found in many Western homes. The authors argued: "The length and frequency of these interactions . . . were determined by the child's persistence and interest, never the mother's" (pp. 14–15).

Children are clearly active in the process of learning to read, in some cases seeming to take on the bulk of the work in that regard (Bissex, 1984; Clark, 1976; Torrey, 1973). However, it would be misleading to leave the impression that children's desire to read is the primary explanatory variable. Clark's early readers grew up in families in which the parents enjoyed reading, had many books around, and were responsive to their children's requests for help. Moreover, although in some cases the process might better be thought of as *learning* to read (focusing on the child's activity), in other cases it is more important to stress the *teaching* aspect, particularly for those children who find it difficult to learn to read (Donaldson, 1984). Reading, as was pointed out earlier, differs in important ways from oral language, particularly in that the word referents are much less easy to understand. Reading may not be "decontextualized" (a picture, the previous sentences and the sense they have provided, and so on all help to provide context), but there is not the same contextual richness as accompanies spoken language (Donaldson, 1984; Smith, 1984). Taking a Vygotskian perspective, much early reading might be conceptualized as both an intra- and an interpsychological process, with more competent others providing the social support that enables the child to make sense of the text (Ninio & Bruner, 1978; Teale, 1984).

Implications of a Co-constructionist Developmental Perspective

When considering culture and cognition from a co-constructionist perspective it would be incorrect to view them as though they were separate "variables." The two are in fact in a continually changing dynamic interaction; it thus makes no sense to ask whether individuals create culture or culture creates individuals, for they are inextricably linked. In the course of experience in, on, and with the existing world (particularly, though by no means exclusively, with the social world), individual thinking develops along cultural pathways while at the same time culture is in the process of being re-created by the new generation. But neither cultures nor the individuals who are formed in them (and simultaneously form them) are ever created exactly according to preexisting patterns. No two individuals have exactly the same experiences, and cultures continually develop.

Books indeed have a relevant role to play in culture transmission. That role, however, is not one that determines the development of reading, but it provides the cultural basis on which the developing person builds his or her construction of the new cultural activity (reading) and, via it, the knowledge base. Thus, beginning readers do not just learn words, they learn about their world. However, even as they are learning words (both orally and in written form) they are changing that world. As Halliday (1975) argued, children do not learn language first and only later apply it. What they do is learn at the same time not only how to read, but also how to write. They create totally new materials to be read, by themselves and by others, and, in the process, transmit something new to contemporary and future generations of readers. Thus in the course of cognitive development (coming to make increasing sense of the world in the course of activities with culturally defined objects, often in conjunction with others who are more competent), an interweaving of culture and individual, of culture and cognition, takes place.

The co-constructive nature of the process of reading is further reinforced by the fact that literacy experiences between caregiver and child exert a clear impact not only on the child but also on the adult: "Book reading seemed to bring with it new ways of talking to the toddler, changed perceptions of the child and of caregiver roles, an increased consciousness of the child's language development, and altered patterns of talking about language" (Heath & Thomas, 1984, p. 70).

Cognitive Activity and Units of Analysis

We have argued that analysis of reading (as one example of cognitive activity) may be informed by a co-constructionist orientation as opposed to a variable-oriented approach. Any discussion of the units of analysis in developmental science brings us to the major general issue that haunts any enterprise claiming the status of "science." That is, what implications does the theoretical orientation have for the everyday practice of empirical investigations? Contributors to this volume have touched upon this issue from a number of divergent standpoints, ranging from loyalty to psychology's traditional methodological stance to the need for a new methodology that fits the theoretical needs of developmental science.

Our analysis of this methodological issue is based on the latter stance. We believe that science requires consistency between the theoretical and empirical realms of knowledge construction (see Kindermann & Valsiner, 1989; Valsiner, 1987, 1991) and that developmental science thus needs a developmentally appropriate methodology. This point was well made more than a half century ago, by both James Mark Baldwin and Lev Vygotsky:

> The Spencerian or quantitative method, brought over into psychology from the exact sciences, physics and chemistry, must be discarded; for its ideal consisted in reducing the more complex to the more simple, the whole into its parts, the later-evolved to the earlier-existent, *thus denying just the factor which constituted or revealed what was truly genetic* [i.e.,

developmental]. New modes of manifestation cannot be stated in atomic terms without doing violence to the more synthetic modes which observation reveals. . . .

A method is therefore called for which will take account of this something left "over and above" the quantitative, something which presents new phases as the genetic [developmental] progression advances. This something reveals itself in a series of qualitative aspects. (1930, pp. 7–8, emphasis added)

Similarly, Vygotsky argued: "In general, any fundamentally new approach to a scientific problem inevitably leads to new methods of investigation and analysis. The invention of new methods that are adequate to the new ways in which problems are posed requires far more than a simple modification of previously accepted methods" (1978, p. 58).

Our methodological position is in agreement with Baldwin's call for a developmental structural-dynamic methodology that retains the phenomena of development. This methodology is ill served by the analytic techniques currently favored, techniques that are nondevelopmental (ontological), static, and atomistic. None of these assumptions fit into the foundation of developmental science as portrayed by many of the contributors to this volume.

Unfortunately, existing disciplines that parallel developmental psychology in their concerns for explaining change do not provide many alternative models (see Valsiner, 1987, Chap. 5, for an overview of some of these approaches). There is no doubt that a novel methodology – a logic of inference of general developmental mechanisms from the high variability of concrete empirical phenomena – needs to be created. Although efforts of this kind have been attempted in the past (Baldwin, 1906; Herbst, 1987), they either have been largely forgotten or have remained unfinished. It is only currently that the issue appears anew on the agenda of researchers (Winegar & Valsiner, 1992). Complete elaboration of these methodological points is beyond the scope of this chapter, but issues relating to them will be illustrated in our discussion of reading.

According to these tenets of developmental science, reading cannot be fully understood by treating it as a unidimensional skill, assessed by the score on a standardized test, by the particular color-coded basal reader currently being used, by the ability to identify letter-sound correspondences, or by scores on tests of sight recognition of words. These indicators of reading all have utility, but they have two problems: First, they are not developmental and, second, they disguise variability in performance by ignoring the fact that context is an unexplored and hidden feature of these tests. Context here is commonly (at least as far as reading tests are concerned) a school classroom or a laboratory in which independent performance is being assessed, in a culture in which reading is a valued activity, and in which scores on a reading test are viewed as signifying, indicating, or uncovering a child's ability and govern expectations about future performance. The meaning of this context is likely to differ in significant ways for the participants, particularly for those who view the test as an opportunity to be praised for their ability and for those who are only too aware of their lack of ability. But this context, and these varying meanings, are considered of little importance in variable-oriented approaches. Typically, the only other critical variable is that of age, "good" reading being related to age norms.

By contrast, a co-constructionist approach requires that attention be paid to reading as a goal-directed activity, the sense of which varies according to the context in which it occurs. The unit of analysis, according to this viewpoint, is therefore neither the context nor the child but the child in the process of doing something in a particular context. A person's ability to read, therefore, rather than being assessed as an "in-the-head" ability, might be better assessed in conjunction with the context in which it is taking place. For example, when dealing with performance differences among a group of 10-year-olds in a schooled society, reading in traditional testing situations might be viewed as one context, and contrasted with reading in other contexts (for example, to achieve different goals than test performance – to find out what is on television that night, to work out how a baseball pitcher has performed previously against an opposing team, to enjoy an activity with someone who is assisting the reading process, and so on). Ability, from this perspective, is not a unitary phenomenon but one that varies from context to context. As Wertsch (1991) has argued, abilities are not things that are possessed by individuals, but are expressed differently in the course of different activities.

Context may also or simultaneously be considered at the historical or cultural level. The assessment of a person's ability to read, when conducted in a literate, technologically complex society, simply takes for granted the culturally appropriate conceptions of what constitutes "good" reading. The cultural context, in other words, is present but invisible. However, what counts as good reading clearly has varied across time and across cultures – among Vai literates, the ability to read or to write a letter for a nonliterate person is crucial (Scribner & Cole, 1981); among nonliterate Ibo, it may be the ability to read sufficiently to keep proper accounts (Akinnaso, 1991); among Brazilian peasants, the ability to read a few words may provide a tremendously empowering feeling and provide status among one's peers (Freire, 1972). In any culture, over time, the same points may be made, with literacy being assessed at one time as the ability to read sections of the Bible or Koran, to keep simple accounts, or to reproduce copperplate writing when at a later time these abilities by themselves would be inadequate indicators of reading.

What does this mean specifically for the study of reading or, for that matter, of any activity being considered from the co-constructionist perspective? As we have demonstrated in this chapter, a co-constructionist approach can hardly be considered "new" any more; nevertheless, methodology and analysis have lagged quite appreciably behind theory. The directions in which methodology and analysis have to go are clear, however. The unit must be the individual in activity, thereby encompassing both time and context.

We will illustrate this with a concrete example. The scenario is that it is the regular storyreading time for a child (49 months) before she goes to bed. She (RZ) has chosen the book *Mike Mulligan and the Steam Shovel* and is sitting with her mother (MS) as the recording starts. Four sections of the transcript are provided, with the passage of time marked in minutes and seconds. (The text of this story is placed within quotation marks.)

> 0.00 MS: "Mike Mulligan and the Steam Shovel." [She turns the page.]
>
> 0.13 RZ: "To Mike"
>
> 0.15 MS: Good. "Mike Mulligan had a steam shovel. A beautiful red steam shovel. Her name was . . ." [MS pauses.]
>
> 0.26 MS: What was her name?
>
> 0.26 RZ: "Marianne"
>
> 0.27 MS: Marianne. "Mike Mulligan was very proud of Marianne."
>
> 1.31 MS: "It was Mike Mulligan and Marianne and some others who cut through the high mountains so that trains could go through. It was Mike Mulligan and Marianne and some others who lowered the hills and straightened the curves to make the long highways for the automobiles."
>
> 1.51 RZ: [Pointing at the picture] And the holes for the um er for the er um cars.
>
> 1.57 MS: Yep, there are some holes for the cars to go through. "It was Mike Mulligan and Marianne and some others who smoothed out the ground and filled in the holes to make the landing fields for the airplanes."
>
> 2.15 MS: RZ, look at this airport. What do you think is strange about that airport? [RZ looks at the picture.]

2.25 MS: Have you ever been to an airport that looked like that? [RZ shakes her head, indicating No.] What's different about that airport? Why does it look different from the airports we've been to?

2.37 RZ: Got houses.

2.38 MS: It's got houses, but that wasn't what I was thinking of. But that's true. I was thinking that the airports that we've been to, the airplane landing is a long rectangular-shaped road called a landing strip, a runway. Is that what this one looks like?

3.04 RZ: [Shakes head, No]

3.05 MS: No. What's different about this one?

3.14 RZ: Don't know.

3.15 MS: It's round! Have you ever seen . . . been to an airport where the airplane landed on a round road?

3.23 RZ: No!

3.23 MS: [Laughs] Pretty strange. Oooh, look at that.

3.50 MS: "Then along came new gasoline shovels, and the new electric shovels and the new diesel motor shovels and took all the jobs away from the steam shovels. Mike Mulligan and Marianne were . . ." [pauses, and looks down at RZ]

4.04 RZ: " . . . very sad."

4.07 MS: Why were they sad?

4.09 RZ: Because they um, because, because um all the um gasoline shovels and all the [looks at MS] [unclear] shovels and all the mo . . . the motor shovels took all the jobs away from her.

4.33 MS: Aaaah [sad]. That's right.

4.37 MS: "All the other steam shovels were sold for . . ." [pauses]

4.41 RZ: ". . . junk . . ."

4.43 MS: " . . . or just left out in old gravel pits just to rust away."

11.55 MS: "'Why not?' said Henry B. Swap, and he smiled in a way that wasn't quite so mean. 'Why not?' said Mrs. McGillicuddy. 'Why not?' said the town constable." [MS pauses, and looks down at RZ.]

12.01 RZ: "'Why not?' said everybody."

12.08 MS: "So they found a ladder and climbed down into the cellar to ask Mike Mulligan and Marianne." [MS pauses, and looks down at RZ.]

12.15 RZ: "'Why not?' /said/"

12.16 MS: "/said/ Mike Mulligan. So it was decided, and everyone was . . ."

12.21 RZ: " . . . happy!"

13.36 RZ: We have to read this one. [She pulls over another book.]

13.39 MS: Shall we read this one?

13.41 RZ: Yep! What name is it?

13.43 MS: "Dumbi the Owl."

13.47 RZ: "Dumbi the Owl."

13.55 MS: "/In the t . . . /"

13.55 RZ: /Read it./

13.57 MS: "In the time before time began the tribe of people lived on the land near the coast."

14.05 RZ: What's . . . where's the coast?

14.07 MS: The coast is where the land meets the water.

14.11 RZ: There [points to picture].

14.12 MS: Yeah, right there.

14.14 MS: "Every day the children would play beside the river."

What is to be the appropriate unit of analysis, when we come to analyze this text? We have argued in the course of this chapter that the co-constructionist perspective requires a unit of analysis that includes more than one level. That is not to say that one cannot derive interesting, useful information from an analysis that focuses solely on one level, but that greater understanding can be gained when more are considered simultaneously. Similarly, one could examine each person as a separate unit (and derive useful information from that analysis), but more information could be obtained from focusing on the dyad as the unit.

When treating each participant as a separate unit of analysis, examining what each brings to the reading process, we could focus on who had what to contribute, and note that the mother takes the lion's share of the text (as judged by the number of words or sentences read, for example) compared to the child. The mother also asks more questions than the child (9 vs. 2), and the mother takes more control of when the child contributes than the child does (7 vs. 2 occasions).

Still keeping an individual unit of analysis, we could conduct a sequential analysis, in an attempt to capture the points at which the child is drawn into the reading process. The most effective strategy would be to focus on the endings of sentences, for on three occasions RZ completes her mother's sentence. One of the difficulties in this type of analysis, however, is a function of the fact that there are far more cases in which RZ does not complete (and is not asked to complete) the sentence; in one case a word is requested (and supplied) in the middle of a sentence, and in one case an entire sentence is requested and supplied. The words RZ supplied could also be analyzed: "To Mike," "Marianne," "very sad," "junk," " 'Why not, said everybody," "Why not," and "happy." It would be difficult to argue that these were words that RZ could read out of context.

We would propose that more could be gained by focusing on the partners in activity, treating the dyad-in-activity as the unit of analysis. This would necessitate focusing on the various levels discussed earlier. If the researcher is concerned with reading at the microgenetic level, studying, for example, the way in which the mother and child read a book together, then the dyad constitutes the appropriate unit. Rather than try to look for what the mother brings to the activity separate from what the child brings, coding must capture both partners. How can the partners be categorized? Is there joint attention, or is the bulk of the work being carried by one? Are both partners responsive to the wishes or demands of the other? Are the cues provided by one partner picked up by the other, and does this happen in a balanced way or is one partner primarily responsible for responding to the cues of the other? Do the partners share understanding of the particular goal, or do they appear to be working at cross-purposes? If shared understanding is being created in the course of reading, and we can assume that we (as researchers) are as able to make sense of the means for creating shared meaning as are the participants themselves, then the extent of shared meaning can be coded (Rogoff & Gauvain, 1986).

Specifically, coding would incorporate the fact that both partners are jointly engaged in the reading process (0.15–0.26; 3.50–4.04; 4.37–4.41; 11.55–12.21) although the mother is taking the larger role (judged by the proportion of words, sentences, etc.). Coding would incorporate the fact that an initial miscommunication (0.15) was handled by a formal request from MS to RZ: "What was her name?" (0.26). From a Vygotskian perspective one would argue that an initial nonverbal gambit on the part of the mother (an extended pause) was insufficient to cue the child as to what was expected. The mother therefore made what was expected quite explicit (0.26), whereupon the child provided the response. Subsequently, the mother's pause was quite sufficient for the child to conclude the sentence appropriately (4.04; 4.41; 12.21) or to supply a full sentence (12.01).

One might conclude from this analysis that the mother was providing appropriate scaffolding experiences for the child, who was filling in text wherever the mother thought she was able – when the context was clear enough for successful completion, because of either the pictures or the child's memory for the story. However, the child does not simply react to the mother's verbal and nonverbal cues. The mother may well have been cued into the fact that her daughter wanted to participate early on in the session when RZ reads, quite spontaneously without suggestion, prodding, or assistance "To Mike" from the 2nd page of the text (0.13). Later (1.51), RZ uses the picture to add her own text to the story. In both cases, MS validates and appreciates her daughter's contribution, either with a "good" (0.15) or by repeating what had been said (1.57). Moreover, not only had RZ chosen this book for reading, but she pulls over a new book and says: "We have to read this one" (13.36). She clearly has an expectation of some degree of control here and knows what her mother should do (13.41; 13.55). RZ also provides us with some insight into the way in which she makes sense of the text – by repeating new phrases (13.47) and by asking explicit questions about parts of the text that are not clear (14.05).

These examples serve to illustrate a number of important points. The first is that the text provides a certain structure, in terms of both words and pictures. On the other hand, that structure is abandoned in places, as questions are asked and points are raised that serve to link the structure quite explicitly to aspects of the participants' experiences. The second is that the interactions are asymmetrical (the mother for the most part takes the lead and moves the reading process along in ways she considers appropriate), serving to illustrate that co-construction does not imply equality of weight in the constructive process. The third point is that the child is far from passive, choosing the books, choosing to participate at all, and interjecting comments and questions into the flow as well as reading some sections.

This way of dealing with the data provides codes that are essentially dyadic and that are assessed over time as the reading session progresses. Moreover, this approach provides a means of comparing dyadic patterns that perhaps differ on these or other dyadically assessed dimensions. However, we also need to know something about the history of these dyads and their previous joint reading sessions if we are to make more sense of the processes we are currently observing. Does this particular dyad read together typically, or is this a single occurrence for the benefit of the researcher? Have previous reading sessions been characterized in the same general ways as the current session? Dyads thus may differ not only in their current interactional patterns, but in their interactional patterns assessed longitudinally. The process of reading is likely to differ according to the age of the child.

Thus, when focusing on the ontogenetic level, one might evaluate this session quite differently if the child were 12 than if she had just turned 4. A 12-year-old having reading difficulties would most likely be given "remedial" reading, in which the reading process would be broken down into its smallest components, with the child responding at the level of letter-sound correspondences, "blends," and so forth. For a young child, this joint reading session in all probability has grown out of a history of being read to from this type of text, a history of being read this particular book (the first one) before, and a history of this type of jointly constructing meaning from text.

Knowing the age of the child also helps make sense of the mother's questioning, getting her daughter to compare what she is reading in the text to reality as she has experienced it (2.15–3.23), and asking her daughter to reflect on the characters' emotional states (4.07–4.33). It also helps us to understand RZ's questioning: "What name is it?" (referring to a new book – 13.41) and "What's . . . where's the coast?" (14.05).

Analysis of the cultural-historical level would take account of the fact that this reading session is taking place in a literate culture, a context in which books are readily available, in which children are expected to have to learn to read, and in which books are written specifically to teach children to read. At the within-society level, the way in which the joint reading process occurs indicates that the mother fits into the pattern displayed by Heath's (1983) white middle-class sample. MS uses the reading session to link, quite explicitly, the text with her daughter's past experiences (2.15–3.23), asking RZ to think about differences between the airport in the picture and airports that she has been to. MS also checks on RZ's understanding of the text by enquiring why the protagonists are sad (4.07). In this culture (unlike some – see Schieffelin, 1990, in which others' emotional states are not believed to be accessible), awareness of others' emotional states is something to be taught, learned, or both.

The level that is least relevant to this analysis is the phylogenetic level, but it serves to illustrate the point that the co-constructionist perspective does not require that analysis of reading take equal account of all levels. A concern with the processes of learning to read would involve consideration of the microgenetic level, but these processes would make little sense without knowing something about the ontogenetic and historical-cultural levels. A concern with dyslexia would involve consideration of the ontogenetic level (with particular focus on individual neurological factors), but more understanding would no doubt be gained from knowing something about the particular microgenetic reading practices that the child is used to in his or her local culture. On the other hand, a concern with the impact of reading on the development of humans' thought processes could involve consideration of either phylogenetic and cultural-historical levels of analysis (with little attention paid to the ontogenetic and microgenetic levels) or ontogenetic and microgenetic, with little attention paid to phylogeny and history.

Conclusion

Returning to the first of Magnusson and Cairns's propositions discussed earlier, the co-constructionist viewpoint is one that explicitly focuses on the ways in which "maturational, experiential, and cultural contributions are fused in ontogeny." We have focused on the relation between culture and cognition, with particular reference to reading, as a way of illustrating the systemic, fused, nature of development.

Development and the contexts in which it occurs cannot be treated as separate phenomena from this perspective. Context, we have argued, may be thought of at a variety of levels. It may be examined at the most immediate of levels, focusing on where the interaction is being assessed – home or school, at a time when reading (or any other cognitive activity) typically occurs for this dyad or at a time when one or other dyad member would rather be doing something different – or upon the perceived motivations of the participants. At another level, it would clearly be inappropriate, from the co-constructionist perspective, to disregard cultural and historical factors that are likely to affect the meaning of the reading process. We would want to know the meaning that reading has for the particular community or culture from which the participants have been drawn. Is the culture literate, is literacy valued, are there culturally prescribed or valued approaches to literacy? Without knowing something about the meaning that reading has for the population from which the dyads have been drawn, it is difficult to make sense of the particular interactions between dyadic members.

This stipulation does not mean that researchers studying reading have to engage in cross-cultural research, but rather that they make explicit the cultural and historical context(s) within which their participants fit. Typically, this is not done, or done only with reference to the fact that the sample is African-American, or working class, without effort to unpackage that "explanatory variable." Otherwise we are in danger of treating the cultural significance of the activities we are studying as simply the taken-for-granted norm, much as fish are unaware of their watery world until pulled from it.

Last, but by no means least, the co-constructionist perspective demands that attention be paid to individuals. Culture, history, context, and the dyad are clearly relevant when trying to make sense of a particular joint reading session. But each of these is expressed in the individual. Each individual has a history, a set of experiences in varying contexts with various other people over time, and individuals bring their histories to each new activity at the same time as they are creating (with help or hindrance) a new and continuing history. To understand our joint readers, we have to know something about their personal histories, the differing ways in which they have appropriated and reconstructed their culture. At a minimum, it is necessary to know the ages of the participants and have some understanding of their current attitudes toward reading, their particular goals, the meaning the situation has for them, and their individual abilities in similar situations.

In essence, then, the co-constructionist approach is systemic, requiring developmental scientists to attend to the multiple levels at which development is simultaneously occurring and to the varying contexts that accompany all development. Researchers are not being asked to undertake a Sisyphean task, always to be striven after, never to be attained. Analysis of any activity simply requires a concern with both the processes of development at whatever level (microgenetic, ontogenetic, etc.) is the primary focus of attention and the links between this level and all others in the system – the individual, social, historical, and cultural contexts within which development occurs.

11   The Making of Developmental Science

Robert B. Cairns, E. Jane Costello, and
Glen H. Elder, Jr.

In this concluding chapter, we note the special opportunities and the special hazards afforded by the emergence of a unified developmental science. We offer some comments on its past, take stock of its present, and speculate about its future.

Scope of Developmental Science

Judging from the review volumes that have been published in the 1990s, there are at least five domains of behavioral investigation that may be subsumed under the rubric developmental science. These loosely connected domains include the development of human personality and social actions, the ontogeny and evolution of the behavioral adaptations in nonhuman animals, the development of perception, movement, and language in infants and young children, the development of psychopathology and emotional disorders, and the development of cognitive processes in children and older adults.[9]

These domains not only frame problems in different ways; they deal with different problems. Even when it appears that the issues are similar on formal grounds, there seems to be scant overlap in research designs and analytic strategies. Links have historically been made across developmental domains only at the highest levels of abstraction. One of the aims in this volume has been to articulate a framework that promotes more direct coordination and evaluation of developmental methods and concepts.

[9] Review volumes have recently been prepared in each of these areas, including social development and social ecology (e.g., Cairns & Cairns, 1994; Elder, Modell, & Parke, 1993; Ford & Lerner, 1992; Moen, Elder, & Lüscher, 1995), developmental psychobiology and ethology (Bateson, 1991; Gottlieb, 1992; Hood, Greenberg, & Tobach, 1995), the dynamic systems approach (Eckerman, 1993a; Hood, 1995; Smith & Thelen, 1993; Thelen & Smith, 1994), developmental psychopathology (e.g., Cicchetti & Cohen, 1995; Hay & Angold, 1993; Rutter & Hay, 1994), and cognitive development (Baltes & Baltes, 1990; Butterworth & Bryant, 1990; van der Veer & Valsiner, 1988).

History provides clues to how a common frame can be achieved despite such divisions and the biases they represent. It seems altogether fitting that the present volume is published on the centennial of James Mark Baldwin's *Mental Development in the Child and the Race* (1895).[10] Although its empirical chapters were concerned with human infancy and the development of movement and perception, *Mental Development in the Child and the Race* and its companion volume, *Social and Ethical Interpretations in Mental Development,* provide an expansive view of the science. Baldwin succeeded in covering three of the five substantive domains that are central to developmental study in the 1990s, and he outlined theoretical principles that have guided research and thinking in a fourth. For Baldwin, the developmental-evolutionary-comparative method was key to behavioral and cognitive investigations.[11]

Comparative analyses continue to be fundamental to the study of development, as emphasized by each of the contemporary traditions. The methods range from the cross-cultural comparisons of anthropology to the cross-generational comparisons of life-course sociology and comparative studies of the development of nonhuman species. In this volume, the authors report on developmental work conducted in multiple settings, including comparisons across diverse societies in North America and Europe. Comparisons are required to determine which principles are general across settings, and which are specific to particular contexts.

By the same logic, investigations of animals can be informative with respect to basic developmental processes. To be sure, human social interactions cannot simply be reduced to the animal models without a loss of the distinctive properties of human beings. Yet there are substantial reasons why the aggressive exploitation of animal models is critical for further advances in human development. Nonhuman investigations permit the

---

[10] It should be noted that the developmental ideas were part of a Zeitgeist in experimental embryology, comparative psychology, and evolutionary theory. For example, Baldwin's emphasis on comparative study was predated by G. Stanley Hall when he founded the first American psychological journal, *Pedagogical Seminary,* in 1891. This journal, retitled in 1929, became *Pedagogical seminary and journal of genetic psychology: Child behavior, animal behavior, and comparative psychology.* Hall's work owed much to the seminal volumes of W. Preyer (Cairns, 1983).

[11] This was not a high recommendation in the eyes of many of Baldwin's contemporaries, for the founders of scientific psychology had relegated historical studies and child psychology to second-class status (behind experimental psychology) in the new discipline. The problem was that it is impossible to experimentally manipulate time, and so these fields were limited to comparisons.

direct manipulation of experience from birth to maturity by tracking effects in social behavior over generations and by conducting studies of the ontogenies of successive generations.

In addition, we can experimentally manipulate interconnections among biological and environmental manipulations over ontogeny. Such research is critical to understanding precisely how biological and social-ecological factors become linked in social behaviors, and how the biology of organisms is influenced by their environments and social interactions. Animal studies can also be valuable because of basic commonalties in how the organismic system is constructed. There are remarkable similarities across mammalian species in brain architecture and functions, along with similarities in neurobiological and endocrinological structures and processes. More generally, the developmental-comparative perspective promises to eventually build a bridge between virtually separate worlds of behavioral inquiry – animal and human investigations.

This conclusion stands in sharp contrast to the view offered by Aslin (1993) and others on the scope of the developmental orientation. In discussing the limitations of the dynamic-systems approach, Aslin notes what he fears as the danger of its "overapplication to inappropriate domains" (1993, p. 386). What makes a domain inappropriate – or appropriate? In Aslin's view, the study of motor performance and motor development is appropriate because there is a rich data base from individuals on movement patterns and because there is a well-articulated theory of the developmental constraints that operate. Other domains that lack this information presumably do not qualify for the application of particular developmental models. In brief, Aslin (1993) articulates why many researchers in developmental psychobiology and dynamic systems have been reluctant to extend their models beyond perception, motor behavior, and infancy.

By contrast, the developmental framework described in this volume is explicitly intended to be inclusive rather than exclusive. Indeed, the domains that stand to benefit most from a systematic developmental perspective – and are most likely to enlarge our understanding of the processes and constraints of behavioral development – are those that have traditionally been excluded from rigorous, controlled microgenetic and ontogenetic investigation, including the study of personality and social development (Bronfenbrenner, 1995; Magnusson, 1995).[12]

---

[12] One early example of such a breakthrough involves the study of cognition and the development of intelligence tests. In contrast to the positions of Cattell and Galton, Binet, and Henri (1895) argued that the elementaristic approach to the

Longitudinal and Intergenerational Investigation

Just as paleologic studies have provided a foundation for understanding biological evolution, longitudinal investigations are essential if we are to unravel the secrets of behavioral and cognitive development. An enormous investment has been made in recent decades in the longitudinal study of human lives in context. Longitudinal designs have brought life-course investigations, developmental-social research, and cognitive-language studies to a common plane of discourse, inquiry, and discovery. The study of human development across the life course has gained momentum over the past 30 years in Europe and North America, with significant advances in the standards for data quality and methods of analysis (Magnusson & Bergman, 1990; Young, Savola, & Phelps, 1991).

Before this era, the field relied mainly on the pioneering child development samples that were carried forward from the 1920s, including the Stanford Studies of Genius (Terman, 1925), the Berkeley longitudinal studies (Eichorn, 1973; Eichorn, Clausen, Haan, Honzik, & Mussen, 1981), and the Fels longitudinal study (Kagan & Moss, 1962). In the new era, longitudinal studies were launched, older samples were followed up, and retrospective life history surveys were devised for contemporary studies (Freedman, Thornton, Camburn, Alwin, & Young-DeMarco, 1988). By the early 1980s, the value of longitudinal studies had become recognized, leading a consultant panel at the National Institutes of Mental Health to recommend that longitudinal studies be actively encouraged and supported (Clausen, 1983).

The new era also includes the monumental Project Talent, which began in the 1960s with over 400,000 high school students (Abeles, Steel, & Wise, 1980); the National Longitudinal Surveys that extend from the birth cohorts of mature men and women to the national cohort of graduating seniors in 1972 and a late-1970s cohort of mothers and children; and the path-breaking Michigan Panel Study of Income Dynamics (Elder, 1985) in North America. Initiated in 1968 to study the nature and persistence of

assessment of intelligence was misguided because of its reductionism. Even if the components of sensation, perception, and memory could be accurately measured, it was unclear how they could be combined and fitted together to account for adaptive functioning in the concrete contexts of living. Binet and Henri (1895) proposed that pragmatic techniques for intellectual assessment should mirror, in controlled circumstances, the cognitive constraints of everyday life. This line of reasoning led to the establishment of assessment procedures that arguably constitute psychology's most influential contribution to the 20th century.

poverty, the panel has been contacted each year up to the present. Sample members who die are replaced by births to sample members. The current sample includes over 20,000 people who span three generations. The great value of this sample for studying environmental change in families and individual lives has led to its replication in numerous European countries, thereby enabling cross-national studies of poverty and socioeconomic stresses in children's lives.

In Great Britain, Denmark, Sweden, and Finland, national studies have been ongoing since the 1940s, covering health, economic, and social issues. These larger samples of the national population are coupled with a substantial number of smaller-scale longitudinal studies that have more explicit developmental objectives.

Because of the focus on individual development in context over a large segment of the life span, it was perhaps inevitable that new parallels would breathe fresh life into traditional sociological and psychological domains of inquiry. Not only did fresh findings become available on the basic issues of continuity and change over the life span, but the study of persons in context forced attention to temporal changes in context, community, and society (Chaps. 2, 3, this volume).

As these findings have become joined, they have precipitated major changes in developmental science. The developmental method requires detailed examination of the concrete features of each measure prior to comparisons across investigations. Comparisons should be as concerned with differences as with similarities in outcomes. The task demands that investigators in the future become intimately acquainted with multiple data sets and that translation rules be formulated to establish similarities and identities in assessment across longitudinal investigations that have been independently formulated. The challenge is to formulate procedures and training that will facilitate rigorous cross-investigation analyses.

Gavin de Beer (1958) has argued that development is not merely about the life span of individuals from conception to death; rather, there must be linkages between successive life courses because intergenerational transmission extends from the embryos of one generation to those of the next. But research on intergenerational transmission in psychology has typically focused on the immediate and enduring outcomes associated with family differences in child rearing. This examination of parent-to-child relations, although valuable for many purposes, is limited to transactions and outcomes that occur across a single generation. For research to qualify as intergenerational according to de Beer's (1958) criterion, offspring in successive generations should be assessed at roughly the same ages and with the same measures across development as their parents were when they were first assessed.

In the future, longitudinal investigations may be joined with experimental interventions over ontogeny and over generations. For example, preventative intervention research designs may be linked with longitudinal and intergenerational strategies in order to determine the long-term outcomes of attempts to shift developmental pathways. On this score, the largest payoffs of preventative interventions in the 1990s will be in the opportunities created for children who become adults in the 2020s, and for their children who reach maturity in the 2050s.

The Dynamics and Plasticity of Individual Adaptations

Major concerns of the developmental orientation are understanding when and how behavioral changes occur and the potential in development for optimal adaptations. As the citation from Baldwin (1895) suggests, the ontogenetic resolution of the nature-nurture debate may be that nature and nurture cooperate rather than compete and that this cooperation is typically biased toward ontogenetic adaptation. The controversies associated with the classic dualisms of behavioral study – the nature versus nurture debate, the effects of early versus late experience – evaporate when development becomes the focus.[13]

The developmental orientation avoids the choice of having to ignore either the pervasive effects of contexts and experiences or the powerful effects of biological and maturational change. Both influence behavior. They are typically interwoven in development, driven by a common goal of achieving adaptation in the midst of changing internal and external conditions. Developmental study is required to determine the pathways by which these influences become synchronized and consolidated over time, and which source takes the lead and under which conditions. Then it may be possible to determine how these influences can be modified. Yet, as this book attests, developmental pathways are essentially probabilistic rather than determined. Events arise during the course of ontogeny from within and without that have the potential to shift the direction of the life course. In this regard, William James wrote: "However closely psychical changes may conform to law, it is safe to say that individual histories and biogra-

---

[13] This point is embedded in the writings of modern contributors to the developmental framework (e.g., Bronfenbrenner, 1979; Bronfenbrenner & Ceci, 1994; Cairns, 1979; Elder, 1974; Gottlieb, 1992; Magnusson, 1995; Sameroff & Fiese, 1990; Suomi, 1991).

phies will never be written in advance no matter how 'evolved' psychology may become" (James, 1890, pp. 576–577).

The core of the developmental orientation is its concern with time and timing in ontogeny. There exist a medley of short-term, intermediate-term, and long-term processes that promote adaptations that are optimal to the then-available circumstances. In the short term, learning clearly plays a major role in short-term social adaptations. The lessons of learning are typically time-bound unless they are interwoven with other changes in the individual and the environment. This time-relativity of learning mechanisms, which is rarely discussed in accounts of social learning, is consistent with the proposal that the effects of early experiences are modified by inevitable changes in contexts and age-related maturation. In recent investigations, it has been shown that small variations in the timing and synchrony of key components of social development can lead to enduring changes in adaptation in ontogeny and microevolution (Cairns, 1993; Hofer, 1994; Rader, 1985; Turkewitz & Devenney, 1993).

Social Applications and the Science of Design

Sheldon White (in press) and Charles Cofer (1986) have proposed that the study of development issues occupies a special niche in modern social science. Cahan and White (1992) distinguish between the "bottom-up" psychology of experimental and physiological psychology and the "top-down" psychology that is involved with social concerns and social applications. White (in press) makes an important point:

> Child study of some sort has to be part and parcel of any social design for children. Though developmental psychology is not, in the traditional sense, a policy science it has nevertheless a significant role to play in the organization and management of systems of governance directed towards children and families. Developmental psychologists build knowledge that helps people in and out of government contend with the powerful centrifugal and centripetal forces at work in the politics of large organizations.

The framework outlined in this book provides guides about how to connect the multiple worlds of developmental investigation. In this regard, the emphasis of the developmental orientation on establishment, plasticity, and change has enormous implications for recent statements on prevention (Coie, Terry, Lenox, Lochman, & Hyman, 1995; Mrazek & Haggerty,

1994; Reiss & Roth, 1993). One of the tasks in developmental psycho-pathology is to create a nosology that takes development seriously. This involves a paradigmatic shift for practitioners and scientists who have spent the last several decades laboring to do precisely the opposite – to fit the emotional and behavioral problems of humanity into a "medical" frame-work that is nondevelopmental in orientation. There is growing evidence that the current nosologies do not fit either clinical wisdom or the problems that drive individuals or parents to seek treatment. Other researchers are committed to the task of bringing our theories of abnormal development into line with our growing understanding of normal development. It is a task whose importance is not only scientific but also political and eco-nomic. Heavy costs are involved in the current system in paying for treat-ment, providing supplementary income support on the basis of the current nosology, or both, and bringing this system into line with developmental reality. It will indeed be a "dangerous business."

Developmental knowledge is necessary for the task of deciding which problems are best treated by prevention and which cannot currently be prevented but can be treated or ameliorated. For example, we have no hints yet of how to prevent schizophrenia, but we do have a growing understand-ing of the diverse early signs and symptoms, and exciting new ways of helping families to create an environment for a vulnerable individual that reduces the risk of relapse. There is now evidence from longitudinal studies of conduct disorders and other antisocial behaviors that opportunities for change recur throughout the lifetime, not merely in the first 2 years of life. In addition, there is a robust linkage between age and deviance, such that the asymptotic age for physical violence occurs between 14 and 22 years of age, then drops off sharply. The task that remains is to determine how to modify these developmental trajectories, change their shape, or reduce their impact.

There always exist dangers of misapplication or misinterpretation of developmental research findings. Whereas errors of logic seem no more prevalent in developmental research than in other domains, interpretation biases are often implicit in socially relevant research designs and analyses. For example, simple correlation is a weak basis upon which to assume causation, even when the correlation also reflects gross sequences in development. Thus, a disturbed mother-child relationship (or a disturbed mother) in infancy is likely to continue to be disturbed in childhood, in adolescence, and in early adulthood. It then becomes a leap of faith that the distal events (infancy) are more basic in causing adjustment differences at maturity than the proximal ones. Yet this leap is typically made in the interpretation of longitudinal data, along with the assumption that the effects of third-order factors are negligible.

The present framework also points to the hazards of applying standard experimental designs to investigate the multidetermined, dynamic phenomena of social development. By way of example, it has been recently argued that research designs that involve random assignment of subjects to experimental and control groups should be the gold standard for prevention research (Mrazek & Haggerty, 1994). This proposition has been broadly accepted within public health, biostatistics, and epidemiology as the principal route to conclude that a prevention-intervention is effective or ineffective. It is argued that the ideal methodology for a clinical drug trial is also the ideal method for evaluating the enduring impact of Head Start experience or of a violence-prevention program.

It is a myth that the experimental-control design is uniformly superior as a research strategy regardless of problem and context. Its shortcomings become transparent when the design is applied to the study of lives in natural contexts. Consider the evaluation of the effects of intervention programs on violence-reduction programs in schools or of Head Start cognitive-enrichment programs. The random-assignment design problems include the high likelihood of experimental contamination (e.g., control parents, teachers, or communities may identify the discrepancy and demand further enrichment for their children), the probability that effects are produced beyond the individual (i.e., parents tend to become aware of the problem and they will explore possible solutions), the movement of individuals across conditions over time (i.e., children and families move, teachers quit, and principals change their minds, creating inevitable confounds in the experimental and control conditions), and the interactive and constructive nature of the processes of social development over time. When modifications in design and unit of analysis are introduced to correct for some of the pragmatic shortcomings, the elegant simplicity and logic of the design is compromised. An example is the Multiple Risk Factors Intervention Trial of cardiovascular risk (MRFIT) in which middle-aged men were randomly assigned to diet, exercise, smoking, and lifestyle interventions. Cardiovascular deaths fell in the intervention group – but they fell to an equal extent in the controls. Apparently, members of the control group picked up on the Zeitgeist of the 1970s and instituted their own lifestyle changes (Kuller, Perper, Dai, & Rutan, 1986).

Assigning potentially powerful social and bidirectional events to "experimental error" virtually guarantees a distorted view both of the phenomena and of the efficacy of any preventive intervention. Alternative research designs are available that take advantage of time, sequence, change, and the dynamics of developmental phenomena rather than attempt to get rid of them. Multilevel microgenetic and ontogenetic analyses capitalize upon the information embedded in short-term and long-term sequential effects. Configural analyses of developmental pathways provide attractive methods for disaggregating samples and providing precise evaluations of prevention effects in social context (see Bergman & Magnusson, 1990).

Just as the developmental investigation of personality and social adaptation points to the involvement of configurations of internal and external characteristics over development rather than to the potency of single variables taken at a single time point, research designs should mirror the developmental-contextual theories that gave rise to the interventions. In this regard, Bronfenbrenner (1943–1944) early described an essential theme of social ecology: "Social development applies not only to the individual but to the social organization of which he is a part. Variations occur not only in the social status of a particular person within the group, but also in the structure of the group itself – that is, in the frequency, strength, pattern, and basis of the interrelationships which bind the group together and give it distinctive character" (p. 363). In a companion article, Bronfenbrenner observed that "piecemeal analysis, fixed in time and space, of isolated aspects is insufficient and even misleading" (Bronfenbrenner, 1944, p. 75). This methodological perspective is fundamental to the developmental framework.

Each Researcher Is a Methodologist

The importance of increasing the scope and rigor of advanced training in developmental research can hardly be overstated. In this regard, Marian Radke Yarrow and her colleagues (Yarrow, Campbell, & Burton, 1968) succinctly describe the essential issues:

> Childrearing research is a curious combination of loose methodology that is tightly interwoven with provocative hypotheses of developmental processes and relationships. The compelling legend of maternal influences on child behavior that has evolved does not have its roots in solid data, and its precise verification remains in many respects a subject for future research. The findings from the preceding analyses of data make it difficult to continue to be complacent about methodology, and difficult to continue to regard replication as a luxury. The child's day-to-day experiences contribute significantly to his behavior and development and are in many respects the essence of developmental theory. An exact understand-

ing is important to science and society. In attempting to build on this knowledge, each researcher is a methodologist and as such has a responsibility for excellence. (p. 152)

Which should come first: the curriculum, the disciplinary area, or the substantive research? Advances in scholarship and research should lead the way, but fresh creative talent must be nurtured in order to extend the work and correct its shortcomings. Hence the contributors to this volume, along with other colleagues, established the Carolina Consortium on Human Development as an institute for advanced studies in development. From its inception, a primary aim of the Consortium – the training component of the Center for Developmental Science – has been to involve young scientists in collaborative research and writing. We believe that there must be a balance between the formalization in training, on the one hand, and the flexibility required for effective developmental research across disciplines, on the other. If teaching and curricula sprint too far ahead of research accomplishments, the field might be poorly served by the creation of premature structures.

Although there is potential strength in diversity, there are also hazards. When areas with different scientific goals and methods coexist, they may be mutually strengthened by a process akin to intellectual heterosis. But any attempt to integrate can be divisive. Tensions arise when, for instance, different domains evolve separate meanings for the same terms or when they compete for hegemony. True interdisciplinary collaboration as opposed to coexistence requires time, rigor, insight, and mutual commitment. The combination, when it occurs, can provide an essential platform from which fresh advances become possible.

Looking Ahead

The developmental framework obviously has strong implications for research designs, methods, measures, and analyses. It also speaks to applications and strategies for social design. To the extent that these issues are boldly stated, they may invite opposition – and sometimes rejection. It is easier to achieve agreement on developmental concepts at a general level than it is to implement the recommendations in concrete issues of measure selection, research design, and statistical analysis.

Much of the unfinished business concerns the details of research and the systematization of theory. If these challenges are taken seriously, the proposals must be supported – even overdetermined – by experimental, longitudinal, and comparative findings. One immediate task is to reexamine designs, statistics, and interpretations across areas in order to bring them into alignment with current models of developmental dynamics. This forward-looking perspective offers fresh hope for the practice and design of the human sciences. Even a modest impact on the design and interpretation of developmental investigations in our time may enhance applications in the next generation.

References

Abeles, R. P., Steel, L., & Wise, L. L. (1980). Patterns and implications of life-course organization: Studies from project talent. In P. B. Baltes & O. G. Brim, Jr. (Eds.), *Life-span development and behavior* (Vol. 1, pp. 307–337). New York: Academic Press.

Achenbach, T. M. (1991). The derivation of taxonomic constructs: A necessary stage in the development of developmental psychopathology. In D. Cicchetti & S. L. Toth (Eds.), *Rochester Symposium on Developmental Psychopathology: Vol. 3. Models and integrations* (pp. 43–74). Rochester, NY: University of Rochester Press.

Achenbach, T. M., & Edelbrock, C. (1983). *Manual for the Child Behavior Checklist and Revised Child Behavior Profile*. Burlington, VT: Achenbach.

Ainsworth, M. D. (1963). The development of infant-mother interaction among the Ganda. In B. M. Foss (Ed.), *Determinants of infant behaviour* (Vol. 2, pp. 67–104). New York: Wiley.

Ainsworth, M. D. S., Bell, S. V., & Stayton, D. J. (1971). Individual differences in strange-situation behavior of one-year-olds. In H. R. Schaffer (Ed.), *The origins of human social relations* (pp. 17–52). London: Academic Press.

Ainsworth, M. D. S., Blehar, M. C., Waters, E., & Wall, S. (1978). *Patterns of attachment: A psychological study of the strange situation.* Hillsdale, NJ: Erlbaum.

Akinnaso, F. N. (1991). Literacy and individual consciousness. In E. M. Jennings & A. C. Purves (Eds.), *Literate systems and individual lives: Perspectives on literacy and schooling* (pp. 73–94). Albany: State University of New York Press.

Allport, G. W., Bruner, J. S., & Jandorf, E. M. (1941). Personality under social catastrophe: Ninety life histories of the Nazi revolution. *Character and Personality, 10,* 1–22.

Almond, G. A., & Verba, S. (1963). *The civic culture: Political attitudes and democracy in five nations.* Princeton, NJ: Princeton University Press.

American Psychiatric Association. (1994). *Diagnostic and statistical manual of mental disorders* (4th ed.). Washington, DC: Author.

Anderson, A. B., & Stokes, S. J. (1984). Social and institutional influences on the development and practice of literacy. In H. Goelman, A. A. Oberg, & F. Smith (Eds.), *Awakening to literacy* (pp. 24–37). Exeter, NH: Heinemann.

Angold, A., & Costello, E. J. (1991). Developing a developmental epidemiology. In D. Cicchetti & S. L. Toth, (Eds.), *Rochester symposium on developmental psychopathology: Vol. 3. Models and integrations* (pp. 75–96). Rochester, NY: University of Rochester Press.

Angold, A., & Costello, E. J. (1992). Comorbidity in children and adolescents with depression. In D. Cantwell (Ed.), *Child and adolescent psychiatric clinics of North America: Vol 1. Mood disorders* (pp. 31–52). Philadelphia: Saunders.

Ariès, P. (1962). *Centuries of childhood* (R. Baldick, Trans.). New York: Knopf.

Asendorpf, J. B., & Baudonnière, P. (1993). Self-awareness and other-awareness: Mirror self-recognition and synchronic imitation among unfamiliar peers. *Developmental Psychology, 29,* 88–95.

Asendorpf, J. [B.], & Valsiner, J. (Eds.). (1992). *Stability and change in development: A study of methodological reasoning.* Newbury Park, CA: Sage.

Aslin, R. N. (1993) Commentary: The strange attractiveness of dynamic systems to development. In L. Smith & E. Thelen (Eds.), *A dynamic systems approach to development: Application* (pp. 385–399). Cambridge, MA: MIT Press.

Atkinson, R. C., & Shiffrin, R. M. (1968). Human memory: A proposed system and its control processes. In K. W. Spence & J. T. Spence (Eds.), *Advances in the psychology of learning and motivation* (Vol. 2, pp. 89–195). New York: Academic Press.

Austin, J. (1962). *How to do things with words.* London: Oxford University Press.

Baer, K. E. von (1828). *Über entwickelungsgeschichte der thiere.* Königsberg: Bornträger.

Baker-Ward, L., Gordon, B. N., Ornstein, P. A., Larus, D. M., & Clubb, P. A. (1993). Young children's long-term retention of a pediatric examination. *Child Development, 64,* 1519–1533.

Baker-Ward, L., Ornstein, P. A., & Gordon, B. N. (1993). A tale of two settings: Young children's memory performance in the laboratory and the field. In G. M. Davies & R. H. Logie (Eds.), *Memory in everyday life* (pp. 13–41). Amsterdam: North-Holland Press.

Baldwin, J. M. (1892). Origin of volition in childhood. *Science, 20,* 286–287.

Baldwin, J. M. (1894a). Imitation: A chapter in the natural history of consciousness. *Mind, 3* (new series), 26–55.

Baldwin, J. M. (1894b). Personality-suggestion. *Psychological Review, 1,* 274–279.

Baldwin, J. M. (1895). *Mental development in the child and the race: Methods and processes.* New York: Macmillan.

Baldwin, J. M. (1897). *Social and ethical interpretations in mental development: A study in social psychology.* New York: Macmillan.

Baldwin, J. M. (1902). *Social and ethical interpretations in mental development: A study in social psychology* (3rd ed., rev. & enl.). New York: Macmillan. (Originally published in 1897)

Baldwin, J. M. (1906). *Thought and things: A study of the development and meaning of thought or genetic logic: Vol. 1. Functional logic, or genetic theory of knowledge.* London: Swan Sonnenschein.

Baldwin, J. M. (1908). *Thought and things: A study of the development and meaning of thought or genetic logic: Vol. 2. Elementary logic, or genetic theory of thought.* London: Swan Sonnenschein.

Baldwin, J. M. (1930). "James Mark Baldwin." In C. Murchison (Ed.), *A history of psychology in autobiography* (Vol. 1, pp. 1–30). Worcester, MA: Clark University Press.

Baltes, P. B. (1987). Theoretical propositions of life-span developmental psychology: On the dynamics between growth and decline. *Developmental Psychology, 23,* 611–626.

Baltes, P. B., & Baltes, M. M. (Eds.). (1990). *Successful aging: Perspectives from the behavioral sciences.* New York: Cambridge University Press.

Baltes, P. B., & Reese, H. W. (1984). The life-span perspective in developmental psychology. In M. H. Bornstein, & M. E. Lamb (Eds.), *Developmental psychology: An advanced textbook* (pp. 493–531). Hillsdale, NJ: Erlbaum.

Banaji, M. R., & Crowder, R. G. (1989). The bankruptcy of everyday memory. *American Psychologist, 44,* 1185–1193.

Bandura, A. (1988). Self-regulation of motivation and action through goal systems. In V. Hamilton, G. H. Bower, & N. H. Frijda (Eds.), *Cognitve perspectives on emotion and motivation* (pp. 37–61). Dordrecht, The Netherlands: Kluwer.

Bandura, A. (Ed.). (1995). *Self-efficacy in changing societies.* New York: Cambridge University Press.

Bates, E., Camaioni, L., & Volterra, V. (1975). The acquisition of performatives prior to speech. *Merrill-Palmer Quarterly, 21,* 205–226.

Bateson, G. (1972). *Steps to an ecology of mind* (Prepared by V. Carroll). New York: Ballantine.

Bateson, P. P. G. (1996). Design for a life. In D. Magnusson (Ed.), *The lifespan development of individuals: Behavioral, neurobiological, and psychosocial perspectives* (pp. 1–20). Cambridge: Cambridge University Press.

Bateson, P. P. G. (Ed.). (1991). *The development and integration of behaviour: Essays in honour of Robert Hinde.* New York: Cambridge University Press.

Bayley, N. (1969). *Manual for the Bayley scales of infant development.* New York: Psychological Corporation.

Beach, F. A. (1950). The snark was a boojum. *American Psychologist, 5,* 115–124.

Beilin, H. (1964). Perceptual-cognitive conflict in the development of an invariant area concept. *Journal of Experimental Child Psychology, 1,* 208–226.

Bell, R. Q. (1968). A reinterpretation of the direction of effects in studies of socialization. *Psychological Review, 75,* 81–95.

Bendersky, M., & Lewis, M. (1990). Early language ability as a function of ventricular dilatation associated with intraventricular hemorrhage. *Developmental and Behavioral Pediatrics, 11,* 17–21.

Berger, P. L., & Luckman, T. (1966). *The social construction of reality: A treatise in the sociology of knowledge*. New York: Doubleday.

Bergman, L. R. (1988). You can't classify all of the people all of the time. *Multivariate Behavioral Research, 23*, 425–441.

Bergman, L. R., & Magnusson, D. (1990). General issues about data quality in longitudinal research. In D. Magnusson & L. R. Bergman (Eds.), *Data quality in longitudinal research* (pp. 1–31). Cambridge: Cambridge University Press.

Berman, C. M. (1992). Immature siblings and mother-infant relationships among free-ranging rhesus on Cayo Santiago. *Animal Behavior, 44*, 247–258.

Bertalanffy, L. von (1962). *Modern theories of development: An introduction to theoretical biology* (J. H. Woodger, Trans.). New York: Harper. (Originally published in 1933)

Binet, A., & Henri, V. (1894a). La mémoire des mots. *L'Année Psychologique, 1*, 1–23.

Binet, A., & Henri, V. (1894b). La mémoire des phrases (memoire des idées). *L'Annee Psychologique, 1*, 24–59.

Binet, A., & Henri, V. (1895). La psychologie individuelle. *L'Annee Psychologique, 2*, 411–465.

Bisanz, J., Morrison, F. J., & Dunn, M. (1995). Effects of age and schooling on the acquisition of elementary quantitative skills. *Developmental Psychology, 31*, 221–236.

Bissex, G. L. (1984). The child as teacher. In H. Goelman, A. A. Oberg, & F. Smith (Eds.), *Awakening to literacy* (pp. 87–101). London: Heinemann.

Bjorklund, D. F. (1985). The role of conceptual knowledge in the development of organization in children's memory. In C. J. Brainerd & M. Pressley (Eds.), *Basic processes in memory development: Progress in cognitive development research* (pp. 103–142). New York: Springer-Verlag.

Bjorklund, D. F. (1987). How age changes in knowledge base contribute to the development of children's memory: An interpretive review. *Developmental Review, 7*, 93–130.

Bjorklund, D. F., & Zeman, B. R. (1982). Children's organization and metamemory awareness in their recall of familiar information. *Child Development, 53*, 799–810.

Blass, E. M. (1990). Suckling: Determinants, changes, mechanisms, and lasting impressions. *Developmental Psychology, 26*, 520–533.

Born, D. E., & Rubel, E. W. (1988). Afferent influences on brain stem auditory nuclei of the chicken: Presynaptic action potentials regulate protein synthesis in nucleus magnocellularis neurons. *Journal of Neuroscience, 8*, 901–919.

Bowlby, J. (1958). The nature of the child's tie to his mother. *International Journal of Psycho-Analysis, 39*, 350–373.

Bowlby, J. (1969). *Attachment and loss: Vol. 1. Attachment*. New York: Basic Books.

Bowlby, J. (1973). *Attachment and loss: Vol. 2. Separation: Anxiety and anger.* New York: Basic Books.

Braine, M. D. S. (1963). The ontogeny of English phrase structure: The first phase. *Language, 39,* 1–13.

Brainerd, C. J. (1978). *Piaget's theory of intelligence.* Englewood Cliffs, NJ: Prentice-Hall.

Brazelton, T. B., Koslowski, B., & Main, M. (1974). The origins of reciprocity: The early mother-infant interaction. In M. Lewis & L. A. Rosenblum (Eds.), *The effect of the infant on its caregiver* (pp. 49–76). New York: Wiley .

Brazy, J. E., Eckerman, C. O., Oehler, J. M., Goldstein, R. F., & O'Rand, A. M. (1991). Nursery neurobiologic risk score: Important factors in predicting outcome in very low birth weight infants. *Journal of Pediatrics, 118,* 783–792.

Brehm, S. S., & Brehm, J. W. (1982). *Psychological reactance: A theory of freedom and control.* New York: Academic Press.

Breland, K., & Breland, M. (1961). The misbehavior of organisms. *American Psychologist, 16,* 681–684.

Broadbent, D. E. (1958). *Perception and communication.* New York: Pergamon Press.

Bronfenbrenner, U. (1943). A constant frame of reference for sociometric research. *Sociometry, 6,* 363–397.

Bronfenbrenner, U. (1944). A constant frame of reference for sociometric research: Part II. Experience and inference. *Sociometry, 7,* 40–75.

Bronfenbrenner, U. (1958). Socialization and social class through time and space. In E. E. Macoby, T. M. Newcomb & E. L. Hartley (Eds.), *Readings in social psychology* (3rd ed.). New York: Holt, Rinehart, & Winston.

Bronfenbrenner, U. (1977). Toward an experimental ecology of human development. *American Psychologist, 32,* 513–531.

Bronfenbrenner, U. (1979). *The ecology of human development.* Cambridge, MA: Harvard University Press.

Bronfenbrenner, U. (1986). Ecology of the family as a context for human development: Research perspectives. *Developmental Psychology, 22,* 723–742.

Bronfenbrenner, U. (1993). The ecology of cognitive development: Research models and fugitive findings. In R. H. Wozniak & K. W. Fischer (Eds.), *Development in context: Acting and thinking in specific environments* (pp. 3–44). Hillsdale, NJ: Erlbaum.

Bronfenbrenner, U. (1995). Developmental ecology through space and time: A future perspective. In P. Moen, G. H. Elder, Jr., & K. Lüscher (Eds.), *Examining lives in context: Perspectives on the ecology of human development* (pp. 619–647). Washington, DC: American Psychological Association.

Bronfenbrenner, U., & Ceci, S. J. (1994). Nature-nurture reconceptualized in developmental perspective: A bioecological model. *Psychological Review, 101,* 568–596.

Bronfenbrenner, U., & Crouter, A. C. (1983). The evolution of environmental models in developmental research. In P. H. Mussen (Gen. Ed.) & W. Kessen (Vol. Ed.), *Handbook of child psychology: Vol. 1. History, theory, methods* (pp. 357–414). New York: Wiley.

Brown, A. L., & DeLoache, J. S. (1978). Skills, plans, and self-regulation. In R. S. Siegler (Ed.), *Children's thinking: What develops?* Hillsdale, NJ: Erlbaum.

Brown, R., & Bellugi, U. (1964). Three processes in the child's acquisition of syntax. *Harvard Educational Review, 34,* 133–151.

Brownell, C. A. (1986). Convergent developments: Cognitive-developmental correlates of growth in infant/toddler peer skills. *Child Development, 57,* 275–286.

Brownell, C. A. (1988). Combinatorial skills: Converging developments over the second year. *Child Development, 59,* 675–685.

Brownell, C. A., & Carriger, M. S. (1991). Collaborations among toddler peers: Individual contributions to social contexts. In L. B. Resnick, J. M. Levine, & S. D. Teasley (Eds.), *Perspectives on socially shared cognition* (pp. 365–383). Washington, DC: American Psychological Association.

Bruner, J. S. (1964). The course of cognitive growth. *American Psychologist, 19,* 1–15.

Bruner, J. S. (1983). *Child's talk: Learning to use language.* New York: Norton.

Brunswick, E. (1952). *The conceptual framework of psychology.* Chicago: University of Chicago Press.

Bryk, A. S., & Raudenbush, S. W. (1992). *Hierarchical linear models: Applications and data analysis methods.* Newbury Park, CA: Sage.

Buchmann, M. (1989). *The script of life in modern society: Entry into adulthood in a changing world.* Chicago: University of Chicago Press.

Bühler, C. (1935). The curve of life as studied in biographies. *Journal of Applied Psychology, 19,* 405–409.

Bullock, M., & Lutkenhaus, P. (1988). The development of volitional behavior in the toddler years. *Child Development, 59,* 664–674.

Burton, L. M., & Bengtson, V. L. (1985). Black grandmothers: Issues of timing and continuity of roles. In V. L. Bengtson & J. F. Robertson (Eds.), *Grandparenthood* (pp. 61–77). Beverly Hills, CA: Sage.

Butterworth, G., & Bryant, P. (Eds.). (1990). *Causes of development: Interdisciplinary perspectives.* Hillsdale: Erlbaum.

Button, J. W. (1989). *Blacks and social change: Impact of the civil rights movement in southern communities.* Princeton, NJ: Princeton University Press.

Cahan, E. D., & White, S. H. (1992). Proposals for a second psychology. *American Psychologist, 47,* 224–235.

Cairns, R. B. (1973). Fighting and punishment from a developmental perspective. In J. K. Cole & D. D. Jensen (Eds.), *Nebraska Symposium on Motivation* (Vol. 20). Lincoln: University of Nebraska Press.

Cairns, R. B. (1979). *Social development: The origins and plasticity of social interchanges.* San Francisco: Freeman.

Cairns, R. B. (1983). The emergence of developmental psychology. In P. H. Mussen (Gen. Ed.) & W. Kessen (Vol. Ed.), *Handbook of child psychology: Vol. 1: History, theory, and methods* (4th ed., pp. 41–102). New York: Wiley.

Cairns, R. B. (1986). Phenomena lost: Issues in the study of development. In J. Valsiner (Ed.), *The individual subject and scientific psychology* (pp. 97–112). New York: Plenum.

Cairns, R. B. (1992). The making of a developmental science: The contributions and intellectual heritage of James Mark Baldwin. *Developmental Psychology, 28,* 17–24.

Cairns, R. B. (1993). Belated but bedazzling: Timing and genetic influence in social development. In G. Turkewitz & D. A. Devenny (Eds.), *Developmental time and timing* (pp. 61–84). Hillsdale, NJ: Erlbaum.

Cairns, R. B., & Cairns, B. D. (1991). Social cognition and social networks: A developmental perspective. In D. Pepler & K. Rubin (Eds.), *The development and treatment of childhood aggression* (pp. 249–278). Hillsdale: Erlbaum.

Cairns, R. B., & Cairns, B. D. (1994). *Lifelines and risks: Pathways of youth in our time.* New York: Cambridge University Press.

Cairns, R. B., Cairns, B. D., & Neckerman, H. J. (1989). Early school dropout: Configurations and determinants. *Child Development, 60,* 1437–1452.

Cairns, R. B., Cairns, B. D., Neckerman, H. J., Ferguson, L. L., & Gariépy, J.-L. (1989). Growth and aggression: I. Childhood to early adolescence. *Developmental Psychology, 25,* 320–330.

Cairns, R. B., Gariépy, J.-L., & Hood, K. E. (1990). Development, microevolution, and social behavior. *Psychological Review, 97,* 49–65.

Cairns, R. B., MacCombie, D. J., & Hood, K. E. (1983). A developmental-genetic analysis of aggressive behavior in mice: I. Behavioral outcomes. *Journal of Comparative Psychology, 97,* 69–89.

Cairns, R. B., McGuire, A. M., & Gariépy, J.-L. (1993). Developmental behavior genetics: Fusion, correlated constraints, and timing. In D. F. Hay & A. Angold (Eds.), *Precursors and causes in development and psychopathology* (pp. 87–122). New York: Wiley.

Cairns, R. B., & Ornstein, P. A. (1979). Developmental psychology. In E. S. Hearst (Ed.), *The first century of experimental psychology* (pp. 459–510). Hillsdale, NJ: Erlbaum.

Cappiocco J. T., & Tassinary L. G. (1990). Inferring psychological significance from physiological signals. *American Psychologist, 45,* 16–28.

Case, R. (1978). Intellectual development from birth to adulthood: A neo-Piagetian approach. In R. S. Siegler (Ed.), *Children's thinking: What develops?* (pp. 37–72). Hillsdale, NJ: Erlbaum.

Case, R. (1985). *Intellectual development: Birth to adulthood.* Orlando, FL: Academic Press.

Caspi, A. (1995). Puberty and the gender organization of schools: How biology and social context shape the adolescent experience. In L. J. Crockett & A. C. Crouter (Eds.), *Pathways through adolescence: Individual development in relation to social context* (pp. 57–74). Mahwah, NJ: Erlbaum.

Caspi, A., Bem, D. J., & Elder, G. H., Jr. (1989). Continuities and consequences of interactional styles across the life course. *Journal of Personality, 57,* 375–406.

Caspi, A., & Moffitt, T. (1991). Individual differences are accentuated during periods of social change: The sample case of girls at puberty. *Journal of Personality and Social Psychology, 61,* 157–168.

Cavalier-Smith, T. (1985). Cell volume and the evolution of eukaryote genome size. In T. Cavalier-Smith (Ed.), *The evolution of genome size* (pp. 105–184). Chichester, England: Wiley.

Ceci, S. J., & Liker, J. (1986). A day at the races: The study of IQ, expertise, and cognitive complexity. *Journal of Experimental Psychology: General, 115,* 225–266.

Ceci, S. J., Toglia, M. P., & Ross, D. F. (Eds.) (1987). *Children's eyewitness memory.* New York: Springer-Verlag.

Champoux, M., Suomi, S. J., & Schneider, M. L. (1994). Temperamental differences in captive Indian- and Chinese-derived rhesus macaque neonates. *Laboratory Animal Science, 44,* 351–357.

Chandler, M. J. (1973). Egocentrism and antisocial behavior: The assessment and training of social perspective-taking skills. *Developmental Psychology, 9,* 326–332.

Changeux, J.-P., & Konishi, M. (Eds.) (1987). *The neural and molecular bases of learning.* Chichester, England: Wiley.

Cherlin, A. J. (1993). *Marriage, divorce, and remarriage.* Cambridge, MA: Harvard University Press.

Chess, S., & Hassibi, M. (1978). *Principles and practice of child psychiatry.* New York: Plenum.

Chess, S., & Hassibi, M. (1986). *Principles and practice of child psychiatry* (2nd ed.). New York: Plenum.

Chi, M. T. H. (1978). Knowledge structures and memory development. In R. S. Siegler (Ed.), *Children's thinking: What develops?* (pp. 73–96). Hillsdale, NJ: Erlbaum.

Chi, M. T. H., & Ceci, S. J. (1987). Content knowledge: Its role, representation, and restructuring in memory development. In H. W. Reese (Ed.), *Advances in child development and behavior* (Vol. 20, pp. 91–142). Orlando, FL: Academic Press.

Chi, M. T. H., & Koeske, R. D. (1983). Network representation of a child's dinosaur knowledge. *Developmental Psychology, 19,* 29–39.

Chomsky, N. (1959). A review of Skinner's *Verbal Behavior. Language, 35,* 26–58.

Cicchetti, D. (1984). The emergence of developmental psychopathology. *Child Development, 55,* 1–7.

Cicchetti, D. (1990). An historical perspective on the discipline of developmental psychopathology. In J. Rolf, A. Masten, D. Cicchetti, K. Neuchterlein, & S. Weintraub (Eds.), *Risk and protective factors in the development of psychopathology* (pp. 1–28). Cambridge: Cambridge University Press.

Cicchetti, D., & Cohen, D. J. (Eds.). (1995). *Developmental psychopathology.* New York: Wiley.

Cierpal, M. A., & McCarty, R. (1987). Hypertension in SHR rats: Contribution of maternal environment. *American Journal of Physiology, 253,* 980–984.

Clark, M. M. (1976). *Young fluent readers: What can they teach us?* London: Heinemann.

Clark, N. M., & Galef, B. G. (1988). Effects of uterine position on rate of sexual development in female mongolian gerbils. *Physiology & Behavior, 42,* 15–18.

Clausen, J. A. (1983). *Behavioral Science Research Review Consultant Panel.* Behavioral sciences research in mental health. Rockville, MD: ADAMHA.

Clausen, J. A. (1993). *American lives: Looking back at the children of the Great Depression.* New York: Free Press; Toronto: Maxwell Macmillan Canada; New York: Maxwell Macmillan International.

Clipp, E. C., & Elder, G. H., Jr. (1996). The aging veteran of World War II: Psychiatric and life course insights. In P. E. Ruskin & J. A. Talbott (Eds.), *Aging and post-traumatic stress disorder* (pp. 19–51). Washington, DC: American Psychiatric Press.

Clipp, E. C., Pavalko, E. K., & Elder, G. H., Jr. (1992). Trajectories of health: In concept and empirical pattern. *Behavior, Health, and Aging, 2(3),* 159–179.

Cofer, C. N. (1986). Human nature and social policy. In L. Friedrich-Cofer (Ed.), *Human nature and public policy: Scientific views of women, children, and families* (pp. 39–96). New York: Praeger.

Coie, J. D., Terry, R., Lenox, K., Lochman, J., & Hyman, C. (1995). Childhood peer rejection and aggression as predictors of stable patterns of adolescent disorder. *Development and Psychopathology, 7,* 697–713.

Cole, M. (1985). The zone of proximal development: Where culture and cognition create each other. In J. V. Wertsch (Ed.), *Culture, communication and cognition: Vygotskian perspectives* (pp. 146–161). Cambridge: Cambridge University Press.

Cole, M., & Scribner, S. (1974). *Culture and thought: A psychological introduction.* New York: Wiley.

Cole, T. R. (1992). *The journey of life: A cultural history of aging in America.* New York: Cambridge University Press.

Coleman, J. S. (1990). *The foundations of social theory.* Cambridge, MA: Harvard University Press.

Conger, R. D., & Elder, G. H., Jr. (1994). *Families in troubled times: Adapting to change in rural America.* Hawthorne, NY: Aldine DeGruyter.

Cooper, R. M., & Zubeck, J. P. (1958). Effects of enriched and restricted early environments on the learning ability of bright and dull rats. *Canadian Journal of Psychology, 12,* 159–164.

Costello, E. J., Benjamin, R., Angold, A., & Silver, D. (1991). Mood variability in adolescents: A study of depressed, nondepressed and comorbid patients. *Journal of Affective Disorders, 23,* 199–212.

Cottrell, L. S. (1942). The analysis of situational fields in social psychology. *American Sociological Review, 7,* 370–382.

Crick, F. (1988). *What mad pursuit: A personal view of scientific discovery.* New York: Basic Books.

Crockenberg, S. B. (1981). Infant irritability, mother responsiveness, and social support influences on the security of infant-mother attachment. *Child Development, 52,* 857–865.

Cronbach, L. J. (1975). Beyond the two disciplines of scientific psychology. *American Psychologist, 30,* 116–127.

Damerow, P. (1988). Individual development and cultural evolution of arithmetical thinking. In S. Strauss (Ed.), *Ontogeny, phylogeny, and historical development* (pp. 125–152). Norwood, NJ: Ablex.

Dannefer, D. (1984). The role of the social in life-span developmental psychology, past and future: Rejoinder to Baltes and Nesselroade. *American Sociological Review, 49,* 847–850.

Danziger, K. (1990). *Constructing the subject: Historical origins of psychological research.* Cambridge: Cambridge University Press.

Darlington, R. B. (1991). The long-term effects of model preschool programs. In L. Okagaki & R. J. Sternberg (Eds.), *Directors of development: Influences on the development of children's thinking* (pp. 203–216). Hillsdale, NJ: Erlbaum.

Darwin, C. (1872). *The expression of the emotions in man and animals.* London: Murray.

Darwin, C. (1877). A biographical sketch of an infant. *Mind, 2,* 285–294.

Davidson, E. H. (1986). *Gene activity in early development* (3rd ed.). Orlando, FL: Academic Press.

Davis, K. (1940). The sociology of parent-youth conflict. *American Sociological Review, 5,* 523–535.

Davydov, V. V., & Radzikhovskii, L. A. (1985). Vygotsky's theory and the activity-oriented approach in psychology. In J. V. Wertsch (Ed.), *Culture, communication and cognition: Vygotskian perspectives* (pp. 35–65). Cambridge: Cambridge University Press.

DeBaryshe, B. D., Caulfield, M. B., Witty, J. P., & Holt, H. E. (1991). *Early language experiences: Picture-book reading in the home.* Unpublished manuscript, University of North Carolina at Greensboro.

de Beer, G. (1958). *Embryos and ancestors* (3rd ed.). Oxford: Oxford University Press.

De Ribaupierre, A. (Ed.). (1989). *Transition mechanisms in child development: The longitudinal perspective.* New York: Cambridge University Press.

deVries, M. W., & Sameroff, A. J. (1984). Culture and temperament: Influences on temperament in three East African societies. *American Journal of Orthopsychiatry, 54,* 83–96.

Dewey, J. (1916). *Democracy and education: An introduction to the philosophy of education.* New York: Macmillan.

Dewey, J., & Bentley, A. F. (1949). *Knowing and the known.* Boston: Beacon.

Dewsbury, D. A. (1978). *Comparative animal behavior.* New York: McGraw-Hill.

DiBerardino, M. A. (1988). Genomic multipotentiality of differentiated somatic cells. In G. Eguchi, T. S. Okada, & L. Saxén (Eds.), *Regulatory mechanism in developmental processes* (pp. 129–136). Amsterdam: Elsevier.

Didow, S. M. (1993). Achieving verbal discourse through nonverbal coordinated action (Doctoral dissertation, Duke University, 1993). *Dissertation Abstracts International, 54* (03), 1691.

Didow, S. M., & Eckerman, C. O. (1991, April). *Developments in toddlers' talk with unfamiliar peers.* Poster presented at the Biannual Meeting of the Society for Research in Child Development, Seattle.

Dittus, W. P. J. (1979). The evolution of behaviors regulating density and age specific ratios in a primate population. *Behavior, 69,* 265–302.

Donald, M. (1991). *Origins of the modern mind: Three stages in the evolution of culture and cognition.* Cambridge, MA: Harvard University Press.

Donaldson, M. (1984). Speech and writing and modes of learning. In H. Goelman, A. A. Oberg, & F. Smith (Eds.), *Awakening to literacy* (pp. 174–184). Exeter, NH: Heinemann.

Dore, J. (1973). A developmental theory of speech act production. *Transactions of the New York Academy of Sciences,* series 2, 35 (8), 623–630.

Dore, J. (1974). A pragmatic description of early language development. *Journal of Psycholinguistic Research, 3,* 343–350.

Doris, J. (Ed.). (1991). *The suggestibility of children's recollections.* Washington, DC: American Psychological Association.

Doyle, A. B. (1973). Listening to distraction: A developmental study of selective attention. *Journal of Experimental Child Psychology, 15,* 100–115.

Draper, P. (1976). Social and economic constraints on child life among the !Kung. In R. B. Lee & E. DeVore (Eds.), *Kalahari hunter gatherers: Studies of the !Kung Son and their neighbors* (pp. 199–217). Cambridge, MA: Harvard University Press.

Driesch, H. (1908/1929). *The science and philosophy of the organism.* London: A. & C. Black. (Second abridged edition used here)

Duranti, A., & Ochs, E. (1986). Literacy instruction in a Samoan village. In B. B. Schieffelin & P. Gallimore (Eds.), *The acquisition of literacy: Ethnographic perspectives* (pp. 213–232). Norwood, NJ: Ablex.

Easterlin, R. A. (1980). *Birth and fortune.* New York: Basic Books.

Ebert, J. D., & Sussex, I. M. (1970). *Interacting systems in development* (2nd ed.), New York: Holt.

Eckerman, C. O. (1993a). Imitation and toddlers' achievement of co-ordinated action with others. In J. Nadel & L. Camaioni (Eds.), *New perspectives in early communicative development* (pp. 116–156). New York: Routledge.

Eckerman, C. O. (1993b). Toddlers' achievement of coordinated action with conspecifics: A dynamic systems perspective. In L. B. Smith & E. Thelen (Eds.), *A dynamic systems approach to development: Applications* (pp. 333–357). Cambridge, MA: MIT Press.

Eckerman, C. O., Davis, C. C., & Didow, S. M. (1989). Toddlers' emerging ways of achieving social coordinations with a peer. *Child Development, 60,* 440–453.

Eckerman, C. O., & Didow, S. M. (1989). Toddlers' social coordinations: Changing responses to another's invitation to play. *Developmental Psychology, 25,* 794–804.

Eckerman, C. O., & Oehler, J. M. (1992). Very-low-birthweight newborns and parents as early social partners. In S. L. Friedman & M. D. Sigman (Eds.), *The psychological development of low birthweight infants.* Norwood, NJ: Ablex.

Eckerman, C. O., Oehler, J. M., Hannan, T. E., & Molitor, A. (1995). The development prior to term age of very-prematurely-born newborns' responsiveness in en face exchanges. *Infant Behavior and Development, 18,* 283–297.

Eckerman, C. O., Oehler, J. M., Medvin, M. B., & Hannan, T. E. (1994). Premature newborns as social partners before term age. *Infant Behavior and Development, 17,* 55–70.

Eckerman, C. O., Oehler, J. M., Molitor, A., Hsu, H., & Smith, D. (1994, June). *Arousal regulation in en face social encounters: Biological risk and prior interactive experience.* Poster presented at International Conference on Infant Studies, Paris.

Eckerman, C. O., & Stein, M. R. (1990). How imitation begets imitation and toddlers' generation of games. *Developmental Psychology, 26,* 370–378.

Eckerman, C. O., Sturm, L. A., & Gross, S. J. (1985). Different developmental courses for very-low-birthweight infants differing in early head growth. *Developmental Psychology, 21,* 813–827.

Edelman, G. M. (1987). *Neural Darwinism: The theory of neuronal group selection.* New York: Basic Books.

Edelman, G. M. (1988). *Topobiology: An introduction to molecular biology.* New York: Basic Books.

Eichorn, D. H., Clausen, J. A., Haan, N., Honzik, M., & Mussen, P. H. (Eds.). (1981). *Present and past in middle life.* New York: Academic Press.

Eisenstein, E. L. (1979). *The printing press as an agent of change: Communications and cultural transformations in early modern Europe.* Cambridge: Cambridge University Press.

Elder, G. H., Jr. (1974). *Children of the Great Depression: Social change in life experience.* Chicago: University of Chicago Press.

Elder, G. H., Jr. (1978). Family history and the life course. In T. K. Hareven (Ed.), *Transitions*. New York: Academic Press.

Elder, G. H., Jr. (1979). Historical change in life patterns and personality. In P. B. Baltes & O. G. Brim, Jr. (Eds.), *Life-span development and behavior* (Vol. 2, pp. 117–159). New York: Academic Press.

Elder, G. H., Jr. (1980). Adolescence in historical perspective. In J. Adelson (Ed.), *Handbook of adolescent psychology* (pp. 3–46). New York: Wiley.

Elder, G. H., Jr. (1985). Perspectives on the life course. In G. H. Elder, Jr. (Ed.), *Life course dynamics: Trajectories and transitions, 1968–1980* (pp. 23–49). Ithaca, NY: Cornell University Press.

Elder, G. H., Jr. (1987). War mobilization and the life course: A cohort of World War II veterans. *Sociological Forum, 2*(3), 449–472.

Elder, G. H., Jr. (1992a, March). *Children of the farm crisis*. Paper presented at the Society for Research on Adolescence, Washington, DC.

Elder, G. H., Jr. (1992b). Life course. In E. Borgatta & M. Borgatta (Eds.), *The encyclopedia of sociology* (Vol. 3, pp. 1120–1130). New York: Macmillan.

Elder, G. H., Jr. (1995). The life course paradigm: Social change and individual development. In P. Moen, G. H. Elder, Jr., & K. Lüscher (Eds.), *Examining lives in context: Perspectives on the ecology of human development* (pp. 101–139). Washington, DC: American Psychological Association.

Elder, G. H., Jr., & Caspi, A. (1988). Economic stress in lives: Developmental perspectives. *Journal of Social Issues, 44,* (4), 25–45.

Elder, G. H., Jr., & Caspi, A. (1990). Studying lives in a changing society: Sociological and personological explorations. In A. I. Rabin, R. A. Zucker, & S. Frank (Eds.), *Studying persons and lives* (pp. 201–247). New York: Springer.

Elder, G. H., Jr., Caspi, A., & Downey, G. (1986). Problem behavior and family relationships: Life course and intergenerational themes. In A. B. Sørensen, F. E. Weinert, & L. R. Sherrod (Eds.), *Human development and the life course: Multidisciplinary perspectives* (pp. 293–340). Hillsdale, NJ: Erlbaum.

Elder, G. H., Jr., Eccles, J. S., Ardelt, M., & Lord, S. (1995). Inner city parents under economic pressure: Perspectives on the strategies of parenting. *Journal of Marriage and the Family, 57,* 771–784.

Elder, G. H., Jr., Liker, J. K., & Cross, C. E. (1984). Parent-child behavior in the Great Depression: Life course and intergenerational influences. In P. B. Baltes & O. G. Brim, Jr. (Eds.), *Life-span development and behavior* (Vol. 6, pp. 109–158). New York: Academic Press.

Elder, G. H., Jr., & O'Rand, A. M. (1995). Adult lives in a changing society. In K. S. Cook, G. A. Fine, & J. S. House (Eds.), *Sociological perspectives on social psychology* (pp. 452–475). New York: Allyn & Bacon.

Elder, G. H., Jr., Pavalko, E. K., & Clipp, E. C. (1993). *Working with archival data: Studying lives*. Newbury Park, CA: Sage Publications.

Elder, G. H., Jr., Shanahan, M. J., & Clipp, E. C. (1994). When war comes to men's lives: Life-course patterns in family, work, and health. *Psychology and Aging,* *9,* 5–16.

Elder, G. H., Jr., Modell, J., & Parke, R. D. (Eds.). (1993). *Children in time and place: Developmental and historical insights.* New York: Cambridge University Press.

Ellis, P. L. (1982). Empathy: A factor in antisocial behavior. *Journal of Abnormal Child Psychology, 10,* 123–134.

Erikson, Erik H. (1950/1963). *Childhood and society* (2nd ed., rev. & enl.). New York: Norton.

Fantz, R. L. (1958). Pattern vision in young infants. *Psychological Record, 8,* 43–47.

Farrington, D. P. (1986). Stepping stones to adult criminal careers. In D. Olweus, J. Block, & M. Radke-Yarrow (Eds.), *Development of antisocial and prosocial behavior: Research, theories and issues* (pp. 359–384). New York: Academic Press.

Farrington, D. P., & West, D. J. (1990). The Cambridge study in delinquent development: A long-term follow-up of 411 London males. In H.-J. Kerner & G. Kaiser (Eds.), *Kriminalität: Persönlichkeit, Lebensgeschichte und Verhalten: Festschrift für Hans Göppler zum 70. Geburtstag* [Criminality: Personality, behavior, and life history]. Berlin: Springer-Verlag. (In German and English)

Featherman, D. L. (1986). Biography, society, and history: Individual development as a population process. In A. B. Sørensen, F. E. Weinert, & L. R. Sherrod (Eds.), *Human development and the life course: Multidisciplinary perspectives* (pp. 99–149). Hillsdale, NJ: Erlbaum.

Feldman, K. A., & Newcomb, T. M. (1969). *The impact of college on students.* San Francisco: Jossey-Bass.

Ferreira, F., & Morrison, F. J. (1994). Children's metalinguistic knowledge of syntactic constituents: Effects of age and schooling. *Developmental Psychology, 30,* 663–678.

Ferreiro, E., & Teberosky, A. (1983). *Literacy before schooling* (K. G. Castro, Trans.). London: Heinemann.

Field, T. (1981). Infant arousal, attention, and affect during early interactions. In L. P. Lipsitt & C. K. Rovee-Collier (Eds.), *Advances in infancy research* (Vol. 1, pp. 157–200). Norwood, NJ: Ablex.

Fischer, K. W. (1980). A theory of cognitive development: The control and construction of hierarchies of skills. *Psychological Review, 87,* 477–531.

Fishbein, H. D. (1976). *Evolution, development, and children's learning.* Pacific Palisades, CA: Goodyear.

Fitzgerald, K., & Needlman, R. (1991). Reach out and read: A pediatric program to support emergent literacy. *Zero to Three, 12,* 17–20.

Fitzhardinge, P. M. (1980). Current outcome of ICU populations. In A. W. Brann & J. J. Volpe (Eds.), *Neonatal neurological assessment and outcome* (Report of the Seventy-seventh Ross Conference on Pediatric Research, pp. 1–5). Columbus, OH: Ross Laboratories.

Fivush, R., Gray, J. T., & Fromhoff, F. A. (1987). Two-year-olds talk about the past. *Cognitive Development, 2,* 393–409.

Fivush, R., Hudson, J. A., & Nelson, K. (1984). Children's long-term memory for a novel event: An exploratory study. *Merrill-Palmer Quarterly, 30,* 303–316.

Fivush, R., & Hudson, J. A. (Eds.). (1990). *Knowing and remembering in young children.* New York: Cambridge University Press.

Flavell, J. H. (1963). *The developmental psychology of Jean Piaget.* Princeton, NJ: Van Nostrand.

Flavell, J. H. (1985). *Cognitive development* (2nd ed.). Englewood Cliffs, NJ: Prentice-Hall.

Flavell, J. H., Beach, D. H., & Chinsky, J. M. (1966). Spontaneous verbal rehearsal in a memory task as a function of age. *Child Development, 37,* 283–299.

Flavell, J. H., & Markman, E. M. (Eds.). (1983). *Handbook of child psychology: Cognitive development* (Vol. 3). New York: Wiley. (P. H. Mussen, Gen. Ed.)

Flynn, J. R. (1984). The mean IQ of Americans: Massive gains 1932–1978. *Psychological Bulletin, 95,* 29–51.

Flynn, J. R. (1987). Massive IQ gains in 14 nations: What IQ tests really measure. *Psychological Bulletin, 101,* 171–191.

Fogel, A., Nwokah, E., Hsu, H., Dedo, J. Y., & Walker, H. (1993). Posture and communication in mother-infant interaction. In G. J. P. Savelsbergh (Ed.), *The development of coordination in infancy* (pp. 395–422). Amsterdam: North-Holland.

Fogel, A., & Thelen, E. (1987). Development of early expressive and communicative action: Reinterpreting the evidence from a dynamic systems perspective. *Developmental Psychology, 23,* 747–761.

Fogel, A., Toda, S., & Kawai, M. (1988). Mother-infant face-to-face interaction in Japan and the United States: A laboratory comparison using 3-month-old infants. *Developmental Psychology, 24,* 398–406.

Folds, T. H., Footo, M. M., Guttentag, R. E., & Ornstein, P. A. (1990). When children mean to remember: Issues of context specificity, strategy effectiveness, and intentionality in the development of memory. In D. F. Bjorklund (Ed.), *Children's strategies: Contemporary views of cognitive development.* Hillsdale, NJ: Erlbaum.

Ford, D. H., & Lerner, R. M. (1992). *Developmental systems theory: An integrative approach.* Newbury Park, CA: Sage.

Freedman, D., Thornton, A., Camburn, D., Alwin, D., & Young-DeMarco, L. (1988). The life history calendar: A technique for collecting retrospective data. *Sociological Methodology, 18,* 37–68.

Freire, P. (1972). *Cultural action for freedom.* Harmondsworth, England: Penguin.

Freud, A. (1965). *Normality and pathology in childhood: Assessment of development.* New York: International Universities Press.

Frye, D. (1991). The origins of intention in infancy. In D. Frye & C. Moore (Eds.), *Children's theories of mind: Mental states and social understanding* (pp. 15–38). Hillsdale, NJ: Erlbaum.

Funder, D. C., Parke, R. D., Tomlinson-Keasey, C., & Widaman, K. (1993). *Studying lives through time: Personality and development.* Washington, DC: American Psychological Association Press.

Furstenberg, F. F., Jr., Eccles, J., Elder, G. H., Jr., Cook, T., & Sameroff, A. J. (Eds.). (in press). *Urban families and adolescent success.* Chicago: University of Chicago Press.

Futuyma, D. J. (1988). *Sturm und Drang* and the evolutionary synthesis. *Evolution, 42,* 217–226.

Garber, J. (1984). Classification of childhood psychopathology: A developmental perspective. *Child Development, 55,* 30–48.

Gariépy, J.-L. (1995). The mediation of aggressive behavior in mice: A discussion of approach-withdrawal processes in social adaptations. In K. E. Hood, G. Greenberg, & E. Tobach (Eds.), *Behavioral development: Concepts of approach/withdrawal and integrative levels* (pp. 231–284). New York: Garland.

Gariépy, J.-L., Gendreau, P. J., Mailman, R. B., Tancer, M., & Lewis, M. H. (1995). Rearing conditions alter social reactivity and D1 dopamine receptors in high and low aggressive mice. *Psychopharmacology, Biochemistry and Behavior, 51,* 767–773.

Gariépy, J.-L., Hood, K. E., & Cairns, R. B. (1988). A developmental-genetic analysis of aggressive behavior in mice: 3. Behavioral mediation by heightened reactivity or increased immobility? *Journal of Comparative Psychology, 102,* 392–399.

Gariépy, J.-L., Lewis, M. H., & Cairns, R. B. (in press). Genes, neurobiology, and aggression: Time frames and functions of social behaviors in adaptation. In D. M. Stoff & R. B Cairns (Eds.), *Aggression and violence: Neurobiological, biosocial and genetic perspectives.* Hillsdale:, NJ: Erlbaum.

Garner, P. W., Landry, S. H., & Richardson, M. A. (1990). *The developmental sequence of joint attention skills for preterm infants: Effects of medical risk status.* Paper presented at the Sixth Biennial Meeting of the International Conference on Infant Studies, Montreal, Canada.

Ge, X., Lorenz, F. O., Conger, R. D., Elder, G. H., Jr., & Simons, R. L. (1994). Trajectories of stressful life events and depressive symptoms during adolescence. *Developmental Psychology, 30,* 467–483.

Geertz, C. (1973). *The interpretation of cultures: Selected essays.* New York: Basic Books.

Gelb, I. J. (1952). *A study of writing: The foundations of grammatology.* Chicago: University of Chicago Press.

Gelman, R. (1969). Conservation acquisition: A problem of learning to attend to relevant attributes. *Journal of Experimental Child Psychology, 7,* 167–187.

Gesell, A. L. (1925). *The mental growth of the pre-school child: A psychological outline of normal development from birth to the sixth year, including a system of developmental diagnosis.* New York: Macmillan.

Gigerenzer, G., Swijtink, Z., Porter, T., Daston, L. J., Beatty, J., & Kruger, L. (1989). *The empire of chance: How probability changed science and everyday life.* Cambridge: Cambridge University Press.

Gleick, J. (1987). *Chaos: Making a new science.* New York: Viking.

Glenn, N. D. (1977). *Cohort analysis.* Beverly Hills, CA: Sage.

Glick, J. (1975). Cognitive development in cross-cultural perspective. In F. D. Horowitz et al. (Eds.), *Review of child development research* (Vol. 4, pp. 595–654). Chicago: University of Chicago Press.

Golinkoff, R. M., & Gordon, L. (1983). In the beginning was the word: A history of the study of language acquisition. In R. M. Golinkoff (Ed.), *The transition from prelinguistic to linguistic communication* (pp. 1–25). Hillsdale, NJ: Erlbaum.

Gollin, E. S. (1981). Development and plasticity. In E. S. Gollin (Ed.), *Developmental plasticity: Behavioral and biological aspects of variations in development.* New York: Academic Press.

Gontard, A. von (1988). The development of child psychiatry in 19th century Britain. *Journal of Child Psychology and Psychiatry, 29,* 569–588.

Goody, J. (1987). *The interface between the written and the oral.* Cambridge: Cambridge University Press.

Gorbman, A., Dickhoff, W. W., Vigna, S. R., Clark, N. B., & Ralph, C. L. (1983). *Comparative endocrinology.* New York: Wiley.

Gordon, B. N., Schroeder, C., Ornstein, P. A., & Baker-Ward, L. E. (1995). Clinical implications of research on memory development. In T. Ney (Ed.), *Allegations of child sexual abuse: Assessment and case management* (pp. 99–124). New York: Brunner/Mazel.

Gordon, E. W., & Armour-Thomas, E. (1991). Culture and cognitive development. In L. Okagaki & R. J. Sternberg (Eds.), *Directors of development: Influences on the development of children's thinking* (pp. 83–99). Hillsdale, NJ: Erlbaum.

Gottlieb, G. (1970). Conceptions of prenatal behavior. In L. R. Aronson, E. Tobach, D. S. Lehrman, & J. S. Rosenblatt (Eds.), *Development and evolution of behavior: Essays in memory of T. C. Schneirla* (pp. 111–137). San Francisco: Freeman.

Gottlieb, G. (1976). The roles of experience in the development of behavior and the nervous system. In G. Gottlieb (Ed.), *Neural and behavioral specificity* (pp. 25–54). New York: Academic Press.

Gottlieb, G. (1981). Roles of early experience in species-specific perceptual development. In R. N. Aslin, J. R. Alberts, & M. Petersen (Eds.), *Development of perception* (Vol. 1, pp. 5–44). New York: Academic Press.

Gottlieb, G. (1983). The psychobiological approach to developmental issues. In P. H. Mussen (Gen Ed.), M. M. Haith, & J. J. Campos (Vol. Eds.), *Handbook of child psychology: Vol. 2. Infancy and developmental psychobiology* (4th ed., pp. 1–26). New York: Wiley.

Gottlieb, G. (1985). Development of species identification in ducklings: XI. Embryonic critical period for species-typical perception in the hatchling. *Animal Behaviour, 33,* 225–233.

Gottlieb, G. (1987). Development of species identification in ducklings: XIII. A comparison of malleable and critical periods of perceptual development. *Developmental Psychobiology, 20,* 393–404.

Gottlieb, G. (1991a). Experiential canalization of behavioral development: Results. *Developmental Psychology, 27,* 35–39.

Gottlieb, G. (1991b). Experiential canalization of behavioral development: Theory. *Developmental Psychology, 27,* 4–13.

Gottlieb, G. (1992). *Individual development and evolution: The genesis of novel behavior.* New York: Oxford University Press.

Gottlieb, G. (1995). Some conceptual deficiencies in "developmental" behavior genetics. *Human Development, 38,* 131–141.

Gottlieb, G., Wahlsten, D., & Lickliter, R. (in press). The significance of biology for human development: A developmental psychobiological systems view. In R. Lerner (Ed.), *Handbook of child psychology: Theoretical models of human development* (5th ed., Vol. 1). New York: Wiley.

Gould, M. S., Wunsch-Hitzig, R., & Dohrenwend, B. P. (1980). Formulation of hypotheses about the prevalence, treatment and prognostic significance of psychiatric disorders in children in the United States. In B. P. Dohrenwend (Ed.), *Mental illness in the United States: Epidemiological estimates* (pp. 9–44). New York: Praeger.

Gould, S. J. (1977). *Ontogeny and phylogeny.* Cambridge, MA: Harvard University Press.

Greenough, W. T., & Chang, F. L. F. (1988). Dendritic pattern formation involves both oriented regression and oriented growth in the barrels of mouse somatosensory cortex. *Developmental Brain Research, 43,* 148–152.

Greenough, W. T., & Juraska, J. M. (1979). Experience-induced changes in brain fine structure: Their behavioral implications. In M. E. Hahn, C. Jensen, & B. C. Dudek (Eds.), *Development and evolution of brain size: Behavioral implications* (pp. 296–320). New York: Academic Press.

Grene, M. G. (1987). Hierarchies in biology. *American Scientist, 75,* 504–510.

Grouse, L. D., Schrier, B. K., Lefendre, C. H., & Nelson, P. G. (1980). RNA sequence complexity in central nervous system development and plasticity. *Current Topics in Developmental Biology, 16,* 381–397.

Guttentag, R. E. (1984). The mental effort requirement of cumulative rehearsal: A developmental study. *Journal of Experimental Child Psychology, 37,* 92–106.

Hack, M., & Breslau, N. (1986). Very low birth weight infants: Effects of brain growth during infancy on intelligence quotient at 3 years of age. *Pediatrics, 77,* 196–202.

Hack, M., Breslau, N., Weissman, B., Aram, D., Klein, N., & Borawski, E. (1991). Effect of very low birth weight and subnormal head size on cognitive abilities at school age. *New England Journal of Medicine, 325,* 231–237.

Hagell, A., & Tudge, J. (in press). Illiterate adults in literate societies: Interactions with a social world. In M. Kohl de Olivera & J. Valsiner (Eds.). *Literacy in human development.* New York: Ablex.

Hagen, J. W., & Hale, G. H. (1973). The development of attention in children. In A. D. Pick (Ed.), *Minnesota symposia on child psychology* (Vol. 7, pp. 117–140). Minneapolis: University of Minnesota Press.

Hagestad, G. O. (1982). Parent and child: Generations in the family. In T. M. Field, A. Huston, H. C. Quay, L. Troll, & G. E. Finley (Eds.), *Review of human development* (pp. 485–499). New York: Wiley.

Hagestad, G. O. (1990). Social perspectives on the life course. In R. H. Binstock & L. K. George (Eds.), *Handbook of aging and the social sciences* (3rd ed., pp. 151–168). New York: Academic Press.

Haith, M. M., & Campos, J. J. (Eds.). (1983). *Handbook of child psychology: Vol. 2. Infancy and developmental psychobiology* (4th ed.). New York: Wiley. (P. H. Mussen, Gen. Ed.)

Hall, B. K. (1988). The embryonic development of bone. *American Scientist, 76,* 174–181.

Hall, G. S. (1885). The new psychology. *Andover Review, 3,* 120–135, 239–248.

Halliday, M. A. K. (1975). *Learning how to mean: Explorations in the development of language.* London: Edward Arnold.

Hamburger, V. (1988). *The heritage of experimental embryology: Hans Spemann and the organizer.* New York: Oxford University Press.

Harding, C. G., & Golinkoff, R. M. (1979). The origins of intentional vocalizations in prelinguistic infants. *Child Development, 50,* 33–40.

Hareven, T. K. (1982). *Family time and industrial time.* New York: Cambridge University Press.

Harlow, H. F. (1958a). The evolution of learning. In A. Roe & G. G. Simpson (Eds.), *Behavior and evolution.* New Haven: Yale University Press.

Harlow, H. F. (1958b). The nature of love. *American Psychologist, 13,* 673–685.

Harlow, H. F., & Harlow, M. K. (1965). The affectional systems. In A. M. Schrier, H. F. Harlow, & F. Stollnitz (Eds.), *Behavior of nonhuman primates* (Vol. 2). New York: Academica Press.

Harlow, H. F., & Zimmerman, R. R. (1959). Affectional responses in the infant monkey. *Science, 130,* 421–432.

Hay, D. F., & Angold, A. (1993). *Introduction: Precursors and causes in development and pathogenesis.* Chichester, England: John Wiley.

Heath, S. B. (1983). *Ways with words: Language, life, and work in communities and classrooms.* Cambridge: Cambridge University Press.

Heath, S. B. (1986a). What no bedtime story means: Narrative skills at home and school. In B. B. Schieffelin & E. Ochs (Eds.), *Language socialization across cultures* (pp. 97–124). Cambridge: Cambridge University Press.

Heath, S. B. (1986b). Critical factors in literacy development. In S. De Castell, A. Luke, & K. Egan (Eds.), *Literacy, society, and schooling: A reader* (pp. 209–229). Cambridge: Cambridge University Press.

Heath, S. B., & Thomas, C. (1984). The achievement of preschool literacy for mother and child. In H. Goelman, A. A. Oberg, & F. Smith (Eds.), *Awakening to literacy* (pp. 51–72). London: Heinemann.

Heckhausen, J. (1987). Balancing for weaknesses and challenging developmental potential: A longitudinal study of mother-infant dyads in apprenticeship interactions. *Developmental Psychology, 23,* 762–770.

Hegmann, J. P., & DeFries, J. C. (1970). Are genetic correlations and environmental correlations correlated? *Nature, 226,* 284–286.

Helson, R., Mitchell, V., & Moane, G. (1984). Personality and patterns of adherence and nonadherence to the social clock. *Journal of Personality and Social Psychology, 46(5),* 1079–1096.

Herbst, D. (1987). Co-genetic logic: The eight process networks. Unpublished Document 1.87 of the Work Research Institute, Oslo, Norway.

Hetherington, E. M., & Baltes, P. B. (1988). Child psychology and life-span development. In E. M. Hetherington, R. M. Lerner, & M. Perlmutter (Eds.), *Child development in life-span perspective* (pp. 1–19). Hillsdale, NJ: Erlbaum.

Heubner, T. (1987). A socio-historical approach to literacy development. In J. A. Langer (Ed.), *Language, literacy, and culture: Issues of society and schooling* (pp. 179–196). Norwood, NJ: Ablex.

Higley, J. D., Hopkins, W. D., Hirsch, R. M., Marra, L. M., & Suomi, S. J. (1987). Preferences of female rhesus monkeys (Macaca mulatta) for infantile coloration. *Developmental Psychobiology, 20,* 7–18.

Hill, R. (1970). *Family development in three generations.* Cambridge, MA: Schenkman.

Hinde, R. A. (1966). *Animal behaviour: A synthesis of ethology and comparative psychology.* New York: McGraw-Hill.

Hinde, R. A., & Stevenson-Hinde, J. (1976). Towards understanding relationships: Dynamic stability. In P. P. G. Bateson & R. A. Hinde (Eds.), *Growing points in ethology* (pp. 451–480). Cambridge: Cambridge University Press.

Ho, M.-W. (1984). Environment and heredity in development and evolution. In M.-W. Ho & P. T. Saunders (Eds.), *Beyond neo-Darwinism: An introduction to the new evolutionary paradigm* (pp. 267–289). London: Academic Press.

Hodapp, R. M., Goldfield, E. C., & Boyatzis, D. J. (1984). The use and effectiveness of maternal scaffolding in mother-infant games. *Child Development, 55,* 772–781.

Hofer, M.A. (1994). Hidden regulators in attachment, separation, and loss. *Monographs of the Society for Research in Child Development, 59(2–3, Serial No. 240).*

Hogan, D. P. (1981). *Transitions and social change: The early lives of American men.* New York: Academic Press.

Hogan, D. P., & Astone, N. M. (1986). The transition to adulthood. *The Annual Review of Sociology* (Vol. 12, pp. 109–130).

Hood, K. E. (1995). Dialectical and dynamical systems of approach and withdrawal: Is fighting a fractal form? In K. E. Hood, G. Greenberg, & E. Tobach (Eds.), *Behavioral development: Concepts of approach/withdrawal and integrative levels* (pp. 19–76). New York: Garland.

Hood, K. E., Greenberg, G., & Tobach, E. (Eds.). (1995). *Behavioral development: Concepts of approach/withdrawal and integrative levels.* New York: Garland.

Horowitz, F. D. (1987). *Exploring developmental theories: Toward a structural/behavioral model of development.* Hillsdale: Erlbaum.

Hudson, J. A., & Fivush, R. (1991). As time goes by: Sixth graders remember a kindergarten experience. *Applied Cognitive Psychology, 5,* 347–360.

Hull, C. L. (1939). The problem of stimulus equivalence in behavior theory. *Psychological Review, 46,* 9–30.

Hull, C. L. (1943). Principles of behavior. New York: Appleton-Century-Crofts.

Huxley, J. S. (1957). The three types of evolutionary progress. *Nature, 180,* 454–455.

Hydén, H., & Egyházi, E. (1962). Nuclear RNA changes of nerve cells during a learning experiment in rats. *Proceedings of the National Academy of Sciences of the United States of America, 48,* 1366–1373.

Hydén, H., & Egyházi, E. (1964). Changes in RNA content and base composition in cortical neurons of rats in a learning experiment involving transfer of handedness. *Proceedings of the National Academy of Sciences of the United States of America, 52,* 1030–1035.

Immelmann, K. (1975). Ecological significance of imprinting and early learning. *Annual Review of Ecology and Systematics, 6,* 15–37.

Ireland, W. W. (1877). *On idiocy and imbecility.* London: Churchill.

Irvine, J. T. (1978). Wolof "magical thinking": Culture and conservation revisited. *Journal of Cross-Cultural Psychology, 9,* 300–310.

James, W. (1890). *The principles of psychology* (Vol. 1). New York: Macmillan.

Janet, P. (1921). The fear of action. *Journal of Abnormal Psychology and Social Psychology, 16,* 151–160.

Janet, P. (1925). *Psychological healing: A historical and clinical study* (E. Paul & C. Paul, Trans.) (Vols. 1–2). London: Allen & Unwin; New York: Macmillan.

Jessor, R., Donovan, J. E., & Costa, F. M. (1991). *Beyond adolescence: Problem behavior and young adult development.* New York: Cambridge University Press.

Johnson, W. H. E. (1950). *Russia's educational heritage.* Pittsburgh: Carnegie Press.

Johnston, T. D. (1987). The persistence of dichotomies in the study of behavioral development. *Developmental Review, 7,* 149–182.

Jones, M. C. (1924). A laboratory study of fear: The case of Peter. *Pedagogical Seminary, 31,* 308–315.

Kadanoff, L. P. (1986). Chaos: A view of complexity in the physical sciences. In *The great ideas today: 1986.* Chicago: Encyclopaedia Britannica.

Kagan, J. (1989). *Unstable ideas: Temperament, cognition, and self.* Cambridge, MA: Harvard University Press.

Kagan, J. (1994). *Galen's prophecy: Temperament in human nature.* New York: Basic Books.

Kagan, J., & Moss, H. A. (1962). *Birth to maturity: A study in psychological development.* New York: Wiley.

Kail, R. V. (1990). *The development of memory in children* (3rd ed.). New York: Freeman.

Kail, R. V., & Bisanz, J. (1982). Information processing and cognitive development. In H. W. Reese (Ed.), *Advances in child development and behavior* (Vol. 17, pp. 45–81). Orlando, FL: Academic Press.

Kanner, L. (1945). *Child psychiatry.* Springfield, IL: C. C. Thomas.

Kanner, L. (1972). *Child psychiatry* (4th ed.). Springfield, IL: C. C. Thomas.

Kaye, K. (1982). *The mental and social life of babies: How parents create persons.* Chicago: University of Chicago Press.

Keeney, T. J., Canizzo, S. R., & Flavell, J. H. (1967). Spontaneous and induced verbal rehearsal in a recall task. *Child Development, 38,* 953–966.

Kemp, M. (1985). Parents as teachers of literacy. In M. M. Clark (Ed.), *New directions in the study of reading* (pp. 153–167). London: Falmer Press.

Kendler, H. H., & Kendler, T. S. (1962). Vertical and horizontal processes in problem solving. *Psychological Review, 69,* 1–16.

Kendler, H. H., & Kendler, T. S. (1975). From discrimination learning to cognitive development: A neobehavioristic odyssey. In W. K. Estes (Ed.), *Handbook of Learning and Cognitive Processes: Vol. 1. Introduction to concepts and issues* (pp. 151–248). Hillsdale, NJ: Erlbaum.

Kertzer, D. I., & Keith, J., (Eds.). (1984). *Age and anthropological theory.* Ithaca, NY: Cornell University Press.

Kessen, W. (1960). Research design in the study of developmental problems. In P. H. Mussen (Ed.), *Handbook of research methods in child development* (pp. 36–70). New York; Wiley.

Kessen, W. (1979).The American child and other cultural inventions. *American Psychologist, 34,* 815–820.

Kessen, W. (1993). The child and other cultural inventions. In F. S. Kessel & A. W. Siegel (Eds.), *The child and other cultural inventions: Houston Symposium 4* (pp. 26–47). New York: Praeger.

Kessen, W., Haith, M. M., & Salapatek, P. H. (1970). Human infancy: A bibliography and guide. In P. H. Mussen (Ed.), *Carmichael's Manual of Child Psychology* (3rd ed., Vol. 1, pp. 287–445). New York: Wiley.

Kessler, D. S., & Melton, D. A. (1994, October 28). Vertebrate embryonic induction: Mesodermal and neural patterning. *Science, 266,* 566–604.

Kindermann, T., & Valsiner, J. (1989). Strategies for empirical research in context-inclusive developmental psychology. In J. Valsiner (Ed.), *Child development in cultural context* (pp. 13–50). Toronto, Canada: Hogrefe & Huber.

King, J. A. (1967). Behavioral modification in the gene pool. In J. Hirsch (Ed.), *Behavior-genetic analysis* (pp. 22–43). New York: McGraw-Hill.

Kitchell, J. A. (1990). The reciprocal interaction of organism and effective environment: Learning more about "and." In R. M. Ross & W. D. Allman (Eds.), *Causes of evolution: A paleontological perspective.* Chicago: University of Chicago Press.

Klahr, D., & Wallace, J. G. (1972). Class inclusion processes. In S. Farnham-Diggory (Ed.), *Information processing in children* (pp. 143–172). New York: Academic Press.

Kohn, M. L. (1969/1977). *Class and conformity: A study in values, with a reassessment* (2nd ed.). Chicago: University of Chicago Press.

Kohn, M. L., & Schooler, C. (1983). *Work and personality: An inquiry into the impact of social stratification.* Norwood, NJ: Ablex.

Kollar, E. J., & Fisher, C. (1980). Tooth induction in chick epithelium: Expression of quiescent genes for enamel synthesis. *Science, 207,* 993–995.

Kovach, J. K., & Wilson, G. (1988). Genetics of color preferences in quail chicks: Major genes and variable buffering by background genotype. *Behavioral Genetics, 18,* 645–661.

Kozulin, A. (1990). *Vygotsky's psychology: A biography of ideas.* Cambridge, MA: Harvard University Press.

Kroger, R. O., & Scheibe, K. E. (1990). A reappraisal of Wundt's influence on social psychology. *Canadian Psychology, 31,* 220–228.

Kuenne, M. R. (1946). Experimental investigation of the relation of language to transposition behavior in young children. *Journal of Experimental Psychology, 36,* 471–490.

Kuller, L. H., Perper, J. A., Dai, W. S., & Rutan, G. (1986). Sudden death and the decline in coronary heart disease mortality. *Journal of Chronic Diseases, 39,* 1001–1019.

Kuo, Z.-Y. (1967). *The dynamics of behavioral development: An epigenetic view.* New York: Random House.

Kuo, Z.-Y. (1976). *The dynamics of behavior development: An epigenetic view* (enlarged ed.). New York: Plenum Press. (Prepared by G. Gottlieb.)

Laboratory of Comparative Human Cognition. (1983). Culture and cognitive development. In P. H. Mussen (Ed.), *Handbook of child psychology: Vol. 1. History, theory, methods* (4th ed., pp. 295–356). New York: Wiley.

Lachman, R., Lachman, J. L., & Butterfield, E. C. (1979). *Cognitive psychology and information processing: An introduction.* Hillsdale, NJ: Erlbaum.

Lamb, M. E., Thompson, R. A., Gardner, W. P., Charnov, E. L., & Estes, D. (1984). Security of infantile attachment as assessed in the "strange situation": Its study and biological interpretation. *Behavioral and Brain Sciences, 7,* 127–147.

Landry, S. H., & Chapieski, M. L. (1988). Visual attention during toy exploration in preterm infants: Effects of medical risk and maternal interactions. *Infant Behavior and Development, 11,* 187–204.

Langer, J. A. (1987). A sociocognitive perspective on literacy. In J. A. Langer (Ed.), *Language, literacy, and culture: Issues of society and schooling* (pp. 1–20). Norwood, NJ: Ablex.

Lapouse, R. L., & Monk, M. A. (1958). An epidemiologic study of behavior characteristics in children. *American Journal of Public Health,* 48, 1134–1144.

Largo, R. H., Molinari, L., Comenale Pinto, L., Weber, M., & Duc, G. (1986). Language development of term and preterm children during the first five years of life. *Developmental Medicine and Child Neurology, 28,* 333–350.

Laufer, R. S., Yager, T., Frey-Wouters, E., & Donnellan, J. (1981). *Legacies of Vietnam: Comparative adjustment of veterans and their peers: Vol. 3. Postwar trauma: Social and psychological problems of Vietnam veterans.* Washington, DC: U.S. Government Printing Office.

Lehrman, D. S. (1953). A critique of Konrad Lorenz's theory of instinctive behavior. *Quarterly Review of Biology, 28,* 337–363.

Lehrman, D. S. (1970). Semantic and conceptual issues in the nature-nurture problem. In L. R. Aronson, D. S. Lehrman, E. Tobach, & J. S. Rosenblatt (Eds.), *Development and evolution of behavior: Essays in memory of T. C. Schneirla* (pp. 17–52). San Francisco: Freeman.

Leichter, H. J. (1984). Families as environments for literacy. In H. Goelman, A. A. Oberg, & F. Smith (Eds.), *Awakening to literacy* (pp. 38–50). Exeter, NH: Heinemann.

Lenneberg, E. (1967). *Biological foundations of language.* New York: John Wiley, 1967.

Leontyev, A. N. (1981). *Problems of the development of mind.* Moscow: Progress Publishers.

Leopold, W. F. (1939, 1947, 1949a, 1949b). *Speech development of a bilingual child: A linguist's record: Vol. 1. Vocabulary growth in the first two years. Vol. 2. Sound-learning in the first two years. Vol. 3. Grammar and general problems in the first two years. Vol 4. Diary from age 2.* Evanston, IL: Northwestern University Press.

Lerner, R. M., & Kaufman, M. B. (1985). The concept of development in contextualism. *Developmental Review, 5,* 309–333.

LeVine, R. A., Dixon, S., Richman, A., Leiderman, P. H., & Keefer, C. H. (1994). *Child care and culture: Lessons from Africa.* Cambridge: Cambridge University Press.

Levine, S., Wiener, S. G., & Coe, C. L. (1993). Temporal and social factors influencing behavioral and hormonal responses to separation in mother and infant squirrel monkeys. *Psychoneuroendocrinology, 18,* 297–306.

Levinson, D. J. (1978). *The seasons of a man's life.* New York: Ballantine.

Lewin, K. (1931). Environmental forces in child behavior and development. In C. Murchison (Ed.), *A handbook of child psychology* (2nd ed., pp. 590–625). Worcester, MA: Clark University Press; London: H. Milford, Oxford University Press.

Lewis, M. H., Gariépy, J.-L., Gendreau, P. J., Nichols, D. E., & Mailman, R. B. (1994). Social reactivity and D1 dopamine receptors: Studies in mice selectively bred for high and low levels of aggression. *Neuropsychopharmacology, 10,* 115–122.

Lewis, M. H., Gariépy, J.-L., Southerland, S. B., Mailman, R., & Cairns, R. B. (1988). Alterations in central dopamine induced by selective breeding. *Society for Neuroscience Abstracts, 14,* 969.

Lilienfeld, A. M., & Lilienfeld, D. E. (1980). *Foundations of Epidemiology* (2nd ed.). New York: Oxford University Press.

Liljequist, R., Henriksson, B. G., Latif, N., Pham, Lissman T., Winblad, B., & Mohammed, A. H. (1993). Subchronic MK-801 treatment to juvenile rats attenuates environmental effects on adult spatial learning. *Behavioural Brain Research, 56,* 107–114.

Lindburg, D. G. (1971). The rhesus monkey in North India: An ecological and behavioral study. In L. A. Rosenblum (Ed.), *Primate behavior: Developments in field and laboratory research* (Vol. 2). New York: Academic Press.

Loeber, R., & Hay, D. F. (1994). Developmental approaches to aggression and conduct problems. In M. Rutter & D. F. Hay (Eds.), *Development through life: A handbook for clinicians* (pp. 488–515). Oxford: Blackwell Scientific.

Loeber, R., & Le Blanc, D. (1990). Toward a developmental criminology. In M. Tonry & N. Morris (Eds.), *Crime and justice: An annual review of research* (Vol. 12, pp. 375–473.) Chicago: University of Chicago Press.

Loftus, E. F. (1991). The glitter of everyday memory . . . and the gold. *American Psychologist, 46,* 16–18.

Lorenz, E. N. (1983). *Irregularity: A fundamental property of the atmosphere. The Crafoord Prize in the Geosciences: 1983.* Stockholm: The Royal Swedish Academy of Sciences.

Lovejoy, C. O. (1981). The origins of man. *Science, 211,* 341–350.

Løvtrup, S. (1987). *Darwinism: The refutation of a myth.* New York: Croom Helm in association with Methuen.

Lozoff, B. (1983). Birth and "bonding" in non-industrial societies. *Developmental Medicine & Child Neurology, 25,* 595–600.

Lumsden, C. J., & Wilson, E. O. (1980). Translation of epigenetic rules of individual behavior into ethnographic patterns. *Proceedings of the National Academy of Sciences of the United States of America, 77,* 4382–4386.

Luria, A. R. (1928). The problem of the cultural behavior of the child. *Pedagogical Seminary and Journal of Genetic Psychology, 35,* 493–506.

Maccoby, E. E., & Konrad, K. W. (1966). Age trends in selective listening. *Journal of Experimental Child Psychology, 3,* 113–122.

Maccoby, E. E., & Masters, J. C. (1970). Attachment and dependency. In P. H. Mussen (Ed.), *Carmichael's Manual of Child Psychology* (3rd ed., Vol. 2, pp. 73–157). New York: Wiley.

Mack, K. J., & Mack, P. A. (1992). Induction of transcription factors in somatosensory cortex after tactile stimulation. *Molecular Brain Research, 12,* 141–147.

Magnusson, D. (1988). *Individual development in paths through life: Vol. 1. A longitudinal study.* Hillsdale, NJ: Erlbaum.

Magnusson, D. (1995). Individual development: A holistic integrated model. In P. Moen, G. H. Elder, Jr., & K. Luscher (Eds.), *Examining lives in context: Perspectives on the ecology of human development* (pp. 19–60). Washington, DC: American Psychological Association.

Magnusson, D. (Ed.). (1996). *The lifespan development of individuals: Behavioral, neurobiological, and psychosocial perspectives: A synthesis.* New York: Cambridge University Press.

Magnusson, D., & Bergman, L. R. (1984). On the study of the development of adjustment problems. In L. Pulkkinen & P. Lyytinen (Eds.), *Human action and personality: Essays in honour of Martti Takala,* Jyväskylä studies in education, psychology, and social research. Jyväskylä, Finland: University of Jyväskylä.

Magnusson, D., & Bergman, L. R. (1990). A pattern approach to the study of pathways from childhood to adulthood. In L. N. Robins & M. Rutter (Eds.), *Straight and devious pathways from childhood to adulthood* (pp. 101–115). Cambridge: Cambridge University Press.

Magnusson, D., & Stattin, H. (in press). Person-context interaction theories. In R. M. Lerner (Vol. Ed.) & J. Damon (Gen. Ed.), *Handbook of child psychology: Theoretical models of human development* (5th ed., Vol. 1). New York: Wiley.

Magnusson, D., & Törestad, B. (1993). A holistic view of personality: A model revisited. *Annual Review of Psychology, 44,* 427–452.

Manis, F., Keating, D. P., & Morrison, F. J. (1980). Developmental differences in the allocation of processing capacity. *Journal of Experimental Child Psychology, 29,* 156–169.

Marler, P., Zoloth, S., & Dooling, R. (1981). Innate programs for perceptual development: An ethological view. In E. Gollin (Ed.), *Developmental plasticity: Behavioral and biological aspects of variations in development* (pp. 135–172). New York: Academic Press.

Marschark, M. (1993). *Psychological development of deaf children.* Oxford: Oxford University Press.

Maudsley, H. (1879). *The pathology of mind* (3rd ed.). London: Macmillan.

Mayer, K. U. (1986). Structural constraints on the life course. *Human Development, 29*(3), 163–170.

Mayer, K. U., & Tuma, N. B. (Eds.). (1990). *Event history analysis in life course research.* Madison: University of Wisconsin Press.

Mayr, E. (1961). Cause and effect in biology. *Science, 134,* 1501–1507.

Mayr, E. (1982). *The growth of biological thought: Diversity, evolution and intelligence.* Cambridge, MA: Belknap Press.

McCarthy, D. (1954). Language development in children. In L. Carmichael (Ed.), *Manual of child psychology* (2nd ed.). New York: Wiley.

McLane, J. B., & McNamee, G. D. (1990). *Early literacy.* Cambridge, MA: Harvard University Press.

McLaughlin, S. D., Melber, B. D., Billy, J. O. G., Zimmerle, D. M., Winges, L. D., & Johnson, T. R. (1988). *The changing lives of American women.* Chapel Hill: University of North Carolina Press.

McLeod, J. D., & Shanahan, M. J. (1994, 25–27 May). *Cumulative effects of poverty and children's mental health.* Paper presented at the Fifth International Conference of Social Stress Research, Honolulu.

McNeill, D. (1966). Developmental psycholinguistics. In F. Smith & G. A. Miller (Eds.), *The genesis of language: A psycholinguistic approach.* Cambridge, MA: MIT Press.

Mead, G. H. (1934). *Mind, self, and society from the standpoint of a social behaviorist.* C. W. Morris (Ed.). Chicago: University of Chicago Press.

Mead, G. H. (1956). *The social psychology of George Herbert Mead.* A. Strauss (Ed.). Chicago: University of Chicago Press.

Mehlman, P. T., Higley, J. D., Faucher, I., Lilly, A. A., Taub, D. M., Vickers, J., Suomi, S. J., & Linnoila, M. (in press). CSF 5-HIAA concentrations are correlated with sociality and the timing of emigration in free-ranging primates. *American Journal of Psychiatry.*

Milko, J. E. (1992). Effects of social experience on the dopaminergic systems of mice selectively bred for high and low levels of aggressiveness. Unpublished honors essay, University of North Carolina at Chapel Hill.

Miller, P. H. (1989). *Theories of developmental psychology* (2nd ed.). New York: Freeman.

Miller, W., & Ervin, S. (1964). The development of grammar in child language. In U. Bellugi & R. W. Brown (Eds.), *The acquisition of language.* Monographs of the Society for Research in Child Development, 29, no. 1, serial no. 92.

Mills, W. (1899). The nature of animal intelligence and the methods of investigating it. *Psychological Review, 6,* 262–274.

Minuchin, P. (1985). Families and individual development: Provocations from the field of family therapy. *Child Development, 56,* 289–302.

Mirsky, A. E., & Ris, H. (1951). The deoxyribonucleic acid content of animal cells and its evolutionary significance. *Journal of General Physiology, 34,* 451–462.

Modell, J. (1989). *Into one's own: From youth to adulthood in the United States, 1920–1975*. Berkeley: University of California Press.

Moen, P., Dempster-McClain, D., & Williams, R. M., Jr. (1992). Successful aging: A life-course perspective on women's multiple roles and health. *American Journal of Sociology, 97,* 1612–1638.

Moen, P., Elder, G. H., Jr., & Lüscher, K. (Eds.). (1995). *Examining lives in context: Perspectives on the ecology of human development.* Washington, DC: American Psychological Association.

Morgan, C. L. (1896). *Habit and instinct.* London: Arnold.

Morrison, F. J. (1987, November). *Making the cut: Contrasting developmental and learning influences on cognitive growth.* Paper presented at the annual meeting of the Psychonomics Society, Seattle.

Morrison, F. J., Griffith, E. M., & Frazier, J. A. (in press). Schooling and the 5 to 7 shift: A natural experiment. In A. Sameroff & M. M. Haith (Eds.), *Reason and responsibility: The passage through childhood.* Chicago: University of Chicago Press.

Morrison, F. J., Holmes, D. J., & Haith, M. M. (1974). A developmental study of the effects of familiarity on short-term visual memory. *Journal of Experimental Child Psychology, 18,* 412–425.

Morrison, F. J., Lord, C. L., & Keating, D. P. (Eds.) (1984). *Applied developmental psychology* (Vol. 1). Orlando, FL: Academic Press.

Morrison, F. J., Smith, L., & Dow-Ehrensberger M. (1995). Education and cognitive development: A natural experiment. *Development Psychology, 31,* 789–799.

Mowrer, O. (1954). The psychologist looks at language. *American Psychologist, 9,* 660–694.

Mrazek, P. J., & Haggerty, R. J. (Eds.) (1994). *Reducing risks for mental disorders: Frontiers for preventive intervention research.* Committee on Prevention of Mental Disorders, Division of BioBehavioral Sciences and Mental Disorders, Institute of Medicine. Washington, DC: National Academy Press.

Myers, M. M., Brunelli, S. A., Shair, H. M., Squire, J. M., & Hofer, M. A. (1989). Relationships between maternal behavior of SHR and WKY dams and adult blood pressures of cross-fostered F1 pups. *Developmental Psychobiology, 22,* 55–67.

Myers, M. M., Brunelli, S. A., Squire, J. M., Shindeldecker, R. D., & Hofer, M. A. (1989). Maternal behavior of SHR rats and its relationships to offspring blood pressure. *Developmental Psychobiology, 22,* 29–53.

Nagel, E. (1957). Determinism and development. In D. B. Harris (Ed.), *The concept of development: An issue in the study of human behavior* (pp. 15–26). Minneapolis: University of Minnesota Press.

National Advisory Mental Health Council. (1990). *National plan for research on child and adolescent mental disorders: A report requested by the U.S. Con-*

gress. Rockville, MD: U.S. Department of Health, National Institute of Mental Health.

Needham, J. (1929). *The skeptical biologist.* London: Chatto.

Needham, J. (1959). *A history of embryology* (2nd ed., rev. with the assistance of A. Hughes). New York: Abelard-Schuman.

Neisser, U. (1967). *Cognitive psychology.* New York: Appleton-Century-Crofts.

Neisser, U. (1978). Memory: What are the important questions? In M. M. Gruneberg, P. E. Morris, & R. N. Sykes (Eds.), *Practical aspects of memory* (pp. 3–24). London: Academic Press.

Nelson, K., with Gruendel, J., et al. (1986). *Event knowledge: Structure and function in development.* Hillsdale, NJ: Erlbaum.

Nelson, K., Fivush, R., Hudson, J., & Lucariello, J. (1983). Scripts and the development of memory. In M. T. H. Chi (Vol. Ed.), *Trends in memory development research: Vol. 9. Contributions to human development* (pp. 52–70). Basel, Switzerland: S. Karger.

Nelson, K., & Hudson, J. (1988). Scripts and memory: Functional relationships in development. In F. E. Weinert & M. Perlmutter (Eds.), *Memory development: Universal changes and individual differences* (pp. 147–168). Hillsdale, NJ: Erlbaum.

Neugarten, B. L., & Datan, N. (1973). Sociological perspectives on the life cycle. In P. B. Baltes, & K. W. Schaie (Eds.), *Life-span developmental psychology: Personality and socialization* (pp. 53–69). New York: Academic Press.

Newcomb, T. M. (1943). *Personality and social change: Attitude formation in a student community.* New York: Dryden Press.

Newman, D., Griffin, P., & Cole, M., with Broyles, S., Petitto, A. L., & Quinsatt, M. G. (1989). *The construction zone: Working for cognitive change in school.* Cambridge: Cambridge University Press.

Ninio, A., & Bruner, J. (1978). The achievement and antecedents of labelling. *Journal of Child Language, 5,* 1–15.

Nyiti, R. M. (1982). The validity of "cultural differences explanations" for crosscultural variation in the rate of Piagetian cognitive development. In D. A. Wagner & H. W. Stevenson (Eds.), *Cultural perspectives on child development* (pp. 146–165). San Francisco: Freeman.

Ogbu, J. U. (1987). Opportunity structure, cultural boundaries, and literacy. In J. A. Langer (Ed.), *Language, literacy, and culture: Issues of society and schooling* (pp. 149–177). Norwood, NJ: Ablex.

Okagaki, L., & Sternberg, R. J. (1991). Cultural and parental influences on cognitive development. In L. Okagaki & R. J. Sternberg (Eds.), *Directors of development: Influences on the development of children's thinking* (pp. 101–120). Hillsdale, NJ: Erlbaum.

O'Rand, A. M., & Krecker, M. L. (1990). Concepts of the life cycle: Their history, meanings and uses in the social sciences. *Annual Review of Sociology* (Vol. 16, pp. 241–262).

Ornstein, P. A. (1978a). Introduction: The study of children's memory. In P. A. Ornstein (Ed.), *Memory development in children* (pp. 1–20). Hillsdale, NJ: Erlbaum.

Ornstein, P. A. (1978b). *Memory development in children.* Hillsdale, NJ: Erlbaum.

Ornstein, P. A., Baker-Ward, L., & Naus, M. J. (1988). The development of mnemonic skill. In F. E. Weinert & M. Perlmutter (Eds.), *Memory development: Universal changes and individual differences* (pp. 31–50). Hillsdale, NJ: Erlbaum.

Ornstein, P. A., Gordon, B. N., Baker-Ward, L. E., & Merritt, K. A. (in press). Children's memory for medical experiences: Implications for testimony. In D. Peters (Ed.), *The child witness in context: Cognitive, social, and legal perspectives.* Dordrecht, The Netherlands: Kluwer Academic Publishers.

Ornstein, P. A., Gordon, B. N., & Larus, D. M. (1992). Children's memory for a personally experienced event: Implications for testimony. *Applied Cognitive Psychology, 6,* 49–60.

Ornstein, P. A., & Naus, M. J. (1978). Rehearsal processes in children's memory. In P. A. Ornstein (Ed.), *Memory development in children* (pp. 69–99). Hillsdale, NJ: Erlbaum.

Ornstein, P. A., & Naus, M. J. (1985). Effects of the knowledge base on children's memory strategies. In H. W. Reese (Ed.), *Advances in child development and behavior* (Vol. 19, pp. 113–148). Orlando, FL: Academic Press.

Ornstein, P. A., Naus, M. J., & Liberty, C. (1975). Rehearsal and organizational processes in children's memory. *Child Development, 46,* 818–830.

Osgood, C. (1963). On understanding and creating sentences. *American Psychologist, 18,* 735–751.

Overton, W. F. (1984). World views and their influence on psychological theory and research: Kuhn-Lakatos-Laudan. In H. W. Reese (Ed.), *Advances in child development and behavior.* (Vol. 18, pp. 191–226). Orlando, FL: Academic Press.

Overton, W. F., & Horowitz, H. A. (1991). Developmental psychopathology: Integrations and differentiations. In D. Cicchetti & S. L. Toth (Eds.), *Rochester symposium on developmental psychopathology: Vol. 3. Models and integrations* (pp. 1–42). Rochester, NY: University of Rochester Press.

Oyama, S. (1985). *The ontogeny of information: Developmental systems and evolution.* Cambridge: Cambridge University Press.

Oyama, S. (1989). Ontogeny and the central dogma: Do we need the concept of genetic programming in order to have an evolutionary perspective? In M. R. Gunnar & E. Thelen (Eds.), *Minnesota Symposia on Child Psychology: Vol. 22. Systems and development* (pp. 1–34). Hillsdale, NJ: Erlbaum.

Papousek, H., & Papousek, M. (1987). Intuitive parenting: A dialectic counterpart to the infant's integrative competence. In J. Osofsky (Ed.), *Handbook of infant development* (2nd ed., pp. 669–720). New York: Wiley.

Papousek, H., Papousek, M., Suomi, S. J., & Rahn, C. W. (1981). Preverbal communication and attachment: Comparative views. In J. L. Gewirtz & W. M. Kurtines (Eds.), *Intersections with attachment.* Hillsdale, NJ: Erlbaum.

Paris, S. G. (1978). Coordination of means and goals in the development of mnemonic skills. In P. A. Ornstein (Ed.), *Memory development in children* (pp. 259–273). Hillsdale, NJ: Erlbaum.

Parke, R. D., Ornstein, P. A., Rieser, J. J., & Zahn-Waxler, C. (1994). The past is prologue: An overview of a century of developmental pyschology. In R. D. Parke, P. A. Ornstein, J. J. Rieser, & C. Zahn-Waxler (Eds.), *A century of developmental psychology* (pp. 1–70). Washington, DC: American Psychological Association.

Parker, S. T., & Gibson, K. R. (1979). A developmental model for the evolution of language and intelligence in early hominids. *Behavioral and Brain Sciences, 2,* 367–408.

Patterson, G. R. (1982). *Coercive family processes.* Eugene, OR: Castalia.

Pepper, S. C. (1942). *World hypotheses: A study in evidence.* Berkeley: University of California Press.

Peterson, L. R., & Peterson, M. J. (1959). Short-term retention of individual verbal items. *Journal of Experimental Psychology, 58,* 193–198.

Piaget, J. (1926). *The language and thought of the child.* New York: Harcourt Brace. (Originally published in 1923)

Piaget, J. (1950). *The psychology of intelligence.* London: Routledge.

Piaget, J. (1951). *Play, dreams, and imitation in childhood.* New York: Norton.

Piaget, J. (1952). *The origins of intelligence in children.* New York: International Universities Press.

Piaget, J. (1954). *The construction of reality in the child.* New York: Basic Books.

Piaget, J. (1967). *Biologie et connaissance* [Biology and knowledge]. Paris: Gallimard.

Piaget, J. (1977). *Etudes sociologiques* [Sociological studies] (3rd ed.). Geneva, Switzerland: Librairie Droz. (Original work published in 1928 and 1945)

Pipp, S., Fisher, K. W., & Jennings, S. (1987). Acquisition of self- and mother knowledge in infancy. *Developmental Psychology, 23,* 86–96.

Platt, S. A., & Sanislow, C. A. (1988). Norm-of-reaction: Definition and misinterpretation of animal research. *Journal of Comparative Psychology, 102,* 254–261.

Powers, W. T. (1973). *Behavior: The control of perception.* Chicago: Aldine.

Prechtl, H. F. R. (1974). The behavioural states of the newborn infant (A review). *Brain Research, 76,* 185–212.

Preyer, W. T. (1888–1889). *The mind of the child* (2 vols.). New York: Appleton.

Prichard, J. C. (1837). *A treatise on insanity and other disorders affecting the mind.* Philadelphia: Haswell, Barrington & Haswell.

Pritchard, D. J. (1986). *Foundations of developmental genetics.* London: Taylor & Francis.

Rader, N. (1985). Change and variation: On the importance of heterochrony for development (Commentary on Bateson). In G. Butterworth, J. Rutkowska, & M. Scaife (Eds.), *Evolution and developmental psychology* (pp. 22–29). New York: St. Martin's Press.

Rasmussen, K. L. R., & Suomi, S. J. (1989). Heart rate and endocrine response to stress in adolescent male rhesus monkeys on Cayo Santiago. *Puerto Rican Health Sciences Journal, 8,* 65–71.

Ratner, H., Smith, B., & Dion, S. (1986). Development of memory for events. *Journal of Experimental Child Psychology, 41,* 411–428.

Ratner, N., & Bruner, J. (1978). Games, social exchange and the acquisition of language. *Journal of Child Language, 5,* 391–401.

Reese, H. W. (1962). Verbal mediation as a function of age level. *Psychological Bulletin, 59,* 502–509.

Reiss, A. J., Jr., & Roth, J. A. (Eds.). (1993). *Understanding and preventing violence.* Washington, DC: National Academy Press.

Reiss, D. (1989). The represented and practicing family: Contrasting visions of family continuity. In A. J. Sameroff & R. N. Emde (Eds.), *Relationship disturbances in early childhood: A development approach* (pp. 191–220). New York: Basic Books.

Renner, M. J., & Rosenzweig, M. R. (1987). *Enriched and impoverished environments: Effects on brain and behavior.* New York: Springer-Verlag.

Rensch, B. (1959). *Evolution above the species level* (Dr. Albevogt, Trans.). New York: Columbia University Press.

Rheingold, H. L. (1969). The social and socializing infant. In D. A. Goslin (Ed.), *Handbook of socialization theory and research.* Chicago: Rand McNally.

Rheingold, H. L. (Ed.). (1963). *Maternal behavior in mammals.* New York: Wiley.

Rheingold, H. L., Gewirtz, J. L., & Ross, H. W. (1959). Social conditioning of vocalization in the infant. *Journal of Comparative and Physiological Psychology, 52,* 68–73.

Riley, M. W., Foner, A., & Waring, J. (1988). The sociology of age. In N. J. Smelser (Ed.), *The handbook of sociology* (pp. 243–290). Newbury Park, CA: Sage.

Riley, M. W., Johnson, M. E., and Foner, A. (Eds.). (1972). *Aging and society: Vol. 3. A sociology of age stratification.* New York: Russell Sage Foundation.

Rindfuss, R. R., Morgan, S. P., & Swicegood, C. G. (1984). The transition to motherhood: The intersection of structure and temporal dimension. *American Sociological Review, 49,* 359–372.

Rindfuss, R. R., Swicegood, C. G., & Rosenfeld, R. (1987). Disorder in the life course: How common and does it matter? *American Sociological Review, 52,* 785–801.

Roberts, G. R. (1969). *Reading in primary schools.* London: Routledge; New York: Humanities Press.

Robins, E., & Guze, S. B. (1970). Establishment of diagnostic validity in psychiatric illness: Its application to schizophrenia. *American Journal of Psychiatry, 126,* 107–111.

Rogoff, B. (1981). Schooling and the development of cognitive skills. In H. C. Triandis & A. Heron (Eds.), *Handbook of cross-cultural psychology: Vol. 4. Developmental psychology* (pp. 233–294). Boston: Allyn & Bacon.

Rogoff, B. (1982). Integrating context and cognitive development. In M. E. Lamb & A. L. Brown (Eds.), *Advances in developmental psychology* (Vol. 2, pp. 125–170). Hillsdale, NJ: Erlbaum.

Rogoff, B. (1990). *Apprenticeship in thinking: Cognitive development in social context.* New York: Oxford University Press.

Rogoff, B., & Gauvain, M. (1986). A method for the analysis of patterns illustrated with data on mother-child instructional interaction. In J. Valsiner (Ed.), *The individual subject and scientific psychology* (pp. 261–289). New York: Plenum.

Rogoff, B., & Lave, J. (1984). *Everyday cognition: Its development in social context.* Cambridge, MA: Harvard University Press.

Romanes, G. J. (1884). *Mental evolution in animals.* New York: Appleton.

Rosenblatt, J. S. (1965). The basis of synchrony in the behavioral interaction between the mother and her offspring in the laboratory rat. In B. M. Foss (Ed.), *Determinants of infant behaviour: Vol. 3. Proceedings.* [New York]: Wiley.

Rossi, A. S., & Rossi, P. H. (1990). *Of human bonding: Parent-child relations across the life course.* New York: Aldine.

Rothman, K. J. (1976). Reviews and commentary: Causes. *American Journal of Epidemiology, 104,* 587–592.

Rubin, H. (1995). Alternatives to molecular mechanism thinking in biology and cancer research. *Frontier Perspectives, 4,* 9–16.

Rutter, M. (1988). *Studies of psychosocial risk: The power of longitudinal data.* Cambridge: Cambridge University Press.

Rutter, M., & Hay, D. F. (Eds.). (1994). *Development through life: A handbook for clinicians.* Oxford: Blackwell Scientific Publications.

Rutter, M., Lebovici, S., & Eisenberg, L. (1969). A tri-axial classification of mental disorders in childhood. *Journal of Child Psychology and Psychiatry, 10,* 41–61.

Ryder, N. B. (1965). The cohort as a concept in the study of social change. *American Sociological Review, 30,* 843–861.

Sade, D. S. (1967). Determinants of social dominance in a group of free-ranging rhesus monkeys. In S. Altmann (Ed.), *Social communication among primates.* Chicago: University of Chicago Press.

Salapatek, P., & Kessen, W. (1966). Visual scanning of triangles by the human newborn. *Journal of Experimental Psychology, 3,* 155–167.

Salthe, S. N. (1985). *Evolving hierarchical systems: Their structure and representation.* New York: Columbia University Press.

Sameroff, A. J. (1983). Developmental systems: Contexts and evolution. In P. H. Mussen (Gen. Ed.) & W. Kessen (Vol. Ed.), *Handbook of child psychology: Vol. 1. History, theory, and methods* (4th ed., pp. 237–294). New York: Wiley.

Sameroff, A. J. (1985, 23–27 August). *Can development be continuous?* Paper presented at Annual Meeting of the American Psychological Association, Los Angeles.

Sameroff, A. J. (1995). General systems theories and developmental psychopathology. In D. Cicchetti & D. Cohen (Eds.), *Manual of developmental psychopathology*. New York: Wiley.

Sameroff, A. J., & Chandler, M. J. (1975). Reproductive risk and the continuum of caretaking casualty. In F. D. Horowitz, E. M. Hetherington, S. Scarr-Salapatek, & G. M. Siegel (Eds.), *Review of child development research* (Vol. 4, pp. 187–244). Chicago: University of Chicago Press.

Sameroff, A. J., & Fiese, B. H. (1990). Transactional regulations and early intervention. In S. J. Meisels and J. P. Shonkoff (Eds.), *Handbook of early childhood intervention* (pp. 119–149). New York: Cambridge.

Savage, A., Ziegler, T. E., & Snowdon, C. T. (1988). Sociosexual development, pair bond formation, and mechanisms of fertility suppression in female cottontop tamarins (Saguinus oedipus oedipus). *American Journal of Primatology, 14*, 345–354.

Scarr, S., & McCartney, K. (1983). How people make their own environments: A theory of genotype–>environment effects. *Child Development, 54*, 424–435.

Scarr-Salapatek, S. (1976). Genetic determinants of infant development: An overstated case. In L. P. Lipsitt (Ed.), *Developmental psychobiology: The significance of infancy* (pp. 59–79). Hillsdale: Erlbaum.

Schaffer, H. R. (1984). *The child's entry into a social world*. London: Academic Press.

Schaffer, H. R. (Ed.). (1977). *Studies in mother-infant interaction*. London: Academic Press.

Schaffer, H. R., & Emerson, P. E. (1964). The development of social attachments in infancy. *Monographs of the Society for Research in Child Development, 29* (3, Serial No. 94).

Schieffelin, B. B. (1990). *The give and take of everyday life: Language socialization of Kaluli children*. Cambridge: Cambridge University Press.

Schieffelin, B. B., & Cochran-Smith, M. (1984). Learning to read culturally: Literacy before schooling. In H. Goelman, A. A. Oberg, & F. Smith (Eds.), *Awakening to literacy* (pp. 3–23). Exeter, NH: Heinemann.

Schieffelin, B. B., & Ochs, E. (1983). A cultural perspective on the transition from prelinguistic to linguistic communication. In R. M. Golinkoff (Ed.), *The transition from prelinguistic to linguistic communication* (pp. 115–131). Hillsdale, NJ: Erlbaum.

Schlossman, S., & Cairns, R. B. (1993). Problem girls: Some observations on past and present. In J. Modell, R. Parke, & G. H. Elder, Jr. (Eds.), *Children in time and place: Interesting historical and developmental insights* (pp. 110–130). New York: Cambridge University Press.

Schmandt-Besserat, D. (1978). The earliest precursor of writing. *Scientific American, 283,* 50–59.

Schmidt, K. (1994, October 28). A puzzle: How similar signals yield different effects. *Science, 266,* 566–567.

Schneider, W., & Pressley, M. (1989). *Memory development between 2 and 20.* New York: Springer-Verlag.

Schneirla, T. C. (1949). Levels in the psychological capacities of animals. In R. W. Sellars, V. J. McGill, & M. Garber (Eds.), *Philosophy for the future: The quest for modern materialism* (pp. 243–286). New York: Macmillan.

Schneirla, T. C. (1959). An evolutionary and developmental theory of biphasic processes underlying approach and withdrawal. In M. R. Jones (Ed.), *Nebraska Symposium on Motivation, 1958* (pp. 1–42). Lincoln: University of Nebraska Press.

Schneirla, T. C. (1961). Instinctive behavior, maturation – experience and development. In B. Kaplan & S. Wapner (Eds.), *Perspectives in psychological theory: Essays in honor of Heinz Werner* (pp. 303–334). New York: International Universities Press.

Schneirla, T. C. (1966). Behavioral development and comparative psychology. *Quarterly Review of Biology, 41,* 283–302.

Scott, J. P. (1967). Comparative psychology and ethology. *Annual Review of Psychology, 18,* 65–86.

Scott, J. P. (1977). Social genetics. *Behavior Genetics, 7,* 327–346.

Scribner, S., & Cole, M. (1981). *The psychology of literacy.* Cambridge, MA: Harvard University Press.

Searle, J. R. (1969). *Speech acts: An essay in the philosophy of language.* London: Cambridge University Press.

Sears, R. R., Maccoby, E. E., & Levin, H. (1957). *Patterns of child rearing.* Evanston, IL: Row, Peterson.

Sears, R. R., Rau, L., & Alpert, R. (1965). *Identification and child rearing.* Stanford: Stanford University Press.

Sells, S. B. (1966). Ecology and the science of psychology. *Multivariate Behavioral Research, 1,* 131–144.

Shanahan, M. J., Valsiner, J., & Gottlieb, G. (in press). Developmental concepts across disciplines. In J. Tudge, J. Valsiner, & M. J. Shanahan (Eds.), *Comparative approaches in developmental science.* New York: Cambridge University Press.

Shapiro, D. Y. (1980). Serial female sex changes after simultaneous removal of males from social groups of a coral reef fish. *Science, 209,* 1136–1137.

Shepherd, M., Oppenheim, B., & Mitchell, S. (1971). *Childhood behaviour and mental health.* London: University of London Press.

Sherrod, L. R. (1981). Issues in cognitive perceptual development: The special case of social stimuli. In M. E. Lamb & L. R. Sherrod (Eds.), *Infant social cognition: Empirical and theoretical considerations.* Hillsdale, NJ: Erlbaum.

Shirley, M. M. (1931). *The first two years. A study of twenty-five babies: Vol. 1. Postural and locomotor development.* Minneapolis: University of Minnesota Press.

Shirley, M. M. (1933a). *The first two years. A study of twenty-five babies: Vol. 2. Intellectual development.* Minneapolis: University of Minnesota Press.

Shirley, M. M. (1933b). *The first two years. A study of twenty-five babies: Vol. 3. Personality manifestations.* Minneapolis: University of Minnesota Press.

Shore, B. (1991). Twice-born, once conceived: Meaning construction and cultural cognition. *American Anthropologist, 93,* 9–27.

Shweder, R. A. (1990). Cultural psychology – What is it? In J. W. Stigler, R. A. Shweder, & G. H. Herdt (Eds.), *Cultural psychology: Essays on comparative human development* (pp. 1–43). Cambridge: Cambridge University Press.

Siegel, L. S., & Brainerd, C. J. (Eds.). (1978). *Alternatives to Piaget: Critical essays on the theory.* New York: Academic Press.

Siegler, R. S. (1976). Three aspects of cognitive development. *Cognitive Psychology, 8,* 481–520.

Siegler, R. S. (1983). Information processing approaches to cognitive development. In P. H. Mussen (Gen. Ed.) & W. Kessen (Vol. Ed.), *Handbook of child psychology: Vol. 1. History, theory, and methods* (4th ed., pp. 129–211). New York: Wiley.

Siegler, R. S. (1989). Mechanisms of cognitive development. *Annual Review of Psychology, 40,* 353–379.

Siegler, R. S. (1992). The other Alfred Binet. *Developmental Psychology, 28,* 179–190.

Siegler, R. S., & Crowley, K. (1991). The microgenetic method: A direct means for studying cognitive development. *American Psychologist, 46,* 606–620.

Siegler, R. S., & Shrager, J. (1984). Strategy choices in addition and subtraction: How do children know what to do? In C. Sophian (Ed.), *Origins of cognitive skills.* Hillsdale, NJ: Erlbaum.

Sigel, I., Stinson, E. T., & Flaugher, J. (1991). Socialization of representational competence in the family: The distancing paradigm. In L. Okagaki & R. J. Sternberg (Eds.), *Directors of development: Influences on the development of children's thinking* (pp. 121–146). Hillsdale, NJ: Erlbaum.

Silva, J. A., & Leiderman, P. H. (1986). The life-span approach to individual therapy: An overview with case presentation. In P. Baltes, D. Featherman, & R. Lerner (Eds.), *Life-span development and behavior* (pp. 113–134). Hillsdale, NJ: Erlbaum.

Simmons, R. G., & Blyth, D. A. (1987). *Moving into adolescence: The impact of pubertal change and school context.* New York: Aldine de Gruyter.

Simpson, G. G. (1970). Uniformitarianism: An inquiry into principle, theory and method in geohistory and biohistory. In M. K. Hecht & W. C. Steere (Eds.), *Essays in evolution and genetics in honor of Theodosius Dobzhansky.* New York: Appleton-Century-Crofts.

Singh, S. D. (1969). Urban monkeys. *Scientific American, 221,* 108–115.

Skae, D. (1874). The Morisonian lectures on insanity for 1873. *Journal of Mental Science, 20,* 491–503.

Skinner, B. F. (1957). *Verbal behavior.* New York: Appleton-Century-Crofts.

Smedslund, J. (1964). Concrete reasoning: A study of intellectual development. *Monographs of the Society for Research in Child Development, 29* (2, Serial No. 93).

Smith, F. (1984). The creative achievement of literacy. In H. Goelman, A. A. Oberg, & F. Smith (Eds.), *Awakening to literacy* (pp. 143–153). London: Heinemann.

Smith, L. B., & Thelen, E. (Eds.). (1993). *A dynamic systems approach to development: Applications.* Cambridge, MA: MIT Press.

Smuts, B. B., Cheney, D. L., Seyfarth, R. M., Wrangham, R. W., & Struhsaker, T. T. (1987). *Primate societies.* Chicago: University of Chicago Press.

Smuts, J. C. (1926). *Holism and evolution.* London: Macmillan.

Snow, C. E., & Ferguson, C. A. (Eds.). (1977). *Talking to children: Language input and acquisition.* Cambridge: Cambridge University Press.

Spemann, H. (1927). Organizers in animal development. *Proceedings of the Royal Society of London, 102,* 177–187.

Sperling, G. (1960). The information available in brief visual presentations. *Psychological Monographs, 74* (Whole No. 176).

Sroufe, L. A., & Rutter, M. (1984). The domain of developmental psychopathology. *Child Development, 55,* 17–29.

Stattin, H., & Magnusson, D. (1990). *Pubertal maturation in female development.* Hillsdale, NJ: Erlbaum.

Steinberg, L. (1987, September). Bound to bicker. *Psychology Today,* 36–39.

Stern, D. N. (1974a). Mother and infant at play. In M. Lewis & L. Rosenblum (Eds.), *The origins of behaviour* (Vol. 1, pp. 187–213). New York: Wiley.

Stern, D. N. (1974b). The goal and structure of mother-infant play. *Journal of American Academy of Child Psychiatry, 13,* 402–421.

Stevenson, H. W., Chen, C., & Uttal, D. H. (1990). Beliefs and achievement: A study of black, white and Hispanic children. *Child Development, 61,* 508–523.

Stevenson, H. W., & Lee, S.-Y., with Chen, C., Stigler, J. W., Hsu, C.-C., & Kitamura, S. (1990). Contexts of achievement. *Monographs of the Society for Research in Child Development, 55* (Nos. 1–2, Serial No. 221).

Suomi, S. J. (1979). Differential development of various social relationships by rhesus monkey infants. In M. Lewis & L. A. Rosenblum (Eds.), *The child and its family.* New York: Plenum Press.

Suomi, S. J. (1987). Genetic and maternal contributions to individual differences in rhesus monkey biobehavioral development. In N. A. Krasnegor, E. M. Blass, M. A. Hofer, & W. P. Somotherman (Eds.), *Perinatal development: A psychobiological perspective.* New York: Academic Press.

Suomi, S. J. (1991). Adolescent depression and depressive symptoms: Insights from studies with rhesus monkeys. *Journal of Youth and Adolescence, 20,* 271–285.

Suomi, S. J. (1995). Influence of Bowlby's Attachment Theory on research on nonhuman primate biobehavioral development. In S. Goldberg, R. Muir, & J. Kerr (Eds.), *Attachment theory: Social, developmental, and clinical perspectives.* Hillsdale, NJ: Analytic Press.

Suomi, S. J., & Harlow, H. F. (1975). The role and reason of peer friendships in rhesus monkeys. In M. Lewis & L. A. Rosenblum (Eds.), *Friendship and peer relationships.* New York: Wiley.

Suomi, S. J., Rasmussen, K. L. R., Higley, J. D. (1992). Primate models of behavioral and physiological change in adolescence. In E. R. McAnarney, R. E. Kriepe, D. P. Orr, & G. D. Comerci (Eds.), *Textbook of adolescent medicine.* Philadelphia: Saunders.

Super, C., Kagan, J., Morrison, F. J., Haith, M. M., & Wieffenbach, J. (1972). Discrepancy and attention in the five-month infant. *Genetic Psychology Monographs, 85,* 305–331.

Teale, W. H. (1984). Reading to young children: Its significance for literacy development. In H. Goelman, A. A. Oberg, & F. Smith (Eds.), *Awakening to literacy* (pp. 110–121). London: Heinemann.

Terman, L. M. (1925). *Genetic studies of genius: Vol. 1. Mental and physical traits of a thousand gifted children.* Stanford: Stanford University Press.

Thelen, E. (1989). Self-organization in developmental processes: Can systems approaches work? In M. R. Gunnar & E. Thelen (Eds.), *Minnesota Symposia on Child Psychology: Vol. 22. Systems and development* (pp. 77–117). Hillsdale, NJ: Erlbaum.

Thelen, E., & Smith, L. B. (Eds.). (1994). *A dynamic systems approach to the development of cognition and action.* Cambridge, MA: MIT Press.

Thieman, T. J., & Brewer, W. F. (1978). Alfred Binet on memory for ideas. *Genetic Psychology Monographs, 97,* 243–264.

Thom, R. (1972). *Stabilité structurelle et morphogénèse; essai d'une théorie générale des modèles.* Reading, MA: Benjamin.

Thomas, W. I., & Znaniecki, F. (1918–1920). *The Polish peasant in Europe and America* (Vols. 1–2). Urbana, Illinois: University of Illinois Press. (Republished in 1974. New York: Octagon.)

Tobach, E. (1969). Developmental aspects of chemoreception in the wistar (DAB) rat: Tonic processes. *Annals of New York Academy of Science, 290,* 226–267.

Torrey, J. W. (1973). Learning to read without a teacher: A case study. In F. Smith (Ed.), *Psycholinguistics and reading* (pp. 147–157). New York: Holt.

Trabasso, T. (1977). The role of memory as a system in making transitive inferences. In R. V. Kail, Jr., & J. W. Hagen (Eds.), *Perspectives on the development of memory and cognition* (pp. 333–366). Hillsdale, NJ: Erlbaum.

Trabasso, T., & Nickels, M. (1992). The development of goal plans of action in the narration of a picture story. *Discourse Processes, 15,* 249–275.

Tronick, E. Z. (1989). Emotions and emotional communication in infants. *American Psychologist, 44,* 112–119.

Tudge, J. R. H. (1973). *The moral aspect of socialization in the Soviet Union: Its development in theory and practice.* Unpublished thesis, Oxford University, Oxford, England.

Tudge, J. R. H. (1990). Vygotsky, the zone of proximal development, and peer collaboration: Implications for classroom practice. In L. C. Moll (Ed.), *Vygotsky and education: Instructional implications and applications of sociohistorical psychology* (pp. 155–172). Cambridge: Cambridge University Press.

Tudge, J. R. H., & Rogoff, B. (1989). Peer influences on cognitive development: Piagetian and Vygotskian perspectives. In M. H. Bornstein & J. S. Bruner (Eds.), *Interaction in human development* (pp. 17–40). Hillsdale, NJ: Erlbaum.

Tudge, J. R. H., & Winterhoff, P. A. (1993). Vygotsky, Piaget, and Bandura: Perspectives on the relation between social interaction and cognitive development. *Human Development, 36,* 61–81.

Tudge, J. R. H., Shanahan, M. J., & Valsiner, J. (Eds.). (in press). *Comparisons in human development: Understanding time and context.* New York: Cambridge University Press.

Tulkin, S. R., & Cohler, B. J. (1973). Childrearing attitudes and mother-child interaction in the first year of life. *Merrill-Palmer Quarterly, 19,* 95–106.

Tulkin, S. R., & Covitz, F. E. (1975). *Mother-infant interaction and intellectual functioning at age six.* East Lansing, MI: National Center for Research on Teacher Learning. (ERIC Document Reproduction Service No. ED 111514)

Tulving, E. (1991). Memory research is not a zero-sum game. *American Psychologist, 46,* 41–42.

Tulviste, P. (1989). Education and the development of concepts: Interpreting results of experiments with adults with and without schooling. *Soviet Psychology, 27,* 5–21.

Tulviste, P. (1991). *The cultural-historical development of verbal thinking* (M. J. Hall, Trans.). Commack, NY: Nova.

Turkewitz, G., & Devenny, D. A. (Eds.). (1993). *Developmental time and timing.* Hillsdale, NJ: Erlbaum.

Turkewitz, G., Gardner, I., & Lewkowicz, C. J. (1984). Sensory/perceptual functioning during early infancy: The implications of a quantitative basis for responding. In G. Greenberg & E. Tobach (Eds.), *Behavioral evolution and integrative levels.* The T. C. Schneirla Series. Hillsdale, NJ: Erlbaum.

Turman, M. C. (1987). *A preface to literacy: An inquiry into pedagogy, practice, and progress.* University: University of Alabama Press.

Upchurch, D. M., Lillard, L. A., & Panis, C. W. A. (1994). *Interdependencies over the life course: Women's fertility, marital, and educational experiences.* Labor and Population Working Paper Series 94–17. [Santa Monica, CA]: Rand.

Uphouse, L. L., & Bonner, J. (1975). Preliminary evidence for the effects of environmental complexity on hybridization of rat brain RNA to rat unique DNA. *Developmental Psychobiology, 8,* 171–178.

Valsiner, J. (1987). *Culture and the development of children's action: A cultural-historical theory of developmental psychology.* Chichester, England: Wiley.

Valsiner, J. (1988a). *Developmental psychology in the Soviet Union.* Brighton, England: Harvester Press.

Valsiner, J. (1988b). Ontogeny of co-construction of culture within socially organized environmental settings. In J. Valsiner (Ed.), *Child development within culturally structured environments: Social co-construction and environmental guidance in development* (Vol. 2., pp. 283–297). Norwood, NJ: Ablex.

Valsiner, J. (1989). *Human development and culture: The social nature of personality and its study.* Lexington, MA: Lexington Books.

Valsiner, J. (1991a). Construction of the mental: From the "cognitive revolution" to the study of development. *Theory and Psychology, 1,* 477–494.

Valsiner, J. (1991b). Social development of human cognitive processes, and its study. *Theory and Psychology, 1* (4).

Valsiner, J. (1991c). Theories and methods in the service of data construction in developmental psychology. In P. van Geert & L. P. Mos (Eds.), *Annals of theoretical psychology* (Vol. 7, pp. 161–175). New York: Plenum.

Valsiner, J. (Ed.). (1986). *The individual subject and scientific psychology.* New York: Plenum.

Valsiner, J., & van der Veer, R. (1988). On the social nature of human cognition: An analysis of the shared intellectual roots of George Herbert Mead and Lev Vygotsky. *Journal for the Theory of Social Behavior, 18,* 117–135.

Valsiner, J., & van der Veer, R. (1993). The encoding of distance: The concept of the zone of proximal development and its interpretations. In R. R. Cocking & K. A. Renninger (Eds.), *The development and meaning of psychological distance* (pp. 35–62). Hillsdale, NJ: Erlbaum.

van der Kolk, B. A. (Ed.). (1984). *Post-traumatic stress disorder: Psychological and physiological sequelae.* Washington, DC: American Psychiatric Press.

van der Veer, R., & Valsiner, J. (1988). Lev Vygotsky and Pierre Janet: On the origin of the concept of sociogenesis. *Developmental Review, 8,* 52–65.

Varnhagen, C. K., Morrison, F. J., & Everall, R. (1994). Age and schooling effects in story recall and story production. *Developmental Psychology, 30,* 969–979.

Vohr, B. R., Garcia-Coll, C., & Oh, W. (1989). Language and neurodevelopmental outcome of low-birthweight infants at three years. *Developmental Medicine and Child Neurology, 31,* 582–590.

Volkart, E. H. (1951). *Social behavior and personality: Contributions of W. I. Thomas to theory and social research.* New York: Social Science Research Council.

Vygotsky, L. S. (1929). The problem of the cultural development of the child. *Journal of Genetic Psychology, 36,* 415–434.

Vygotsky, L. S. (1962). *Thought and language.* Cambridge, MA: MIT Press.

Vygotsky, L. S. (1978). *Mind in society: The development of higher psychological processes.* Cambridge, MA: Harvard University Press.

Vygotsky, L. S. (1981). The instrumental method in psychology. In J. V. Wertsch (Ed.), *The concept of activity in Soviet psychology* (J. V. Wertsch, Trans., pp. 134–143). Armonk, NY: Sharpe.

Vygotsky, L. S. (1984). Orudie i znak v razvitii rebenka [Tool and symbol in child development]. In L. S. Vygotsky (Ed.), *Sobranie sochinenii* (Vol. 6, pp. 6–90). Moscow: Pedagogika.

Vygotsky, L. S. (1987). *The collected works of L. S. Vygotsky: Vol. 1. Problems of general psychology.* New York: Plenum.

Vygotsky, L. S., & Luria, A. R. (1930). Tool and symbol in child development. Unpublished manuscript in English. (Russian back-translation published as Vygotsky, 1984)

Waal, F. B. M. de (1982). *Chimpanzee politics: Power and sex among apes.* New York: Harper & Row.

Waddington, C. H. (1957). *The strategy of the genes: A discussion of some aspects of theoretical biology.* London: Allen & Unwin.

Wagner, D. A. (1978). Memories of Morocco: The influences of age, schooling, and environment on memory. *Cognitive Psychology, 10,* 1–28.

Wagner, D. A. (1991). Literacy as culture: Emic and etic perspectives. In E. M. Jennings & A. C. Purves (Eds.), *Literate systems and individual lives: Perspectives on literacy and schooling* (pp. 11–19). Albany: State University of New York Press.

Wallman, J. (1979). A minimal visual restriction experiment: Preventing chicks from seeing their feet affects later responses to mealworms. *Developmental Psychobiology, 12,* 391–397.

Watson, J. B. (1913). Psychology as the behaviorist views it. *Psychological Review, 20,* 158–177.

Watson, J. B., & Rayner, R. A. (1920). Conditioned emotional reactions. *Journal of Experimental Psychology, 3,* 1–14.

Weinert, F., & Schneider, W. (Eds.). (1993). *The Munich longitudinal study on the genesis of individual competencies (LOGIC). Report No. 10: Assessment procedures and results of wave seven.* Munich: Max Planck Institute for Psychological Research.

Weismann, A. (1894). *The effect of external influences upon development.* London: Henry Frowde.

Weiss, P. (1939/1969). *Principles of development.* New York: Hafner.

Weiss, P. (1959). Cellular dynamics. *Reviews of Modern Physics, 31,* 11–20.

Wells, C. G. (1981). *Learning through interaction: The study of language development.* Cambridge: Cambridge University Press.

Wertsch, J. V. (1985). *Vygotsky and the social formation of mind.* Cambridge, MA: Harvard University Press.

Wertsch, J. V. (1991). *Voices of the mind: A sociocultural approach to mediated action.* Cambridge, MA: Harvard University Press.

Wertsch, J. V., & Rogoff, B. (1984). Editors' notes. In B. Rogoff & J. V. Wertsch (Eds.), *Children's learning in the "zone of proximal development." New Directions for Child Development* (No. 23, pp.1–6). San Francisco: Jossey-Bass.

Wessells, N. K. (1977). *Tissue interactions and development.* Menlo Park, CA: W. A. Benjamin.

Whitbeck, L. B., Hoyt, D. R., Simons, R. L., Conger, R. D., Elder, G. H., Jr., Lorenz, F. O., & Huck, S. (1992). Intergenerational continuity of parental rejection and depressed affect. *Journal of Personality and Social Psychology, 63*(6), 1036–1045.

White, S. H. (in press). The relationships of developmental psychology to social policy. In S. H. White (Ed.), *Developmental psychology and social policy.*

Whiting, B. B. (1976). The problem of the packaged variable. In K. F. Riegel & J. A. Meacham (Eds.), *The developing individual in a changing world: Vol. 1. Historical and cultural issues* (pp. 310–321). Chicago: Aldine.

Whiting, J. W. M. (1981). Environmental constraints on infant care practices. In R. L. Munroe, R. H. Munroe, & B. B. Whiting (Eds.), *Handbook of cross-cultural human development* (pp. 155–179). New York: Garland.

Wilson, E. O. (1975). *Sociobiology: The new synthesis.* Cambridge, MA: Belknap Press of Harvard University Press.

Winegar, L. T., & Valsiner, J. (Eds.). (1992). *Children's development within social context* (Vols. 1–2). Hillsdale, NJ: Erlbaum.

Wohlwill, J. F. (1973). *The study of behavioral development.* New York: Academic Press.

Wolpert, L. (1994). Do we understand development? *Science, 266,* 571–572.

Worthman, C. M. (1993). Bio-cultural interactions in human development. In M. E. Pereira & L. A. Fairbanks (Eds.), *Juvenile primates: Life history, development and behavior.* New York: Oxford University Press.

Wozniak, R. (1986). Notes toward a co-constructive theory of the emotion-cognition relationship. In D. J. Bearison & H. Zimiles (Eds.), *Thought and emotion: Developmental perspectives* (pp. 39–64). Hillsdale, NJ: Erlbaum.

Wright, S. (1968). *Evolution and the genetics of populations: Vol. 1. Genetic and biometric foundations.* Chicago: University of Chicago Press.

Wundt, W. (1916). *Elements of folk psychology: Outlines of a psychology history of the development of mankind.* New York: Macmillan.

Yarrow, M. R., Campbell, J. D., & Burton, R. V. (1968). *Child rearing: An inquiry in research and methods.* San Francisco: Jossey-Bass.

Young, C. H., Savola, K. L., & Phelps, E. (1991). *Inventory of longitudinal studies in the social sciences.* Newbury Park, CA: Sage.

Zamenhof, S., & van Marthens, E. (1978). Nutritional influences on prenatal brain development. In G. Gottlieb (Ed.), *Early influences* (pp. 149–186). New York: Academic Press.

Zamenhof, S., & van Marthens, E. (1979). Brain weight, brain chemical content, and their early manipulation. In M. E. Hahn, C. Jensen, & B. C. Dudek (Eds.), *Development and evolution of brain size: Behavioral implications* (pp. 164–185). New York: Academic Press.

Zeaman, D., & House, B. J. (1963). The role of attention in retardate discrimination learning. In N. R. Ellis (Ed.), *Handbook of mental deficiency: Psychological theory and research* (pp. 159–223). New York: McGraw-Hill.

Zeeman, E. C. (1976). Catastrophe theory. *Scientific American, 234,* 65–83.

Zinchenko, V. P. (1985). Vygotsky's ideas about units for the analysis of mind. In J. V. Wertsch (Ed.), *Culture, communication, and cognition: Vygotskian perspectives* (pp. 94–118). Cambridge: Cambridge University Press.

Author Index

Abeles, R. P., 226
Achenbach, T. M., 176, 183
Ainsworth, M. D. S., 139, 140
Akinnaso, F. N., 204, 214
Allport, G. W., 57
Almond, G. A., 32
Alpert, R., 137
Alwin, D., 42, 226
Anderson, A. B., 208
Angold, A., 179, 180, 185, 188, 195, 223
Aram, D., 149
Ardelt, M., 61
Ariès, P., 108
Armour-Thomas, E., 130
Asendorpf, J. B., 159, 197
Aslin, R. N., 225
Astone, N. M., 39
Atkinson, R. C., 126
Austin, J., 143

Baer, K. E. von, 21
Baker-Ward, L. E., 129, 130, 132, 133
Baldwin, J. M., 2, 11, 83, 143, 198, 213, 224, 228
Baltes, M. M., 29, 223
Baltes, P. B., 29, 34, 44, 48, 223
Banaji, M. R., 132
Bandura, A., 38, 56
Bates, E., 143
Bateson, G., 195
Bateson, P. P. G., 2, 100, 223
Baudonniere, P., 159
Bayley, N., 149
Beach, D. H., 126
Beach, F. A., 80
Beatty, J., 197
Beilin, H., 125
Bell, R. Q., 137, 140
Bell, S. V., 140
Bellugi, U., 142
Bem, D. J., 46
Bendersky, M., 151
Bengtson, V. L., 41

Benjamin, R., 188
Bentley, A. F., 63
Berger, P. L., 99
Bergman, L. R., 3, 20, 22, 25, 29, 226, 232
Berman, C. M., 114
Bertalanffy, L. von, 2, 13, 63
Binet, A., 121, 225, 226
Bisanz, J., 124, 130, 132
Bissex, G. L., 210
Bjorklund, D. F., 129, 130
Blass, E. M., 108
Blehar, M. C., 140
Blythe, D. A., 18
Bonner, J., 73
Borawski, E., 149
Born, D. E., 71
Bowlby, J., 107, 139
Boyatzis, D. J., 147
Braine, M. D. S., 142
Brainerd, C. J., 125, 128
Brazelton, T. B., 140
Brazy, J. E., 149, 150
Brehm, J. W., 56
Brehm, S. S., 56
Breland, K., 27
Breland, M., 27
Breslau, N., 149
Brewer, W. F., 122
Broadbent, D. E., 123
Bronfenbrenner, U., xv, 2, 10, 14, 35, 48, 63, 87, 101, 102, 103, 111, 194, 195, 200, 225, 228, 232
Brown, A. L., 127, 130
Brown, R., 142
Brownell, C. A., 159
Brunelli, S. A., 75
Bruner, J. S., 57, 124, 125, 142, 143, 147, 152, 155, 156, 211
Brunswick, E., 83
Bryant, P., 71, 223
Bryk, A. S., 40
Buchmann, M., 35
Bühler, C., 34

279

LeVine, R. A., 105
Levine, S., 117
Levinson, D. J., 45
Lewin, K., 2
Lewis, M. H., 15, 91, 92, 93, 94, 95, 151
Lewkowicz, C. J., 81
Liberty, C., 126
Lickliter, R., 68
Liker, J. K., 54, 129
Lilienfeld, A. M., 188
Lilienfeld, D. E., 188
Liljequist, R., 92
Lillard, L. A., 40
Lindburg, D. G., 109, 111
Lochman, J., 229
Loeber, R., 22, 185
Loftus, E. F., 132
Lord, C. L., 127
Lord, S., 61
Lorenz, E. N., 28
Lovejoy, C. O., 109
Løvtrup, S., 72
Lozoff, B., 105
Lucariello, J., 132
Luckman, T., 99
Lumsden, C. J., 66
Luria, A. R., 199
Lüscher, K., 2, 223
Lutkenhaus, P., 159

Maccoby, E. E., 124, 137
MacCombie, D. J., 91
Mack, K. J., 71
Mack, P. A., 71
Magnusson, D., 2, 3, 7, 9, 10, 12, 14, 15, 18, 20, 22, 25, 29, 35, 63, 79, 84, 190, 225, 226, 228, 232
Mailman, R. B., 91, 94
Main, M., 140
Manis, F., 130
Markman, E. M., 128
Marler, P., 66
Marschark, M., 207
Masters, J. C., 137
Maudsley, H., 169, 171, 172
Mayer, K. U., 35, 44
Mayr, E., 77, 106, 179
McCarthy, D., 141
McCartney, K., 38
McCarty, R., 74
McGuire, A. M., 21, 85
McLane, J. B., 207
McLaughlin, S. D., 49
McLeod, J. D., 40
McNamee, G. D., 207
McNeill, D., 142
Mead, G. H., 200

Medvin, M. B., 150
Mehlman, P. T., 115, 116
Melton, D. A., 99
Merritt, K. A., 132
Milko, J. E., 92
Miller, P. H., 65
Miller, W., 142
Mills, J. W., 11, 22
Minuchin, P., 54
Mirsky, A. E., 73
Mitchell, S., 175
Mitchell, V., 38
Moane, G., 38
Modell, J., 37, 41, 223
Moen, P., 2, 36, 40, 223
Moffitt, T., x, 9, 10
Molinari, L., 151
Molitor, A., 150, 152
Monk, M. A., 175
Morgan, C. L., 11
Morgan, S. P., 49
Morrison, F. J., 18, 121, 124, 126, 127, 130, 131, 132, 192
Moss, H. A., 226
Mowrer, O., 141
Mrazek,P. J., 230, 231
Mussen, P. H., 31, 226
Myers, M. M., 75

Nagel, E., 179
Naus, M. J., 126, 128, 129, 130
Neckerman, H. J., 16, 25, 26
Needham, J., 68, 80
Needlman, R., 210
Neisser, U., 123, 132
Nelson, K., 132
Nelson, P. G., 73
Neugarten, B. L., 39, 41
Newcomb, T. M., 57
Newman, D., 201
Nichols, D. E., 94
Nickels, M., 121, 130
Ninio, A., 143, 152, 156, 211
Nwokah, E., 161
Nyiti, R. M., 193

Ochs, E., 144, 154, 204, 206
Oehler, J. M., 149, 150, 152
Ogbu, J. U., 207
Oh, W., 151
Okagaki, L., 130
Oppenheim, B., 175
O'Rand, A. M., 38, 43, 149
Ornstein, P. A., 121, 122, 126, 128, 129, 130, 132, 133, 192
Osgood, C., 141
Overton, W. F., 186, 195, 196

Subject Index

abilities, 214
accelerated development, 18
acceleration, 17
accentuation principle, 57
accommodation, 85–6, 198
adapted state, 81–6
addiction, 4
adolescence, 9–13, 51, 104, 107, 108, 114
African-Americans, 149, 221
age grading, 38, 41; as timetable, 47
age-invariant diagnostic criteria, 186
aggregate data, 13
aggressive behavior, 11, 17, 26; subtype of, 186
ambient print, 208
anagenesis, 79–81
anamnestic strategy, 187
animal-model work, 167
apes, 118
applied perspectives, 133–4
Arabic, 207
assimilation, 198
attachment, 139–40, 144, 186
autocatalytic, human society as, 120

basal readers, 208
Bayley Scales of Infant Development, 149
behavioral development as leading edge, 30
behavioral novelties, 137, 140
behavioral organization, 159
behaviorism, 122–3
Berkeley Guidance and Growth Study, 37, 42, 54–5
Bible, 215
bidirectional events, 231
bidirectional influence, 64, 71, 73, 84, 146
bidirectional interactions, 82
bidirectional nature, 164
bidirectional paths, 163
bidirectional perspective, 194
bidirectional processes, 15
bidirectionality, 8, 14, 16, 64, 71, 73, 81, 84, 86–7

biographies, 229
biological constraints, 28, 97
biological processes, 11
biological reductionism, 16
birth, 49–51
black-families studies, 207
Brazilian, 214
butterfly effect, 18

calendars, 42, 44
cardiac system, 13
Carolina Consortium on Human Development, xix, 6, 233
Carolina Longitudinal Study, 53, 55
catastrophe theory, 19
categories versus continua, 183
change, 232
chaos theory, 99
child abuse, 184
child psychiatry, 169
child psychopathology, 168, 177
child study, 229
Children of the Great Depression, 32, 34–5, 51, 53–4
chimpanzee, 97
circular reaction, 198
clinical child psychology, 169
coaction, significance of, for individual development, 68–73
co-constructionist approach, 194, 195, 200, 203, 209, 212, 214–15, 220–2
coding, 218
coevolved adaptations of mothers and infants, 139
cognition, 158–9, 163–4, 190; basic and applied perspectives on, 133–4; and cognitive-psychology influences, 123–6; development of, 121–34; foundational approaches to, 121–3; Piagetian approaches to, 124–6
cognitive activity, 212
cognitive psychologists, 123–6, 192
cohorts: birth, 49–51; effects of, 49